A Place at the Table

A Place at the Table

George Eldon Ladd and the Rehabilitation of Evangelical Scholarship in America

JOHN A. D'ELIA

OXFORD
UNIVERSITY PRESS
2008

OXFORD
UNIVERSITY PRESS

Oxford University Press, Inc., publishes works that further
Oxford University's objective of excellence
in research, scholarship, and education.

Oxford   New York
Auckland   Cape Town   Dar es Salaam   Hong Kong   Karachi
Kuala Lumpur   Madrid   Melbourne   Mexico City   Nairobi
New Delhi   Shanghai   Taipei   Toronto

With offices in
Argentina   Austria   Brazil   Chile   Czech Republic   France   Greece
Guatemala   Hungary   Italy   Japan   Poland   Portugal   Singapore
South Korea   Switzerland   Thailand   Turkey   Ukraine   Vietnam

Published by Oxford University Press, Inc.
198 Madison Avenue, New York, New York 10016

www.oup.com

Oxford is a registered trademark of Oxford University Press

Library of Congress Cataloging-in-Publication Data
D'Elia, John A.
A place at the table : George Eldon Ladd and the rehabilitation of
evangelical scholarship in America / John A. D'Elia.
   p. cm.
Includes bibliographical references and index.
ISBN 978-0-19-534167-6
1. Ladd, George Eldon, 1911–1982.   2. Bible. N.T.—Theology.
3. Evangelicalism–United States.   I. Title.
BX4827.L15D45 2008
230'.04624092—dc22   2007040452

9 8 7 6 5 4 3 2 1

Printed in the United States of America
on acid-free paper

For Julie,
who inspired me to begin
and provoked me to finish

Introduction

In a letter to a friend in 1971, George Eldon Ladd celebrated a message
he had received from a student at Princeton Seminary. The young
man had told Ladd that his little book, *The New Testament and Criticism*, "had put him, as an evangelical, on his feet with reference to
New Testament criticism and had helped him to see daylight."[1] The
news pleased Ladd greatly. Much of his career was devoted to precisely
this effort—setting evangelicalism on its feet regarding the value of
biblical criticism and helping it emerge from its self-imposed darkness. To put it a different way, George Ladd spent the better part of his
thirty-year career as a scholar attempting to rehabilitate what he perceived to be a weak and irrelevant evangelical movement in the United
States, especially in its contribution to intellectual life. Conservative
Christianity had been shut out—when it had not separated on its
own—from the critical discussions taking place over the very book
that gave evangelicals their identity, and Ladd wanted to come back in.
In Ladd's estimation, evangelicals had stopped publishing scholarly
literature that was worthy of consideration by the great universities.
They had abandoned the field just when the broader academic world
was addressing crucial questions about the central doctrines of the
Christian faith. Ladd's response to this crisis is the fundamental
theme of the present work.

George Eldon Ladd was born in 1911 and reared in New England,
where he served as a pastor in several Baptist churches. After receiving a doctorate from Harvard in 1949, Ladd became one of the

most important authors in an evangelical scholarly resurgence over the next three decades. The author of fourteen books and numerous academic and popular articles, Ladd demonstrated an erudition and intellectual vigor that played a vital role in raising the profile of evangelicals in the broader academy. He is perhaps best known for his writings on the doctrine of the Kingdom of God, but Ladd also made significant contributions to the understanding of history and biblical criticism among evangelicals and worked tirelessly to identify points of agreement both within and beyond the borders of conservative evangelicalism. After thirty years on the faculty at Fuller Theological Seminary in California, Ladd died in 1982.

Why is George Ladd important? Why look to a sectarian theologian—a recipe for obscurity if ever there was one—at this particular point in history? Certainly there is value in seeing how an individual who was brought up in a narrow religious tradition learned to live and participate in a broader and more secular culture than he would have chosen for himself. Rightly or wrongly, religion is perceived to be the root of much of the world's trouble. Perhaps a look at someone who tried to live his faith in the modern culture without demonizing those who did not would be beneficial. Further, conservative evangelicalism in America appears to be experiencing a rebirth of the militancy and anti-intellectualism that led to its marginalization and paralysis in the early twentieth century. It is crucial for contemporary readers, especially those unfamiliar with the conservative evangelical world, to know that this was not always the case. Indeed, there were giants and near giants who faithfully tried to resist the slide to the periphery. It is too easy to see the contemporary scene as descending in a straight unbroken line from the militancy of the 1920s and 1930s. The story arc of American evangelicals is actually far more textured and interesting than that, as we shall see. Finally and most important, Ladd is worthy of study because he represents, in all his brilliance, hubris, brokenness, and discipline, the most complete and self-conscious attempt by an individual to rehabilitate the intellectual vigor of the movement that gave him life.

How did George Ladd attempt to rehabilitate evangelical scholarship in America? His evolving strategy can be divided into two main elements. First, Ladd sought to raise the level of discourse within evangelicalism—to improve the quality of its scholarly content. He was disciplined—at times obsessed—in his study of the Bible and of critical works from scholars across the theological spectrum. He also developed a reputation as a rigorous and demanding—and occasionally intimidating—seminary professor who required his students to do the highest-quality work possible. If they were to earn the right to represent the gospel in the world, they first had to master its study in his classroom.

But there was an external component to his strategy as well. Ladd believed that, in order for evangelical scholars to be accepted as equals in the best institutions and societies, he and others like him had to earn their way in and prove their worthiness to participate. To this end Ladd submitted articles to prestigious journals, joined the academic organizations that would have him, and had his magnum opus printed by a publishing house outside the evangelical world. He also encouraged the brightest of his students to pursue doctoral work themselves, mentored them in their studies, and supported their applications to universities around the world. Ladd devoted his life to this two-pronged strategy for rehabilitating evangelicalism both in content and in image. His success in this quest—and that is not too strong a term to describe it—is evident in the results of a 1984 survey. When the members of an evangelical academic society were asked to identify the theologian who had influenced them the most, George Ladd shared top billing with John Calvin.[2] This book examines George Ladd's life and work as they are reflected in his strategy for including evangelicalism in the mainstream of theological scholarship.

What exactly was Ladd attempting to rehabilitate? To answer this question it is important to recall the important role evangelicalism had played in American culture in the nineteenth century. In William McLoughlin's words, "The story of American Evangelicalism is the story of America itself in the years 1800 to 1900. . . . [T]o understand it is to understand the whole temper of American life in the nineteenth century."[3] From the days of the Second Great Awakening in the early part of that century to the dynamism of Dwight L. Moody's revivalism at its close, evangelicalism was a dominant spiritual, cultural, and social force in the United States. By the turn of the twentieth century, however, urbanization and the massive immigration of Roman Catholics and Jews from Europe had forever altered the religious landscape of American society.[4] More important for this thesis, the influence of modern science, the growing secularization of the academy, and the critical study of the Bible threatened and ultimately shattered the cultural hegemony that evangelicalism had enjoyed for nearly a hundred years.[5] At first there was an attempt to incorporate these developments into the evangelical expression of Christian faith, but gradually many conservative Protestants in the United States found themselves marginalized within their own society, especially in relation to the role the Bible would play in interpreting history, shaping cultural norms for the present, and defining a hope for the future.

The perceived challenge to the Bible's authority served as a catalyst for several important developments. A series of prophecy-oriented conferences championed a literalistic approach to the interpretation of the Bible and helped to spread millennialist views.[6] There were denominational and interdenominational efforts to define and defend specific doctrines of the Christian faith. In 1910 the general assembly of the Presbyterian Church approved a five-point declaration of essential doctrines, followed in the next decade by string of similar statements uniting conservatives across multiple traditions.[7] In the years between 1910 and 1915 two wealthy oilmen from California published a series of pamphlets called "The Fundamentals," from which the term *fundamentalism* would later be derived.[8] These essays were fair and reasoned expositions of Christian doctrines written by conservative pastors and scholars from the United States and Great Britain. Though based on important differences over foundational principles for many Christians, these conflicts were, for the most part, relatively peaceful. In the early years of the twentieth century these doctrinal debates took place between fellow travelers in still-unified traditions. That would change dramatically after the First World War.

One of the critical fault lines that threatened to divide American Protestantism was the issue of human evolution. The challenge to the biblical account of the origins of human life acted as a breaking point between Christians who interpreted the Bible literally and those who accepted only modern scientific explanations for natural phenomena. In several states fundamentalists succeeded in having the teaching of evolutionary theory prohibited in public schools. In 1925 a group that comprised local leaders in Tennessee and the American Civil Liberties Union (ACLU) challenged the new law during the trial of a science teacher, and the resulting publicity served to humiliate, then radicalize, many fundamentalists in America.[9] Militant conservatives began to separate from denominations, from educational institutions, and in many ways from public life. They established loose confederations of churches and schools dedicated to the defense of conservative doctrines and the separation from an increasingly secularizing culture and consequently found themselves cut off from academic life in the United States. For many fundamentalists this was just fine. In their perception the intellectual life led inevitably to the liberalization of doctrine, and so they considered it an appropriate hedge against apostasy to resist the teachings of modern science and other disciplines.[10] Many of the Bible colleges that were founded in response to the threat from secular education offered instead a narrow curriculum of biblically based courses that promoted conservative doctrinal teaching.[11] Such was the state of evangelical higher education on the eve of the Second World War.

The relationship between conservative evangelical higher education and the mainstream academy was even more fractured.[12] Battles over the role that

faith commitments would play within public education pitted fundamentalists against secular academic leaders. As a result, conservative Christianity
came to be seen as a villain that stifled the culture's quest for knowledge in
favor of a backward faith. The president of the American Association of
University Professors, Joseph V. Denny (1862–1935), claimed in 1923 that
fundamentalism was "the most sinister force that has yet attacked freedom of
teaching."[13] In the years preceding and immediately following the Second
World War, all but the most superficial expressions of Christianity took on
outsider status in American universities, and even institutions with Christian
origins limited the practice of Christianity to its most inclusive functions.[14] It
would be difficult to overstate the extent to which conservative evangelicals
were marginalized within academic life in the United States.

Around the end of the 1930s, however, a movement arose that self-consciously rejected the militant separatism of fundamentalism—and the general
indifference from the secular mainstream—and began to reengage society.
This "new evangelicalism," as it was called, represented several important
shifts in the level of cultural participation among conservative Protestants in
America.[15] The National Association of Evangelicals (NAE), founded in 1942,
initiated a domestic program of cooperative evangelism, uniting Christian
denominations and traditions in promoting the faith even if they may have
disagreed on some points of doctrine.[16] Evangelicals had always proselytized,
to be sure, but more often than not their evangelistic work was accomplished
as outsiders, separate even from other Christian traditions. The NAE was able
to bring like-minded groups together for the greater good.

Related to this effort was the resurgence of an increasingly united program in foreign missions. The New Tribes Mission (1942), the Evangelical
Foreign Missions Association (1945), and the Far Eastern Gospel Crusade
(1947) transcended denominational and sectarian boundaries in their work
of spreading the Christian message around the world.[17] Most significant
for the present study is the group of scholars who had been brought up in
fundamentalist traditions but had rejected the strict separatism and anti-
intellectualism of their own movement in favor of training at elite universities.[18] These men, including George Eldon Ladd, became the intellectual
leaders for an entire generation of nonmilitant conservative evangelicals.
Connected to this final development was the founding and growth of Fuller
Theological Seminary. Created to raise the standard of academic training for
conservative evangelical leaders, Fuller became the key institution in the resurgent intellectual life of American evangelicalism.[19]

The historiography of postwar evangelicalism and especially the intellectual progress of the new evangelical movement is certainly incomplete. Joel

Carpenter has successfully revised our understanding of conservative evangelicalism in the years between the Scopes trial and the rise of Billy Graham's evangelistic crusades. Against the traditional appraisal, which saw fundamentalism as shattered and ineffectual, Carpenter argues that American fundamentalists were a thriving subculture that developed new institutions and innovative methods for achieving their goals and objectives.[20] Carpenter understates the destructive role of the most militant and separatistic wing of fundamentalism, but he is correct in rejecting the notion that conservative evangelicals had become completely inactive.

Mark Noll has provided a helpful study of evangelical biblical scholarship during this period, especially with regard to the relationship between those who hold traditional views of inspiration and revelation and modern critical methodologies.[21] Evangelical scholarship, especially in the area of biblical studies, has moved forward dramatically since 1950, led by the scholars who earned their degrees at elite universities the preceding decade. Perhaps the most helpful assessment of modern evangelical scholarship is the outsider's view provided by Gary Dorrien. Mirroring Ladd's call for evangelicalism to be counted among other leading theological traditions, Dorrien also credits evangelical theology with overseeing its own renewal, directed by the biblical scholars who argued for a more historically sensitive understanding of the Bible during the second half of the twentieth century.[22]

Others have sought to assess various aspects of the new evangelical movement. David Russell correctly charts the hope among some evangelicals after the Second World War of achieving a "respectable position" for evangelical thought.[23] However, he emphasizes the role of philosopher-theologians such as Edward John Carnell at the expense of those in technical disciplines. In the end it would be the historians and biblical scholars who succeeded in reestablishing evangelicals in the academy. Jon Stone takes a darker view of new evangelical scholarship as a whole. While he is correct in saying that the postwar evangelicals "were determined to wrest control of the helm of orthodoxy and direct a course toward theological and cultural respectability," he gives only a partial view of how this was accomplished.[24] Stone argues that the new evangelicals were obsessed with setting and defending theological and ecclesial boundaries and that what unified—and divided—them was essentially a preoccupation with self-definition. This, however, is only part of the story. Progressive evangelical scholars in the postwar era—George Ladd especially—shattered many traditional boundaries in their attempt to earn a hearing for evangelical scholarship in the broader academic world. Thus, while Stone accurately identifies the desire on the part of some evangelicals for a measure of "respectability," he ignores the cost they were willing to pay in order to achieve it.

Closer to the present topic is George Marsden's institutional history of Fuller Seminary, *Reforming Fundamentalism* (1987). Marsden traces the development of the institution back to Reformed—and largely Presbyterian—dreams of cultural transformation. His book effectively tells the complicated story of the various strands within the evangelical coalition and the way in which the progressives among them struggled to reassert evangelicalism in American intellectual life. However, he also emphasizes, as the title states, the "reforming" of fundamentalism rather than the repudiation of its excesses and thus leaves out an important part of the tale.[25] Marsden's Reformed-Princeton emphasis omits another important influence as well. Several key members of Fuller's early faculty were veterans of the irenic evangelical atmosphere at Gordon College in Massachusetts.[26] This was an important mitigating influence on the later conflicts at Fuller. Rudolph Nelson's biography of Fuller professor and president Edward John Carnell is also a helpful study.[27] Nelson shows how Carnell was driven by his desire to create a Christian apologetic that would stand among the great philosophical positions in modern culture. Nelson exposes a bifurcation in Carnell's thought, however, which allowed him to publish works that stayed within the boundaries of traditional Protestant orthodoxy even as the ambiguities of modernity were challenging his personal beliefs.[28] As Nelson states, Carnell acted as an important foil to Ladd, who had many of the same outward struggles as Carnell: a sense of failure, mental or emotional instability, and frustrating interactions with the academy at large. Unlike Carnell, however, Ladd did not need his theological position to be accepted as much as he craved acceptance for himself as a scholar. This subtle difference made some aspects of Ladd's career easier and some clearly more difficult, as we shall see.

While there have been several examinations of George Ladd's theology, little has been written about his life and personal development. In fact, the only biographical studies of him are sketches in dictionaries and catalogues of theologians.[29] Further, many of Ladd's life details in these short pieces are based on his faulty recollections as communicated to a colleague in 1978.[30] The present study is the first attempt at an examination of Ladd's life and work using his personal papers as source material. On the other hand, several studies discuss his theological positions. James Bibza examines Ladd's position on the historicity of the resurrection of Jesus and correctly sees him as attempting to join traditional faith with a critical understanding of historical inquiry.[31] Robert Yarbrough probes deeper into Ladd as an evangelical proponent of the *Heilsgeschichte* position.[32] While concluding that Ladd is too rigid in his interpretative method to shift the direction of modern biblical studies, Yarbrough adds that he deserves a place in the scholarly pantheon for having produced one of the few twentieth-century New Testament theologies in the Anglo-Saxon world.[33] Most balanced is the work by Bradley Harper on Ladd's understanding of the doctrine of the Kingdom of God in the context of American evangelical theology.[34] Harper reveals Ladd's willingness to engage and appropriate modern critical scholarship in his own writing and argues convincingly for Ladd's influence on contemporary evangelical thought. What Harper's study lacks (and this is largely an issue related to the availability of source material) is an understanding of what compelled Ladd to pursue the scholarly directions that define his career.

The purpose of this book is to examine the motivation for George Ladd's contribution to evangelical scholarship. It is not, consequently, solely an analysis of his theological position or a retracing of his exegetical steps. Biblical scholars and theologians will do a better job of that and in some cases already have. Of primary concern for the present study is more *why* Ladd wrote rather than simply an examination of *what* he wrote. Ladd was driven, as I have already stated, by the need to rehabilitate the content and image of evangelical scholarship, and he executed a strategy for accomplishing that goal. However, he was also motivated by personal issues that were equally powerful influences on both his life and his career as a scholar. It is at the confluence of Ladd's personal and professional motives that his life story comes into focus. This book, then, traces the development of Ladd's thought over the course of his life and pays special attention to the forces that animated that evolution and inspired his contribution to evangelical scholarship. The story is not a painless one but nonetheless serves to illuminate a life that has made an important and lasting impact on American evangelicalism.

Chapter 1 traces the impact of Ladd's family life and academic training on his later career as a scholar. Ladd's relationships to his parents and brother were problematic in ways that shaped his personality and foreshadowed his reactions to conflict throughout his life. The chapter encompasses Ladd's academic training at Gordon College and Harvard University, especially the influence of New Testament scholar Henry J. Cadbury. Special attention is also given to his work as a Baptist minister in the contentious Northern Baptist Convention and his decision to leave the ministry for a scholastic career. Ladd emerged from this early period with strong academic credentials, an evolving but still conservative theological position, and a quest to create a work of evangelical scholarship that the rest of the world could not ignore.

Chapter 2 examines Ladd's first five years at Fuller Seminary and the emergence of his strategy to rehabilitate evangelical scholarship. Ladd chose to offer a detailed critique of dispensationalism (the dominant theological system within conservative evangelicalism) from an almost equally conservative point of view. As a part of this strategy he initiated a dialogue with John Walvoord, a leader at the academic home of dispensational theology, and this interaction set the tone for Ladd's relationship to the conservative wing of his own movement. Ladd also assumed a leadership role in several collaborative projects with colleagues at Fuller Seminary, only to see them collapse along the same fissures that divided the broader evangelical world.

Chapter 3 shows Ladd as an established scholar who was willing to take on the militant wing of his own movement to achieve his goal of acceptance for evangelical scholarship. Ladd's relationship with Walvoord evolved into one between equals, and Ladd was sharper in his criticism of the dispensationalist interpretative model during this period. He also sided with the more progressive developments within evangelicalism such as Billy Graham's cooperative evangelism and support for the Revised Standard Version translation of the Bible. These moves effectively separated Ladd from the militant wing of evangelicalism and mirrored the division between conservative and progressive evangelicals taking place at every level.

Chapter 4 traces Ladd's transition from his focus on evangelical issues to his greater interaction with the greater mainstream of theological scholarship. The relationship with Walvoord and the emphasis on correcting dispensationalism were abandoned in favor of this new element of his strategy. Ladd involved himself in a scholarly discussion of the historicity of the resurrection of Jesus that was taking place beyond the boundaries of evangelicalism. He began to communicate his understanding of biblical miracles in terms of modern historical thought and defended traditional views using these contemporary categories. Ladd also provided the first thorough assessment of Rudolf Bultmann's theology from a conservative viewpoint. That Ladd disagreed with Bultmann on many foundational points was not nearly so important as the fact that he engaged him at all. These interactions were positive experiences for Ladd and energized his strategy for dealing with theological scholarship beyond his own tradition. He began to work relentlessly to complete his magnum opus, the goal toward which his entire career was aimed.

Chapter 5 examines the completion and release of Ladd's *Jesus and the Kingdom* (1964) and his response to the critical reaction. Ladd had worked on this book for more than a decade and dreamed of producing a major work of scholarship for twice that long. He intentionally sought a publisher outside the evangelical world, and when Harper and Row accepted it, Ladd felt as though his goal was within reach. However, he was devastated by a review of his book by British theologian Norman Perrin and descended into a time of bitter depression and alcohol abuse from which he would never fully recover. In the aftermath of the review Ladd lashed out indiscriminately, even at friends who tried to console him, and decided to abandon the quest that had driven his career from the earliest days.

Chapter 6 reveals Ladd in personal and professional crisis as he surrendered his dream of earning a place for himself in the broader theological discussion. There was tension in his family, severe alcoholism, and disciplinary action at Fuller Seminary. Ladd's reputation as the leading evangelical biblical scholar in the United States was threatened as word of his personal problems spread. Yet it was in this period that Ladd solidified his place in evangelical scholarship with the publication of his *Theology of the New Testament* in 1974, as well as other important works. As he neared retirement Ladd was recognized as a star in the world of conservative biblical scholarship, but he ended his career believing that he had been a failure in his mission to earn a place for evangelicalism in the wider world of academic theology.

The primary source materials I used offer a fascinating glimpse into the history of modern American evangelicalism. After George Ladd was debilitated by a stroke in 1980, Robert Meye, then the dean of the School of Theology at Fuller Seminary, moved Ladd's files to his home, where they remained until he offered them for use in my project. The files contain a massive record of Ladd's personal and academic history: course notes from undergraduate days, a diary of his courtship with the woman who would become his wife, hundreds of sermon outlines, seminar papers from his doctoral program at Harvard, meticulous notes from his study of various books and Bible passages, manuscripts of his published and unpublished works, and correspondence with many of the principal players across the spectrum of theological scholarship. Processing these papers—choosing what to use and what to set aside—took more than a year in itself. Ladd himself made it easy to emphasize the correspondence over, say, the sermon outlines. Perhaps anticipating his role in the evangelical world or simply wanting to keep a record of his many dialogues, Ladd kept carbon copies of virtually all of the letters he wrote. As a result, the collection of his papers presents both sides of the conversations he maintained with theologians, pastors, colleagues, and the many people who wrote to comment on something he had written or preached. It is in these exchanges that we learn the most about Ladd's motivation for writing and thinking the way he did. All of the references to manuscript materials in this book, unless otherwise noted, are from the George Eldon Ladd Papers.

Other books and manuscripts provided valuable perspective on Ladd's life and work. The archival collections at Gordon College and Harvard University gave detail and structure to the understanding of Ladd's education and training for his career. The Archives Center of the American Baptist Historical Society offered a glimpse into Ladd's ministerial work and his relationship to the Northern (later, American) Baptist Convention. Several private collections have also been particularly helpful. In 1989 a student at Fuller Seminary, Rebecca Jane Duncan, wrote a paper on Ladd's spiritual development.[35] In the process she spoke with Ladd's family members and colleagues, most of whom have died in the years since, and made her original interview notes available to me. These papers are the only surviving firsthand accounts of Ladd's early life and his relationships with his parents, brother, wife, and children and were invaluable in helping me to understand the childhood and adolescent wounds at the root of his later pathologies.

On the professional side of things, David Allan Hubbard, the late president of Fuller Seminary, gave me full access to Ladd's personnel file and provided particulars on sabbatical leaves, committee work, and, later, disciplinary actions. The letters and papers of Calvin Mercer, Norman Perrin's biographer, supplied important details on the life of this important figure in Ladd's career and prevented him from becoming a one-dimensional villain. The correspondence between George Marsden, the historian of Fuller Seminary, and Daniel Payton Fuller, the son of the seminary's founder, offered helpful information about events at the institution. The published writings of Ladd's contemporaries, especially those with whom Ladd interacted in his own work, are considered primary source material (see bibliography).

Though George Eldon Ladd was a conservative evangelical, it is not necessary to share his faith to recognize his contribution or the value of his story. George Marsden and others have argued convincingly that it is impossible to comprehend American social and intellectual history without acknowledging the impact of evangelicalism, and this is certainly true.[36] The role of conservative Christianity in the creation of American institutions, mores, literature, and political discourse has been dramatic or pervasive, depending upon one's own experience of the movement. Marsden correctly argues that "The failure of the American educational establishment to provide perspective for understanding exclusivist religion in our midst is surely one reason why so many Americans have difficulty fathoming the dynamics of exclusivist religion abroad."[37] Attempting to make sound historical judgments about a Christian scholar without acknowledging the validity of his faith—at least for his own experience—is a bit like studying automotive science without reference to gasoline. It is important, then, at least to acknowledge that the faith experiences of Ladd and other evangelicals are central to their individual and corporate stories. Making this concession will allow Ladd's passion for the rehabilitation of evangelical scholarship—and his remarkable influence on evangelicals in America—to have their full force.

Excursus: Fundamentalism, Evangelicalism, and Dispensationalism

The terms *evangelicalism* and *fundamentalism* in their American context are disputed enough to warrant some brief comment, and the influence of dispensationalism on both is central to this study.[38] The oldest and broadest of the terms, evangelicalism encompasses a category of Bible-believing, soul-saving, revival-seeking Christians. Because of their influence on the colonial period, their leadership role in American society during the nineteenth century, and their resurgent participation in American culture and politics in the late twentieth century, evangelicals have played a central part in U.S. history. Under this rubric we find Reformed, Baptist, Holiness, and Pentecostal groups, among others, both in identified evangelical traditions and as conservative voices within more liberal denominational traditions. Certainly evangelical beliefs and practices will vary across this diverse gathering, but David Bebbington's definition of the movement is helpful for this study. He has described evangelicalism as including any person or group that adheres to the following characteristics: *biblicism*, or the belief that the Bible is the unique, supernaturally inspired revelation of God; *conversionism*, or the belief that an individual must make a decision to follow the Christian faith; *activism*, or the emphasis on extending the influence of Christianity; and *crucicentrism*, the focus on the cross of Jesus (i.e., the doctrine of the atonement) as the central theme of Christian preaching and teaching.[39] The attention given to crucicentrism among evangelicals should be seen in contrast to the emphasis on the moral example of Jesus found in more liberal traditions. Bebbington's quadrilateral serves as the foundation for the use of the term *evangelicalism* in this book.

Fundamentalism represents the more conservative outgrowth of evangelicalism in response to modernizing influences around the turn of the twentieth century. Early fundamentalism was really a call to return to what were seen as traditional formulas of orthodox Christian doctrinal positions, often from within established denominations. What might be labeled *middle fun-*

damentalism was the more militant and separatistic variety that attacked those who were perceived as threats to doctrinal orthodoxy and retreated from denominations, schools, and other institutions that strayed beyond traditional boundaries. Later fundamentalism broke with the broader evangelicalism in 1957 over the cooperative evangelism of Billy Graham's ministry, a split that largely persists to the present day.[40] In this book fundamentalism is used only to describe specific individuals or groups that fit into these categories.

Dispensationalism was overwhelmingly the most dominant and influential system of biblical interpretation among conservative Protestant churches and groups and is thus significant for the present work.[41] In the dispensationalist model, history is divided into seven economies, or dispensations, each representing a unique facet of the relationship between God and his people, each providing a distinct matrix for redemption when humankind cannot measure up to the divine standard, and each ending in some form of human catastrophe. The dispensations are not simply periods of time; rather, they are individual economies of salvation that demonstrate the complex nature of humankind's dependence upon God. Traditionally, the seven dispensations correlate to the seven days of creation in Genesis, although some proponents have listed as few as three or as many as nine. The seventh, or Sabbath, day, in most systems, was thematically connected to the establishment of an earthly millennial kingdom, an aspect of dispensationalism that I discuss later. In the model championed by C. I. Scofield, by far the most influential dispensationalist of the twentieth century, the dispensations were innocency, conscience, human government, promise, law, grace, and kingdom.[42]

However, beyond the divisions of human history, one key characteristic of modern dispensationalism is the total separation between Israel and the church. The number of dispensations can vary as long as there is one for Israel (or "the law"), one for the church (or "grace"), and one for the future earthly millennial kingdom; Dallas Theological Seminary, the intellectual center of dispensational thought in the United States, requires only these three dispensations in its doctrinal statement.[43] The "parenthetical" nature of the church is a component of this dispensational system. If God's plan is focused primarily on his chosen people and the final act of this drama will be a second redemptive gesture to those people, then the church functions only as a bridge or "parenthesis" amid the true purpose of history: the redemption of Israel. This separation of Israel from the church is key to understanding the interpretative model of dispensational theology, as it requires faithful readers to approach biblical texts according to their relationship to one or the other. This separation of "law texts" from "grace texts" is called, in dispensational terms, "rightly dividing the Word of truth" and is the key to any examination of dispensational hermeneutics.[44]

Central to dispensationalism is its literal interpretation of the Bible, especially the prophetic writings. Indeed, some early premillennialists did not refer to themselves as such but rather as "literalists."[45] In the face of increasing skepticism about the claims of Christianity and as the religious landscape diversified through immigration and the rise of new homegrown religions, the dispensationalist model sought to reassert the primacy of Christianity—and the Bible—in American culture, though with a pessimistic twist. In the midst of political, economic, and religious chaos, the dispensationalists proclaimed that God was actively involved in human history and that he would soon bring it to a violent close. God had a plan, they argued, but it could be discerned only if one were willing to abandon what the dispensationalists perceived as the modernist tendency to allegorize the prophetic teachings of scripture and instead interpret them literally. In the United States, literalism became a battle cry for dispensationalists in the twentieth century and certainly functioned as a litmus test for inclusion in their vision of the true church. Moreover, as they became virtually indistinguishable from the slightly broader fundamentalist movement, their emphasis on the literal interpretation of scripture provided a foundation for the inerrancy debates of that century.

Biblical literalism has not been the only source of conflict for dispensationalists. The relegation of the church to second-tier status effectively created an ecclesiology that has proved to be problematic, if not inherently destructive. Since the church is really only an "in-between" institution and thus not a permanent part of redemptive history and since it will be a major source of evil according to dispensational eschatology, dispensationalists often brought with them a radically low view of organized religion. John Nelson Darby, the most important figure in the translation of dispensational views from Great Britain to the United States, argued that the true believer should have nothing to do with the institutional church.[46] This emphasis on separation did not endear the movement to denominational leaders, though many of their followers were adopting dispensational views. Further, in dispensational eschatology one of the signs of the end will be the rise of apostasy within the church. For those who were longing for the consummation of history, this created a built-in need to find infidels among the brethren not only in churches but in colleges, seminaries, and other Christian organizations as well. The result was (and has remained) a seemingly endless series of divisions and conflicts among dispensationalists in the conservative Protestant movement.

The eschatology of dispensationalism has become its most widely known feature.[47] In the dispensationalist model, the church age will close with a series of clearly identifiable events, announcing that the final stage of human history has come. With some variation, this order of events is predicted as follows: First, in the pretribulational secret rapture, all believers will be "taken up" to meet with Christ in the air, leaving behind all who rejected the offer of faith in their lifetimes. Second, in the Great Tribulation, the Antichrist will join forces with the apostate church to rule the world for seven years. The tribulation itself is divided into two equal periods of three and a half years, the second of which will be a horrible time of suffering. Third, Christ and the saints will join to crush the Antichrist and his army at Armageddon, ending the tribulation and ushering in the next chapter, Christ's millennial reign on earth. During the millennium, Satan will be bound and rendered powerless until he is released for one final revolt at the end of the thousand years. Once he is permanently defeated, the dead will rise in a great resurrection, and human history will end after the Last Judgment. Interest in this futuristic component of dispensationalism is largely responsible for the spread of the system as a whole. The conferences and publications that made dispensationalism such an influential factor in American evangelicalism did not achieve their dominance by emphasizing minutiae regarding the age of innocency. Rather, it was this futurist element of dispensationalism that caught the attention of evangelicalism in the United States and beyond.

Cyrus I. Scofield produced the most influential work of the dispensationalist tradition, a widely read edition of the King James Bible. Scofield consolidated his interpretation of prophetic detail into an elaborate system of Bible notes, and more than any other published work, the Scofield Bible is credited with the spread of dispensationalist views.[48] First published in 1909 (with revisions in 1917 and 1967), the Scofield Bible sold more than 5 million copies between 1909 and 1967, plus an additional 2.5 million copies of the 1967 revision.[49] Considering that virtually all ministers and Bible teachers in the dispensational tradition, as well as many of their followers, would have used the Scofield notes to interpret the Bible, its influence is impossible to determine with any accuracy. It is also impossible to overstate. One such preacher, Leander Munhall, preached, on average, two sermons per day for fifty years and was heard by an estimated seventeen million people.[50]

For generations of dispensationalists, the interpretative scheme in the Scofield notes became inextricably connected to the text of the Bible itself; for many of them, it came as a surprise to learn that any other method of interpretation was possible.[51] A parody of a popular hymn pokes fun at the widespread influence of the Scofield Bible: "My hope is built on nothing less than Scofield's notes and Moody Press."[52] The consulting editors of the Scofield Bible mirrored the leadership roster of the prophecy conferences and included dispensationalist luminaries such as Arno Gaebelein, James Gray, William Erdman, A. T. Pierson, and W. G. Moorehead.[53] The participation of these leaders in the development of the Scofield Bible served to communicate their views to an even wider audience than the conferences had been able to achieve and played a major role in the spread of dispensationalist theology.

A final word of introduction: George Eldon Ladd's career as a scholar must be seen in the context of the history of American evangelicalism. He was certainly influenced by the general sense of loss within his movement: loss of prestige, loss of influence, and loss of intellectual vigor. I contend that much of Ladd's career was spent trying to reclaim for evangelicalism the qualities and status it had once enjoyed. But there is more to Ladd than simply a nostalgic desire to recover some faded glory. The image of the table, then, becomes an appropriate symbol for that for which Ladd strove during his career. Certainly it works within the Christian frame of mind, both in the solemnity of Communion and the joyous celebration of the various feast days. However, for Ladd it meant more than that. The table represented inclusion in the broader discussion of the crucial theological issues of the day, and Ladd wanted to sit there. Nonetheless, Ladd was above all an evangelical and certainly would have described himself as a fundamentalist, at least until the breach over Billy Graham in 1957. As such his goals must always be seen through the filter of his desire to win converts to the Christian faith; Ladd himself subordinated his own quest to the priority of world evangelization, as we shall see. The personal and professional ambitions that drove George Ladd rest—however imperfectly—in his identity as an evangelical Christian whose life was devoted to seeing the gospel preached "in all the world for a witness unto all nations."[54]

A Place at the Table

I

Early Life and Academic Preparation (1911–1950)

George Eldon Ladd was born 31 July 1911 in Chauvin, Alberta, Canada, the eldest son in a troubled working-class family.[1] Ladd's father was an ill-tempered man who had left home at the age of fourteen to escape the abuse of his own violent father. Elmer Eugene Ladd (1869–1929) was born in Nashua, New Hampshire, and lived in northern New England for much of his early life.[2] A gifted singer in his younger years, Elmer Ladd studied briefly at the Boston Conservatory in the 1890s while working as an assistant to a local doctor. He decided to pursue a career in medicine and, though he never finished high school, was admitted to the medical school at Yale College. In 1896 he completed his training in the undergraduate medical program at Dartmouth College in New Hampshire.

Elmer Ladd had been married in his younger years, but his wife had left him and taken their young daughter, Una, with her. He married again sometime around 1900 to the former Mary Cowan and settled in New Hampshire. Almost immediately he contracted tuberculosis, which threatened his life and damaged his hearing, and abruptly moved with his wife to Canada in search of a drier climate. It is there that George was born. The family struggled to carve out a life in rural Canada, but because U.S. medical licenses were not recognized there, the family spent this period in severe poverty. To make matters worse, Mary Ladd contracted scarlet fever in the forbidding conditions of the Canadian prairie and, soon after regaining her health, was stricken with typhoid. These illnesses gradually destroyed her hearing as well, and in her later years she communicated only with great difficulty, depending on an ear trumpet. Already a stern, pious woman, Ladd's mother was made even more remote by her disability. In 1913 the Ladds moved back to New Hampshire, where a second son, James Mathon, was born the next year.

Frail, shy, and bookish almost from the beginning, young George retreated from his unhappy life into popular fiction, particularly stories that focused on the American West. For much of his early life and beyond, Ladd was drawn especially to the characters in the novels of Zane Grey (1872–1939).[3] Grey created an image of the West as a moral battleground in which his characters are either destroyed because of their inability to change or redeemed through a final confrontation with their past.[4] Grey's characters often find themselves unjustly accused of crimes and subsequently have to go outside the law to accomplish what the legal system cannot.[5] Ladd gleaned from these characters an image of what a man should be, think, and do. He came to admire—even as he hoped to personify—this paragon of manliness, the strong, clean-cut, moral man who loved the outdoors and was guided by an uncomplicated view of the world.[6] To his great disappointment, Ladd would never see any of these qualities in his own life, though he often recognized—and occasionally envied—them in others.[7] Ladd's difficult early life provides a glimpse into the origins of his sense of inferiority and devastatingly low self-image.

Despite the difficulties in their lives, Ladd's mother and father remained committed to the Christian faith, though neither had strong denominational ties, and this shared faith represented the nearest thing to a sense of connection between George and his parents. Ladd's father had "experienced a great change of life at conversion" and remained religiously active for the rest of his life.[8] Ladd remembered his father as a "constant church attendant and worker" who lived as a "fine example of Christian belief and character."[9] The spiritual backbone of the family was Ladd's mother, who taught her children Bible stories and the basics of evangelical piety. Ladd learned to pray, he recalled later, "at his mother's knee."[10]

Still, George Ladd's early life was largely joyless. As a child he suffered from poor health and as an adolescent was awkward and extremely shy. Life was generally difficult for the entire family. Despite his education, the elder Ladd never seemed to be able to earn enough to secure a stable residence for his family. George spent most of his early years moving around New England, where his father found itinerant work as a country doctor, and the family attended a range of Baptist, Methodist, and Congregational churches during that time. The financial struggles of Ladd's family were burdensome at times, as evidenced by the constant relocation from town to town, and the strain left Ladd with strong feelings of alienation.

Moreover, it did not help that George was unusually tall, thin, and clumsy as a youth, a fact that made it even harder for him to find his niche at school. Ladd would later tell students that his nickname in high school was "Freak," an epithet he hated and one that served only to intensify his sense of exclusion and isolation.[11] Worse, Ladd's brother, James, was developing into a bright, handsome, athletic, and personable young man. Ladd's father clearly favored his younger son, belittling George for his lack of manliness while taking James with him to visit patients.[12] That Ladd's parents were limited in their abilities to communicate exacerbated the problems, and his father's tendency toward physical abuse drove the final wedge between them.[13] For much of his young life, Ladd saw himself as anything but the classic Zane Grey hero. Rather, he felt humiliated, rejected, and *unheard* both at home and at school. At an early age the seeds were planted that caused Ladd to react—and overreact—emotionally to the slightest provocation.[14]

Ladd began his high school studies at Plymouth High School in New Hampshire and finished, after yet another move, at Kent's Hill Seminary for Boys in Maine. In 1928, immediately after graduation from high school, the family moved again, this time to another village in Maine, where Ladd's life would change dramatically. During his teen years Ladd did not show much serious interest in his parents' faith, but at a local Methodist church a young woman preached a sermon that led to his conversion. Ladd could remember her only as "Miss Cash," but her influence was as important as any in his early years. Cora Regina Cash attended Gordon College in Boston from 1924 to 1926 as part of a two-year training program for men and women in Christian service. A woman training for Christian leadership was not out of the ordinary at Gordon. Indeed, of Cash's class of forty-four students, twenty-three were women.[15] It was only after the fundamentalist controversies of the late 1920s and 1930s that gender restrictions became an unofficial test of orthodoxy; Cash's role as a pulpit supply preacher would not have raised an eyebrow in 1928.[16]

Ladd said that through Cash's preaching, "Christ became a reality to me.... I resolved that evening when the invitation was given to take my stand for Christ and to make an open confession of Him. It was a struggle, one of the most difficult things I have done in my life, but I did it."[17] Ladd participated in regular Bible studies and lessons in "dispensational truth and Eschatology" and resolved that summer to enter the ministry. The presence of dispensational teaching in a Methodist church would not have been incongruous in the early 1930s. Many conservative evangelicals within American denominations at that time would have embraced dispensationalism to some degree without feeling compelled to separate.[18] Ladd's presence in this and several other Methodist churches is more a reflection of convenience than denominational loyalty. Often in the smallest towns and villages of Maine, only one church served the local population, especially after Methodist and Baptist churches supplanted Congregationalism in the early nineteenth century.[19] The Ladds simply found themselves residing in villages with Methodist congregations.[20] Following in the footsteps of Cora Cash, Ladd made plans to attend Gordon College. When she was called to another town, Ladd took the pulpit at the Methodist church for six Sundays, an event that helped to form his sense of call.[21]

Nevertheless, the fact remains that at the time of his conversion Ladd perceived himself as poor, physically awkward, and freakish, as well as intensely jealous of his younger brother—wounds that never completely healed. To make matters worse, Ladd's father died suddenly, four days after George began classes at Gordon. Never much of a businessman, Ladd's father left his family with debts they could not afford to pay and uncollected fees they would never recover.[22] Destitute, the family lacked even the funds to cover the funeral expenses.[23]

Ladd's mother subsequently went to work in a local textile mill.[24] In the 1930s the New England mill industry was in serious decline, and wages paid to women there were pathetically low. It is a sign of the Ladd family's desperate straits that mill work was even an option.[25] George was forced to work for a year to support his mother and brother before continuing his studies, ensuring that he would begin college just as poor as he had been in high school. He spent what would have been his freshman year of college as a day laborer on local farms and road-building crews.[26] While it is difficult to quantify with precision the impact Ladd's difficult upbringing had on the rest of his life, the related themes of inferiority, obsession with status, and his desperate need to be heard remained apparent until his death.

In 1929 Ladd began studying for his first degree at Gordon College of Theology and Missions in suburban Boston. Gordon was one of the original institutions in the Bible school movement, which provided safe alternatives for higher education to theologically conservative men and women.[27] At least as significantly for Ladd, Gordon charged no tuition and only nominal fees for residence. Founded as an evangelical vocational school in 1889 by Baptist missionary Adoniram Judson Gordon (1836–1895), Gordon College was far less militant than many of the other schools that sprouted up around the same time. The school's leadership intentionally cultivated a genteel atmosphere at the institution. Nathan Wood (1874–1961), dean and later president of Gordon, emphasized not only basic education and conservative evangelical doctrine but also "the high type of culture" he attributed to the historic British universi-ties.[28] Learning itself was important at Gordon, and Ladd happily embraced this principle. The school's theological outlook, though clearly conservative, predominantly Baptist, and largely dispensationalist in practice, was never coercively so.[29] Gordon's first public doctrinal statement, published in the 1922–1923 academic year catalogue, was rare in its avoidance of key divisive issues such as inerrancy or premillennialism.[30] The statement emphasized instead the more universally agreed-upon evangelical essentials such as the deity, virgin birth, the bodily resurrection of Christ, the inspiration of the Bible, and a traditional understanding of the Trinity. The only eschatological decla-ration was an affirmation of Christ's "triumphal return." In Gordon College Ladd found a place where he could prepare for Christian ministry, free from significant doctrinal conflict and without regard to his difficult financial situation.[31]

Gordon also promoted and maintained unusually rigorous academic stan-dards for a Bible college, even as many other conservative institutions became militantly anti-intellectual. In the 1915 catalogue the school declared that "It is believed at Gordon that the problems of the day including the 'higher criticism' should be frankly and fearlessly faced."[32] To this end Gordon College was highly selective in its admissions policies. In 1915 Nathan Wood, dean of the college, reported to the trustees that he had accepted only "about ⅓ of the applicants."[33] The next year Wood proudly told the trustees that two-thirds of the students at Gordon were "doing work of college or university grade."[34] Gordon's mission, as defined by Wood, was to train men and women to be both doctrinally and culturally literate. He was not above reminding students of their responsibility to work hard at their studies, especially given the absence of tuition. In the 1933 catalogue Wood stated that for their bargain education, he expected "in return a worthy standard in the scholastic work of the students."[35] The educational atmosphere at Gordon reflected the twin priorities of evan-gelical witness and academic excellence, and by the time Ladd arrived there, President Wood's emphasis on transmitting culture through a rigorous evangelical liberal arts program was firmly in place.[36] Like many institutions in the Bible college movement, however, Gordon did not yet merit the same level of accreditation that the more established schools enjoyed. For most students headed toward ministry within the conservative movement this was not an issue, but for Ladd it would prove to be disastrous. Still, Gordon College in 1929, with its combination of scholarly atmosphere and minimal cost, served Ladd well at this stage of his education.

Ladd attempted, as many do, to reinvent himself during his college years. He joined the basketball team and played at the varsity level for two years. A fine singer (as his father had been), Ladd also sang in the Radio Chorus, a choir that, in addition to performing in churches and at other gatherings around Boston, was featured twice each week on local radio programs.[37] Adopting Gordon's Baptist ethos, Ladd returned to Maine on his first summer break and preached for sixteen consecutive Sundays at the Baptist Church of Clifton, an arrangement made through the college. The work of studying and preaching thrilled Ladd, and the response to his sermons provided yet another layer of confirmation that he belonged in the pastorate. Ladd left Clifton for Gordon believing that he "could never be happy in any other work than in God's ministry" and approached his studies with new resolve.[38]

In 1932 Ladd was elected president of the League of Evangelical Students, a service organization that visited hospitals and "homes for the aged" and distributed religious tracts in and around Boston.[39] With the lack of money still an ever-present issue, Ladd found work "cutting butter and cracking eggs" at a nearby creamery and waited on tables at nearby restaurants.[40] In his junior year Ladd began service as a student pastor at the Baptist church in Gilford, a small town in central New Hampshire, where he worked with youth groups and occasionally preached. This position required significant initiative on Ladd's part. With no car, he had to take a train from Boston to Laconia (a distance of about one hundred miles) and walk the remaining six miles to Gilford, only to make the return trip when his duties were completed.[41] All of this was a strain on his time and energies, especially as a working student, but Ladd thrived in the role of pastor and devoted himself to both his education and service. This new sense of purpose and belonging marked Ladd as one to watch in his graduating class, and at his commencement service in 1933 he was one of five students chosen to give an address.[42] During his four years as an undergraduate at Gordon, Ladd was able to shed some—though by no means all—of the stigma from his days as the "Freak."

Ladd's academic work as an undergraduate was solid, though not particularly stellar. In his first year he earned as many top grades as lesser ones, but as a senior he earned straight As and A minuses. He took Greek courses every year, moving from Bs as a freshman to As at the time of his graduation. True to Gordon's emphasis on liberal studies, Ladd completed coursework in psychology, European history, biology and literature, alongside his Bible, theology and ministry work.[43] Ladd's work in one Old Testament course revealed some of his own brewing inner struggle. Asked to write a character study of a significant biblical figure, Ladd chose King Saul, about whom he said that "although his life was a failure spiritually, his early life was very promising and hopeful... [and] the downward steps may be followed from the heights of humbleness and service to the depths of selfishness and hatred of a better man."[44] Without drawing too much from a single undergraduate paper, this glimpse into Ladd's choice of subject matter and his handling of it shed some light on his priorities and values. Ladd's feelings of inferiority, as we will see, would lead later to bouts of envy in relation to friends, colleagues, and family, not unlike those of the biblical King Saul. Further, he would eventually come to see his own life as a spiritual failure, despite his obvious promise and accomplishment as a preacher and scholar. Whatever pathologies appeared in Ladd's later years, the seeds were visible virtually from the start.

In 1933 Ladd's adult life and career began to take shape. He graduated from Gordon with a Bachelor of Theology degree and was ordained by the ministers of the Belknap Association in the Northern Baptist Convention (NBC). That same year Ladd was called to pastor the Gilford church he had served as a student and prepared for his move to New Hampshire. On 11 July 1933, just a month after graduating from Gordon, Ladd married Winifred Webber, a Gordon alumna who had finished her degree two years before Ladd and had been working as a secretary.[45] Winnie, as she was known, was four years older than George and suffered from her own set of humiliating physical and familial problems. Several times she was ill enough to leave Gordon and return to her home in Worcester, about fifty miles from Boston. The day before their wedding, Winnie's dental bridge came loose and needed to be repaired.[46] She was also the product of a difficult family. One of four sisters, Winnie competed for love from two difficult parents. Even relatives on George's side of the family remember Winnie's father as "miserly . . . cold and distant" and stated that her mother similarly exhibited little personal warmth.[47] Still, George's diary makes it clear that he doted on Winnie: "At last, I've found real love, and a real lover, and best of all, God is leading us . . . . I know she is the only girl for me, and I hope I may always be worthy of her love."[48]

Together the newlyweds went to Belmont, near Gilford, to live with Ladd's mother, and Ladd began his first full-time pastorate. In 1934 the Ladds had their first child, Norma, and three years later a son, Larry. Also in 1934 Ladd enrolled at Gordon Divinity School to begin his work toward a Bachelor of Divinity degree. All of these activities taxed his time and strength, but Ladd was accustomed to hard work. He completed several courses toward the BD while working as a full-time pastor and young father and continued to thrive in his public role. By all accounts the pastorate in Gilford was a successful one. Ladd sang with the choir, worked with the youth of the town, and organized sports leagues. During the winter months he arranged skating parties for church members at a local pond.[49] Ladd earned $20 per week at the forty-member church, barely enough to get by even during the worst years of the Depression, and by 1936 it was time to move on.[50]

Even at this early stage in his career, Ladd was growing uncomfortable with his Baptist affiliation. The NBC was formed in 1907, with the Arminian Free Will Baptists joining the affiliation in 1911.[51] The organization was beset by conflict virtually from the beginning over topics as diverse as doctrine, authority, and the centralization of authority. Beginning in 1923, fundamentalist groups had seceded or partially seceded from the NBC after the formation of the Baptist Bible Union (BBU), which organized separately but whose congregations stayed in the NBC. The BBU evolved into the fully separated General Association of Regular Baptist Churches (GARBC) in 1932, and by 1947 the Conservative Baptist Fellowship, which had formed only the year before with the intention to remain in the NBC, left the convention completely as the Conservative Baptist Association (CBA). Ladd had participated in the CBA movement from its start but remained in the NBC after the split.[52]

Ladd participated in various aspects of the NBC leadership but was distressed by both its increasing level of liberalism and the simmering militancy of the fundamentalist agitators. In 1936 he wrote to Robert Ketcham (1889–1978), a fundamentalist pastor who was a leader of the BBU and the GARBC, complaining that several belligerent New England Baptist pastors were disrupting the NBC's work.[53] The response was less than helpful. Ketcham was a virulent critic of any centralized denominational organization and had led all of his congregations out of their convention memberships.[54] Ketcham told Ladd that "one of the ways to have avoided the arising of leadership in New England with which you cannot cooperate, would have been for you to have started out on this matter yourself a long time ago."[55] Ketcham continued:

> I find it necessary in my own case to go along with a lot of men who do things and say things that, if I were doing them and saying them, it would be different, but I cannot run every man through my own personal mould, so wherever I find a man who is sincerely out and out for Christ and His truth, I try to throw my forces with him. I certainly think this is a better plan than to retreat into the old Convention where there is insincerity, infidelity, Modernism and Communism.[56]

Ladd could see where this was heading. The fundamentalists in the GARBC had directed the break with the NBC in 1932 and treated anyone who showed sympathy for the "old convention" with suspicion. Ladd was twenty-five years of age and had a young family, and it was the middle of the Depression. Despite his unease with the theological direction of the NBC, it was better at this point for Ladd to stay within the convention than to join the more militant separatists.

Before leaving Gilford, Ladd made a successful application to join the New England Fellowship (NEF) as a radio and conference preacher. Founded in 1931 by J. Elwin Wright (1890–1973) as a cooperative effort to evangelize the region, the NEF played an important foundational role in what would become the new evangelical movement after World War II. In the 1930s, separatist attitudes kept most conservative churches and groups of churches from working together, even in tasks on which they did not disagree. Wright, an evangelist from New Hampshire, founded the NEF on the principle that Christians from diverse traditions could concur on the necessity for evangelism in the New England region.[57] Wright hosted evangelistic meetings, conferences for pastors, and youth camps from his base in Rumney, New Hampshire. The NEF model of cooperative evangelism laid the groundwork for the 1942 launching of the National Association of Evangelicals, which was a national version of the NEF and also founded by Wright, as well as Fuller Theological Seminary (1947) and the ministry of Billy Graham.[58] The NEF succeeded because it emphasized evangelistic work over tests of doctrinal purity. Wright's motto, from the seventeenth-century Lutheran Peter Meiderlin, was as follows: "In essentials, unity; in non-essentials, liberty; in all things, charity."[59]

The NEF had a doctrinal statement, to be sure, but like that of Gordon College it avoided controversial issues such as inerrancy and eschatology. Leaders who attended the early conferences were amazed at the unified atmosphere. One commented that the meetings "demonstrated that twenty denominational groups, with very diverse views on many theological questions, could submerge their unessential differences and unite in perfect fellowship in a period of worship, spiritual inspiration, and prayer." Another said of the NEF leadership that he "would not be surprised if those dear people [were] quietly making history."[60] Indeed they were. The young ministers, teachers, and graduate students who participated in the early NEF conferences became the vanguard of the cooperative evangelical enterprises of the second half of the twentieth century. The irenic NEF provided Ladd with another influential example of how evangelical ministry could be accomplished without militancy or separatism. Ladd worked with the NEF at least until 1948, teaching at pastors' conferences and giving radio sermons.[61] In 1948 he represented the NEF at the convention of the National Association of Evangelicals, where he chaired the commission on youth literature.[62]

Ladd's application and surviving sermon manuscripts provide a glimpse into his theological views at the time. To whatever extent his early Christian faith was influenced by the dispensationalism of Cora Cash, it appears to have been tempered by his time at Gordon College. The statement of faith that Ladd submitted to the NEF around 1936 can be placed squarely in the mainstream of the evangelical tradition, thereby avoiding any of the divisive questions related to the nature of the Bible or eschatology.[63] He affirms the inspiration of the Bible but draws a line between his own views and those that would say that the Bible was "dictated" by God. He allows that the "personality and training" of each biblical author are present in the writings, though not to the point of interfering with the divine message.

Regarding the doctrine of salvation, Ladd reveals a moderately Arminian position. He states that "on the cross Christ took the place of all men" but acknowledges that "salvation is effective only for those who accept." He would not have believed in the Calvinist doctrine of unconditional election: "A man must give the assent of his will to the work of Christ to make Salvation his own."[64] In the area of eschatology Ladd affirms the "visible bodily personal return" of Jesus but bypasses contentious mainstays of dispensationalist vocabulary such as *tribulation, rapture,* and the *Antichrist.* Further, his understanding of the purpose of scripture is significant. He says that the Bible is "God's message to men of the facts they cannot naturally learn."[65] This appraisal of the biblical documents as sources of facts would shape Ladd's work for years to come. More important, especially in light of its role in Ladd's later academic career, he makes no mention of millennial belief in any form. Whether this moderate statement was an accurate reflection of all that he believed or was crafted for the nonmilitant readers at the NEF cannot be known with certainty. What is clear is that in 1936 Ladd was already becoming aware of the finesse that would be required of him in order to avoid conflicts over doctrinal issues.

In 1936, just as he was beginning his work with the NEF, Ladd was called to serve as the pastor of the First Baptist Church in Montpelier, Vermont. The move to a new community and a slightly larger church was a happy one for the Ladds. They developed close friendships, were involved in local recreational activities, and enjoyed the new church community. The impact of the Depression still dominated economic conditions in the United States, and Montpelier, though a larger city and capital of the state, suffered during that time. The pay was meager, just $22 per month, and often the Ladds would receive regular gifts of vegetables and fruit from members of their church.[66] Friends in Montpelier remember both couples being "very poor" but also recall the Ladds sharing their donated food with them.[67]

Still striving to emulate the qualities of his cherished Zane Grey characters, George developed a love for outdoor sports in his twenties and was known to recruit friends from the midweek Bible study group to go skiing on weekends and evenings. He and Winnie regularly shared meals with friends, "each bringing whatever [they] had on hand."[68] Though Ladd was remembered as being "very dogmatic," even by close friends at the Montpelier church, some of his mother's pietist influence emerged in his preaching ministry. Members of his church recall that he often said, "I know Jesus lives because I know it in my heart."[69] This reliance upon inner confirmation differs strongly from the coercive doctrinal conformity of militant fundamentalism and indicates Ladd's evolving individuation from that movement. At Montpelier, Ladd learned that he loved to teach the Bible and started several study groups, which grew substantially during his time there. But he also remained poor, with two children growing up in much the same financial distress as he had experienced as a boy. To earn an extra $1.80 per week, Ladd assumed the preaching duties for another local church, a position he held for two years. Between his pastoral duties, his newfound love of teaching, and his continuing academic work at Gordon, Ladd's plans for himself began to change. He told friends that he "always felt the need to get more education, to better serve the Lord."[70] It was during his time at Montpelier that Ladd decided to pursue an advanced degree and focus his career on teaching and writing.

Why the shift in direction? Certainly there were financial considerations. Even at Gordon College the professors were earning significantly higher salaries than those of rural pastors.[71] So much of Ladd's life had been lived on the brink of abject poverty that, after a few years of serving as an underpaid minister, an academic career must have seemed appealing. There may have been status considerations as well. Ladd's interactions with professors exhibit a deference he was unlikely to show to many others. For a man with a fragile sense of self-esteem and overdeveloped feelings of being an outsider, the respect commanded by—and authority granted to—a professor would have held a magnetic draw.

Most significant in Ladd's decision to pursue an academic career, however, was his growing tendency to retreat from his family into long hours of study. The Ladds' marriage was increasingly an unhappy one, with Winnie needing far more fatherly attention from George than he would ever be able to provide. Further, George found it extremely difficult to establish a loving connection with his own children. His daughter, Norma, had a much closer relationship with George's brother, James, whom she clearly saw as her father figure, a development that also forged a new layer of bad feeling between the brothers.[72] Larry, who did not yet show the signs of his later emotional and physical problems, was still a mystery to George, who responded by ignoring him. This combination of a difficult marriage, the challenges of parenthood, renewed jealousy toward his brother, and his demanding work schedule caused Ladd to escape into books. The decision to pursue an advanced degree and a career in academia provided him with an outwardly respectable way to distance himself from those who demanded—and threatened—emotional closeness. And while this move set Ladd on the path to prominence as a scholar, it also marked the beginning of the end of his relationship to his family.

With his sights set on an academic career, Ladd's next objective was to choose a school in which to continue his studies. The task proved to be challenging—even humiliating at times—as he tried to make the sizable leap from provincial evangelical Bible college to a respected seminary or university. Ladd's propensity to see himself as an unwelcome outsider certainly aggravated his response to the process. Ironically—or perhaps fittingly—it was Ladd's evangelical training that made this next crucial step so difficult.

The necessity for a postgraduate degree had been impressed upon Ladd early in this time of transition. In 1938 Ladd wrote to J. Oliver Buswell (1895–1977), then president of Wheaton College in Illinois, to ask for a teaching position. Wheaton at that time represented the pinnacle of evangelical liberal arts education, and Ladd's query, while unrealistic, makes sense in light of that fact.[73] Buswell recognized the value of education for the evangelical movement, and as president of Wheaton from 1926 to 1940 he was largely responsible for facilitating the school's growth in size and academic stature.[74] To Ladd's inquiry, which explained in some detail his plans for an academic career, Buswell stated that Wheaton did not employ as instructors "any who do not have the earned doctor's degree or who are not practically ready to receive that degree."[75] At this point Ladd held only his BTh from Gordon, not exactly a top-notch credential. Buswell further advised Ladd: "If you are interested in college teaching, I should suggest that you continue straight forward toward your Ph.D. I should be glad to hear from you when you are nearly ready to receive it." Ladd was disappointed but took this advice to heart and began to look for a doctoral program that might accept him.

Ladd was clearly aware that his choice of institutions would impact his ability to make the transition from pastor to scholar, a fact that intensified the pain of each closed door. In early 1939 Ladd wrote to John R. Sampey (1863–1946), president of the Southern Baptist Theological Seminary in Kentucky, and asked whether his work at Gordon would be enough for admission to doctoral study and whether financial support might be available.[76] The blunt answer to Ladd's query regarding finances, according to Sampey, was that he must be prepared to pay the costs himself.[77]

Ladd wrote immediately to the dean, W. Hersey Davis, only to find more disappointment as Davis informed him that admission to the doctoral program required both BA and BD degrees. Davis may also have initiated some suspicion on Ladd's part regarding the degree he had already earned by informing him that it could not be accepted in lieu of a BA from an accredited institution.[78] Given Ladd's desire to make the transition to an academic career, the refusal to recognize his Gordon degree was a significant blow. Ladd wrote back, pleading for acceptance and asking whether an MA would satisfy the entrance requirements.[79] Davis replied in the affirmative, though with the restriction that Ladd could be admitted only for the ThD, a lesser degree.[80] Ladd wrote back, once again begging to be admitted for doctoral studies and promising to earn the necessary credentials at the University of Vermont or Boston University, only to be told that the seminary no longer offered the PhD degree.[81]

Ladd decided at this point to pursue an MA degree at an accredited institution and began the process of applying to the philosophy department at Boston University. He proposed a course of study there that met the requirements for the degree and also corrected the deficiencies identified in his failed doctoral applications.[82] Edgar Brightman (1884–1953), the head of the department, responded positively to Ladd's proposal, though Ladd chose not to attend at that time. In his note to Ladd, Brightman gently scolded his prospective student for his carelessly written application: "Let me suggest that you brush up on spelling. Last time we had an odd version of the *Timaeus*, and this time 'Inter-Testimental' appears. After all, a graduate student should have his *termini technici* in proper shape!"[83] For someone with a growing obsession to achieve some level of academic standing, Brightman's criticisms of Ladd may have had more impact than they warranted. In any case, there was no further communication between Ladd and Brightman. The next year Ladd applied again, this time to Yale University for a BD degree, but was rejected once more. Luther Weigle (1880–1976), dean of the divinity school, wrote personally (and kindly) to express his "high regard and regret" for Ladd and to assure him that the determining factor was that the school had a severely limited number of openings.[84]

By 1939 and 1940 it was clear to Ladd that he would not achieve his goal of a doctoral degree unless he improved his credentials. However, he also knew that with a wife and two small children, his financial situation left him few options. He took steps to complete his BD at Gordon Divinity School by increasing his course load and burying himself in study. To improve his chances of gaining admission to a university doctoral program he also began taking courses at Vermont Junior College, not far from his church in Montpelier. There Ladd completed a full year of Latin coursework and a semester each of German, French, sociology, and chemistry.[85] Since several of the university doctoral programs required some laboratory experience, Ladd also completed a semester in a chemistry laboratory. These were exhausting days for the young pastor as he balanced home and church responsibilities, along with coursework at two institutions, but he was determined, if at all possible, to avoid the humiliation and rejection he had experienced from 1938 to 1940.

To complicate this time of uncertainty, Ladd was finding that Christian leadership could be dangerous as well. In 1940 he received a reminder of how sensitive certain issues could be within the world of conservative evangelicalism. At the end of his Latin class at Vermont Junior College, the students held a celebratory feast in the style of first-century Rome. A local newspaper publicized the event, including a menu of the dinner, which included wine, and also a list of the participating students. Ladd was immediately called before the board of deacons to explain his partaking of alcohol, to which he responded that the goblets were filled with grape juice only. Despite this explanation the board censured him for allowing his name to appear in a story that included a positive reference to the drinking of wine.[86]

Ladd's search for a postgraduate program continued through 1941 and into 1942, but with only limited success. He wrote to a Methodist friend, J. Homer Slutz, in early 1941 to ask about the possibility of studying at Duke University in North Carolina. Slutz offered to send a letter of reference on his behalf to H. Earl Myers, a professor at Duke, and encouraged Ladd to apply.[87] Ladd wrote to Myers himself almost immediately, and the response gave him hope. Myers had contacted several Baptist leaders in the Durham area and found that pulpit openings were plentiful and that several were substantial enough to fund Ladd's studies.[88] Clearly Ladd's further study at Vermont College and Gordon Divinity School had minimized the question of his academic preparation, and the discussion focused exclusively on financial matters. As a training school for Methodist clergy, the area around Duke represented a broad range of opportunities for a Baptist student. While Methodist students competed for a limited number of pulpits, Ladd, as an experienced Baptist minister, would have had his choice of several church positions. Nevertheless, while the financial and academic prospects looked exceedingly favorable at Duke, the application process was halted. Whether this decision was the outcome of a conflict between George and Winnie Ladd is not known, but it seems strange that such an opportunity should be summarily rejected. Nevertheless, the Ladds decided to stay in the Northeast, and George focused on building his academic résumé.

However, little would deter Ladd's search for a postgraduate program. In 1941 he wrote to the Eastern Baptist Theological Seminary in Philadelphia, where he hoped to have greater success with his more complete training and Baptist background. At this point Ladd was almost finished with his BD degree at Gordon and was confident that the next round of applications would be more satisfying than the first. But disappointment loomed again. Carl H. Morgan (1901–1983), the dean of Eastern Seminary, advised Ladd to abandon his hope of teaching biblical languages, claiming that many institutions were beginning

to move them out of the required curriculum.[89] Certainly this was more reflective of conditions in the Northern Baptist Convention, which had strong
liberal influences, and not the evangelical academy as a whole. Indeed, what
often separated conservative curricula from those of moderate or liberal institutions was the rigorous requirement for the study of Hebrew and Greek.

Moreover, that was not the only bad news from Eastern. Morgan was
dismissive of Ladd's academic preparation, even with his added remedial
studies. Responding to Ladd's desire to teach in a seminary setting, Morgan
advised him that "most seminaries require that their faculty members have at
least one graduate degree *not* in *theology*."[90] Morgan recommended an MA
from an established university. Then, as if this were not bruising enough to
Ladd's fragile ego, Morgan told him that "it will be necessary, of course, for you
to get your A.B.," a statement that must have come as a crushing blow to Ladd,
who had spent the previous two years completing a BD degree plus extra
coursework. Morgan closes the letter by saying that it would not "be wise to
suggest that you seek admission to Eastern until after you have had more
academic training."

The response from Eastern added a new level of desperation to Ladd's quest
for a doctoral program that would accept him. In early 1941 Ladd sent his typed
transcripts and a proposal for study to the University of Pennsylvania and received what must have seemed to him a standardized response. A dean's assistant, Paul C. Kitchen, wrote back, saying that Ladd's academic preparation did
not fulfill the university's requirements and recommended that Ladd complete
several courses in science or mathematics to remove the deficiencies.[91] The best
Kitchen could promise was that "if all [remedial] course requirements were met,
your Bachelor of Theology degree would not prevent you from undertaking work
for the doctor's degree here at Pennsylvania." He advised Ladd to bring proof of
the added coursework to his office when it was completed.

At that moment Ladd must have reached some type of breaking point. He
packed a box of catalogues and official transcripts of his academic record and
traveled to Philadelphia—a distance of more than four hundred miles—to
show them to Kitchen. Arriving at the university on a Saturday, Ladd found the
offices closed, left the box and an application at Kitchen's door, and went back
to Vermont. Kitchen read through Ladd's academic history and determined
that he still did not meet the requirements for admission to the university.[92]
Ladd wrote back immediately and demanded to know why his application had
been rejected but received a similar answer from Kitchen.[93] In May of 1941
Ladd gave up on the University of Pennsylvania.

Even without enrolling in a graduate program, Ladd maintained an extremely demanding schedule. At his church in Montpelier he preached twice

a week, taught Bible classes, carried a full schedule of visitation and admin-istrative duties, and led the youth group. From 1936 to 1937 he earned $1,040 annually and $1,200 for the remainder of his tenure.[94] The lack of money continued to be a problem, so to augment his income Ladd also preached a weekly sermon at a Freewill Baptist church in nearby Shady Rill, a position for which he was theologically suited and which added $182 annually to his in-come.[95] In addition, Ladd worked toward his BD degree at Gordon, which he completed in 1941, while simultaneously taking his remedial courses at Ver-mont College. Married with two young children, Ladd spent most of his time either in pastoral duties or obsessively working toward his goal of an academic career and left the parenting to Winnie. Family life for the Ladds revolved around George's work and study, which regularly occupied him late into the night.[96]

As George Ladd was working toward an academic degree and career, his brother, James, was making a name for himself as well. James followed his brother to Gordon, where he graduated in 1937, and also served as a pastor in several churches affiliated with the Northern Baptist Convention. In 1942 James enrolled at the U.S. Army Chaplain Training School at Harvard and for the next year worked on army bases in New York State. In July of 1943 he was promoted to the rank of captain and in November was sent to England to serve the troops preparing for the invasion of Europe.[97] James earned some renown in 1944, when it was learned that he and several soldiers had built a jeep out of scrap parts, which enabled the chaplain to lead services over a wider range of Ninth Air Force encampments.[98] In 1946 James was awarded the Bronze Star for meritorious service as a war chaplain. He retired from the military in 1950 and earned a PhD in speech communication from the Oklahoma State Uni-versity in 1960.[99] He spent the remainder of his life as a professor and served as head of the speech department at Phillips University for twenty years.[100]

It is ironic that James Ladd came to personify many of the idealized qualities of Zane Grey's heroes, a fact that permanently damaged his rela-tionship with George. James was an outgoing, attractive person who enjoyed his large and loving family (he had six children) and a wide circle of friends, in addition to being an accomplished university professor.[101] Further, even George's own children felt closer to their uncle than to their father, a fact that drove the intensely resentful George deeper into his studies. Still, on those occasions when Ladd's fragile emotional state prevented him from completing a sermon, it was James who came to his rescue by finishing the writing for his brother.[102] A less-wounded man would have been grateful to his brother for this sort of help, but George found it humiliating and maintained a cool dis-tance from James.

Ladd made another attempt in 1942 to find a doctoral program that would accept him, this time at the University of Chicago Divinity School. Although affiliated with the Northern Baptist Convention, Chicago clearly represented the theological left wing of the tradition. Surprisingly, however, Chicago looked like a real option for Ladd. Theologian Bernard Loomer (b. 1912), who later became a prominent Unitarian Universalist, answered Ladd's query and encouraged him to complete the application process. The deficiencies that had scuttled his earlier applications remained, but according to Loomer they could be easily remedied. Here, finally, Ladd found someone willing to work with—if not overlook—his earlier academic record. Loomer assured Ladd that his extra work at Vermont College would satisfy most, if not all, of Chicago's entrance requirements.[103] Ladd must have been overjoyed. Loomer implicitly promised Ladd admission to the program and declared that "these [remedial] requirements do not have to be gotten out of the way before you actually enter the Divinity School. They can be made up while you are working for a degree."

Why the sudden change in Ladd's fortunes? It may simply be that his academic potential and obvious tenacity made him a desirable candidate for admission. More likely, however, the beginning of World War II left Chicago and other institutions short on students, leading to greater flexibility in the admissions process. In any case, Ladd immediately inquired about money and was informed not only that financial assistance was available but that "in all probability [he would] be granted a scholarship."[104] Despite these positive indications, Ladd, as he had with Duke the year before, elected to stay in New England. The question remains unanswered as to the role Winnie played in the decisions to turn down these opportunities, but given Ladd's growing desperation to find a program that would accept him, one may assume a growing level of tension between them. There was no further communication between Ladd and the University of Chicago.

Ladd completed his BD degree at Gordon Divinity School in 1941, hoping that this added credential would help him secure a place in a doctoral program. His thesis, a study of Pauline eschatology, was titled "Did Paul Change His Mind about the Time of the Second Coming of Christ?"[105] In it Ladd addresses the major theories of the day regarding Paul's apparently evolving views of Christ's return, specifically, that his earlier writings predicted an imminent return and the later ones a postponed coming. Challenging the proposal that Paul had simply changed his mind over time, Ladd argues that Paul is consistent throughout and that any evolutionary interpretation of Paul's thought ignores the fact that his entire message was the product of divine revelation and thus could not shift over time. Ladd's logic for defending the consistency of Paul's thought betrays a sort of blind spot in his intellectual development.

Ladd argues that since Paul claimed to have received his knowledge by revelation, this premise itself "must be recognized and the evidence studied in the light of his claim."[106] This stance would later hurt him in his attempt to be considered a credible scholar, but within the evangelical confines of Gordon Divinity School it caused him no problems. Ultimately Ladd argues that Paul simply did not know when the second coming would take place and that this lack of knowledge was consistent with the teachings of Jesus himself in Matthew 24:36.[107]

Commenting on the thesis, Nathan Wood praised Ladd's "clarity of thought and style," as well as his "almost constant logical mind."[108] More significantly, Wood identified several characteristics of Ladd's method of forming an argument that would both serve him and haunt him in the years to come: "You never once seem to be trying to prove a point, but always simply to reach a fair conclusion. With this is a very pleasant attitude. In more than one place, where you need to show that the statements of a group of critics are absurd, you use the statements of a group of better interpreters about the absurdities, and so avoid an ex cathedra attitude on your part, and then proceed to draw impartial conclusions of your own."[109]

Ladd's ability to handle sensitive theological issues with an objective tone would become a hallmark of his later writings on a wide range of topics. This "pleasant attitude" served Ladd as he endeavored to correct the excesses of militant fundamentalism and sought the approval of scholars outside the evangelical world. Nonetheless, Wood also inadvertently names another strain in Ladd's work that would wound him in the coming years. Ladd, according to Wood, is willing to use the work of other scholars to make his most important or damaging arguments. Later critics would attack Ladd for his tendency either to hide behind other scholars' conclusions or to use their work out of context for his benefit. These habits would eventually make several appearances in Ladd's life.

Ladd's choice of topic for his thesis introduces a pair of themes that reappeared throughout his academic career. In the opening paragraph of the first chapter Ladd writes the following: "Several years ago, the statement was made within the hearing of the writer that there was no single study that adequately treated the question of a possible change in the mind of Saint Paul with reference to his thought on the time of the Second Advent of Jesus Christ. It is the purpose of this study to investigate this question, and to bring within the scope of a single study the evidence and the problems related thereto."[110] The first matter is the recognition of a gap or deficiency in the scholarly literature regarding an important doctrinal issue. Ladd would often look for the definitive study or "final word" on a particular topic, only to find that such a work did not exist. More importantly, the second subject emerges as Ladd often names himself as the one to whom the burden falls to create the definitive piece of scholarship. This need for a "final word" exposes Ladd's related hopes for both the certainty of his faith and the ability of his scholarship to define and defend that certainty. These themes ultimately became significant sources of both motivation and pain as they played out in the course of Ladd's academic life.

In 1942 Ladd left his church in Montpelier to become the pastor of Blaney Memorial Church in Boston, a move that helped to determine the rest of his life and career. Blaney Church, founded in 1882, had a membership of about six hundred people when Ladd was called to assume this new position.[111] It was a conservative church, situated in a historic section of Dorchester, one of the oldest neighborhoods in Boston.[112] The financial terms of the larger Blaney pastorate alleviated some of the Ladd family's financial difficulties and placed George in the heart of Boston, then the center of the academic world. The position paid him $2,100 per year (more than double his salary at Gilford and $900 more than he earned in Montpelier), allowed the use of the parsonage, covered local telephone expenses, and made the standard contributions to a retirement fund.[113] Hoping to leave rural Vermont for the richer possibilities that Boston represented, Ladd had pursued this church for a while. Earlier in 1942 Ladd had written to Merrill Tenney (1904–1985), a doctoral student at Harvard and an instructor at Gordon, who was serving as the interim pastor at Blaney. Tenney had been one of Ladd's New Testament professors at Gordon in 1940 and 1941, and they remained friends for decades. Aware of Ladd's academic plans, Tenney asked whether Ladd understood that the increased responsibilities might force him to "forego extensive study for the sake of the church."[114] "Blaney is at the place now," Tenney warned, "where it will take all of one man's time to do the job well." Ladd dismissed the words of caution, accepted the position, and continued his search for admission to graduate school. The move to Boston also allowed him to inquire about a teaching position at Gordon College. Undaunted by the workload, he was hired in 1942 to teach elementary Greek in the undergraduate program and settled into his new life balancing pastoral responsibilities, part-time teaching, and preparation for academic study. He was also heavily involved in the leadership of the Boston South Baptist Association, with which Blaney Memorial was affiliated. Ladd served on the Missionary Cooperation Committee and the Ordination and Ministerial Committee in 1943 and 1944 and the Evangelism Committee in 1944 and 1945.[115]

In his participation in the various Baptist conventions during the 1930s and 1940s, Ladd consistently sought to be a moderate advocate for the conservative wing within the broader Baptist community. Through his personal relationships with other pastors and the writings of the disgruntled Baptist fundamentalists who had not yet separated, he was aware that the conservatives were being marginalized. Ladd's response was to work for change from within the political structure of his state convention. In 1945, however, it became clear to him that his attempts to work peacefully for change were doomed to failure. Serving as clerk for the program committee of the Massachusetts Baptist Convention, Ladd objected to the proposed slate of nominees for the main convention speaker. The New York office of the NBC had suggested three moderate pastors, a reflection of the close partnership between the state and larger conventions. Among them were Norman Vincent Peale, liberal Reformed author of *The Power of Positive Thinking*, and Daniel Poling, editor of the *Christian Herald*, social activist and Peale's predecessor at New York's Marble Collegiate Church. The minutes of the meeting state that Ladd "expressed the opinion that he would like to have a speaker who would appeal to the conservative men in the state," and he suggested fellow conservatives John Bradbury and Clarence Roddy.[116] Bradbury was a pastor in Boston, while Roddy was a popular preacher who had served congregations from New York City to Portland, Maine. Both were trustees of Gordon College. Both were also rejected by the program committee, even after Ladd's impassioned defense. The record shows that immediately after the vote, the clerk—Ladd—"had to leave the meeting because of another engagement."[117] The next day Ladd resigned from the committee and never again participated in the leadership of either the Massachusetts Baptist Convention or the NBC.[118]

As Ladd enjoyed his dual careers as pastor and academic, he attempted to determine what his role might be in the world of evangelical scholarship. He wrote a series of letters to prominent Christian scholars and leaders around the country and asked them to recommend the best works of evangelical Christian philosophy. Again, as in his academic work at Gordon, we see Ladd searching for the final word on faith and theology. The responses, though largely disappointing, identified for him an opportunity to make a contribution to the world of scholarship and set him on the path he would follow for the rest of his career. Gordon Clark of Wheaton College suggested two Christian books written before the turn of the century and several others written by men he referred to as a humanist and an infidel, respectively. The best Clark could suggest was a series of syllabi by Cornelius Van Til of Westminster Seminary, though he characterized them as "difficult" to the point of being "discouraging."[119] William Mueller of Eastern Baptist Seminary offered a better variety of sources, though Ladd would have considered only two of the twelve acceptably conservative. Mueller recommended a handful of nineteenth-century German scholars, most notably Martin Kähler, a writer whose thought would have an important influence on Ladd's later work.[120] In addition, H. Emerson Rosenberger of Houghton College tried to steer Ladd away from philosophical or theological works entirely and toward psychological studies. He recommended the writings of Harvard psychology professor William James as guides to "the practical aspects of religious faith," though it is doubtful that James was the kind of thinker Ladd was looking for.[121]

The response from T. Leonard Lewis, then of Northern Baptist Seminary, was the most detailed and best predicted the driving force behind Ladd's career as a scholar. Lewis wrote that the conservative champion of evangelical philosophy "[had] not yet been discovered" because "our conservative men are so occupied with evangelism and preaching that they haven't time to write."[122] Lewis's next comment was even more telling. He admitted that "some apology has to be made for every book one might suggest because the neo-conservatives who have written have not come far enough to suit many of us." He closed his letter with a challenge to Ladd: "May it be possible that you in the future can put in print your views and make a contribution to the field?" Ladd's unsuccessful attempt to find a respected and credible expression of conservative evangelical theology provided the animating spirit for his scholastic life. For the next quarter century he made it his personal goal to write a book that would make the broader academic world take notice of evangelical thought.

But how to prepare? Joining the faculty at Gordon College and, later on, Gordon Divinity School were important steps in Ladd's development, and their influence would stay with him throughout his career. In addition to the irenic spirit of the institution, the presence of dynamic evangelical scholars who were pursuing their advanced degrees in nearby Boston created a community of fellow travelers for Ladd. Of the twenty-four members of the faculty in the 1948–1949 academic year, for example, six were completing doctoral-level studies at Harvard, and two were at Boston University. Twenty members of the faculty had completed some part of their education at the university level, outside the confines of evangelical higher education.[123] These young instructors added to the atmosphere of serious inquiry at the school and encouraged a more critical approach to the issues of the day.

The work at Gordon, coupled with the responses to his letters, renewed Ladd's desire to pursue doctoral studies, and Boston provided him with multiple opportunities. Living in the Boston area gave Ladd another occasion to consider Boston University, though this time not in philosophy. Ladd's teaching experience confirmed his initial plan to study Greek, and he began the process of seeking admission to Boston's department of classics. The war years created openings for promising students with dubious qualifications, and Ladd was admitted to the doctoral program in classics at Boston University, an enormous relief after his long search.

While at Boston Ladd studied with the mercurial Robert H. Pfeiffer (1892–1958), an expert in Semitic languages and the intertestamental period. Pfeiffer wrote on a wide range of topics, most related to the study of the Old Testament and ancient alphabets.[124] Pfeiffer inspired Ladd's interest in the pseudepigrapha, a collection of noncanonical works distinct from those that appear in the apocrypha, as well as in the relationship between Jewish and early Christian expressions of the Kingdom of God, and encouraged him to pursue this topic in his doctoral work. Ladd in turn excelled in his studies, earning high grades for his papers and seminar presentations.[125] Pfeiffer, who held dual appointments at Boston and Harvard, presumably advised Ladd to transfer to Harvard in order to take advantage of its joint program in classics and New Testament Greek. In 1944, after two years at Boston University, Ladd was accepted into Harvard University's doctoral program in biblical and patristic Greek.

In the 1940s a remarkable group of young men who had been raised in fundamentalist traditions earned advanced degrees at Harvard.[126] The list of graduates reads, as one writer has described, "like an honor roll of mid- to late-twentieth-century American evangelicalism."[127] Indeed, the twelve conservative evangelical or fundamentalist men who studied for doctoral degrees from Harvard during this period became prominent leaders in evangelical academic and publishing institutions. Like their secular counterparts in Harvard's Business School, these men changed the landscape—and arguably the culture—of their chosen fields.[128] The fundamentalist presence at Harvard represented a dramatic step away from the anti-intellectual sentiment of the movement and foreshadowed a growing division between separatist and non-separatist evangelicals. However, little of this surfaced while the men were still students, leaving them free to prepare for academic careers without suffering militant attacks.

The apparently counterintuitive notion of fundamentalists studying at Harvard actually made sense for both sides in the 1940s.[129] Many students preparing for the ministry or academic careers were simply choosing other schools, leaving openings for candidates outside the traditional Harvard constituency. Furthermore, the war had taken many prospective students out of the pool from which Harvard recruited. Virtually all of the Harvard fundamentalists began their studies before the onslaught of GI Bill students entered the mix in 1946. This need for students created a level of access to the divinity school that had not existed before and would not continue for very long after the period in question.

Nevertheless, there was clear benefit to the new group of students as well. First, Harvard's historical—and generally theologically neutral—approach to biblical studies allowed conservative students to pursue their studies without significant challenge to the content of their beliefs.[130] As long as they were willing to learn the critical methodology of the Harvard school, they could succeed in their academic work. Second, Harvard's heavily endowed scholarship program offered generous financial support for its students; a Harvard education in the 1940s, odd as it sounds, was a bargain compared to that of many lesser institutions. Finally and most significantly was the issue of reputation. Harvard was—as it remains—among the most highly regarded academic institutions in the United States. For this unusual generation of young scholars raised behind the walls of fundamentalism, what better place than Harvard to reengage the broader world of culture and intellectual life? In the fall of 1944 Ladd entered into this mutually beneficial arrangement to complete his doctoral studies at the Harvard Divinity School.

The years at Harvard were a period of intellectual awakening and validation for George Ladd. His acceptance there ended the humiliating search for a graduate school that would recognize his academic promise, and the faculty he found there perfectly suited his need for a pragmatic course of study rooted in facts and technical skill. Ladd also made friends at Harvard, but the focus was on academic matters, not socializing. Most of Ladd's fellow students were married with children and held full-time teaching or pastoral positions as well. It took a significant commitment of energy to complete the Harvard doctoral program, especially in light of the stress of venturing into such daunting territory.

Ladd later remembered entering Harvard with "fear and trembling," only to be relieved as he discovered that his professors "didn't care what he believed as long as he produced good work."[131] In that merit-based system he eventually realized that "he was as good a student as any of the rest." The challenge—and intellectual freedom—of Harvard deeply influenced the rest of Ladd's life and career as a scholar, giving him a new framework through which he could support his evangelical faith. Years later Ladd recalled that "Harvard didn't change what I believed, but it certainly did change the way I held my belief."[132] This is true for the most part, though it is important to note that the new critical manner in which Ladd learned to *hold his belief* allowed him to shed not only the methodology but also much of what remained of the theological content of his earlier dispensationalist faith.

Ladd blossomed in the Harvard program, where he earned several merit fellowships and thrived in the challenging but straightforward system of training. In 1945 the university awarded him the Albert and Anna Howard

Fellowship for Classics, which provided a renewable $1,000 stipend beginning with the 1945–1946 academic year.[133] The funds, when coupled with Ladd's salary as an instructor at the newly constituted Gordon Divinity School, permitted him to leave Blaney Memorial Church and the rigors of pastoral ministry for the last time. In his letter of resignation Ladd admitted that his teaching at Gordon and studies at Harvard prevented him from "doing justice to the heavy requirements of parish work which Blaney makes upon its pastor."[134] The resignation would be final in time for him to enter full-time studies at Harvard in the autumn of 1945. Ladd was finally a working scholar: He was teaching in an evangelical college and completing his training in an institution at the pinnacle of the intellectual world.

The Harvard Divinity School faculty in the 1940s consisted of a truly dazzling—and intimidating—array of scholars. British intellectual Arthur Darby Nock (1902–1963), a brilliant historian of early Christianity and classics, could be brutal in the classroom when facing an unprepared student.[135] Still, many from the era remember Nock as one of the most influential professors at the divinity school; Ladd recalled him as an example of "fair, honest scholarship."[136] Arthur Stanley Pease (1881–1964), another classicist, was also a world-renowned amateur botanist and was at least as well known for his work on the names of orchids as he was for his study of the Hellenic period.

At the same time, Robert Pfeiffer remained a strong influence on Ladd because of both his brilliance and his orthodox piety. Pfeiffer was at the height of his career during the mid-1940s. He had written important works on the biblical book of Job, as well as an edition of the Hammurabi Code. His *Introduction to the Old Testament* was already a standard seminary textbook. Pfeiffer also served as curator of Harvard's Semitic Museum and was instrumental in establishing the university's reputation in Near Eastern studies. Fluent in English, Italian, French, German, Latin, Greek, Hebrew, and a handful of Semitic languages, Pfeiffer exhibited the kind of excellence in scholarship Ladd admired and wanted to achieve. Werner Jaeger (1888–1961), a towering figure in classical studies after the publication in English of his authoritative, three-volume *Paideia* (1934, 1944, 1947), also taught in the divinity school and was to be the secondary examiner of Ladd's dissertation. In this heady atmosphere, where academic excellence was both modeled and required, Ladd thrived.

The most important influence on George Ladd during his time at Harvard, however, was Henry J. Cadbury (1883–1974). Cadbury was a brilliant New Testament scholar and holder of the oldest endowed professorship in the United States, the Hollis Chair in Divinity.[137] Cadbury was in many ways an unlikely mentor for Ladd. He was a pacifist Quaker, a liberal critic in the nineteenth-century European sense of the term, and a thoroughgoing skeptic regarding the supernatural claims of the Bible. But Cadbury was also a brilliant exegete and teacher, a compassionate advisor, and a practitioner of a rigorous historical approach to the study of biblical texts. It is not an overstatement to say that Ladd clearly loved Cadbury as a son would love a father and that the relationship between them was enormously significant in Ladd's development as a scholar. Certainly Ladd was awed by Cadbury's accomplishments. The Harvard professor had published several books both in the area of Quaker history and on the origins of the biblical Luke-Acts, was an active participant in national politics, and was known as a leader in the movement to produce a modern translation of the Bible. As Ladd worked through his doctoral program, his professor not only supervised the completion of the New Testament section of the Revised Standard Version of the Bible (1946) but also accepted the Nobel Peace Prize for his work with the American Friends Service Committee (1947). If Ladd was hoping that Harvard would provide someone to prepare him to make a significant impact on the broader culture, he had clearly found the right professor.

Cadbury's first book on the Luke-Acts writings remains a classic study in the historical-critical tradition and provides an indication of why he was so successful with his conservative students. The focus of his work was strictly limited to the history of the text itself, often—and often aggressively so— without reference to or concern for the events described in the text being studied. In the introduction Cadbury wrote that "Unless one believes in an inerrant tradition and a supernatural church as organs of transmission, one can hardly suppose that much reliable information about Jesus would have been handed down through generations of unchecked oral repetition."[138]

Of course, some of the conservative evangelical students at Harvard— including Ladd—in fact believed in an "inerrant tradition and a supernatural church," but as long as they were willing to set those presuppositions aside and address the historical data, they would survive the program. Cadbury demonstrated a relentless allegiance to the scientific study of biblical writings without regard to their theological message. This clarity of focus has for years made Cadbury accessible—and acceptable—to readers at opposite ends of the theological spectrum.[139] To Ladd, Cadbury's methodology offered an opportunity to study biblical texts according to their historical development without engaging the truth of their claims. Ladd thrived in this objective environment, with its emphasis on "facts," as did many of his fellow evangelical students.[140] Fundamentalists—especially those influenced by dispensationalism—saw the Bible as a source of facts that were apparent to all who were willing to see.[141] This focus on the facts contained in biblical writings would have created a sense—a false sense, perhaps—of impartiality in the approach to those texts taken by the Harvard faculty. Even Ladd's degree focus under Cadbury (biblical and patristic Greek) seemed theologically neutral. Cadbury's scholarship and the style of mentorship that proceeded from it created an ideal setting for Ladd and others to develop their critical abilities.

Under Cadbury Ladd was exposed to an unflinchingly critical variant of liberal biblical scholarship. While Ladd may already have been acquainted with modern critical methodologies, it was under Cadbury that he saw those methods rigorously applied to the sacred texts of the New Testament. Cadbury led his students on a journey through the most controversial questions about the historicity and message of the Christian faith, including the debate over the sources of the gospels, archaeological evidence of biblical events, divergent chronologies of the biblical record, and the value of form criticism (*Formgeschichte*).[142] With regard to form critical analysis Cadbury argued that "There is nothing in the form of a miracle story that can determine the validity or non-validity of it. A genuine miracle would assume the same pattern [as one that was fabricated]."[143] For the conservative students, Ladd included, this was a radical statement. They believed the biblical record to be inspired—if not verbally dictated—by God alone, and they would have perceived any prima facie questioning of the witness of the biblical text as nothing less than revolutionary, if not heretical. However, this was precisely why Ladd and the other evangelical students were at Harvard in the first place. If they were to engage the world of contemporary theological scholarship, they would have to pass through the crucible of learning it from its ablest practitioners. Cadbury's courses challenged many of the evangelical students' cherished beliefs but also acted as a sort of initiation for the task ahead.

While Cadbury's academic prowess drew Ladd and others to Harvard, it was his kindness and moral character that left the deepest impression. A former student wrote that Cadbury's classes "were never conventional: he did his teaching by adding observations and corrections to the comments he encouraged from his students. Reverence for his subject and the whole subsequent tradition typified his teaching."[144] Another wrote of Cadbury's classroom style that "he has inspired both ministers and teachers, through his genial kindliness, scrupulous fairness, and outstanding scholarship."[145]

This was not to say, however, that the Harvard program lacked rigor. Cadbury was known for his Socratic teaching methods and his challenges to conservative students to be honest in their handling of biblical writings. Besides, Arthur Darby Nock remained committed to keeping things from becoming too congenial. Still, it was Cadbury's ability to create a peaceful environment within which to pursue academic excellence that students remembered. This gracious comportment dominates recollections of Cadbury's influence. When Cadbury retired from Harvard in 1954, his colleagues prepared a book in his honor, *The Harvard Divinity School: Its Place in Harvard University and the American Culture*, edited by George Hunston Williams. The dedication credited Cadbury with knowing how to "balance the scholarly claims of the past with the urgent necessities of the hour" and praised him as "the very embodiment of the ideals of the community of memory and hope chronicled in the pages of our book."[146] Ladd was equally effusive in his praise of Cadbury's influence. He later wrote the following to Cadbury: "You are the man who first got me started in critical thinking, and I consciously pattern my methodology after yours. I owe you a debt which cannot be repaid, and I am sure that while my basic theological convictions have not changed, my orientation toward scholarship, particularly my desire to understand and interact with other positions in honest empathy, had its source in your example."[147] This was the key to Cadbury's impact on Ladd and his other conservative students. Biblical scholarship became a neutral tool in his hands, one to be used cooperatively in the shared quest for understanding rather than a base from which to launch polemical attacks.

Harvard's historical orientation, coupled with Cadbury's calm guidance, made room for Ladd to concentrate his research safely on a noncanonical topic. Ladd's dissertation, "The Eschatology of the *Didache*," was a close study of the eschatological content of the controversial ancient document, discovered in 1875.[148] The dissertation project allowed Ladd to pursue the same types of questions (date, setting, purpose, authorship) that he would in any examination of a biblical text without the added danger of challenging accepted conservative conclusions about the Bible itself. He was thus free to exercise his critical muscles in determining the eschatological content and historical setting of the document and to satisfy Henry Cadbury's academic demands. It was this fusion of freedom and scholarly rigor that prompted Ladd to state that "It is difficult to analyze with true objectivity the purpose of the eschatology such that is found in the *Didache*, but the attempt must be made."[149] Here Ladd returned to the sense of singular duty that marked virtually all of his academic writing: The work must be done, and only he was in a position to accomplish it. The main thesis of Ladd's dissertation was that the answers to the historical questions raised by the *Didache* lay in its eschatological content. It is in the Jewish and early Christian sources of this eschatological teaching, according to Ladd, that one can determine the origins of the *Didache*.[150]

There is no indication that the dissertation caused any stir in the academic community. Henry Cadbury and Werner Jaeger, two of the giants in the Harvard firmament, approved Ladd's completed work, and the degree was awarded in 1949. But the debate over the date and influence of the *Didache* appears to have been unaffected, and Ladd's later writings neither mention the dissertation nor say very much about the *Didache* itself.

Even though the dissertation triggered no upheaval in the study of ancient Christian documents, it did shed light on Ladd's growing distance from dispensationalism. Certainly the years at Harvard caused Ladd to temper many of the methodological presuppositions he had brought with him from Gordon and Cora Cash and thus throw into question his claim that Harvard changed only the way he "held" his belief. The historical-critical approach simply would not have allowed him to maintain the content of dispensationalist theology because it would have destroyed its underlying presuppositions about the nature of the biblical texts. The particular form of inerrancy necessary to support dispensationalist conclusions could not have survived the critical scrutiny Ladd applied to it under Cadbury. Only what the text actually said was important, Ladd had come to believe, and any interpretative model that did not begin at this point should be discarded. The evaluation of ancient Christian eschatology in Ladd's dissertation, then, represented a foreshadowing of his critique of dispensationalist eschatology in the decade to come. Specifically, Ladd attributed to the Didachists the motivation of preparing their audience for "the difficulties of the end." Far from the traditional dispensationalist view of the blessed hope, in which the church will be "taken up" before the time of tribulation, the Didachists passionately call their readers to renewed faithfulness so that they will not be "turned away."[151] Furthermore, though he does not find it in the writings of the Didachists, Ladd is clearly looking for some indication of both present and future aspects of the Kingdom of God. Pure dispensationalism had relegated the kingdom texts to a future time only, but Ladd came to challenge that view. In his dissertation, however, he can say only that there "may be in the writer's mind the concept of a present spiritual kingdom, but this is not certain."[152]

In the summer of 1949, just after completing his PhD at Harvard, Ladd taught a graduate course on the pastoral epistles at Wheaton College, the school that had rejected his application eleven years earlier. By this time Ladd had become not only a trained scholar but a gifted teacher as well. One student in particular benefited from Ladd's tutelage. Raymond Elliott (b. 1924), a graduate student at Wheaton in the late 1940s, was preparing for missionary service. Elliott recalled that the course was rigorous and that he had difficulty keeping up with the assigned readings. Still, he credited this one class with helping him set a course for the work that would occupy much of his life. In Ladd he found a mentor who was committed to both the text of scripture and the use of the biblical text to communicate the gospel to every nation: "This more than anything else made Greek begin to act like a language that was communicating something, instead of just a series of word problems. I consider that to have been very significant to me, in the light of later work."[153] That later work was the translation of the New Testament into the language of the Ixil Indian tribe of Guatemala with Wycliffe Bible Translators, an evangelical missionary organization. Ladd was beginning to see how his academic training and spiritual passion could influence the lives of students. He returned to Gordon Divinity School with a renewed sense of his place in evangelical theological education.

Ladd was made a full professor of New Testament at Gordon at the start of the 1949–1950 academic year, providing a raise in status if not in compensation. Ladd's salary increased by $300 to $3,900 in the final year of his doctoral program but was not raised at his promotion.[154] Although Ladd was armed with his newly minted PhD from Harvard University, his elevation was not as rapid as it may seem; he was nearly forty years of age, and even among Gordon's unusually well-educated faculty his credentials were special. Further, promotion became Gordon's way of trying to keep its faculty from moving to other institutions when they were finished studying in the Boston area. Ladd, who had rejected opportunities to leave New England in the past, threw himself into this new role, leading the reorganization of not only his own department but the teaching of Greek as well. In addition he chaired the thesis committee for Gordon's Bachelor of Divinity program and served on committees overseeing institutional planning, faculty lectureships, literary expression, the library, and academic standing. He was rooted in the community, committed to Gordon as an institution, and influential in shaping the curriculum that would prepare hundreds of Gordon graduates. On the surface it would appear that Ladd had found the position he had craved when he decided in Montpelier to pursue an academic career. However, the teaching load at Gordon was four courses per semester, in addition to administrative duties, and the pace left Ladd with little time to research and write.[155] Faced with postponing his dream of writing great books, Ladd began to look for ways to spend more of his time doing precisely that.

In the autumn of 1949, at the encouragement of Robert Pfeiffer, Ladd applied for a U.S. government grant under the Fulbright Act, which he hoped would fund a year of research in England.[156] The subject of Ladd's proposed research was "The Kingdom of God in Jewish and Early Christian Thought," which provides a glimpse into his later academic focus. True to form Ladd argues, citing Adolph Harnack, that "a thorough history of Chiliasm has not yet appeared."[157] In this application Ladd maintains that he is the one to complete this work, saying that though "it is confessedly an ambitious project and the areas which must be controlled are extensive," he is "sure that such a book could be published."[158] In his application Ladd proposed to go to the University of Manchester to study with T. W. Manson (1893–1958), a New Testament scholar, and H. H. Rowley (1890–1969), a professor of Old Testament, both of whom were conservative in theology and had particular expertise in Ladd's area of interest. The proposed study formed an outline of the research that would represent much of Ladd's most successful and enduring academic product. His application for the grant was rejected, however, and he continued in his duties at Gordon.

In 1950 Ladd received an invitation from a fledgling institution in Southern California, one that he hoped would offer him the resources and freedom to accomplish his goal. Fuller Theological Seminary occupies a key place in the history of the postwar evangelical resurgence.[159] Radio evangelist Charles Fuller (1887–1969) and Harold John Ockenga (1905–1985), pastor of Park Street Church in Boston, decided to open a theological training center to prepare ministers and missionaries for service. Ockenga was also on the board of trustees at Gordon Divinity School and a leader in both the NEF and the NAE and was the most likely source of Ladd's invitation. The founders recruited well-educated evangelical scholars to join the faculty, and Fuller Seminary welcomed its inaugural class to its Pasadena, California, campus in the autumn of 1947.

Fuller Seminary distinguished itself from other conservative institutions of the day by placing a high value on intellectual achievement and interaction with the broader academic world. University degrees, far from drawing suspicion, were prized, if not specifically required. Fuller was to be a place where evangelical Christian leaders prepared to respond to the challenges of the modern world through engagement rather than separation, and excellence in academic work would be expected both from students and faculty. Professors were given competitive salaries and relatively light teaching loads, and each was expected to produce, according to Ockenga, "a new book in his field every two or three years."[160] Dazzled by the offer of reduced teaching responsibilities and time for research and writing, Ladd accepted the invitation to join the faculty and moved with his family to California in the summer of 1950.[161] That the salary offered by Fuller Seminary—$6,000 per year—was $2,100 more than he earned at Gordon (a 54 percent increase) must have played a decisive role in the Ladds' decision finally to leave New England.[162] With time to write and an income that far surpassed anything he had ever earned before, Ladd could at last see himself as a success. He was thirty-nine years old.

This period of preparation introduces some of the influences and ideas that would define the rest of Ladd's life and career. His obsessive quest for a place in a respectable doctoral program exposed some of the psychological wounds from his childhood, wounds that dogged him until his death. The feelings of inferiority and inadequacy he developed as a result of his family's poverty and lack of a secure home caused his overreaction to the rejection he felt in his search for a school. In both his pastoral and academic work, however, he found a measure of acceptance and healing of those earlier injuries. Certainly being accepted at Harvard soothed some of his negative self-perception, and completing the program with distinction still more. But the wounds were deep and persistent, and as Ladd moved into his life as a professional scholar we see an emotional brittleness that is a direct result of those early events. Far from being a Zane Grey hero, Ladd struggled with his sense of inferiority for the rest of his life. Looking back, he remembered parents who could not hear him and a brother he deeply resented and envied, and as a consequence he saw himself as the perpetual outsider, longing for acceptance. In apposition to these negative family legacies, the twin academic influences of Gordon and Harvard provided important counterbalances to the psychological turmoil in Ladd's life. Harvard provided a baptism by immersion in the highest level of academic work, while Gordon's irenic spirit helped Ladd navigate the doctrinal battles to come. By 1950 he was ready for the chance to focus more of his time and energy on research and writing and to make his mark in the world of theological scholarship. The move to Fuller Seminary would provide that opportunity.

2

The Emergence of a Strategy
(1950–1954)

George Ladd moved with his family to Pasadena in the summer of 1950 and began his teaching career at Fuller Theological Seminary, a tenure that would last for more than a quarter century. The institution, though barely three years old, boasted a faculty of mostly young evangelical stars, and Ladd was thrilled to be a part of the team. Fuller was still developing its own character in those early years, especially in relation to three key issues facing the evangelical movement at large: the nature of the Bible and the definition and functions of biblical inerrancy, ecumenism and the practice of ecclesiological separatism, and the extent to which dispensationalist eschatology would shape theological discussion and ecclesiology.[1] These issues were crucial to the role evangelicalism would play in American culture in the years after World War II, and they provided the talking points—and later the battle lines—in the process of shaping the seminary's identity.

The year 1950 was marked by a heightened sense of anxiety in American religious, social, and political life, as all three passed through a period of change and conflict.[2] Membership in the mainline denominations (Episcopalian, Presbyterian, Congregational, Methodist, Baptist, and Lutheran) grew at double the rate of the general population (3 percent versus 1.5 percent).[3] The National Council of Churches (NCC), founded in 1950, represented 33 million church members in 143,000 congregations and sought to present a unified program of Protestant Christian advocacy in American society.[4] Roman Catholics, excluded from the NCC, numbered more than 30 million in 1950 and in that year had 26,322 men training for the priesthood in 388 seminaries in the United States alone.[5] Evangelicals were also experiencing significant growth in numbers, as Charles Fuller's *Old Fashioned Revival Hour*, the National Association of Evangelicals, Youth for Christ, and the Billy Graham evangelistic crusades each enjoyed great influence.[6] But despite these advances, there was a growing sense that the technological advances of the era were somehow making religion obsolete. Paradoxically, given the mass appeal of mainstream, Roman Catholic, and certain evangelical efforts, some worried that Christianity might be pushed irrevocably to the margins of modern society. Robert Ellwood has argued that a "disturbing uncertainty lingered as to whether religionists were not intruding as ambivalent outsiders who could never really be at home in the new world being born."[7] This was certainly true for the new evangelicals and served as a primary motivating factor for George Ladd.

In the midst of this period of dramatic change Ladd joined a Fuller faculty with mostly impressive academic credentials and equally strong opinions on the course the seminary should take. The original four included Carl F. H. Henry (1913–2004), a former journalist who held a ThD from Northern Baptist Theological Seminary in Chicago and would soon complete a PhD in philosophy from Boston University. Henry's first book, *The Uneasy Conscience of Modern Fundamentalism*, was a challenge to conservative Protestants to reengage the social issues of the day in order to gain a hearing for the conversionist message of the Christian gospel.[8] He was joined on the faculty by Harold Lindsell (1913–1998), who held a PhD in history from New York University and brought administrative skills—with a large dose of plain ambition—to the group. Lindsell, who had the weakest background in theological scholarship, was nevertheless a gifted debater who would champion a strict form of inerrancy for the rest of his public life.[9] The third to join was Everett Harrison (1902–1999), an irenic man who had earned a ThD from Dallas Theological Seminary, where he had also served on the faculty, and a PhD from the University of Pennsylvania. Though dispensationalist in orientation, Harrison had struggled with some of the more militant aspects of the system and had been made to feel unwelcome at Dallas Seminary.[10]

Wilbur Smith (1894–1968) was the best known of the four original members of the faculty. A voracious reader with a gregarious personality, Smith had the weakest academic credentials of that first group—he was the only member who lacked an earned doctorate—but the strongest reputation in the evangelical world. He was also a vocal proponent of dispensationalist theology, having published numerous books and articles on the subject, though he was not committed to strict ecclesiological separatism. Ironically for a seminary founded to serve as the intellectual home of evangelicalism, it was Smith who was by far the most commanding and influential presence.[11] Several others had joined the faculty by the time Ladd arrived. Among them were Edward Carnell (1919–1967), Gleason Archer (1916–2004), and William Sanford LaSor (1911–1991). Bela Vassady (1902–1992), an important theologian in the Hungarian Reformed tradition, had been offered a place in 1948 but had not survived Fuller's peculiarly American conservative test of theological orthodoxy.[12] Charles Woodbridge (1902–1992), a popular conference speaker in the fundamentalist tradition, joined the faculty in the same year as Ladd.[13]

The mission and mandate at Fuller Seminary were to produce and promote quality theological scholarship from an evangelical orientation.[14] From the outset Charles Fuller had sought to create an institution that was "academically stronger" than the typical Bible college of the day.[15] Harold John Ockenga's vision for the seminary was that it would become a West Coast counterpart to Princeton Theological Seminary, a place where books would be written that would set the course for theological discussion.[16] The early faculty, dominated as it was by men who had trained at elite universities, understood that the creation of scholarly works was to be their primary responsibility. Carnell, who was clearly the young star of the seminary, had come to Fuller specifically because it offered him more time to write.[17] Two years later Ladd came for the same reason. Fuller Seminary offered him an opportunity to work alongside—and together with—the best of the new generation of evangelical thinkers. He could make a name for himself and move closer to writing the great work of evangelical scholarship. "Fuller is a great school," Ladd told a friend, "and I am convinced that the future is with it."[18]

The members of Ladd's family, on the other hand, were less sanguine. Moving to California from New England meant leaving not only familiar territory but extended family as well. In the fragile, distant, and contentious atmosphere of the Ladds' home life, other close relatives provided a sort of emotional safety net, and now that important network lay three thousand miles away. For the first time, George and Winnie lived outside the shadow—and beyond the immediate support—of their strong-willed mothers. And while moving away from these imposing influences may have been a welcome bonus to the opportunity to teach at Fuller, it also represented a dramatic upheaval in the Ladds' family system.

This radical shift was felt most acutely by the children, Norma and Larry, who were then sixteen and thirteen years of age respectively. Both had been born during the Great Depression and spent their early childhood years surrounded by news of the horrors of World War II, factors that were compounded by the Ladds' financial problems and the moves from church to church. To make matters worse they were being raised in an increasingly unhappy home by parents who were relationally brittle, if not emotionally stunted. The move to Pasadena took Norma away from her Uncle James, who had become her surrogate father and acted as a warm and loving counterpart to George's detached indifference.[19] Larry also began to show signs during this period of the physical and psychological limitations that would handicap him in the future. He suffered from a condition known as cryptorchidism, or un-descended testicles, which could have been corrected in early childhood.[20] The condition affected Larry's development at puberty and created wounds that would grow into mental illness when he reached adulthood. The Ladd family, already barely functioning, suffered tremendously in the years after George's move to Fuller.

The relocation to Pasadena also provided Ladd with an opportunity to escape some brewing trouble within the Baptist world. He was often coy about his own sympathies, but he maintained close friendships with pastors in both the Northern Baptist Convention (NBC) and newly formed Conservative Baptist Association (CBA) even though pressured to join the separatist movement.[21] He was careful not to allow the appearance of divisiveness to interfere with his goals as a scholar. Still, there was strong pressure to choose a side. Many of the CBA leaders were Ladd's friends from his days in the NBC, including Earl Kalland (1910–1992), an Old Testament scholar who had studied with Ladd at Gordon. Kalland, who was the president at a CBA seminary in Oregon, wrote to Ladd: "We make many mistakes and have our share of problems, but I hope you will find yourself more and more in sympathy with and integrated into the Conservative Baptist movement here in the West."[22] The presumption was that Ladd would sever his NBC ties and join the CBA when he left New England for California, but though he was uncomfortable with the liberalizing tendencies in his home denomination, he would not yet fully leave it. This ambiguity regarding his allegiances, coupled with his relative remoteness in Southern California, initially gave Ladd some freedom to participate in either tradition as he liked.

Ladd's academic career was moving into high gear. In order to accomplish his overall objective he sought first to establish himself as a respected scholar in the evangelical world and beyond and second to write a major work of scholarship that could not be ignored. He was thus perfectly placed at Fuller, given its own institutional goals, and in those first few years a strategy began to emerge that Ladd hoped would help him achieve his personal dream. First, he knew that in order to gain a hearing before a broader audience he—and his institution—would need to model a level of erudition that had been seen only infrequently from conservative evangelical writers. Second, Ladd recognized a need within evangelicalism for an expression of the nature of the Bible that acknowledged the contributions of modern biblical criticism while staying within the boundaries of conservative theology. In those early years Ladd was the only member of Fuller's faculty who "felt a call" to engage historical-critical challenges to the Bible.[23] Third and most urgently, Ladd resolved to distance himself from dispensationalism by critiquing its origins and intellectual foundations. These strategic elements could backfire at times, as we shall see, but they provided some direction for Ladd as he began his career as a biblical scholar.

In 1951 Ladd was invited to present the midyear lectures at the Western Conservative Baptist Theological Seminary in Portland, Oregon. Western Seminary was affiliated with the CBA, the dissenting coalition of churches and missionary organizations that had split from the NBC in 1947, and Ladd largely agreed with their theological views, though not with their separatist aims.[24] The invitation to come to Western should be seen in light of the attempt on the part of Kalland and others to recruit Ladd to the CBA. Western itself was a growing institution with a strong faculty. In 1952 five of the eight faculty members—including all of the instructors in academic areas—held earned doctoral degrees.[25] New buildings were being added to the campus, and the enrolment was expanding.[26] It was an honor for Ladd to be invited to give the midyear lectures (once again he followed his friend and mentor, Merrill Tenney of Wheaton, who had given the lectures the previous year), and he decided to use the opportunity to present a critique of a specific dispensational doctrine.

In November 1951, as Ladd was preparing his lectures, he wrote to Howard Ferrin, president of Providence Bible College in Rhode Island. Ferrin (1898–1993) was a veteran of radio evangelist Paul Rader's radio ministry, a graduate of both Northwestern University and Moody Bible Institute, and a charter member of the National Association of Evangelicals (NAE).[27] Ladd and Ferrin had worked together in the New England Fellowship and shared views on the negative impact of militant dispensationalism on contemporary evangelicalism.[28] The lectures at Western would be Ladd's first chance to play a leading role in an academic event, and he knew that eyes would be on him as he represented both himself and Fuller Seminary. Ladd was "deeply concerned," he said, "about this whole matter of strategy in eschatology," and he was seeking advice.[29] Ladd wanted to test some of what he had learned about the Kingdom of God in his studies at Harvard, only this time before a conservative audience. Already planning to publish these lectures, Ladd said:

> I would much prefer that my first book be one which is not negative or critical of the dispensational position. But the Lord has not ordered things in this way, and I have tried to go along with His leading. I have no zeal or personal ambition in this matter for myself, and in some ways I would far prefer to write on subjects which are not so controversial.... However, I realize that now I am in a position which entails considerable responsibility, and since I have hitherto written nothing and am quite unknown in American evangelicalism, the reaction to my first book may well set a pattern with which I will have to live for the rest of my life and which may condition everything else which I shall do.[30]

He concluded:

> I am working on a much larger project which will take several more years of study and which I trust will resolve in a rather extensive volume which treats in the most comprehensive fashion and from a more positive point of view the whole question of the kingdom of God in the New Testament. This latter work will be more technical than these lectures, and I hope will fill a real need in contemporary evangelical literature.[31]

Ladd closed with a request for advice from his trusted friend, knowing that he was about to take a major step that would influence the rest of his professional life. Ferrin wrote back, encouraging Ladd in his desire to offer correction to the dispensationalist system. He acknowledged that the older generation of leaders could not turn from the positions upon which their careers were made. Ferrin wrote that "there is a sense in which one generation must pass and another come. You are of the new generation.... We need a new generation to lead, and I feel that God has raised you up to provide leadership in this field.... I believe you will benefit the whole evangelical movement, and especially our evangelical schools."[32] Ferrin could not know how influential his letter would be.

This exchange reveals much about Ladd's mind at the earliest stage of his tenure at Fuller Seminary. First, he was self-consciously setting the course for what he believed would be an important academic career, one that he hoped would see him personally help evangelicalism regain its place in American culture. Second, in order to accomplish this goal, he was willing to stretch the acceptable boundaries of his theological community through his use of critical sources and methods. Third, though he abhorred conflict in virtually any form, he was willing to confront the best-organized and most militant wing of conservative evangelicalism—dispensationalism—in order to gain the respect he craved. Finally, we see Ladd already making mental space for the creation of his magnum opus, which would once and for all place conservative evangelicalism on an equal footing with the other theological systems of the day.

In his lectures at Western Ladd sought to correct—as an insider—some of the excesses of dispensationalism. Applying his critical training to this system of thought, he found dispensationalism intellectually wanting and sought to correct what he perceived to be its most embarrassing propositions. Focusing on specific aspects of dispensationalism at this early stage of his career, Ladd indeed "set a pattern" for much of his academic life, one that would enable him to influence a generation of conservative evangelicals. But this effort was not without danger. The militant wing of American evangelicalism wielded enormous influence over the public's perception of theological orthodoxy. Within that most conservative faction, dispensationalism functioned virtually as an essential doctrine, much like the deity of Christ or the triune nature of God.[33] To stray too far or to side too closely with nonevangelicals often brought with it the risk of being pronounced "liberal" or "apostate" by the self-proclaimed watchdogs of theological boundaries and of thus losing one's voice in the debate. By taking aim at dispensational theology Ladd was venturing into this perilous atmosphere at the very beginning of his career at Fuller.

Ladd's decision to engage dispensationalism thus placed him in direct conflict with not only the dominant theological outlook among conservative evangelicals but also a trusted fellow member of his own faculty, Wilbur Smith. Still, Ladd was undaunted in his desire to provide a corrective to the dispensationalist system, and he was being encouraged in that endeavor by friends around the country. An Illinois Baptist minister and writer, J. C. Macaulay, cheered Ladd's desire to challenge dispensationalism. He added that he believed the young scholars "at Fuller have a better opportunity to study problems free from 'traditional trammels' than most institutions."[34] Ladd agreed:

> God has placed us in a strategic position here at Fuller, and I am very conscious of a sense of responsibility. My deepest concern is to be faithful to the stewardship entrusted to me. I trust that I am not incorrect in feeling that the time is ripe for a fresh approach to New Testament eschatology.... However, there is what might be called a "strategy of publication." One cannot strike out here and there at random. I am unknown across the country.[35]

Ladd was about to be significantly less "unknown" after the publication of his first book, and his strategy for critiquing dispensationalism from the inside was already taking shape. In books, articles, speeches, and letters Ladd applied the critical methods he learned at Harvard to a system of thought that he saw as a hindrance to full participation in the broader world of academic theology. By so doing he initiated the process of liberating a generation of evangelicals from the constraints of strict dispensationalism.[36]

The lectures at Western, titled "Crucial Questions about the Kingdom," took place before capacity crowds and by all accounts were well received.[37] Though the topic itself was controversial, the public discussion was remained at a "high level," a fact attributed to Ladd's "genial personality and fair presentation."[38] Ladd had sent a rough draft of his presentation to William Eerdmans in October of 1951 and was offered a book contract before the lectures had even been given.[39] Ladd's strategy in sending his manuscript to Eerdmans was to secure a niche for himself in the spectrum of published works on prophetic topics. "[T]here does not exist in the English language," Ladd argued, "an up-to-date book which deals with the Kingdom of God in the New Testament from the point of view of pre-millennial but undispensational eschatology."[40] Eerdmans agreed and gave his approval for the book to be published.[41] Upon his return to Fuller Ladd completed the preparation of the lectures for publication.

Other projects were keeping Ladd busy at Fuller as well. During his first years there he participated in several enterprises that incorporated one or more aspects of his overall strategy for building his academic reputation and that of evangelicalism as a whole. In 1950 the Fuller Faculty Club had begun to discuss the twin issues of the inspiration and interpretation of the Bible at their meetings, and the possibility of publishing a collaborative statement was proposed. The Faculty Club was a colloquium of professors who gathered to discuss current theological topics. Ladd was chosen to chair the project even though he had been a member of the faculty for only a few months, and in 1951 he sent a draft of an outline to Harold Ockenga, then presiding in absentia from Boston. The outline represented a substantial piece of scholarship, with proposed chapters by Carl F. H. Henry, William Sanford LaSor, Gleason Archer, Harold Lindsell, Edward John Carnell, Charles Woodbridge, Wilbur Smith, Everett Harrison, Bela Vassady, and Ladd.[42] Impressed with the proposal, Ockenga responded to Ladd's report. He agreed that the book was necessary and stated that the doctrine of inspiration needed to be "defended against the modern attack."[43] Ockenga rather naively admitted his hope "that our faculty will not only be unanimous in its conviction as to the meaning of inspiration and revelation but also will be able to produce some kind of book which will serve to guide the thinking of countless thousands of young people and of many ministers on this very subject."[44]

A little over a year later, still unable to find any consensus, Ladd wrote again to Ockenga and said that the faculty "had reached a stalemate" and that the Faculty Club meetings had been "discontinued by unspoken mutual consent." The problem, according to Ladd, was that no one on the Fuller faculty had made "revelation and inspiration the central theme of his research." Ladd, clearly uncomfortable in the role of leadership in this project, suggested that "initiative for further activity" would have to rest "with the President of the Seminary."[45] When Ockenga responded, he ignored the hint of discord among the faculty and put off any decision but took the time to report on the weather in Boston.[46]

At the May 1952 faculty meetings Ockenga met with the Faculty Club and asked each member to select a single section of the proposed research and work on it for a year. The following spring, according to Ockenga's plan, the group would devote a month to study and interaction and then produce a draft of the book. Though the members of the Faculty Club had initially agreed to the plan, within a month the project had again derailed. It fell to Ladd to report this development to Ockenga, and he wrote a long letter of explanation. Once more the overriding issue was the lack of focus among the faculty on the topics of inspiration and revelation. While there was general interest in the study, no one wanted to make it his first priority. Most important and related to the issues of time and effort, the project was a distraction from the group's—and Ladd's—goal of creating works of evangelical scholarship that the broader academic community would notice:

> One of the greatest contributions to Evangelical Scholarship which the Seminary can make is the production of monographs which will gain the recognition of technical scholars of all schools. I think you will agree with the Committee that few of the productions of the Faculty have been of this magnitude. Witness to this fact the failure to gain recognition of any of the major publishing houses. We have, to be sure, "arrived" so far as a good part of the Evangelical world is concerned, but hardly so far as American Biblical and Theological Scholarship as a whole is concerned. We are not producing articles which are appearing in the standard theological journals to any appreciable degree. We seriously question the strategy of asking men to lay aside projects which are aimed in this direction and which would bring general scholarly recognition to the Seminary, for a project whose result is at best uncertain.[47]

To immerse himself in this research would interfere with Ladd's strategy for creating the kind of evangelical scholarship that the world would have to notice. For this reason alone Ladd wanted to shelve the project. In an earlier draft of the same letter Ladd continued:

May I illustrate my own case? My lectures at Western [Seminary], to appear in September on the Kingdom of God [as *Crucial Questions*], are aimed at millenarian circles in American Evangelicalism, and do not pretend to be a work of critical scholarship. [Henry] Cadbury would read it and shake his head in disappointment. The book, I feel, needed to be written; I trust it will have a ministry. But there is a greater need for a critical, comprehensive, conservative study of the Kingdom which I would not hesitate to place in Cadbury's hands. My plans had been to proceed directly to this larger work and to complete the reading of the German and French literature which I have begun. Ought such a project to be laid aside? The load of re-search will demand the bulk of my time for two or three more years. German is still hard work. I am sorry that I have had to turn aside this summer, and at the moment the project has congealed. If we go on with the project on Inspiration, it will mean to me the indefi-nite postponement of this work. The Faculty should not omit a cal-culated evaluation of the loss that will ensue in all of the departments if such projects are laid aside.[48]

This section was omitted in the letter sent to Ockenga perhaps because Ladd did not want to be perceived as being difficult, and the book was never com-pleted. Ladd did, however, recommend that a smaller group of scholars take on a similar project if the need arose.[49]

After the project was abandoned, Ladd turned his focus to the release of his first monograph. Published in 1952 under the title *Crucial Questions about the Kingdom of God*, Ladd's book was a firm challenge to the dispensationalist conception of the kingdom. As in his lectures at Western, the main thesis of *Crucial Questions* is that the Kingdom of God is both a present and a future reality as opposed to the dispensationalists' purely futuristic conception. The book is structured around four questions: Have the problems about the King-dom of God been solved? Can the kingdom be both future and present? Was the Kingdom of Heaven postponed? How is the kingdom of Revelation 20 to be interpreted?[50]

Early in the book Ladd lays down the challenge: "It is easy to accept an inherited position uncritically and to espouse it dogmatically; but scholarship, even though it may achieve theological positions which are maintained dog-matically, must continually purify itself by the criticisms of others and criti-cize itself in the light of all the findings of theological studies."[51] This statement is reminiscent of his "but the attempt must be made" proclamation in his dissertation. It announces that he intends to approach his subject with as ob-

jective an eye as possible, at least in his own estimation, and that this motivation is good and necessary. Nonetheless, it also exposes him to criticism from
precisely the dogmatic tradition he is engaging. From the start Ladd is clear in
his intent to correct those aspects of the conservative tradition that are accepted
"uncritically" and espoused "dogmatically," eventually to create a more favorable image for evangelical thought in the broader world of theological studies.
In this intention we can have no doubt that he was speaking of dispensationalism and no doubt that the dispensationalists would respond.

The first important dispensationalist challenge to Ladd's views in *Crucial
Questions* occurs in the first pages of the book itself. Certainly it was an honor
for Ladd to have Wilbur Smith write the preface to the junior scholar's first
book. Smith's reputation was unimpeachable among dispensationalists across
the nation, and his public connection to the book ensured that it would be
widely read. Smith introduced Ladd, asking "for this young man a very careful
hearing."[52] But Smith did not concur with Ladd's conclusions, and it is an
important marker in the coming conflict between dispensationalists and
nondispensational evangelicals that he did not publicly attack the book. Smith
disagreed with Ladd's refusal to distinguish between the kingdom in the New
Testament and the messianic kingdom promised in the prophetic literature.
Again, however, this did not lead Smith to dismiss the book as unorthodox.
Rather, he called it a "joy to commend" and a "carefully executed work of my
beloved friend and colleague."[53]

Privately Smith was no less effusive. In a letter congratulating Ladd on the
publication of *Crucial Questions*, Smith proclaimed that this was only the beginning of a "long series of notable contributions" that would "strengthen the
faith of many."[54] He also said that the book would "awaken an initial interest in
the minds of many New Testament scholars on both sides of the water, so the
day will come when everything you publish will be eagerly read."[55] Ten years
later he would not have been able to sound so magnanimous in his estimation
of his junior colleague, but in 1952 Smith was impressed with the quality of
Ladd's work and willing to allow that there was room for disagreement among
scholars of faith.

Ladd opens the book with a review of eschatological thought from antiq-
uity through the medieval period and on to its place in modern scholarship.
Along the way he exhibits his mastery of the source material, especially that of
the early church era. In the summary of modern eschatological positions, he
devotes most of his space—more than twice as much as to any other system—
to the dispensationalist variety and quotes extensively from the dispensationalist *Systematic Theology* of Lewis Sperry Chafer (1871–1952), the founder of
Dallas Seminary.[56] The dispensational conception of the kingdom, in Ladd's

discussion of Chafer, hinged on the postponement theory, in which the Davidic kingdom, having been initiated in the coming of Christ but rejected by Israel, became hidden in a "mystery form" to be offered again in the form of Christ's millennial reign. In this system the kingdom is purely a future event, and the point of Ladd's book is to argue for some aspect of that kingdom to be reserved for the present time.

Ladd's critique of dispensationalism is couched in language that would protect him from the fiercest conservative attacks. After posing the question of the present and future kingdom, Ladd says that "This problem must not be solved by abstract theological reasoning but by the exegesis of the Scriptures. The point of departure must always be, What do the Scriptures teach? Rather than, What does logic allow? We shall turn therefore to the New Testament, particularly to the teachings of our Lord, for the answer."[57]

This was not the attack of an outsider. Ladd's critique earned its conservative readership precisely because of statements like this, which affirmed the Bible's ultimate authority and arbitrative role. This was a critical approach that the dispensationalists could not repel simply with an avalanche of biblical texts. Ladd was using the same formulaic defense of the biblical texts as those in the dispensationalist camp, a fact that made him far more persuasive to his audience and infinitely more dangerous to those in his critical path.

Ladd's solution to the problem posed by the "future and present Kingdom" begins with a new—for conservative evangelicals—exegesis of the Greek term *basileia*, most often translated as "kingdom." The question was whether this kingdom represented a "realm" or a "reign" of God. Dispensationalists, with their emphasis on an earthly, political kingdom under Christ's rule, spoke of the kingdom as God's realm. Ladd argued that there was "practically unanimous agreement" among modern scholars that *basileia* represented the reign of God and that this development provided a clearer, more exegetically sound interpretation of the New Testament kingdom passages.[58] Ladd thus concludes his discussion of *basileia* by saying that "the kingdom of God is the sovereign rule of God, manifested in the person and work of Christ, creating a people over whom he reigns, and issuing a realm or realms in which the power of his reign is realized."[59]

However, Ladd did not stop there. In direct challenge to the dispensationalist view of the purely temporal kingdom, he argued that the true kingdom was God's historical process of redeeming his people and stated that the "*history* of the kingdom of God is therefore the history of redemption, viewed from the aspect of God's sovereign and kingly power."[60] The Kingdom of God, he contended, could not be contained in any one place or dispensation. Rather, it was the very power of God that was intervening in human history to save all wayward people. Later in his career Ladd would make a more fully developed turn to the theological system known as *Heilsgeschichte*, or salvation history. His redefinition of the biblical concept of the *basileia* was an early step in that process.

The final section of *Crucial Questions* deals with the interpretation of Revelation 20:1–6, the only passage in the Bible that explicitly describes a future thousand-year reign of Christ.[61] Clearly more aggressive here, Ladd states from the outset that:

> There are two ways of approaching the question of the millennium: the question of its implications and its place in one's system of theology; and the question of what the Scriptures actually teach.... One cannot come to the Scriptures with a system of eschatology and fit the records into one's system. One must always ask, What do the Scriptures teach? and then on the basis of the answer derived build his theological system.[62]

While his thinly veiled indictment of those who conform biblical passages to their own system would have been an insult to virtually all dispensationalist readers, Ladd protected himself from attack by appealing to "what the Scriptures actually teach." Certainly few among Ladd's conservative evangelical audience could contradict him on this point without drawing suspicion upon themselves, and it is into this pause that Ladd is able make his case without suffering outright rejection. The crux of his case is that blind literalism produces bad theology. Ladd argues for a more informed hermeneutic, one that allows for some logical freedoms in interpretation and, in one of his boldest challenges to dispensationalism, allows the New Testament to set the terms by which the Old Testament is interpreted. If the New could interpret the Old, then the difficulties related to the biblical Israel would be significantly diminished, and evangelicalism could take a rather large step toward the world of modern theological thought. However, despite his proposal for a more forward-looking hermeneutic, Ladd ends this section with a call to a literal interpretation of Revelation 20. Further, he argues that any nonliteral construal of the passage is a result of "theological presuppositions of an anti-millenarian character."[63]

With regard to the trajectory of Ladd's thought and career, we can make three important observations about *Crucial Questions*. First, Ladd's appeal to modern critical sources represented a radical shift in the way conservative evangelical theology was produced and defended. Ladd was educated at Harvard in the most current literature and methodologies, and he applied that training to his engagement with dispensationalism. His use of Kittel's

Theologisches Wörterbuch zum Neuen Testament and W. G. Kümmel's *Kirch-enbegriff und Geschichtsbewusstsein in der Urgemeinde und bei Jesus*, both in the original German, placed Ladd among the new generation of evangelical scholars.[64] The ease with which Ladd maneuvered through these German sources, while holding on to his conservative theology, made them far less threatening to evangelical students and teachers. By his own example Ladd was able to remove the perception of automatic tainting from works of critical biblical scholarship. In 1952 this alone was a major achievement.

Second, Ladd offered a critically reasoned challenge—from within the fold—to some of the most cherished doctrines in the dispensationalist system. Using his expertise in critical sources, biblical languages, and exegesis, Ladd argued for a shift in the theological understanding of the Kingdom of God, as well as of the related doctrine of the postponed kingdom theory. Up to that time, no insider had ever accomplished this feat without being anathematized by the dispensationalist arbiters of truth. Ladd would have to wait to see how he would be perceived when the book was published.

Finally and more problematically, Ladd showed in *Crucial Questions* an unwillingness to critically examine the literal interpretation of Revelation 20. Why does he appear to retreat here? It is possible that his hermeneutic was not as fully developed or deployed as even he was aware. The literal thousand-year reign of Christ may have been so deeply ingrained in his thinking that he simply neglected to pass it through the filter of his critical method. More likely, Ladd knew that his defense of premillennialism was vital to his acceptance in conservative evangelical circles. His challenge to his own audience could go only so far before he found himself on the wrong side of dispensationalism's strict separatist boundaries. This unwillingness to reexamine the Revelation 20 text, while ensuring Ladd's acceptability in conservative circles, would later hinder his efforts to achieve a hearing in the broader theological world.

Crucial Questions received widespread attention after its publication in 1952. In many ways it earned precisely the recognition Ladd had expected (or at least hoped for) when he began his career as a biblical scholar. Several academic journals published reviews, as did still more popular evangelical and prophetically oriented magazines. He also received letters from professors, Christian leaders, and a handful of avid amateur students of biblical prophecy. Most were positive, though there was a handful of expected challenges from the more committed dispensationalists in Ladd's reading audience. Ladd responded to nearly every letter written to him, sometimes sparking exchanges that lasted for years. The conservative evangelical community functioned in many ways like a small town in the early 1950s, and Ladd presided over an informal town hall meeting discussing the details of his book.

The academic responses to *Crucial Questions* fitted rather neatly along the lines of contemporary theological debate. Delbert Rose of Asbury Theological Seminary wrote in the *Journal of Bible and Religion* that Ladd's work provided "the most consistent exegesis of the kingdom-concept in the diverse Scriptural passages on the theme."[65] Rose continued by saying that "while this volume will not satisfy either the liberal scholar or the rigid dispensationalist, nevertheless here is a scholarly attempt to present from a 'conservative' standpoint the Kingdom of God in its present and future aspects." For Ladd, though Rose offered no sense of agreement with his position, it was gratifying to be acknowledged as having made a "scholarly attempt" to wrestle with the issues.

British evangelical scholar F. F. Bruce was more positive. Writing in the *Evangelical Quarterly*, Bruce hailed Ladd as "one of the leading conservative New Testament scholars of the younger American generation."[66] Though Bruce was barely a year older than Ladd, he had already established himself in Britain as a prominent biblical scholar, and his approval was important to Ladd's standing as a new academic. Bruce was also familiar with the intricacies of dispensationalism, albeit of a less militant variety, having been raised in the moderate Open Brethren offshoot of the Plymouth Brethren tradition.[67] Bruce thus appreciated Ladd's distinction between historic premillennialism and dispensationalism, while recognizing that this point of conflict was more relevant to American audiences. In his discussion of Ladd's chapter on the postponement theory Bruce states that "It is an eloquent commentary on the difference between American and British evangelicalism that it should be thought necessary in an academic course of lectures to devote time to prove that the kingdom of God and the kingdom of heaven are not different but identical."[68]

And yet, precisely to achieve the purpose Ladd had in mind for *Crucial Questions*, it was necessary to make the case for a kingdom that had both present and future reality. This was one of the cracks in the dispensational system through which Ladd would launch his attack. That this emphasis would have been less necessary in Britain should not diminish its importance in the American evangelical context. Nothing about the kingdom as Ladd saw it could survive unless it was permitted to invade time and become, at least in part, a present reality. Bruce ultimately affirmed the extent to which Ladd was willing to test his early conservative eschatological positions and acknowledged the intellectual growth reflected in both the questions and conclusions this book described. He concludes his review by praising Ladd in his role as spokesman for the millennialist position and expressing the hope that he might "write further books."[69]

First, however, Ladd had to contend with the dispensationalist establishment, led by John Walvoord, president of Dallas Theological Seminary (DTS).

Dallas Seminary was the intellectual and institutional home of dispensationalism in the United States, and Walvoord had assumed the role of defender of that system during his tenure as chief executive. Dallas Seminary had taken over the journal *Bibliotheca Sacra* in 1934 and made it into the most influential academic medium for the publication of dispensationalist theology and review. The pages of the journal were dominated by John Walvoord and other members of the DTS faculty, as well as by Lewis Sperry Chafer, the seminary's former president.[70] The journal also reprinted no fewer than nine articles by C. I. Scofield, editor of the dispensationalist-oriented Bible, who had been dead since 1921. Still, this was clearly Walvoord's journal. Between 1934 and 1970 it published 113 of his articles, virtually all of which treated aspects of dispensationalist doctrine or interpretation.

Bibliotheca Sacra was an extremely influential journal among American conservatives, having cultivated its role as arbiter of theological orthodoxy, which in this case was measured by the level of conformity to dispensational theology. Because Ladd had negotiated to write a series of articles on the Old Testament references to the Kingdom of God in the 1952–1953 issues, he was known to the journal's editors. He would also have been known simply for having been a part of the newly founded Fuller Seminary, which at that time could still have gone either way in the debate over dispensationalism. It is a measure of the level of concern with which Dallas Seminary viewed Ladd's book that Walvoord himself wrote a full-length review article, something he did only three times in his entire tenure as president—twice for Ladd—and that it appeared on the first page of the issue rather than with the other reviews.[71] If Ladd was looking to make a splash in the conservative evangelical community with the release of his first book, he was clearly successful.

The relationship between Ladd and Walvoord is an important part of Ladd's interaction with dispensationalism as a whole. Ladd wrote to Walvoord at the completion of his first year on the faculty at Fuller, ostensibly to ask for some clarification on a point of dispensational theology but really to initiate what he hoped would be a fruitful academic relationship. Ladd said, "I hope it will be my pleasure to come to know you in days to come," adding, "I will greatly appreciate your kindness in this problem; I am anxious to make no statements that do not correspond with the facts [sic]."[72]

Early the next year Ladd was commissioned to write a series of articles on eschatology in the Apocrypha, building on his dissertation studies. The response to his series was a blow to Ladd's grand hopes of publishing critical studies in *Bibliotheca Sacra*. Walvoord wrote that there were concerns on his end that Ladd's "theological perspective is not the same as that of Dallas Seminary."[73] Moreover, while Walvoord assured Ladd that he remained eager to publish his work, he also informed the young scholar that, for procedural reasons, the series could not run for the agreed-upon twelve issues.[74] Wounded by this new development, Ladd assumed that the critical nature of the articles had raised the alarm about his dispensational orthodoxy and that this alarm was the true reason for the reduction of the series. He wrote back to Walvoord, defending his work: "I am careful in these articles not to permit my different interpretation of New Testament data to intrude . . . and am attempting to do what I think no one in our Conservative circles has ever done, to write a rather thorough history of the Kingdom concept in the literature which arose in New Testament days."[75] Nevertheless, the series ended after the fourth article.[76]

Walvoord's review of *Crucial Questions*, while relatively calm in tone, painstakingly charts each of Ladd's deviations from dispensational orthodoxy. Complimenting Ladd's diligence and command of the sources, Walvoord's review also reveals a defensiveness toward the potential impact of Ladd's work. He says in the first paragraph that *Crucial Questions* "is a critique of the dispensational concept of the Kingdom of God. To some this will be the most significant contribution."[77] Walvoord, in his role as defender of the faith, was apparently concerned that the enemies of dispensationalism would use Ladd's book as ammunition. In this vein, the reviewer repeatedly lists points of agreement between Ladd's work and amillennialist views and says that Ladd's view of the kingdom "would be happily accepted by amillenarians as it expresses their concept exactly. . . . [Ladd] will have the hearty approval of all enemies of premillennialism."[78] The difficulty in this particular evaluation is that Ladd repeatedly states his support of the premillennialist position. True to the dispensationalist pattern of marking boundaries between their theological worldview and the rest, Walvoord attempted to color Ladd by association with the enemies of the "true faith."

Ladd also, according to Walvoord, overemphasizes the New Testament kingdom passages at the expense of the Old Testament record, which is tantamount to "ignoring the foundation of a building in order to concentrate on the superstructure." Ladd may have agreed with this assessment of his method but not with the analogy used to illustrate it. He firmly believed that the New Testament interpreted the Old, and not the other way around. Ultimately, according to Walvoord, Ladd's view of the kingdom "will distress dispensationalists . . . [and] is actually a compromise position which at once has the strength of modesty and the weakness of too many concessions to the opposition."[79]

Walvoord sent Ladd a draft of his review in November of 1952. In the accompanying letter he warns Ladd of his criticisms but is otherwise friendly and cordial, saying that "there is nothing personal in a doctrinal discussion of this kind."[80] Walvoord added that "I know it is a trial to one's soul to have a labor of love such as your book reviewed somewhat critically. I recall some very unfair reviews of a book which I published some years ago. I wish that we could have recommended the work without any reservation."[81] Ladd read the draft review carefully, made marks throughout, and even wrote a letter to Walvoord objecting to his characterization of his views as in the tradition of covenant theology.[82] Walvoord made the change.[83] In the letter informing Ladd of the revision, Walvoord said he was "glad to learn that you are not a covenant theologian" but warned Ladd that his "view is certainly very similar to it." The review was published in *Bibliotheca Sacra* in early 1953.

Ladd was concerned that he might be perceived as an enemy of Dallas Seminary. In a long explanatory letter to Walvoord, he tried to heal what he already sensed was a damaged relationship with the national spokesman for dispensational theology:

> I was troubled last week when one of my colleagues told me that he had heard the rumor abroad that I had deliberately selected the Dallas position as an object of attack. This is as untrue as it could be, and I long hesitated to send the manuscript to the publishers for fear that it might be so construed.... I trust that you will sense that I tried to write my book as an objective scholar and not with any spirit inimical to what Dallas stands for. I meant genuinely the statement in the foreword that I would much prefer to agree with people with whom I find myself parting company.... I too am anxious to foster the warmest possible relationship between our two institutions, for we are essentially committed to the same ministry of the Word.[84]

At this stage in his career Ladd needed Walvoord's approval or at least the appearance of a peaceful relationship. Walvoord was president of an established seminary and was trusted and revered by Charles Fuller's radio constituency, and Ladd could ill afford to make him an enemy. Ladd, on the other hand, was a junior scholar at a fledgling seminary, a fact that gave Walvoord tremendous sway as long as their comparative positions in the evangelical world remained unequal. Still, with his Harvard PhD, premillennialist beliefs, and a conservative view of Scripture, Ladd was potentially a formidable foe. Walvoord needed to make the differences between Ladd's views and traditional dispensationalism as clear as possible without antagonizing him too much. Ladd in turn needed to make his name as an evangelical scholar without being branded a liberal by Walvoord and thus losing any chance of influencing the conservative evangelical world. Still, for all their kind words and apparent peacemaking, after 1953 Ladd was never again invited to publish an article in *Bibliotheca Sacra*.

Ladd also received numerous letters from readers around the country, both in and out of Christian leadership. Two leaders of the Conservative Baptist movement wrote to him, both generally in favor of the book. Raymond Buker praised Ladd especially for his handling of the Scofield Bible, which Ladd had not condemned in *Crucial Questions*.[85] Ladd responded particularly to the Scofield question and assured Buker that he wanted to honor "the circle of men who represent the so-called Scofield position."[86] Vincent Brushwyler, the head of the Conservative Baptist Foreign Mission Society, also wrote to praise Ladd's book and thank him for his moderation in dealing with the Scofield Bible.[87] Ladd wrote back immediately, thanking Brushwyler for his support and doing his best to underscore the distinction between his work and that of those attacking Scofield: "I have been grieved by the inimical attitude of a number of writers toward dispensationalism and the Scofield Bible, and one of my deepest desires is that while I have been led to depart from some of the so-called Scofield Bible positions, I be not classed with those bitter critics of the dispensationalist tradition."[88]

Ladd's gentle treatment of the men in the Scofield tradition was an act of guarding his theological flank. In his private letters and conversations, as we shall later see, Ladd could be aggressive in his criticism of dispensationalism and particularly of the Scofield Bible. Still, keeping those views hidden from public view was prudent. The Conservative Baptists were beginning to purge their seminary faculties of anyone they deemed unorthodox, chiefly over questions of eschatology. In the middle of just his second year at Fuller, Ladd had no intention of unnecessarily antagonizing the militant wing of his own movement.

Still, *Crucial Questions* was being read and discussed in conferences and seminaries around the country. Bernard Ramm (1916–1992), a progressive evangelical scholar with whom Ladd carried on a long and meaningful correspondence, sent him a postcard describing discussions at a recent meeting of the Evangelical Theological Society (ETS). During a conversation about Ladd's book, according to Ramm, John E. Luchies, a philosophy professor at Wheaton, stated in John Walvoord's presence that "dispensationalism had failed to sustain itself with adequate scholarship."[89] Martin Wyngaarden, a professor of Old Testament at Calvin College, was even more "extensive and enthusiastic," according to Ramm. Vernon Grounds, of the Conservative Baptist Theological Seminary in Denver, wrote Ladd to encourage him: "No doubt you will be hotly criticized—and probably have been already. But don't let that deter you. Perhaps your work will be used of God to spearhead a new movement in premillennialism, redeeming it from arid scholasticism."[90] Sherman Roddy, son of Fuller professor Clarence Roddy and a colleague of Grounds in Denver, told Ladd that "I suppose the reason I enjoyed the book so much was the fact that at last someone, obviously competent, has expressed my own ideas!"[91] Roddy later broke completely with Conservative Baptist fundamentalism and turned to the Presbyterian pastorate.[92]

There were more letters from friends. Merrill Tenney, then dean of Wheaton College, wrote Ladd to compliment him on his "intellectual first-born" He cited the "general excellence of the work" but warned him that "controversy may grow out of this book."[93] Tenney also mentioned the "larger work" Ladd was developing, a theme in many of the letters and reviews that addressed *Crucial Questions*. Ladd wrote back to Tenney to thank him and discussed his hope of producing more extensive study: "The larger work will be a more 'critical' work, addressed not so much to the distinctive evangelical circle but to the world of scholarship at large. It is a rather ambitious project, for it would not only review the entire current literature but would work into the course of the discussion most of the important viewpoints discussed in this literature."[94] Ladd was making a name for himself through his interaction with dispensationalism, but it was also clear that he had his eyes on a bigger prize. Wilbur Smith alluded to this in a letter congratulating Ladd on the publication of his first book, assuring him that "the day will come when everything you publish will be eagerly read."[95]

However, another conflict was brewing within conservative evangelical-ism, one that would reach a flashpoint in the early 1950s: the release of the Revised Standard Version of the Bible (RSV). The RSV was a thoroughgoing restructuring and retranslation based on the American Standard Version (ASV), which first appeared in 1901.[96] Initiated in 1929 and funded by the National Council of Churches of Christ (NCCC), the RSV was based on the latest historical and textual discoveries and was written in clear, American English. The project sought to join current biblical scholarship with church life in the English-speaking world. With one notable exception, the thirty-two translators who worked on the first editions of the RSV were chosen from established universities and divinity schools and represented the major mainstream denominational groups in the United States. Of the original team, nineteen were from universities or university divinity schools, and twelve were from theological seminaries. Henry J. Cadbury of Harvard University, Ladd's doctoral supervisor, was on the New Testament committee. The one true ex-ception among the translators was Harry Orlinsky, a Jewish scholar of the Hebrew Bible from Hebrew Union College. A first edition of the New Testa-ment appeared in 1946, but it was revised when the first full Bible was pub-lished in 1952.

The prevailing philosophy of the RSV translation team was that a theo-logically neutral version of the Bible, one that reflected the best of current biblical and linguistic scholarship, was essential for modern church life. One member of the original team, William A. Irwin of the University of Chicago, argued that "the responsibility of the translator is clear. Representing the best extant understanding of the language with which he deals, he is charged to tell as accurately as he can in his own language precisely what the original says."[97] He continued:

> Linguistic science knows no theology; those of most contradictory views can meet on common ground devoid of polemic, agreed that Hebrew words mean such and such, and their inflection and syntactical relations imply this or that. These facts establish an agreed translation.... The Bible translator is not an expositor; however pronounced his views about Biblical doctrines, he has no right whatever to intrude his opinions in the translation, or to permit his dogmatic convictions to qualify or shape its wording.[98]

Rigorous and dispassionate scholarship, then, was the guiding principle of the RSV translation team. Through critical examination of each word in its own context, followed by reasoned and consistent translation into modern English, the creators of the RSV hoped to produce a Bible that would replace the King James Version, with its outdated language and obsolete or inaccurate sources.

To a large extent, the RSV accomplished its mission. It was released to great fanfare on the festival day of Saint Jerome, with 3,418 observances held in the United States and Canada.[99] In the first thirty years after the RSV appeared, over fifty million copies were sold.[100] The RSV became the Bible of choice for most mainline denominations, and was the preferred version in colleges and universities.[101] A second edition, which included many corrections and other improvements, was issued in 1962.

Although extreme conservatives clearly expressed their opposition to the RSV, the intensity of the response took many of those involved in the project by surprise. Robert G. Lee, pastor of the Bellevue Baptist Church in Memphis, Tennessee, said he was "sorry that the Revised Version ever was gotten out.... I resent the National Council of Churches of Christ in America seeking to establish it as the authorized version of Protestantism."[102] Allan MacRae, president of Faith Theological Seminary and a professor of Old Testament, proclaimed the following: "I cannot trust a single passage in the RSV Old Testament unless I have before me also my Hebrew Bible."[103]

Yet these were tame compared to some of the other articles and pamphlets that attacked virtually every aspect of the RSV. Fundamentalist pastor T. S. Jackson referred to it as "this genius of modernism—this Frankenstein of the spirit—this monstrosity erupted from the womb of hell."[104] In those tense political times it became popular for the militant critics to accuse the RSV committee of using Communist principles in their translation work. In a politely titled article ("Whose Unclean Fingers Have Been Tampering with the Holy Bible, God's Pure, Infallible, Verbally Inspired Word?"), the writer begins with this statement: "Every informed and intelligent person knows that our government is crawling with communists, or those who sanction and encourage communism."[105] Not surprisingly, given this attack, several members of the translation team were investigated during Sen. Joseph McCarthy's search for Communists in the early 1950s. Eventually the charges were challenged and dropped by the House of Representatives.[106] One American preacher responded to the release of the RSV by attempting (unsuccessfully) to burn a copy with a blowtorch in his pulpit, proclaiming that the source of the difficulty was the similarity of the new translation to the devil himself.[107]

Dallas Theological Seminary's response to the RSV was predictably critical. A symposium by four professors in its English Bible department evaluated the source and content of the RSV and in each instance pronounced it unfit for Christian consumption.[108] When writing the "General Considerations," C. F. Lincoln focused his attacks on the link between the RSV and the NCCC. The sponsoring organization, according to Lincoln, has "proved to be unBiblical [sic] in its objectives, socialistic in its aims, and destructively modernistic in its doctrine."[109] Merrill Unger, evaluating the Old Testament of the RSV, argued that not only did the creators of the new version choose the wrong Hebrew texts to translate but that they translated them incorrectly as well.[110] In the New Testament section, S. Lewis Johnson rather boldly asserts that the RSV translators had only a "superficial insight into the exegesis of the Greek New Testament."[111] The closing argument against the RSV was provided by J. Ellwood Evans, who asserts that "the preceding discussion has demonstrated that the Revised Standard Version is a translation which can never receive the approval of conservative scholars."[112] He closes the article with the following comment:

> The continued use, therefore, in public and private of either the King James Version or the American Standard Version of 1901 is still recommended. There is no solid ground for assuming that the Revised Standard Version has supplanted or ever will supplant previous versions. The Scofield Reference Edition of the King James Version is especially recommended, not only for its excellent notes and other helps but because it gives the important corrections in text as found in manuscripts discovered since 1611.[113]

The next article in this issue of *Bibliotheca Sacra* is titled "The Historical Setting of the Ecumenical Movement," a dispensationalist broadside against any moves to unify the various traditions within the Christian world.

At Fuller Seminary, however, the progressives on the faculty saw the RSV as a great leap forward, and in late 1952 a small group of professors made plans to publish an assessment for the seminary's audience. Initiated by Old Testament scholar William Sanford LaSor and designed along the lines of George Ladd's compromise proposal to Ockenga earlier that year, the project group included only LaSor, Everett Harrison, Gleason Archer, and Ladd.[114] The early records of the project begin with the following philosophical statement:

> The members of the Biblical language departments of the Fuller Theological Seminary, under editorship of Dr. LaSor, are undertaking a critical study of the RSV, to evaluate it and to determine what will be the Seminary's attitude toward it. Since this work will be considered as representing the Seminary's position, even though only four members of the Faculty are at work on it, the Editor proposes to seek the counsel of the Faculty and to solicit assistance within reasonable limits.[115]

The book was to have eight chapters that assessed the RSV's use of original texts, its objectivity, its handling of "difficult" texts, and its use of idiomatic expressions.[116] LaSor was to write the introduction, while the others would share duties in the chapters according to their area of expertise. Ladd would write the final full chapter and provide answers to questions such as "Is the RSV worthy to be called the word of God?" "Is the committee representative?" and "Can the Holy Spirit work through [the RSV]?"

Ladd took responsibility for negotiating the publication of the Fuller assessment. He wrote to William Eerdmans in December of 1952, informing him of the project and making it clear that the work going on at Fuller would challenge the unfair criticisms of the RSV. He also let Eerdmans know that the book coming out of Fuller would represent a qualified approval of the new translation.[117] Eerdmans responded enthusiastically, pledging to "bear the cost and risk" of the project and offering favorable financial terms. When Ladd wrote back, he informed Eerdmans that the project was well under way but that he was hesitant to enter into a contract until a draft was completed.[118] Ladd did, however, interject some of the positive reports he was hearing about the response to *Crucial Questions* and asked how the book was selling.

The project was well known to the senior members of the faculty and administration. Each draft of a chapter was sent to Harold Lindsell and Charles Woodbridge for comment, a move designed to preempt attacks from the conservative wing within Fuller.[119] Lindsell and Woodbridge were the strongest defenders of traditional inerrancy among the leadership at the seminary, and their responses helped to shape the book before its publication. Harold Ockenga, president of Fuller at the time, also knew of the project. In May 1954 Ladd received a letter from Russell Hitt, executive editor of *Eternity* magazine. Led by Donald Grey Barnhouse (1895–1960), *Eternity* represented a moderate voice among fundamentalist publications. Hitt told Ladd that Ockenga had mentioned the RSV project to him at a meeting in Philadelphia, and he expressed to Ladd his interest in publishing the work.[120] When Ladd responded a few weeks later, he expressed frustration over the progress of the work. He said that "because it is a corporate work of four men, there has been revision after revision and we have made painfully slow progress toward the finished manuscript. We have not made final plans yet as to publication."[121] Despite the four authors' shared progressive views on the project, the process of agreeing on the final assessment of the RSV proved to be exceedingly difficult.

However, that was not the only threat to the project. Despite (or perhaps because of) the knowledge and encouragement of the project among the leadership at Fuller, Charles Fuller became worried about the book's impact on his radio audience. The seminary was still largely dependent on donations from the *Old Fashioned Revival Hour*, and as a result, that constituency held a measure of influence over the institution.[122] In a special mailing to his radio supporters, Fuller said that, although he did not approve of the RSV himself, the faculty of the seminary had the freedom to examine the work for themselves.[123] Nonetheless, he received letters condemning his weak response to a book that "some did not want to keep . . . in their homes," and he complained to his son Dan that the controversy was costing him listeners.[124] Sometime in 1955 or 1956, though much of the work had already been completed, Charles Fuller ordered his faculty to abandon the RSV project and to refrain from any public mention of the issue.[125] The book was never published.

Ladd's observations regarding the RSV translators and their product reveal several facets of his own thought related to the nature and use of the Bible. First, he saw the Bible, at least in part, as something given in history. As such it could not be damaged—or presumably enhanced in some way—according to the various theological positions of those who would translate and edit it. As a historical phenomenon, the Bible demanded only to be rendered accurately, but beyond that the personality of the technician was irrelevant. In the end, only the quality of the work mattered.[126] Second, as "the word of God," the Bible retained its supernatural origins and conveyed its own saving message regardless of who might translate or even read it. This sacred text had an identity that was completely apart from history and emerged from the words of its writings no matter who was involved in the communication. Finally, in Ladd's reasoned approach to this new translation, we see the unmistakable influence of Harvard's theologically neutral approach to biblical study. Cadbury had taught Ladd—in word and deed—that excellence in scholarship was not always joined to doctrinal orthodoxy, and in Ladd's assessment of the RSV we see that the lesson had taken root. This rigorous method, integrated with conservative faith, formed the basis for Ladd's approach to biblical scholarship for the remainder of his life.

By 1953 Ladd had settled into his role as scholar-teacher at Fuller Seminary. He developed—and cultivated—a reputation as a rigorous, demanding professor and was known for bluntly exposing any student who did not come fully prepared to class.[127] When Ladd became the seminary's acting librarian at the end of 1952, he assumed responsibility for building the collection and scouring bookshops around the country for necessary texts. In these early years, Fuller Seminary survived by using primarily the massive personal library of Wilbur Smith, augmented by whatever Ladd could bring in on his meager budget. It was a difficult process. In a letter to Roger Nicole, former colleague and librarian at Gordon College, Ladd complained that "there is not a good research library in Southern California," but "we are doing our best to make a start toward building one."[128] Nicole, who freely held an amillennialist position in the gentler atmosphere of Gordon College, teased Ladd about his recently published *Crucial Questions*: "The fact that you are not agreeing with the amils does not risk to endanger our friendship . . . [and] I will not shed any tears if I find that your views differ from those of Darby and Scofield."[129] Amid the brewing doctrinal controversies at Fuller and among the Conservative Baptists, Ladd must have felt a certain wistfulness about Gordon, where scholars who disagreed could remain close friends.

This was becoming less the case at Fuller Seminary. The seeds of future conflict found room to grow in the issue of the seminary presidency. After years of presiding from Boston, where he was the immensely popular pastor of Park Street Congregational Church, Harold Ockenga finally decided in 1954 that he would not move to Pasadena and assume the duties of president.[130] In a surprising move, Edward John Carnell was chosen as president over Harold Lindsell and the better-known Carl Henry, which angered the conservative—and mostly dispensationalist—old guard.[131] Carnell was a brilliant young scholar with great dreams of Fuller's role in the world of evangelical scholarship. Like Ladd, Carnell believed that evangelicalism had abandoned its high place in American culture and, like Ladd, saw himself as playing an important part in reassuming a position of leadership. Carnell had completed two doctoral degrees simultaneously, one at Harvard and the other at Boston University, and had already published several books. Almost immediately after taking over the presidency, Carnell began the process of eliminating what he perceived as the primary stumbling block to Fuller's future as an academic institution: the premillennialism clause in the seminary's statement of faith. In a letter to Harold Ockenga, Carnell argued that Fuller could never achieve greatness as long as its faculty were required to assent to this doctrine, noting that "neither Calvin, Warfield, Hodge, nor Machen could teach at Fuller Seminary."[132]

Though Ladd was satisfied with the progress toward his ultimate goal of advancing his academic career in those first years at Fuller Seminary, it was not without cost. He often complained that he was not suited to controversy and that he wanted to be left alone to carry out his scholarly work. The interaction with John Walvoord and the militant dispensationalists took a toll on Ladd, even though he initiated the conflict, and left him bruised and fearful. At Fuller the failure of the two collaborative projects, as well as the growing rift between the old guard and the progressives, drove Ladd to focus on his own work. After 1952 there is no record at Fuller of further joint scholarly enterprises on the scale of the inspiration or RSV assessment ventures. At home Ladd was still demanding silence so that he could work into the evening and complaining that he could never get it.[133] Norma Ladd was finishing high school, and her relationship to her father was increasingly strained. Her brother, Larry, fifteen years old in 1952, now began to manifest the physical and emotional problems that would haunt him—and his father—for the rest of his life. The cumulative impact of these psychological stressors began to have an effect on Ladd's own health between 1951 and 1953. He had headaches that, in addition to being painful, interfered with his study. The problem had started while Ladd was at Harvard but became more severe after the arrival at Fuller.[134] When traditional remedies failed to alleviate the pain, Ladd turned to an experimental treatment known as radionics, administered by a local psychologist.[135]

Radionics is a frankly bizarre method of homeopathic treatment that involves the detection and manipulation of radio waves or "life energies" using modern-looking electronic devices. Just as Ladd was experiencing its supposed benefits, the procedure was in the process of being discredited in a well-publicized trial.[136] The corrective worked for a time, but the headaches foreshadowed a pattern of personal stress manifesting itself in Ladd's life in the form of physical or emotional pain, as well as the lengths he would travel in his desperate search for relief.

Ladd entered the Carnell era as one of the rising stars in the new evangelical movement. He was respected—if not feared—as a teacher and trusted to play an important role in Fuller Seminary's quest to become a well-regarded academic institution. Ladd's leadership in the faculty writing projects, even though they ended in failure, were indications of the esteem he had earned in his short time at the seminary. His active participation in building the seminary's library holdings was also a sign of his central role in shaping Fuller's stature in the academic world. Most importantly, Ladd established himself in the first four years of his tenure there as a conservative scholar willing to critique his own movement rigorously and unflinchingly. In 1954 he told a friend that "neither a theological position nor personal devotion can take the place of the hardest sort of work in scholarly pursuits." He went on to say that he had learned more "from liberal authors than from all the conservative literature which exists."[137] He was willing to engage theological scholarship on its own merits, even when he disagreed with its premises and conclusions. It was the quality and precision of the work that mattered most, and Ladd believed that colleagues on the conservative side had not yet learned to pull their weight. He thus saw himself as one—if not the only one—who could lift conservative scholarship out of its lowly place, and with this resolve Ladd entered the next phase of his career.

3

Old Battles and Partial
Victories (1954–1959)

George Ladd emerged from his first major engagement with dispensationalism as one of the preeminent representatives of progressive evangelicalism. He had met Dallas Seminary—and by extension John Walvoord—on its own ground, and although he did not score a decisive victory, he survived the encounter with some distinction. But critiquing dispensationalism was not what Ladd had in mind as the focus of his career, and he was beginning even at this early date to chafe at the role in which he found himself. Ladd's reaction was to redouble his efforts to complete his critical study of the Kingdom of God. This would be the scholarly achievement that would rescue conservative evangelicals from themselves and from irrelevance in the broader world of ideas. By 1953 Ladd was again working on his magnum opus, with the provisional title "Promise, Fulfillment and Consummation," as well as on a series of important journal articles.

In the midst of his effort to differentiate progressive evangelical theology from that of dispensationalism, Ladd was also looking ahead to a time when he might freely participate in the broader discussions of biblical studies and theology. In a letter to Richard Clearwaters (1900–1996), a separatist Conservative Baptist pastor in Minnesota who was a militant defender of the King James Version of the Bible, Ladd cautiously affirmed the possibility that a "liberal" theologian might have something to offer the careful evangelical reader. "A liberal can be right at given points," according to Ladd, "even though his structure as a whole is wrong." Ladd further stated that "a liberal and a conservative should be able to agree as to what the Bible teaches, even though they violently disagree as to the relevance and the truthfulness of what is taught."[1] This was an important step in Ladd's understanding of both the Bible and biblical studies, not to mention a significant concession regarding the value of liberal scholarship. Scholars of differing views could agree on what the Bible teaches only if they could concur—at least in part—on its historical origins, and Ladd's statement shows that he was willing to meet the other side somewhere nearer the middle:

> If it is principally wrong to quote from liberal scholars, then it is
> equally wrong for our schools and seminaries to desire teachers
> who have university doctorates; for almost invariably such degrees are
> taken under liberals. However it is being increasingly realized
> that correctness of position and quality of scholarship are not iden-
> tical; and in our generation conservatives, who we believe have the
> only correct position, have nearly capitulated the field of scholarship
> to the liberals, whose position is wrong. It has been gratifying to
> me, as a matter of great moment, to find a growing recognition for a
> scholarship that can meet the liberal on his ground, without any
> surrender of our historical conservative position.[2]

In this letter Ladd revealed his willingness to move outside the circles of evangelicalism in order to earn a hearing for evangelical theology. He also acknowledged the weakness in much of the evangelical scholarship of the day and the necessity of engagement as a means by which to improve the state of affairs. This new level of participation in the broader academic world was an important part of Ladd's evolving strategy for establishing the content and image of evangelical thought.

Ladd's advocacy of this broad view came just as he was finalizing his move from the Northern Baptist Convention (NBC) to the Conservative Baptist Association (CBA). There was no single precipitating event, but one can presume that the conservative atmosphere at Fuller and the strong presence of CBA ministerial candidates at the seminary made the choice easier for Ladd. The church where Ladd had his membership, Immanuel Baptist in Pasadena, was sympathetic to the CBA but remained in the NBC. However, even that ended up becoming a source of some pressure. One CB leader confided to Ladd his "hope that the Immanuel church in Pasadena shall be soon in the association."[3] This did not come to pass, but in 1956 Ladd slipped out of his membership on the ministerial rolls of the American Baptist Convention (the name change took place in 1950).[4]

The mid-1950s were troubled times for conservative evangelicals—mostly of their own making—and Ladd's efforts to broaden evangelicalism came just as the most conservative wing of his own movement was seeking to place limits on the impulse toward cooperation. Edward Carnell, the newly installed president of Fuller Seminary, who represented such promise for the future of evangelical theological scholarship, was blasted for his call to tolerance in his 1955 inaugural address at Fuller.[5] The controversies surrounding the publication of the Revised Standard Version of the Bible continued to divide churches and institutions. Race and civil rights issues were moving into prominence, especially after the landmark *Brown v. Board of Education* decision by the U.S. Supreme Court in 1954.[6]

Many evangelicals in the United States were increasingly troubled by the rise in influence of the ecumenical movement, represented first by the National Council of Churches of Christ (NCCC) and later by the World Council of Churches (WCC). The WCC held its 1954 meetings in Evanston, Illinois, receiving widespread media coverage and provoking attacks from those who saw its unifying work as a sign of the end times. Most significantly, because it tore at the unity of the evangelical movement from within, battle lines were forming over issues related to eschatology. Even among those who saw the Bible as the supernaturally inspired word of God, divisions arose over the precise timing and ordering of end-times events. The faculty at Fuller itself was deeply split over these issues, a fact that belied its image as a harmonious refuge for theological study. Ladd was certainly not oblivious to these developments or to their impact on the evangelical enterprise, but it was not until another seminary split over issues of eschatology occurred that he became significantly distracted from his plans to complete a major work of critical scholarship.

By 1955 the Fuller Seminary faculty had settled into two distinct and occasionally contentious theological camps.[7] On one side was the old guard, largely dispensationalist and still holding some separatist tendencies. This group included Wilbur Smith, Harold Lindsell, Charles Woodbridge, Gleason Archer, Everett Harrison, and Carl Henry. In 1953 Lindsell and Woodbridge had co-written a theological primer designed to clarify the boundaries of conservative faith to a lay audience.[8] On the other side were the younger, more critically trained members of the faculty, drawn to Fuller by the opportunity to create serious evangelical scholarship. This group was represented by Carnell, Ladd, Paul King Jewett, Clarence Roddy, and Daniel Payton Fuller, son of the founder and a new instructor at the seminary. A top priority for the progressive faction was the removal of the clause that required premillennialism in Fuller's doctrinal statement.[9] It is significant that the three established leaders of this progressive wing (Carnell, Ladd, and Jewett) were all veterans of Gordon College's tolerant atmosphere, where eschatological issues were left to conscience. Still, Daniel Fuller's contribution to this effort was the only hope for its success since only he could convince his father, still committed to dispensationalist theology, to go along. The best they could accomplish at that time was to secure Charles Fuller's promise that the clause could be removed after his death.[10] This debate exposed serious theological divisions among the faculty and precipitated the fractious times to come. Carnell's presidency was marked by conflict, dissension, and outright mutiny at several points, leading to his eventual emotional and psychological collapse.[11] But as the conflicts centered on the presidency of Carnell, Ladd continued to mount his attack on the dispensationalist edifice.

An important aspect of this campaign was Ladd's strategic mentoring of Dan Fuller. Though groomed to take over his father's radio ministry empire, Dan Fuller was a reluctant successor. Slightly introverted but brilliant, Dan became a replacement instructor after he graduated from Fuller in 1951. He loved teaching, and his students—some of whom had been his classmates the year before—remember him as one of the best instructors they had.[12] This experience gave Dan aspirations of becoming a scholar and teaching at his father's school, and in 1953 he went to Northern Baptist Theological Seminary in Chicago to pursue a ThD in the field of hermeneutics.

During this period Dan looked to Ladd (as a Harvard graduate and rising star in evangelical biblical scholarship) for guidance in the development of his academic training. Ladd responded by recommending books, courses, and even topics for papers. Ladd knew that Dan would have enormous influence on the direction of the seminary and nudged him toward making dispensationalism a focus of his study of hermeneutics. The oldest surviving letter in this correspondence reveals Ladd's role in pointing Dan Fuller toward the work that would eventually dominate most of his academic career, a study of the continuity between the Old and New Testaments. Ladd wrote that the "crucial point at which dispensationalists and nondispensationalists differ is at the point of the interpretation of the two Testaments."[13] Dan wrote back, saying he was "a little more aware now that there is a real problem to be faced in dispensationalism."[14]

For his dissertation Dan decided preliminarily to "set down the basic principles of historical-grammatical interpretation and then apply them to the crucial eschatological passages of the Bible to see where they lead."[15] The result was "The Hermeneutics of Dispensationalism," a landmark broadside against the core interpretative principles of the entire tradition, which earned Dan his doctorate in 1957.[16] In his last letter to Ladd before returning from Northern Dan wrote: "I am convinced that we ought to teach Classical Premillennialism.

I have seen how Dispensationalism can debilitate Christianity."[17] Ladd had recruited an able ally indeed in his challenge to dispensationalism.[18]

The most influential event for Ladd during this period, one that diverted his attention yet again from his magnum opus, was the conflict that rocked Western Seminary in Portland, Oregon.[19] Founded in 1927 in partnership with the Oregon State Baptist Convention and at least in part as a response to liberal influences at other Baptist institutions, Western Baptist Theological Seminary had mirrored many of the contemporary divisions affecting Baptists in the rest of North America.[20] Western's doctrinal statement, while conservative and thoroughly Baptist, originally avoided contentious issues such as inerrancy and dispensational eschatology. Further, and initially as a way to prevent a slide toward liberalism, the bylaws of the institution prohibited any changes to the original statement of faith. The founders and early leaders of Western saw it as a partner institution with Gordon in Boston, Northern in Chicago, and Eastern in Philadelphia, all created as alternatives to local Baptist institutions with strong liberal influences. As had those institutions, Western avoided, at least at first, the militancy of the most conservative groups within the NBC.[21] But in the 1940s the situation began to change.

The doctrinal conflicts that rocked the NBC after the Second World War, coupled with the institution's practice of allowing students to attend without cost, put Western in serious financial difficulties.[22] Most of the faculty members were owed salary payments and were working in local churches to support themselves. Tuition was introduced in 1946, further strengthening the seminary's financial state, and in 1948 Western Seminary seemed to be on solid ground once again. However, by this time doctrinal issues were taking center stage. In 1946 the NBC refused to recognize Western as an acceptable institution for Baptist ministerial candidates, despite the fact that the nearest alternative was Berkeley Baptist Divinity School, more than six hundred miles away in California.[23] Presumably this decision was based on the presence of some militancy in the Oregon State Convention, though not then among the leadership of the seminary itself.

At the meeting of Western's board in December of 1948, conservative chairman Albert Johnson refused to seat any members appointed by the state convention, which had in his view acquiesced too easily to the NBC's leadership. By 1951 the seminary had aligned itself with the CBA and changed the name of the institution to Western Conservative Baptist Theological Seminary. Johnson had grown suspicious of Western's faculty during the early 1950s because he believed they were not sufficiently committed to theological separatism. Indeed, Earl Kalland, president of Western Seminary and a friend of Ladd's from Gordon, had admitted as much before the Oregon Baptist State

Convention.[24] Clearly this educational philosophy could not coexist with the growing sense of militant separatism present in the Conservative Baptist movement. The CBA had avoided questions related to eschatology in its original doctrinal statements but in the early 1950s moved to add a strict premillennialist and pretribulationist clause to the beliefs required for fellowship. This act was proposed at the CBA meetings in Saint Paul, Minnesota, and confirmed at the next year's gathering in Portland, the home of Western Seminary.[25] At the 1954 meetings rumors were spreading that members of the faculty at Western were resisting compliance with the new doctrinal boundaries, and the board of the seminary felt compelled to act.

In March of 1955 Johnson led Western's board to add a premillennialist and pretribulationist clause to the statement of faith, as well as a declaration of Western's commitment to "be separatist in spirit and direction."[26] However, this revision turned out to be impossible. Protected as it was by the seminary's own charter from any addition or other alteration, Western's doctrinal statement was inviolable. Ironically, it was this defense against liberalism that prevented Johnson from making the statement more "conservative." Not to be denied, Johnson adopted a new strategy that affirmed the doctrinal change at the board level and then later required the faculty to assent "without equivocation."[27] A meeting was held between the board and the entire faculty, but according to Johnson, "Little understanding or good resulted." In July of 1955 Earl Kalland resigned his presidency and academic post and, over the next year, was followed by five other professors.[28] By a unanimous vote of the board, Albert Johnson was elected to replace Kalland as president of the seminary.

Why the urgency from Johnson and the rest of Western's board? Why the willingness to decimate a committed faculty? Certainly issues related to eschatology were taking center stage in the boundary-making efforts of conservative Baptists. The CBA was in general agreement that both premillennialism and pretribulationism were rising to the level of essential doctrinal positions. Johnson and the other leading trustees concurred with the CBA, but there was more to their drastic resolution to the issue. In its own explanatory document the board allows for another significant factor in its decision. Western Seminary, while not in the dire financial straits it had experienced in the 1930s and 1940s, was not particularly wealthy or well endowed, either. In its preliminary statement the board affirms that its decision would "aid immeasurably in attracting financial support which is now going to other institutions."[29]

Repeatedly the concern over the "national constituency" is raised; it appears nine times in the first seven pages of the pamphlet, all reflecting the fear that financial stability and student enrolment would suffer if the doctrinal problems were not resolved. To add to the intensity of the issue, there was a threat of a new CBA-affiliated seminary on the West Coast, born out of a perceived "lack of confidence" in the faculty of Western Seminary.[30] Clearly the unforgiving marketplace of conservative higher education had been at the core of the actions by Western's board. Any drop in donations from the seminary's constituency, coupled with diminished enrolments of new students, might have sent the institution into bankruptcy.

Largely in response to the events at Western, Ladd shifted his focus back to the world of dispensationalism and began to examine how its controversial doctrine of the second coming of Christ functioned within Baptist churches and organizations.[31] At issue in this phase of Ladd's struggle against dispensationalism was the practice at some Conservative Baptist institutions of making pretribulationism a test of orthodoxy. As part of his research Ladd sent letters to several churches and organizations asking them for their doctrinal statements.[32] While not constituting a broad sample by any measure, none that he received required pretribulationism, but this fact may have only increased Ladd's drive to continue his study since he was convinced the requirement was being enforced. He knew that Western and other institutions were purging faculty members who would not sign a pretribulationist doctrinal statement and concluded that he was working within a temporary window of opportunity that might soon close. In a letter to Peter de Visser, Ladd's contact at Eerdmans Publishing Company, Ladd wrote that he felt a "burden in [his] heart" for the way this issue was tearing apart his denomination. He shared his shock with de Visser at the fact that the "Baptist Seminary at Portland, Ore. turned out its Faculty because they would not go along with pretribulationism." He also complained that "our [Fuller's] alumni have continual problems with ordination councils because they do not hold to the 'party line.' "[33] Ladd's distress over events in his own Baptist family, in addition to his passion for critical exegesis, must be seen as primary motivations for continuing his engagement with dispensationalism.[34]

In addition to his exegetical research, Ladd began a correspondence with Charles Erdman (1866–1960) of Princeton Seminary. Erdman's father, William (1834–1923), had been a prominent leader in the Niagara Prophetic Conferences, an important series of events in the rise of dispensationalism in the United States, as well as a contributing editor to the revision of the Scofield Bible. Ladd was attempting to get a better understanding of the historical background of dispensational eschatology, hoping that a more accurate perspective might temper the growing militancy of the debate: "I deplore the narrow dogmatic attitude which prevails in many circles of contemporary American Fundamentalism, especially with regard to the interpretation of dispensational truth. If I gather historical information which will place the entire discussion against a saner historical background, I shall be very happy."[35]

Erdman complimented Ladd's efforts: "There is surely a great need of bringing Dispensationalists to a more irenic state of mind.... Anything which can remove the doctrine of the coming of Christ from the field of bitter controversy is to be highly praised."[36] Erdman provided Ladd with firsthand accounts of the Niagara conferences and discussed the leaders' reaction to his father's abandonment of pretribulationism. The change in position, according to Erdman, "caused my father to be deserted by many of his former friends," some of whom treated him "with little courtesy or Christian consideration."[37] Erdman's recollections influenced Ladd's understanding of the historical issues and also underscored his belief that, for years, pretribulationism's attendant militancy had been causing more harm than good.

Ladd also wrote a remarkable series of letters to evangelical leaders around the nation who he believed might support his challenge to the pretribulational aspect of dispensationalism.[38] A letter went to John McNicol of Toronto Bible College, who had been one of the nondispensationalist contributors to *The Fundamentals*. Explaining that he was doing research for a book on eschatology, Ladd asked McNicol whether he remembered any other contributors who had shared his views. Apart from those of whom Ladd was already aware, McNicol could not add to the list. He did, however, express his dismay "at the position taken by the pretribulationists" and encouraged Ladd in his efforts.[39]

Ladd also wrote to G. Allen Fleece, president of Columbia Bible College, someone Ladd knew as a postribulationist. In each letter Ladd began with a description of how pretribulationism was being used as a test of orthodoxy and used the example of Western Seminary. Ladd asked first whether Fleece had ever made his own opinions known and second whether a Doctor McQuilkin had ever published similar beliefs. Finally, Ladd asked whether Fleece would point him in the direction of anyone else who might oppose the pretribulationist position.[40] Fleece's response is telling:

> The answer to your first and second questions inquiring whether Dr. McQuilkin or I have ever expressed ourselves in print on the subject of the Church and the Rapture is no. Dr. McQuilkin was quite cautious about any such expression, and indeed never expressed to me personally his conviction on the subject.... In my own case, I have followed his example as far as public utterances are concerned. However, people are good at making inferences![41]

In this phase of his research Ladd was finding something he clearly already suspected: Few people in Fleece's position could afford to make their views known for fear of being ostracized from the militant wing of the conservative evangelical community.

Ladd received a milder reaction from Philip Newell of Moody Bible Institute. Moody was a staunchly dispensationalist school at the time and certainly the most visible evangelical institution in the United States. Newell praised Ladd's intention to champion the cause of unity in the body of believers: "I deeply deplore the almost hostile position of many of our esteemed brethren regarding this vital question."[42] He explained that he had dabbled in the posttribulation position, "and for several years was definitely committed to it" but now found himself "reluctant to be dogmatic." Newell named a few other posttribulationists and wished Ladd the best on his project.

The final exchange provides a revealing glimpse into the crisis that faced evangelicals in the mid-1950s. Ladd sent one of his query letters to Howard Ferrin, president of Providence-Barrington Bible College in Rhode Island, whose encouragement had prompted Ladd to enter this debate in the first place.[43] As in the previous letters, Ladd asked whether Ferrin knew of any other leaders in the conservative movement whose eschatological views differed from the militant pretribulationist position. He also asked whether Ferrin had published his own position, which Ladd knew to be outside the conservative mainstream. In his response, Ferrin stated that he was "frankly concerned about the growing tension which is developing over the pre-tribulation rapture issue."[44] He told Ladd that he had attempted the same sort of peacemaking effort in 1948 but sensed even then that the issue was becoming overly divisive. He then offered a rambling explanation of the reason he did not want his name attached to Ladd's new campaign:

> Now concerning your request. I cannot feel, my brother, that at this time I would want to make known my own personal position on this matter—and for reasons I shall shortly present—nor name any men in the Bible school movement in America who hold the posttribulation view. . . . I do not want to be guilty of quoting men when they themselves have not made some public or written statement that is, by them, meant to be a public pronouncement of their position.[45]

Ferrin continued to backtrack:

> The questions I raised about the pre-tribulation rapture have led some to quote me as holding to the post-tribulation view—but I have never said that I held to this view. Frankly, I have questions about both views that I cannot answer. Perhaps it might be cowardice that

> I do not state my position unequivocally, but I rather consider it as
> taking a cautious view. . . . I fear this whole issue is so encased in
> emotionalism that I fear we will never get uniformity in thinking on
> it. . . . I fear that the fundamentalist family is going to be upset again
> over what I consider a non-essential prophetic interpretation con-
> cerning the blessed truth of our Lord's appearing.[46]

The fear of being exposed as having views outside the bounds of dispensational orthodoxy was palpable, equivalent in those times to being branded a
Communist. No one wanted to unnecessarily repeat the trauma of Western
Seminary. If Ladd was looking for support in his quest to bring peace and
tolerance to the evangelical debate over eschatology, he was destined for disappointment. It was clear to Ladd as he went to work on his next book that he
would have to act largely alone in his effort.

As Ladd was completing the manuscript for *The Blessed Hope*, he was
invited to speak at the 1956 meetings of the Conservative Baptist Association in
Brooklyn. He was asked to be a member of a panel on the timing of the
tribulation in relation to the millennium and to argue for the posttribulation
position. This was an important opportunity to make his case for latitude in the
area of eschatology, though it was not without danger.[47] Ladd's position was
similar to that which had been central to the catastrophe at Western Seminary.
Hoping to set the tone for the exchange prior to the actual event, he sent
preemptive letters to the other participants on the panel. Ladd wrote to his old
friend Merrill Tenney, who would be presenting the midtribulation position.
He stated that his own main objective would be to offer "a defense of the
right of a man to hold a posttribulation position without being labeled a
'pinko liberalist.'" Here again was the fear that straying too far from the
theological line might be interpreted as some form of incipient Communist
sympathy.

Moreover, Ladd admitted to Tenney that he had not intended to get involved in the controversy over eschatology but that the "tragic events at Western" had forced his hand, and "none of the brethren who have greater
influence . . . [would] speak out." Ladd's goal was to see the different positions
discussed without rancor or suspicion: "[T]he way this question is presented is
infinitely more important than the position taken."[48] It was a bold assertion—
not one shared by many in the Conservative Baptist movement—to say that the
tone and civility of a debate mattered "infinitely more" than one's doctrinal
position and reveals Ladd's developing strategy for lifting conservative evangelicalism out of its self-imposed ghetto of irrelevance.

Ladd also wrote to the presenter of the pretribulation position, potentially a much more dangerous communication. But he was relieved to learn that the representative of the stricter dispensationalist position was E. Schuyler English (1899–1984), editor of *Our Hope*, a prophecy-oriented magazine in the dispensationalist tradition and later an editor as well of the New Scofield Bible. English had been critical of the RSV in *Our Hope*, in which he challenged its methodologies and results, but Ladd had been impressed with the irenic tone of the review.[49] In his letter Ladd stated that he was looking forward to the presentation and assured English that he had "little zeal to convert anyone to a posttribulation position." Ladd's concern was that some in the CBA were "designating any departure from a pretribulation dispensational eschatology as a new form of liberalism," and he expressed his hope that the convention might "respect the integrity and the conscience and the devotion of men who hold a different position."[50] Ladd's appeal to the Baptist ethos of individual liberty was apparently effective with English, who responded with a pledge that his address would "not be given in a controversial way or with any thought of attacking brethren who hold a different view."[51]

The presentation itself was accomplished without contention. Ladd offered his credentials as one who had been a committed dispensationalist but whose views had changed through his study of the Bible. "I have not chosen posttribulationism," he proclaimed, using the refrain that had protected him from charges of liberalism, "God's Word has driven me to it."[52] The primary focus of his address, though, was less theological and more to argue for liberty in the area of eschatological interpretation. The question should not be whether a particular position is orthodox or liberal, Ladd argued, but rather whether it is based on the Bible's authority. If the Bible is held as the ultimate arbiter of truth, then the rest is a question of interpretation and should fall under the protection of individual soul liberty. Though he was making an explicit call for peaceful interaction, Ladd could not resist the temptation to fire a shot at John Walvoord. The president of Dallas Seminary, Ladd told the convention, "is on record in print as affirming that the Word of God does not explicitly affirm a pre-tribulational rapture of the Church. He admits that it is an inference." Still, the central theme of Ladd's presentation was a call to unity: "My hope for the future is not a millennium, it is the Lord Jesus Christ. Let's not make great truths stand in the way of that which is the greatest reality.... Beloved, from the depths of my heart, I believe that the greatest hindrance to revival in America is division among the people of God."[53]

To Ladd's great comfort, the other two presenters felt much the same way. Tenney echoed Ladd's belief that "interpretations vary" and appealed only to the "authority of the Word of God."[54] True Christians, Tenney argued, "should be united" and allow "room for free discussion." English was even stronger in his statement. Bible-believing Christians, he declared, "must not equate premillennialism with pretribulationism. . . . Differences of viewpoint [have] nothing to do with heresy."

Ladd, however, came away from Brooklyn deeply troubled by what he had seen and heard and feeling as though he had stepped irretrievably into a theological "no man's land."[55] There is no record of any confrontation with critics, but it is possible that in the conversations after the session on eschatology, Ladd was challenged by someone who thought his position was inappropriate. This would not be beyond the realm of possibility—these were, after all, some of the same people who had presided over the bloodbath at Western just ten months before. In a revealing letter to E. Schuyler English written just after the CBA meetings, Ladd sounded strangely defeated. He repeated the defense of his own dispensationalist credentials in order to establish his right to critique the system. Ladd told English that he had been brought up on the Scofield Bible and that "as a boy preacher still in my teens was preaching dispensationalism."[56]

Ladd's desire to raise the level of scholarly discourse among evangelicals, however, was still tempered by his desire to keep the peace. He clearly believed that dispensationalism was a key hindrance to intellectual credibility for evangelical thought, though he went out of his never to say so.[57] "I do not consider it *ipso facto* unscholarly," Ladd said, "to hold dispensational views," though in reality he certainly did.[58] Rather, Ladd said that if he could "find the teaching in the Scripture," he would support it "with all vigor." "My authority," Ladd claimed, "is not scholarship but the Word of God."[59]

And yet this claim to biblical authority, which had given Ladd a sense of protection in the pages of *Crucial Questions* (and would seem to again in *The Blessed Hope*), now created in him a sense of isolation. "Modern scholarship" (he referred to it in monolithic terms) would not allow him to base his views "on the premise of an inspired Word of God" without dismissing him as an "obscurantist." "I have been compelled by the Word of God," Ladd complained to English, "to take a position which will make it impossible for me to move in circles where I can enjoy the fellowship of men like yourself." Clearly Ladd feared that, despite the peaceful dialogue of the CBA meetings, the division over eschatology was destined to crumble into the same sort of conflict that had occurred at Western Seminary. "My own position," he concluded, "is one which satisfies no one—neither dispensationalists nor the so-called reformed theologians. However, our responsibility is to the Word, not to men." So Ladd pressed on, challenging the premises of the dispensationalist system and, ironically, finding himself separated from the separatists in his own Baptist tradition. Within a few years he quietly left the CBA and by 1959 was again registered, this time as a "minister in special service," on the rolls of the American Baptist Convention.[60]

The Blessed Hope, released in 1956, is Ladd's critique of the pretribulation rapture position and a direct challenge to the divisive way dispensationalists were using this doctrine. The book represents the next step in Ladd's maturation as a scholar and writer, as well as his growing stature within the evangelical community. No third-party foreword was necessary to provide a stamp of approval, and a firmer hand is evident in the structure and writing of the book. It is also far more aggressive in its attack on cherished dispensationalist doctrines. By 1956 Ladd was the established insider critic of dispensationalism and had built for himself an audience of conservative evangelicals who found in his work an acceptable expression of premillennial faith, without the excesses of dispensational futurism. The *Blessed Hope* would solidify Ladd's place as a leading evangelical scholar, at least among evangelicals, and place him further outside the orbit of those aligned with Dallas Seminary.

Ladd's introduction to the book is both a firm warning of the argument to come and a call to peace and understanding among those who were sure to disagree with his conclusions. While premillennialism and pretribulationism have much in common, according to Ladd, "pretribulationism adds several other features which are not essential to the main outlines of premillennial truth. Thus premillennialism and pretribulationism are not synonymous."[61] He argues that the wide influence of this position is a direct result of the Scofield Bible and those associated with the related prophetic movements. Ladd assessed this influence:

> No instrument has been more influential than the Scofield Reference Bible in implanting this view in the thinking of millions of Christians. . . . So deeply entrenched has it become that many pastors and Christian leaders have been led to assume that this teaching has been an essential doctrine in the history of the Church extending back to apostolic times and has prevailed widely in all ages among believers who have had a sincere love for the Word of God and who have cherished the Blessed Hope of Christ's return.[62]

However, even those leaders could not agree, according to Ladd. Some among the early prophetic movement did not accept the pretribulationist formula, though they continued their work together and allowed for differences of opinion. Ladd is clearly trying to influence the contemporary debate by recalling a gentler time when he believed doctrinal disputes were less rancorous and divisive. He writes that despite these doctrinal differences, "this deviation was not considered to be ground for attacking their essential soundness, orthodoxy, and loyalty to the Word of God."[63] Whether Ladd is calling for peace in the church, trying to avoid attacks on his own work, or both, he is sure that evangelicals have strayed from these conciliatory practices. Now, Ladd charged, "some Christian institutions and leaders appear to be genuinely fearful that any deviation from a pretribulation eschatology is a step toward liberalism."[64] He saw his book as a direct confrontation not only to the doctrine of pretribulationism but also to the behavior of those who militantly defended this belief.

In his introduction Ladd bluntly states that "the Blessed Hope is the second coming of Jesus Christ and not a pretribulation rapture." Though no sane person would choose to go through this horrifying experience, he argues, there appears to be no choice. "The question is not," he states, "what do we want, but, what does the Word of God teach?"[65] Ladd's views, though in direct opposition to those of the dispensationalists, were protected by his appeal to Scripture. However, the dispensationalists also called upon certain passages of Scripture for corroboration. Did that not give them the same weight? Here Ladd plays the Scripture card with a level of aggression not seen in his earlier writing: "Such a line of reasoning is persuasive; but if it happens not to agree with the teachings of Scripture, it is dangerous for that very reason. Persuasiveness is no authority; the one question must be, what does the Word of God teach?"[66] Twice in twelve lines Ladd appeals to the teaching of Scripture as the ultimate—the only—authority, making his thesis difficult indeed to attack. He closes the introduction by calling attention to his "irenic purpose" for writing and petitioning for "unity of the Spirit in the bond of peace."[67]

Blessed Hope begins with a survey of the history of prophetic interpretation. In the first paragraph of the first chapter Ladd states that "if the *Blessed Hope* is in fact a pretribulation rapture, then the Church has never known that hope through most of its history, for the idea of a pretribulation rapture did not appear in prophetic interpretation until the nineteenth century."[68] Each subsequent chapter begins with an equally blunt rejection of some aspect of pretribulationalist thought. In the second chapter Ladd traces the history of pretribulationism in the modern English-speaking world, establishing its trajectory of influence in the prophetic conferences in Britain and the United States at the turn of the twentieth century. Again decrying the militancy that had become the hallmark of the pretribulationalist camp, Ladd called for peaceful coexistence among all of those who "love his appearing," reminding his readers that even the writers of *The Fundamentals* disagreed significantly on the details of eschatology.[69] "Why," asked Ladd, "can such unity not be demonstrated today?" Even the conservative wing of the Northern Baptists, as they formed the first fundamentalist movement within their denomination, allowed for extensive differences in eschatology, Ladd argued. He continued: "If those who are set for the defense of the faith can stand together in the same spirit of basic unity in spite of differences in details, they will win far more ground than they will if they squander their energies in controversy."[70] Nonetheless, even as he called for peace and reasoned disagreement, Ladd took aim at the heart of the dispensationalist tradition.

After addressing the linguistic and exegetical issues of the key biblical eschatological passages, Ladd launches his strongest offensive against the dispensationalist method of interpreting Scripture. In a chapter pointedly titled "Rightly Dividing the Word," he challenges what he acknowledges to be "the major premise of dispensationalism."[71] The title refers to the dispensationalist method of interpreting Scripture, wherein some passages are for the present age or the church and others for the future millennial kingdom and Israel. Attributing this premise to John Nelson Darby, Ladd quotes a Plymouth Brethren critic who called the method "the height of speculative nonsense." Moreover, in a vague, uncited reference to Lewis Sperry Chafer's *Systematic Theology*, Ladd claims that "the most recent vigorous defense of pretribulationism devotes an early chapter to the establishment of this principle as the foundation for the entire subsequent discussion."[72] In addition, "There appears to be no valid reason, therefore, no assertion of Scripture which would require or even suggest that we must apply the prophecies about the Tribulation to a restored Jewish nation rather than to the redeemed of the New Testament, the Church. On the contrary, we have ample reason to apply the prophecies about the Great Tribulation both to Israel and to the Church."[73] Despite Ladd's "irenic purpose," he used this study of pretribulationism to attack the core interpretative methodology of the entire dispensationalist tradition.

Ladd finishes the book with his own proposal for the content of the *Blessed Hope*. For Ladd, this hope was the return of Christ to bring the divine plan to consummation by gathering his people to himself and casting out all those who do not believe. In this broad definition of the hope, Ladd finds eschatological kinship with some amillennialists, primarily conservative Reformed believers.[74] This claim had two sharp edges, however. As much as it put into practice Ladd's call to unity and charity among faithful believers, it also opened him to criticism for being soft on amillennialists, a charge we will see shortly. Still, in the last chapter of *Blessed Hope*, Ladd's attack fades into an impassioned call for a shared sense of unity and urgency in communicating the gospel to the world. He concludes by recovering the "irenic purpose" with which he began:

> Having said this, we would revert to our original thesis, only to
> broaden it: neither pretribulationism nor posttribulationism should
> be made a ground of fellowship, a test of orthodoxy, or a neces-
> sary element in Christian doctrine. There should be liberty and
> charity toward both views. That which is essential is the expectation
> of "the blessed hope and appearing of the glory of our great God
> and Saviour Jesus Christ."[75]

Ladd's proposal required a relaxation in the demand among dispensationalists—and others, to be fair—for strict, uncritical submission to the
methodology and detail of their particular system. Only when evangelicals
could live in some sort of peace with one another could they lay claim to a place
and have a voice in the broader Christian world.

Blessed Hope received mixed responses from some of those who read the
book in draft form, and even Ladd expressed some second thoughts about the
project. In a note to Wilbur Smith, he confessed:

> This is a book I do not want to write. But the time has come when I
> cannot live with myself without speaking out. I fully realize that
> this book is going to make me many enemies and close a hundred
> doors which I wish might someday be open.... But the adherents
> of pretribulationism have gone to such lengths of unreasonable-
> ness that someone has got to speak to the issue, cost what
> it may.[76]

Again one hears the refrain from Ladd's dissertation project: "but the attempt
must be made." Ladd by this time has consciously assumed responsibility not
only for exposing the problematic hermeneutical principles of the dispensationalists but also for rebuking their militancy. Smith did not wait to
finish the manuscript before responding to Ladd. After reading only fifty pages
he challenges Ladd's choice of title by saying that it was misleading. Smith
argued that since Ladd was really writing an attack on pretribulationism, he
should have had the courage to make that his title.[77] Three days later Smith
wrote to Ladd again, this time more favorably, though still not in complete
agreement. He closes this letter with a grudging compliment: "I feel there is an
aspect of this inexhaustible book [the Bible] which perhaps most of us have
been ignoring through the years."[78] Ladd's critique had forced even Wilbur
Smith to acknowledge that the Bible may offer a broader range of views than
those that he held.

Harold Lindsell had other objections. Lindsell was the administrative dean
of Fuller Seminary and in that role acted as an adviser on any issue that might

affect the seminary's public image.[79] He was concerned that Ladd's repeated use of the phrase "unproven inference" might give the impression of "hitting the reader on the head several times."[80] Though the book might offend some in the *Old Fashioned Revival Hour*'s listening audience, a major source of funding for the seminary, Lindsell promised Ladd he would "resist strongly any pressure from any quarter that would take away your liberty at this point." This concern was not a frivolous one. Homer Stanley Morgan, a Baptist leader from New York, had written to Charles Fuller for assurance that he had not abandoned his pretribulationist views.[81] The letter was a barely veiled threat of separation. Morgan praises Fuller for his ministry and even encloses a small donation to the *Revival Hour*. He then mentions that he had led the evangelistic meetings in which Ladd and his brother were "saved" and shares some memories about Ladd's father.[82]

In the next paragraph, with no explicit connection to the mention of Ladd, Morgan writes the following: "Some months ago I was made very happy to hear your broadcast in which you stated that you did not believe that the Church went through the tribulation, for their [*sic*] was an ugly rumor in New York that you believed that the Church did go through the tribulation. I am so glad you made it clear what you do believe on that blessed hope. I fear this rumor lessened your support."[83] Morgan's letter illustrates the pervasive tension at Fuller Seminary between academic freedom and the seminary's financial dependence on *Revival Hour* revenues.[84] In the competitive world of evangelical mass media, the impact of any attack on one's orthodoxy could be measured in dollars. Ladd's work, beyond the risk it posed to his own reputation in evangelical circles, had the potential to cost the seminary significant funding.

Ladd's Baptist pastor, E. B. Hart, had already been convinced by Ladd that pretribulationism was in error and wrote in praise of *Blessed Hope*.[85] Ladd responded, again claiming not to have "wanted to write this book . . . for I do not like to be the center of controversy."[86] Ladd lamented the state of his Baptist tradition: "I would prefer to get out of the entire situation into an environment where such narrow, unbiblical dogmatism has no place. But I am a Conservative Baptist, and I cannot help myself." This remarkable statement illustrates how Ladd's challenge to the dispensationalist tradition had taken on the weight and obsessive quality of a quest or, worse, a holy war. He simply could not help but challenge what he perceived as a threat to the purity and mission of his tradition. The blunt tone of his attack on dispensationalism thus makes much more sense in light of his own perceived inability to avoid it.

The critical response to *The Blessed Hope* was as mixed as that to *Crucial Questions*. Old Testament scholar J. E. Fison (1906–1972), who would later become the bishop of Salisbury, expressed a slightly harsher version of British befuddlement with the American theological landscape than F. F. Bruce had voiced earlier in his review of Ladd's first book.[87] Fison begins by identifying Ladd as "an American and a Fundamentalist" and adds that perhaps only someone in that context could truly understand the purpose of the book. Although Fison looks favorably on Ladd's work, he echoes Bruce's concern about whether the debate should take place at all, calling the issues "strangely remote and irrelevant." Then he continues: "The idea that disagreement upon minutiae of prophetic biblical exegesis can involve practical excommunication would be surprising in a totalitarian atheistic tyranny; in an enlightened Christian democracy it seems well-nigh incredible."[88]

Incredible or not, this was the reality in which Ladd wrote and taught. Divergence from the eschatological grid of fundamentalism's militant wing often meant public attack, ostracism, and other forms of practical excommunication. Ladd's interaction with dispensationalism was all the more courageous in light of the risk to his standing as an evangelical scholar. In the end Fison equivocally acknowledged Ladd's effort: "If this book can save anyone from such pathetic absurdity, we can say a heartfelt "Hallelujah!," but the fact that any who profess and call themselves Christians should need such salvation can only evoke an unutterable groan of anguish."[89] Fison's self-proclaimed "outside opinion" actually provides a trenchant commentary on the volatile conditions that plagued the American evangelical enterprise. For all the talk of "cooperative evangelism" in the postwar era, the reality was far less cooperative and far less focused on evangelistic work.

John Walvoord reviewed *Blessed Hope* for the academic dispensationalist audience, again signifying its importance by placing the review article at the front of *Bibliotheca Sacra* and interrupting his own series on premillennialism.[90] Not surprisingly, the review is heavily critical of Ladd's conclusions, and Ladd's own copy of the review is littered with marginalia critical of the critique. Ladd "ably presents a spirited defense of posttribulationism," according to Walvoord, yet does "not sustain adequately the posttribulational position."[91] Mirroring Ladd's promise to keep the debate on an academic level, Walvoord assures his readers on the first page that "no personal criticism or discourtesy to the author is intended." Still, none of Ladd's pointed attacks on the dispensationalist system escaped Walvoord's eye. He wrote that in Ladd's view, "the promises given to Israel in the Old Testament have a dual fulfillment, i.e., both in the Church and Israel."[92]

In Ladd's copy of the review he wrote "some, not all" in the margin.[93] After comparing Ladd's views to those of covenant theology, Walvoord settles on the main issue in Ladd's treatment of pretribulationism, the fact that it is truly an attack on dispensationalism as a whole: "His rejection of a clear distinction between Israel and the church as well as opposition to other dispensational teachings undoubtedly is a major causal factor in his rejection of pretribulationism. This is recognized by the fact that the author spends an entire chapter refuting dispensationalism as a step in his argument against pretribulationism."[94]

Walvoord is critical of Ladd's historical survey of pretribulationist views and in his comments identifies a criticism of Ladd's work that would wound him in the future:

> It should be clear that citation from eight fathers over a period of three hundred years is not unquestionable proof that the entire early church was posttribulational. The historical argument is more of a psychological than a theological one. Truth cannot be proved simply by counting scholars, even ancient ones. Dr. Ladd is obviously selective and considers only the facts which support his thesis.[95]

Ladd wrote "this is unfair" in the margin by this comment. And yet it was fair to a certain extent. Ladd had done precisely what Walvoord claimed: He had taken the early church fathers who had agreed with his position and neglected to admit that a commonly held doctrine of imminence also existed in the early church.

Walvoord, however, was not above making weak claims himself, including rather conveniently obvious misrepresentations of Ladd's arguments. He criticizes Ladd's list of prominent scholars in the prophetic conference movement who had abandoned pretribulationism: "[T]here had never been [in the conferences] a clear understanding of the true basis for pretribulationism. They were obviously superficial followers of pretribulationism."[96] Walvoord's tone becomes shrill as he refutes Ladd's argument with a reductio ad absurdum: "[O]n the same basis, one could prove that modern liberals are right in their rejection of orthodoxy.... If a departure from an accepted doctrine is its own justification, then unbelief and apostasy are justified and faith refuted."[97] Walvoord concedes several times that pretribulationism did not extend back to the early church, something Ladd notes extensively in his margin notes, but argues that this proves only that the questions "were not formally considered." Finally, in response to Ladd's call for a shift of focus away from eschatology and toward evangelism, Walvoord reaffirms and defends the practicality of the issue: "[P]remillennialists who are pretribulational are immune to modern liberalism."[98] He concludes from these disagreements that "Dr. Ladd does not understand dispensationalism," though it is clear that there was enough misunderstanding to go around.[99]

Again the difficult relationship between Ladd and Walvoord provides a glimpse into evangelical politics in the 1950s. Just as *Blessed Hope* was being published, Ladd wrote to Walvoord and pleaded with him to use his position of leadership to "make it clear that men may differ in the Lord on such matters while they submit themselves equally to the authority of the Word of God."[100] Conservative Baptists were dividing over eschatology, as one wing of the movement attempted to make dispensationalism the test of orthodoxy for the entire denomination. Whenever disagreement surfaced, Ladd complained, the militants "waved the red flag of liberalism" and brought "chaos and disruption into the people of God." He recognized that only a leader of Walvoord's stature—and theological orientation—could stop the disintegration of the conservative wing. He asked Walvoord to publish an article in the moderate evangelical magazine *Christian Life* in order to provide "a tempering evaluation of these issues." Ladd wrote that "there should be utter room for difference of interpretation in the bonds of Christian love" and reminded Walvoord that he had personally invited the president of Dallas Seminary to speak in the chapel at Fuller.

Firing back, Walvoord declined Ladd's request that he write an article and blamed the bulk of the present conflict on Fuller's lack of a firm doctrinal statement:[101]

It would seem to me that Fuller Seminary might be able to prevent some of the criticisms which have arisen if steps were taken to present more positively the theological position you espouse. In other words, if a question exists in people's minds as to what you believe, it seems to me that it is up to you to be clear on the subject. There has been quite a bit of publicity along the line that you do not have any specific theological distinctives, that you have no convictions on the question of the time of the rapture, and that the philosophic and apologetic issues of our day are more important than eschatological issues. I believe one of your professors has suggested that evolution is right in part and that, while man is the subject of immediate creation, there may have been an evolutionary development of animals. You also have to some extent disassociated yourself from fundamentalism while affirming evangelicalism. One of your professors, whom I highly respect, is quoted as saying that inspiration needs to be re-examined, a statement which has been interpreted as meaning that the traditional verbal and plenary inspiration is not tenable any longer. . . . If you have been misrepresented, you owe it to your constituency to correct the error.[102]

In this single paragraph, ostensibly a refusal to assist in the peacemaking effort, Walvoord manages to question Ladd and Fuller on the four most dangerous boundary issues in American evangelicalism at the time: eschatology, evolution, separatism, and inerrancy. There is the clear sense that the militant wing of the movement was watching the members of the faculty at Fuller and that the behavior of the latter would determine their fate.

Ladd was wounded by Walvoord's letter and wrote back to reiterate his call for tolerance among conservative evangelicals. Along the way he admits to being "deeply grieved" that, in Walvoord's view, "a man cannot be a fundamentalist unless he is a dispensationalist."[103] Ladd expressed his disappointment that Walvoord had refused to include himself "among those who plead for tolerance in difference of opinion on this question." Walvoord wrote back, assuring Ladd that he would defend his orthodoxy in the pages of *Bibliotheca Sacra*. He said, "I am going out of my way to point out that there should be no question about your loyalty to the Scriptures or general orthodoxy . . . and no ground whatever for designating your position as liberal."[104] This admission that part of his task was to decide who would and would not be "designated liberal" was an acknowledgement of the difficulties inherent in the sort of tolerance Ladd was proposing. Pretribulationism was in fact a test of orthodoxy at Dallas Seminary, and Walvoord had to give his assent, as would any member of the faculty. He simply could not, then, as a point of logic, "issue a statement . . . to the effect that the issue is minor and irrelevant to conservatism as a whole." Walvoord was precluded by the restrictions of his own tradition (even if he had wanted to participate) from the irenic exchange of ideas that Ladd proposed in *Blessed Hope*. This fact did not bode well for the coming conflicts among conservative evangelicals in America.

Ladd's encounters with dispensationalism in the 1950s represent his first professional steps toward his goal of academic respect and acceptance. He had survived Harvard with his faith intact and had committed himself from his earliest years at Fuller to using his critical skills to elevate the standing of conservative evangelical thought. The hindrance, as he saw it, was the divisive influence of dispensational theology. The broader academic world would never take evangelicals seriously so long as their dominant system of theology was anti-intellectual, anticritical, and militantly separatist. If evangelicals could not allow for differences in peripheral details among themselves, how could they expect the greater theological world to take them seriously?

This question was answered, at least in part, in the fallout over Billy Graham's 1957 evangelistic crusades in New York City. Graham (b. 1918) rose to prominence in the years after World War II as a dynamic speaker in the Youth for Christ organization.[105] In 1949 he led a successful crusade in Los

Angeles that garnered national press coverage and, like many American evangelists, set his eyes on New York City as the key target for his evangelistic work. In the early 1950s Graham developed his "cooperative evangelism" strategy for reaching new communities, a process that included partnership with local church leaders. Fundamentalist separatist leader Carl McIntire (1906–2002) was regularly critical of this methodology because it diminished the role of doctrinal separation in favor of visible unity, and he began to question Graham's worthiness as an evangelist.[106] McIntire was a veteran of the controversies that split the Presbyterian denomination in the 1930s and left him deprived of his Presbyterian ordination. He was also a militant anti-Communist and the host of a radio program in competition with Charles Fuller's *Old Fashioned Revival Hour*.

In 1955 McIntire published an attack against the ecumenical movement, *Servants of Apostasy*, which called for militant resistance in the face of this threat to Christian liberty.[107] McIntire, of course, found a way to connect Fuller Seminary's nonseparatist posture with political subversion by saying that Fuller's "philosophy of love and peace is the line that is being used by the Communists to conquer the rest of the world."[108] John R. Rice (1895–1980), a militant fundamentalist himself, came to Graham's defense in the name of the higher priority of world evangelization.[109] In April of 1955 Rice joined Graham in Scotland, the site of Graham's latest campaign, in order to prepare a defense that would rebut McIntire's criticisms, but the damage was apparently already done.[110]

From 1955 to 1957 conservative evangelicals found themselves forced to choose sides in the debate over Graham. In April of 1956 Graham himself drew the final line in the sand. In a letter to the *Baptist Standard*, a conservative publication, Graham placed his full support behind a Baptist program that promoted the concept of cooperative evangelism and challenged the prevailing view that the church's primary role was to preserve sound doctrine.[111] Despite the pleadings of conservative leaders such as Donald Grey Barnhouse, who exhorted all evangelicals to "show our oneness with Billy," the breach could not be repaired.[112] Even John R. Rice had to retreat at this point, and in the year before the New York campaign in 1957, conservative evangelicalism split into two distinct camps: the militant separatists, who would be called fundamentalists, and the moderate nonseparatists, who would be called evangelicals.[113]

The opposing camps within evangelicalism (apart from theological issues or the market share of the competing radio ministries) drew their battle lines around the question of participation versus separation. The militant side took a literal view of the biblical injunction to "come out from among them, and be ye separate."[114] Separatism, in its basic form, was the avoidance of fellowship with those who held less-than-orthodox theological views. For some of the most extreme fundamentalists, however, this was not enough. In the aftermath of the controversy over Billy Graham's cooperative movement, there arose in fundamentalism the practice of "second-order separatism," by which the militants rejected the company not only of those with whom they disagreed but also of those who did not separate from those with whom they disagreed. This justified the otherwise counterintuitive division between the militant fundamentalists and the premillennialist, inerrantist, conversionist, and exclusivist Billy Graham.

Fuller Seminary was certainly not immune to the impact of this conflict and even played a role in its eventual settlement. In the aftermath of the division over Graham's cooperative evangelism, Fuller, along with the National Association of Evangelicals (NAE) and the newly founded *Christianity Today*, came to be seen as the institutional backbone of the new evangelical movement. This trio of organizations was already deeply connected, with Harold Ockenga playing a key role in the founding of the NAE in 1942 and Carl Henry filling the position as *Christianity Today*'s first editor. After 1957 each of these organizations maintained close ties with Billy Graham's evangelistic efforts, and each appropriated some measure of Graham's tolerant attitudes.

The disintegration and reorganization taking place in evangelicalism were mirrored by dramatic developments in Ladd's personal life as well. Larry Ladd, who turned eighteen in 1955, now fully exhibited the symptoms of his various disorders, and George began to complain about his son's condition to anyone who would listen. In a tearful speech to an audience in Minnesota in 1957, Ladd (who was supposed to be speaking on Fuller's behalf) told the assembly about the problem of his son's undescended testicles.[115] Norma, by that time deeply estranged from her father, had moved to Chicago to attend nursing school in 1952.[116] Though she would later marry one of George's favorite students, Norma never would never forgive her father for his lack of affection toward Larry and kept her distance from him until his death. Ladd also began to experience a loss of his hearing during this time, certainly raising fears that he might eventually be completely deaf, as his parents had become.[117]

Another significant development during this period was the death of Ladd's mother in 1956. Ladd had remained dutiful, if not close, to his mother in the years after the move to California. They had taken trips together on occasion, and Ladd saw her on his visits to the East Coast, where she lived with George's brother, James.[118] But he had, it appears, been relieved to be away from her and after her death sent a terse note to his sister-in-law, saying only "thank you for taking care of my mother."[119] Ladd received a small inheritance from his mother and used the money to fund a sabbatical trip with Winnie to

Heidelberg, Germany, in 1957.[120] Perhaps due to the crumbling relationships with his wife and children, combined with the pressures of battling dispensationalism, severe headaches, and loss of hearing, Ladd began to drink heavily during his time in Germany.[121] There were indications that Ladd had been hiding a worsening problem with alcohol before the stay in Heidelberg, but after the trip it became more an open secret.[122]

Ladd returned to Pasadena clearly frustrated, certainly with his own life but also with the internal battles within his movement, conflicts that distracted and paralyzed conservative evangelicals. He told one student couple in 1958 that he had written everything he wanted to write and threatened to retire and "vegetate" for the rest of his life.[123] Worse, he began to press the boundaries of appropriate behavior with the wife of at least one student, who experienced unwanted advances from her husband's professor.[124] Ladd was clearly not the same when he returned from Heidelberg. Colleague Paul King Jewett recalled later that Ladd seemed physically different after 1957 and that his speech was impaired.[125]

Frustration had been brewing even before the trip to Germany. Ladd was discouraged by the process of finding an instructor who could teach his courses while he was abroad. At that time Fuller Seminary required its faculty to recruit their own replacements for sabbatical leaves, so Ladd offered the position to Glenn Barker (1920–1984), a former colleague at Gordon and one of the Harvard evangelicals.[126] Barker, however, could not leave his responsibilities at Gordon and did not accept the invitation.[127] Ladd appears to have decided at this point that a more junior scholar might be more willing to accept the position, and he began to invite Fuller graduates who were either pursuing graduate studies in other universities or had recently completed their doctorates.

Ladd's first choice was Charles Carlston, who would be the first Fuller graduate to earn a PhD from Harvard.[128] Carlston, however, turned down the offer, stating that after his critical studies he could no longer sign Fuller's strict doctrinal statement.[129] Ladd's next choice was Eldon J. Epp, a Fuller graduate who had just begun a PhD program, also at Harvard.[130] Epp initially agreed, and plans had been set in motion to complete the official paperwork when Epp had a change of heart. After reviewing Fuller Seminary's catalogue and doctrinal stance, Epp wrote the following to Ladd: "I am convinced that my present theological temper and presuppositions are out of harmony with the general spirit of the Seminary"; he added that it was his critical training at Harvard that led him to this conclusion.[131]

Ladd was caught between his desire to bring back one of his protégés to teach his courses and his awareness that Fuller's mandatory doctrinal position effectively precluded many of them from returning. This movement beyond the theological boundaries of Fuller, however, was not inevitable. Ladd turned to David Wallace, the first Fuller graduate to earn a PhD abroad, under Matthew Black at New College, Edinburgh.[132] A committed Baptist and an accomplished young scholar, Wallace accepted the invitation eagerly. In the end, despite the negative responses from Carlston and Epp, Ladd was able to secure precisely the sort of instructor he had wanted for his courses. Why ask Carlston and Epp, who were still working on their degrees, before approaching Wallace, who was already finished? It may be as simple as Ladd's hoping to have a Harvard doctoral candidate, a representative of his own alma mater, to signal that Fuller—and Ladd—had arrived. The result, however, was a reminder that Fuller in fact had not arrived and that there was work yet to do to make the institution into what it claimed to be.

Despite the seriousness of Ladd's personal issues, the sabbatical to Heidelberg was important intellectually. This was Ladd's opportunity to improve his understanding of the German language and immerse himself in current writings not yet available in English. The research on eschatology over the previous seven years had focused Ladd's attention on internal conflicts within evangelicalism, but in Heidelberg Ladd turned his eye back to the mainstream of theological scholarship and thus back to his strategy of participation in that world. This exposure to continental theological works in their original languages marked a significant turning point in Ladd's own scholarship and paved the way for his later engagement with moderate and liberal theologians.[133] Ladd devoured the work of Oscar Cullmann (1902–1999), the influential proponent of *Heilsgeschichte* (redemptive history), and from 1957 on, Ladd referred to his own position as being aligned with Cullmann's redemptive-historical orientation. He also read the work of Martin Kähler during this time and began to develop a deeper understanding of the relationship between theology and modern historical thought.[134] Kähler's distinction between *Historie* (the facts of history) and *Geschichte* (the meaning of history) would transform Ladd's understanding and expression of his own theology.

The Heidelberg sabbatical provided Ladd with several key opportunities to raise not only his own stature but Fuller Seminary's as well. Edward Carnell asked him to visit Great Britain and approach Geoffrey Bromiley, then a lecturer at New College, Edinburgh, to determine his interest in a position at Fuller Seminary.[135] Bromiley was a historian of German theological movements who later earned fame (and a measure of awe) as the translator into English of not only Gerhard Kittel's *Theological Dictionary of the New Testament* (10 vols.) but also, along with Thomas Torrance, the complete *Church Dogmatics* (14 vols.) by Karl Barth. Bromiley was a member of the Tyndale Fellowship, a group of British evangelicals that also included F. F. Bruce, J. Stafford Wright, John Wenham, and Andrew Walls.[136]

Ladd was clearly impressed by Bromiley, who passed easily through the doctrinal thicket that had frustrated the recruitment of Bela Vassady a decade earlier. Ladd sent a positive report to Carnell, and in 1958 Bromiley was hired. While in Britain Ladd was honored to learn that he had been nominated (by F. F. Bruce and Henry Cadbury) for membership in the prestigious Society of New Testament Studies and eagerly awaited his election.[137] There was a problem, however, when an objection was raised as to the standing of Fuller Seminary as a proper academic institution. The preliminary decision was to postpone membership for a year until the issues could be addressed, but at the urging of Matthew Black (1908–1994), a prominent Old Testament scholar at Saint Andrews University, the objection to Fuller was lifted, and Ladd was elected to full membership. Significantly, what carried the day was Black's high regard for the students from Fuller who had pursued doctoral studies with him at New College, Edinburgh, and Saint Andrews.[138] Although Ladd lamented that "as far as European scholarship is concerned, we [Fuller] do not exist," he was proud that "our grads are spreading our fame." This pride was buoyed by the news, which Ladd received in Germany, of Fuller's accreditation as an academic institution.[139] Ladd's election to membership in the Society of New Testament Studies, joined with Fuller's accreditation and the achievement of the seminary's students in doctoral work, were important victories in the ongoing strategy of improving the image of evangelicalism in the wider academic world on the merits of individual and institutional scholarship.

In 1957, Ladd also began submitting articles to major journals outside the conservative evangelical world, another sign of his turning to the broader academy.[140] The only journal to publish Ladd's work up to this point was the dispensationalist *Bibliotheca Sacra*, but with that door now closed Ladd shifted his focus to those publications that served the world of critical scholarship to see whether he passed muster. The articles Ladd published in 1957 represented another significant step in his strategy of establishing the place of evangelical thought—and of Ladd himself—in the world of theological scholarship. Further, these articles show Ladd's understanding of the relationship between theology and history to be maturing. "Biblical theology," he writes, "may be defined as the description and interpretation of redemptive history."[141] This shows Cullmann's influence, filtered through Ladd's more traditional, conservative theological position. Ladd differentiates his stance from that of the pure "scientific" historian, who "insists that the very word 'history,' by definition, must limit its study and discussion to those persons, events, forces, and influences which can be described only in terms of ordinary human experiences."[142] Ladd offers his own view of the relationship between historical events and God's redemptive purpose:

It must be admitted that all of these matters cannot be reduced to the historical control demanded by the secular historian; for in all of these "supernatural" events, the cause of the event is God, not man. . . . They are "historical" in that something actually happened in terms of human experience; but they transcend the ordinary historical in that the cause is not "historical" but suprahistorical—God.[143]

This application of the distinction between the "historical" and the "suprahistorical" was essentially the position Ladd would maintain for the rest of his academic life and represents his self-conscious shift of focus from conservative evangelical concerns to communication with the larger academic world. He did not abandon writing for evangelical publications completely, however. He was also able—finally—to publish in *Christianity Today* his positive assessment of the Revised Standard Version of the Bible—in 1957, five years after he wrote it.[144]

Another important aspect of that shift was Ladd's decision to address some of the questions regarding eschatology in mainstream scholarship, moving him back to the subject of his magnum opus. These were not issues of who would or would not have to endure the Great Tribulation but rather technical subjects of the nature of apocalyptic literature and its significance for understanding larger theological matters. The critical debate centered on making clear distinctions between the prophetic and the apocalyptic in Jesus' teachings on eschatology. The prophetic viewpoint construed these teachings as predicting an imminent, earthly, realized, historical kingdom, which needed to be reinterpreted in light of the fact that this kingdom did not appear. Others saw Jesus' predictions as apocalyptic, requiring a catastrophic event that would usher in a radically new age. "In this apocalyptic eschatology," Ladd argued, "the kingdom is entirely beyond history in a new and different world."[145] Ladd's proposition, which reflected his view of the kingdom as present and future, was to argue for an eschatology that held both interpretations together. In his article "Why Not Prophetic-Apocalyptic?" Ladd summarized his position:

> Thus the kingdom of God has a twofold manifestation: in the apocalyptic consummation and in the historical mission of Jesus and the church. These two are not antithetical or mutually exclusive, for they are both manifestations of the kingly power of the one God in carrying out his soteriologic purpose for man and the world. The meaning of the kingdom of God is therefore to be found within history itself, in the coming of the kingdom of God into the midst of the stream of history in the person of Christ; but the resolution of the

problems of history will be found only in the age to come when the kingdom of God attains its glorious consummation.[146]

Here is Ladd's critical stance, addressing issues that are relevant in the academic mainstream from his conservative theological position. Through this and other articles published in respected journals, Ladd hoped to establish a place for evangelicalism in the wider scholarly world.[147]

The expanding of Ladd's focus is evident in his next book, *The Gospel of the Kingdom*, a brief study published in 1959.[148] Gone are the direct references and challenges to dispensationalism in favor of a more positive affirmation of Ladd's conservative, evangelical theological position. In this sense *Gospel of the Kingdom* represents an important passage in Ladd's thought and a turning point in his career. The book begins by charting the various definitions of the Kingdom of God, including the important distinction between kingdom as *realm* and kingdom as *reign*, then devotes a chapter each to the kingdom as future and as present realities. The next chapters describe the "mystery," the "life," the "righteousness," and the "demand" of the kingdom, while the final two sections treat the relationship between the church and Israel and the timing of Christ's return. Ladd's discussion of timing introduces a theme that was present for the remainder of his life: the link between world evangelization and Christ's return, as described in Matthew 24:14.[149] Ladd would remain a passionate advocate for the missionary enterprise, largely due to his belief that the timing of the second coming of Christ was in some way determined by the completion of that task. The "Kingdom of God in the New Testament," he concludes, "is the redemptive work of God active in history for the defeat of His enemies, bringing to men the blessings of the divine reign."[150]

The Gospel of the Kingdom represents a fairly radical shift in the relationship between Ladd's writing and the audience he hoped to reach. while not explicitly attacking dispensationalism, he nevertheless subtly challenges that system's understanding of the doctrine of the kingdom. Here Ladd argues again that the New Testament references to the "Kingdom of God" and the "Kingdom of Heaven" are in fact describing the same thing.[151] He also challenges—indirectly—the dispensationalist notion of "leaven" in the parables of Jesus as representing the insidious influence of apostasy. The presence of leaven in a story about baking, Ladd argued, was merely an attempt to establish verisimilitude on the part of the storyteller. The parables have details, according to him, "which do not convey spiritual truth and which therefore are not to be pressed in the interpretation."[152]

However, these details appear in more extensive discussions of the kingdom aimed at nondispensational readers and are uniformly artful in their avoidance of direct challenge. More importantly for Ladd in his desire to reach a new audience was his use of source material in his research. Of course, the exegetical work, which makes up the majority of the study, is Ladd's, but it is significant that he does not call on a single conservative author to support—or contrast—his thesis. Rather, the only theologians mentioned in the entire book, apart from Ladd himself, are Rudolf Bultmann, Oscar Cullmann, British scholar C. H. Dodd (1884–1973), German liberal icon Adolf von Harnack (1851–1930), and famed scholar-missionary Albert Schweitzer (1875–1965).[153] Ladd had cited these theologians in his previous works, to be sure, but never without the balancing presence of an equal number of conservative authors.[154] The exclusive use of European critical scholars in *Gospel of the Kingdom* is a departure for Ladd and an important strategic step in his quest to reach a wider audience with his scholarly work.

The critical response to *Gospel of the Kingdom* was muted in comparison to that of his first two books, largely due to its nonpolemical tone and more general focus. The book was reviewed in five academic journals and *Christianity Today*, for the most part with positive comment. Recognizing the shift in Ladd's outlook and audience, one reviewer comments that Ladd has swept away "the uncritical debris which has spoiled the view of this exciting Biblical teaching," and to a great extent this was true.[155] Another described the book as having been written "with both clarity and charity... sanely presented."[156]

Moreover, *The Reformed Review*, a journal based at the Dutch Reformed Western Theological Seminary in Michigan, perceptively called the book "another milestone in the progressive decline of dispensationalism" and stated that it promised "to bring... 'fundamentalism' back toward the mainstream of evangelical Christianity."[157] But this review also identifies what would be seen as a weakness in Ladd's thought as he attempted to find acceptance outside the boundaries of conservative evangelicalism. The reviewer says that "the only basic note in the book which seemed unsatisfactory was Ladd's chiliasm" and that even Ladd "seemed unconvinced at times that this millennium really fits into the structure of things."[158] While this last comment is certainly overstated—Ladd was thoroughly convinced that the millennium fitted quite nicely into the "structure of things"—his literalistic millennial views clashed with his otherwise critically astute handling of biblical texts. A member of the faculty at Gordon-Conwell Divinity School at the time, J. Ramsey Michaels (1930–), agreed with the critique of Ladd's strong millennial position even as he praised the book for its "proclamation rather than polemic."[159] Still, though he worked hard to separate himself from dispensational premillennialism, Ladd's dogged defense of millennialism would become a hindrance to his full acceptance in broader academic circles.

John Walvoord reviewed *Gospel of the Kingdom* for *Christianity Today* rather than *Bibliotheca Sacra*, at once seeking a larger audience for his concerns while also recognizing that the book was not a direct attack on dispensationalism.[160] The review challenges Ladd on all the usual points: the redemptive character of the kingdom over the governmental, neglect of the Old Testament as an interpretative filter, and, significantly, the use of contemporary mainstream scholarship in place of more conservative theological texts. The "vast premillennial literature on the doctrine of the Kingdom is ignored, and not a single premillennial scholar or work on the Kingdom is mentioned."[161]

Once again Walvoord sent a copy of the review to Ladd before it was published, and Ladd took the opportunity to vent his frustrations at Walvoord's ongoing practice of painting anyone who moved beyond "dispensational truth" as a liberal: "Now I read from your pen words which represent what to me is an utterly untrue and an intolerant position, in representing your position alone as the true defenders of the Bible. What shall I do? Shall I continue to plead for tolerance? Shall I ignore this tragic development in the interests of Christian charity? Or shall I protest this divisive tendency."[162] Ladd ultimately chose all three, depending on the situation. He continued to plead with scholars on the right and the left for tolerance in theological dialogue, while also allowing some attacks to pass if opposing them did not suit his needs or concerns. He also continued to protest the use of nonessential doctrines as tests of faith and fellowship, though not in correspondence with Walvoord. Ladd's methodical rejection of Walvoord's criticisms and his indictment of Walvoord's divisiveness signaled the end of their attempt to forge a constructive relationship. After this exchange there was no further correspondence between the two.[163]

In a sense Ladd's career during this period mirrored his own "already but not yet" understanding of the kingdom. By 1959 he was firmly established as a leading New Testament scholar in the evangelical tradition but had not yet earned acceptance and respect outside his own community. Despite his attempt to focus on his major work of scholarship, Ladd was pulled back into the intramural conflict over dispensational eschatology. The events at Western Seminary had shaken him, and John Walvoord's intransigence had proved too deeply rooted to reverse, so Ladd chose to move beyond them. After the publication of *The Gospel of the Kingdom* and the attempt to foster dialogue among conservatives of various stripes, Ladd disengaged not only from dispensationalism but also from its most influential proponent. Now he could turn his full attention and energy toward engaging the broader academic world and earning a place for evangelical theology—and himself—in it.

4

Beyond the Borders
(1959–1963)

As the 1950s came to a close, Ladd crystallized his assessment of evangelical thought—and his vision for improving its content and image—in an address celebrating the opening of a library at the North American Baptist Theological Seminary in South Dakota. His presentation, titled "Renaissance in Evangelicalism," was an indictment of the pervasive and contentious anti-intellectualism of the conservative evangelical movement, as well as a call to participation in the life of the mind of the broader culture.[1] He argued that evangelicals had surrendered their intellectual and spiritual leadership in American life. The conservative response to the academy's threats to the faith, according to Ladd, was to dismiss rather than engage them; the result was "the impression that evangelical Christianity is for the illiterate."[2]

In the area of spiritual leadership, evangelicals had too often "substituted doctrine for love as the norm of the Christian life and orthodoxy," which resulted in the impression that they spent the majority of their time "fighting among themselves, quarreling, bickering, contending."[3] Naming dispensationalism explicitly as the culprit, Ladd blasted the tendency of some evangelicals to practice "status by negation," a way of defining one's position and identity by what they are not, and also "purity by separation," keeping clear of people and writings that do not conform to a strict doctrinal system.[4] How should evangelicals behave instead? Ladd called for three responses. First, a return to the rigorous study of theology, which would unite people "who are true to the Word of God but who also are able to interact with the broad stream of human learning and who have a passion to produce a scholarly evangelical literature."[5]

Second, he appealed to his audience to "restore the ethic of love" to their understanding of the normative Christian experience.[6] Doctrine is vitally important, he argued, but added that "right belief without love is wrong belief." Finally, Ladd called for a "restoration of the Biblical doctrine of the Church," defined by a shared faith rather than adherence to the doctrine and practices of a particular tradition. He stopped short of endorsing the ecumenical movement—still a capital crime in those contentious days—and focused instead on the image evangelicals were presenting to the culture. "Until God's people quit fighting one another and dividing up and quarreling over all sorts of doctrinal details," he urged, "and begin to manifest in some sort of tangible expression the fact that there is a oneness in Jesus Christ, revival will not come to America."[7]

"Renaissance in Evangelicalism" was a coming-out party of sorts for George Ladd. The address encompassed the various animating factors that drove Ladd in his pursuit of acceptance and influence in the world of theological scholarship. It galled Ladd, as it had when he received the responses to his queries regarding Christian scholarship in 1942, that it remained too easy to dismiss evangelicals in the academy because they had contributed little worthy of notice for decades. Ladd's call to excellence in Christian scholarship was an important motivation in his career, but it is important to keep in mind that Ladd had spiritual concerns as well. His theology was not only written and defended but also believed and lived. He was passionate about the church's responsibility to evangelize the world, not least because of the link in his own theology between that effort and the second coming of Christ. Ladd believed, as Matthew 24:14 states, that Christ would return when all the nations had heard the Christian message. The conflicts over nonessential doctrines among evangelicals, disagreements that destroyed institutions and individual careers, in addition to rendering the Christian faith impotent and irrelevant in the culture, were hindrances to accomplishing the great ends of the church. In "Renaissance in Evangelicalism" we see Ladd's maturing integration of his scholarly aspirations and pastoral concerns, as well as his completed individuation from the militant wing of the conservative evangelical movement.

Ladd's quest for participation as an evangelical in broader academic circles led him to examine the intersection between history and theology. As was true in much of his work, he engaged these issues on both conservative and broader scholarly fronts and published frequently in popular and academic periodicals on both sides of the theological fence. To his conservative audience Ladd functioned as an interpreter of developments considered by some to be be-wildering and dangerous to the traditional understanding of faith. Ladd's work as a critic of dispensationalism, while certainly creating enemies in the con-servative camp, also earned him a measure of freedom as a critical scholar who remained sympathetic to evangelical belief. This latitude allowed him to write on topics and move in circles that would have branded other conservative scholars with a fatal mark of suspicion and diminished the impact of their work.

However, Ladd also sought to get his message out beyond the narrow world of conservative evangelicals. In articles he published in mainstream theological journals, Ladd defended traditional doctrinal conclusions even as he appropriated the terms of modern critical methods to reach them. This two-pronged strategy allowed Ladd to make important strides on both sides of his quest to rehabilitate the content and image of evangelical scholarship. In his writings to conservative readers, Ladd believed he was bringing them into a more reasonable expression of their traditional faith, thus enhancing the in-herent credibility of the conservative movement. But this development would be meaningless if it did not engage the world at large. Ladd's work in moder-ate and liberal circles was designed to build the stature and respectability of evangelicals beyond their parochial borders and to help them regain their place in the world of ideas.

Ladd's mature view of the relationship between theology and history was based, at least in part, on a loophole.[8] His embrace of the terms and concepts of modern historical thought grew out of his belief that, when narrowly un-derstood, they allowed for what he called "supranatural" events. If scientific historical methodologies dealt only with that which could be measured, proved, and repeated, then divine actions—which by their very nature occurred outside of natural processes—could exist alongside without contradicting modern sensibilities. Thus Ladd, as we will see, could defend the resurrection as an event beyond history—and presumably beyond the limitations of historical laws—because it did not rely on natural evidentiary principles.

Ladd's historical thought was influenced by James M. Robinson (b. 1924), a second-generation biblical scholar in a more progressive tradition, whom Ladd admired greatly.[9] In an enthusiastic review of Robinson's groundbreak-ing book, *A New Quest of the Historical Jesus* (1959), Ladd cheered Robinson's assertion that pure historical method could never capture the transcendent aspects of religious faith, calling it "refreshing and stimulating."[10] He con-cluded the review with a statement of his own position:

> The heart of the Gospel is the redemptive acts of God in history. Here
> is history which modern historiography must critically examine;

but here is also the work of God about which the historian *qua* historian can make no final judgment. Christ died; this is history. Christ died for our sins; this is theology. Christ rose from the dead; this is an event in history for which there can be no "historical" explanation, for the cause of the resurrection is not an antecedent historical event, but the *unmediated* act of God.[11]

Here, then, is Ladd's defense of the Christian doctrine of the resurrection in contrast to the critical view, using the rules of modern historical thought against itself to preclude its challenge to the idea. Ladd would use variations of this formula in his encounter with theological scholarship beyond the conservative evangelical world.

Despite Ladd's progress toward his goal of engaging the academic culture in general, his troubled personal life continued to pose problems. His abuse of alcohol persisted, though his wife, Winnie, worked hard to keep his behavior in check and protect his reputation.[12] Winnie would not allow alcohol to be used openly in their home, and when George's drinking prevented him from keeping engagements, his wife regularly made excuses for him.[13] By this time the Ladds had settled into a cold and distant partnership. He studied late into the night, and Winnie, in addition to shielding George's alcoholism, mothered him, typed his manuscripts, and prepared his work for publication.[14] In 1961 Ladd traveled to Vienna and Basel for a six-month sabbatical, and it is an indication of the distance between them that Winnie did not go with him even though there were no small children at home.[15]

Larry Ladd's condition, though undoubtedly serious, had not changed dramatically since 1957, when they left him at home during their time in Heidelberg. During the time in Vienna, Ladd appears to have allowed some of his darker impulses to have free rein. Without the constraining influences of Fuller Seminary, the evangelical community, and especially Winnie to keep him in check, Ladd drank heavily and sampled some of the city's tawdrier attractions.[16] As with his time in Heidelberg, Ladd returned from his sabbatical somehow altered or, more accurately, impaired. With his marriage and family in increasing disarray, his work took on even greater significance for his self-image. The relationships closest to him were failing, but he could still—in his eyes—prove his worth by creating quality scholarship. He settled back into life at Fuller and continued his relentless study schedule, reading widely, writing magazine and journal articles, and working on his magnum opus.

To accomplish his aim of engaging the world of scholarship, Ladd chose Rudolf Bultmann (1884–1976) to be the focus of his theological appreciation and critique. In the years before and after World War II, the connection between modern historical thought and Christian faith found a dynamic voice in Bultmann's work. With the possible exception of Karl Barth, no scholar had as great an impact on European and American theology, and as his books became available in English in the 1950s and 1960s, his influence extended to popular circles as well. Bultmann studied theology at the University of Tübingen, then Berlin, and eventually at Marburg University, where he worked under Wilhelm Herrmann and Johannes Weiss.[17] After obtaining his first theological degree in 1906, the following year Bultmann returned to Marburg, where he began doctoral studies and immersed himself in the history-of-religions methodology of Wilhelm Heitmüller. He completed his PhD in 1910 and his postdoctoral dissertation in 1912. In 1921 he published *The History of the Synoptic Tradition* and that same year succeeded Heitmüller at Marburg, where he stayed until his retirement in 1951.

The University of Marburg was an intellectual hotbed at the start of the twentieth century.[18] German theological scholarship at the time was dominated by the descendants of historical theologian Albrecht Ritschl (1822–1889), and Marburg represented the extreme left wing of that tradition. Ritschl rejected what he perceived to be the arid lifelessness of Protestant orthodoxy, which relied—too much, in his view—on philosophical categories. Philosophy, in seeking to provide an explanation for everything, did not offer unique enough language for God and the things of God, and Ritschl argued that this was inadequate. He placed a higher value on how individual believers experienced God rather than on what they could know through Christian dogma, leaving in question the role historical facts would play in the development of theology. One of his students, Wilhelm Herrmann (1846–1922), among the most revered theologians in Germany, carried on the principles of the Ritschlian school. Herrmann agreed that historical facts could not be the source or foundation of faith, though he still relied on them as secondary support for Christian ortho- doxy. Herrmann's scholarship reflected Ritschl's views for much of his career, though by the end of his life he had moved beyond Ritschl and into his own original thought. In any case Herrmann was soon challenged by a famous pair of his own students at Marburg, Karl Barth and especially Rudolf Bultmann.

Early in his career Bultmann reacted against much of his theological training.[19] The quest of the historical Jesus, which dominated nineteenth- century German theology, endeavored to develop a composite picture of Jesus using New Testament texts.[20] The goal was to separate the Jesus of history from the Christ of the early church and thus establish a historical basis for faith. In 1906, the same year that Bultmann began his doctoral studies, Albert Schweitzer published *The Quest of the Historical Jesus*, in which he traced the development and ultimate failure of the search to achieve its goals:

It is not given to history to disengage that which is abiding and eternal in the being of Jesus from the historical forms in which it worked itself out, and to introduce it into our world as a living influence. It has toiled in vain at this undertaking.... The abiding and eternal in Jesus is absolutely independent of historical knowledge and can only be understood by contact with His spirit which is still at work in the world.[21]

Bultmann took this view one step further. Whereas Schweitzer wanted to interpret the historical Jesus through "contact with His spirit," Bultmann attempted to make him irrelevant altogether. Theologian Roger Johnson accurately summarizes Bultmann's view of the purpose of theology: It is "to speak of God not as identified with some particular time of the past but as the power of the eternal to break into our present."[22] Bultmann thus distanced himself from the historically oriented foundations of his tradition (and even from Herrmann's halfway position) on his way to proposing a radically new approach to New Testament theology.

Bultmann was primarily concerned about the communication of the Christian gospel to modern hearers. The New Testament witness was obscured by the ancient, mythical worldview of its writers, according to him, and the result was that the modern hearer missed the *kerygma*, or its saving message. He posed the problem as follows:

We are therefore bound to ask whether, when we preach the Gospel to-day, we expect our converts to accept not only the Gospel message, but also the mythical view of the world in which it is set. If not, does the New Testament embody a truth which is quite independent of its mythical setting? If it does, theology must undertake the task of stripping the Kerygma from its mythical framework, of "demythologizing" it.[23]

It is this concept of "demythologizing" for which Bultmann is best known and upon which the rest of his methodology is based. Miracles, demons, angels, and any other supernatural beings or occurrences were to be excised, leaving only the call to faith in the "unseen, intangible realities" of the gospel.[24] If modern people were to come to a true understanding of themselves and the Christ of faith, Bultmann argued, they must resist the temptation to rely on "all[25] self-contrived security." Ultimately, this stripping away set its sights on the most important of traditional Christian tenets, that of the resurrection of Jesus. Bultmann applied his methodology without hesitation to this crucial doctrine, calling it a "mythical event pure and simple."[26] The cross and resurrection are central to the kerygma of the church, he maintained, but they "cannot be a miraculous proof by which the skeptic might be compelled to believe in Christ. . . . An historical fact which involves a resurrection from the dead is utterly inconceivable!"[27] Here, then, is the crux of the Bultmannian program: that the historicity of the resurrection of Jesus, far from being an encouragement to faith, actually becomes a hindrance to belief for the modern person and as such should be rejected altogether.[28]

Bultmann's theological system presented obvious challenges to traditional evangelical belief. Certainly his approach to the Bible placed him beyond the pale for those with a more conservative, positivistic view of the texts of Scripture. Much of the doctrinal controversy that dominated the early twentieth century centered on the extent to which one assented to the Bible's verbal inspiration, and Bultmann's methodology, with its thorough demythologizing, willfully denied any transcendent, divine hand in the origin of the biblical text. Second, Bultmann's attempt to make the kerygma acceptable to the modern mind by necessity excluded the various accounts of miraculous intervention in human history. There could be no God interfering in the historical processes, according to Bultmann, and no effect that could not be attributed to a natural cause. This made any hope of a second coming of Christ impossible, on its face because it reflected a first-century worldview and at its core because it represented an interruption of historical development. More specifically and most importantly, Bultmann's rejection of the historicity of the resurrection posed an insurmountable stumbling block between his work and the evangelical faith. Most American evangelicals would have taken seriously the injunction from the Apostle Paul that, if the resurrection had not occurred in some real way, then believers were "to be pitied above all men."[29] Bultmann's unwillingness to consider the resurrection as a historical event became, even more than his hermeneutic, the central point of conflict between his views and those of American evangelicals.

In 1961 the "Dare We Follow Bultmann?" articles that appeared in *Christianity Today* were the first attempts to mediate Bultmann's program to the evangelical academic world.[30] Two of the articles deserve attention here. The first was written by Fuller Seminary's Geoffrey Bromiley, who argued that Bultmann's attempt to eliminate the mythological aspect of the New Testament record in fact created a new mythology.[31] The strength of this piece is in its central thesis and its identification of Bultmann's rejection of historicity as the crucial problem for conservatives. The serious weakness of this essay is its refusal to allow that Bultmann's motivation for writing—modern people need to hear a gospel they can believe—had any value at all. For all of his apparent evangelical orthodoxy, Bromiley does not recognize the needs of the modern person as effectively as does Bultmann, and it is clear in his tone that he finds little of value in the Bultmannian program. The second article, which is by Herman Ridderbos, a Dutch Reformed scholar, is the strongest of the series.[32] While also ultimately critical of Bultmann's views, Ridderbos offers a much fairer representation of the pastoral motivation behind their formulation. For Bultmann, according to Ridderbos, demythologizing is necessary "not only as prerequisite to the acceptance of the Gospel by modern man, but also because modern man is confronted with the truth of the Gospel only in this way." Even in rejecting Bultmann's conclusions, Ridderbos assures the reader that he is not insensitive to "the problem which arises when modern people hear the biblical *kerygma*."[33]

George Ladd echoed this more sophisticated understanding of Bultmann's scholarship. Ladd had read Hans Werner Bartsch's assessment of Bultmann's thought, *Kerygma and Myth*, not long after it was translated into English and after 1957 was comfortable reading Bultmann in his native German.[34] While many conservative evangelicals in America attacked Bultmann for his approach to biblical texts, Ladd challenged his use of modern historical concepts and his distinctive methodology. In three articles and two short books, Ladd became an important interpreter of Bultmann's work to the evangelical audience. In this engagement Ladd continued to work out the implications of his historical training at Harvard and in the process was able to critique Bultmann's work at a deeper level than many of his colleagues. Ladd understood the issues raised by modern historical science and was able to move easily between Bultmann's writings and his own evangelical faith. Further, Ladd's critique of the Bultmannian program reflected his grasp of the intricacies of German historical philosophies and their great influence on the theological enterprise. But beyond the content of Ladd's analysis, the most striking features of these writings are the respect and admiration Ladd shows for Bultmann. Unlike some in the evangelical camp, Ladd saw and was able to appreciate the relentless commitment to quality scholarship in Bultmann's writings, even when he rejected the conclusions of that work.

In his earliest published critique of Bultmann in 1962, Ladd immediately acknowledged one of the crucial issues raised by the German theologian. Writing in *Eternity* magazine, a moderate evangelical publication edited by Donald Grey Barnhouse, Ladd argues that "the central problem which Bultmann has tried to solve is the problem of the relationship of God to history."[35] This problem, according to Ladd, centered in the task of reconciling the claims of the biblical record with the boundaries and categories of historical science. Ladd uses an analogy of a German university to illustrate the relationship of diverse academic disciplines and the demands they make on one another in the process of teaching and research. With theological faculties functioning alongside the other university disciplines, each must work within the same—or at least compatible—interpretative model. There cannot be two contradictory definitions of historical truth. The German theologian, working among professors in other areas, thus

> lectures as a historian. He views Jesus strictly as an historical personage, a first century Jew, speaking the language of first century Judaism—Aramaic. . . . In constructing his lectures, the professor of theology must draw upon all the historical disciplines. He must be a philologian and completely handle New Testament Greek against both its Hellenistic and Semitic backgrounds. He must be a textual critic in order to establish a trustworthy text. He must be a literary critic to deal with involved questions of date, authorship, composition, and sources of the Gospels. He must be an historian of religions to compare and contrast the Gospels with their Jewish background. He must be familiar with Jewish history and xinstitutions, as well as the entire Mediterranean world to understand the political, economic and religious status of Judaism in the Roman empire.[36]

Bultmann's concern, according to Ladd, was the question of whether history "can mean two different things to these two university professors? Is the theologian allowed, because he is Christian, to understand and interpret 'history' differently in reconstructing the life and significance of Jesus than does his secular colleague down the hall?"[37] For Bultmann, the answer was emphatically in the negative because the alternative would "put God at the disposal of the historian." The saving message of the kerygma, in Ladd's restating of Bultmann's views, "can never become an event of the past; it must always be a present meaningful reality. God's action cannot become the object of critical study. The historian cannot sit in criticism and judgment on God's deeds. . . . [The] 'laws' of historical experience must be the same in the Gospels as elsewhere, and the same critical principles must be employed in their study." Ladd argues that Bultmann's solution to this problem is to make "a sharp distinction between history and the Christian message." Bultmann's case, Ladd continues, is that if New Testament history must follow the rules of historical science, then we are better off without giving any attention to the historical details of Jesus' life and ministry. Bultmann's view, according to Ladd, was that "Christian faith must be independent, self-validating. Christian faith rises not from a recital of historical events, but from the proclamation of the Christian *kerygma*—the Gospel."[38]

In his response Ladd agreed that historical research was indeed limited in its attempt to understand the role of God but contended that the process of interpreting the New Testament message involved more. The very transcendence of God, according to Ladd, frees God from the constraints of historical science, thereby giving history an important, though not a unique or an isolated, role in the believer's faith. He maintains that "in the events of redemptive history is to be found a dimension which cannot be handled or explained by the 'historical method.' "[39] Still, the historical origins of the Christian faith cannot be denied. Ladd offers a challenge on this point:

> Therefore, when Bultmann divorces the kerygma from the redeeming acts of God in history, he has struck at the heart of the Gospel. The saving act of God for Bultmann occurs not in what the historical Jesus did, but in what God does in me when I hear the Gospel. This is not the New Testament Gospel. The saving act of God is both what God has done for me in Jesus and what God does in me now.[40]

Thus, the problem of provability posed by historical science is not the fatal impediment to faith as Bultmann had argued. Rather, in its proper place, history becomes the catalyst, the invitation to saving faith in the kerygma. In the end, Ladd defends the necessity of this historical basis for Christian faith while agreeing with Bultmann that the kerygma cannot be limited to that which can be proven through historical research.

Though Bultmann's theology was the primary focus of this article, Ladd also revisits the issue of evangelical intellectual credibility, still an important motivating factor in his life and work. He posed a challenge to evangelicals who dismissed Bultmann or attempted to "put him in his place" by acknowledging that he was "wrestling with real problems." Further, Ladd argued, while historical research was crucial to the full understanding and experience of the Christian message, evangelicals had largely ignored the need for scholarship in that area. In a stinging indictment of the evangelical intellectual enterprise Ladd wrote:

> History can only be mastered by scholarly study. Evangelicals should be the first to promote the finest and most thorough scholarship. This has not been the case. Evangelicals have majored in evangelism, missions, and popular Bible teaching, but not in scholarship. We have left this to men like Bultmann. This is one of the reasons why evangelical Christianity has largely surrendered theological leadership. It is time for the evangelical churches to repent of their un-

balanced perspective and to seek to recover a new measure of theological stature.[41]

It was not enough for evangelicals to be sure of their position, according to Ladd. If they wanted a voice in the development of theological scholarship, they were going to have to work for it. The question remained: Where should this work begin?

In the final section of this article Ladd suggested a first step. Echoing his earlier challenge to the simplistic and reductionistic hermeneutic of dispensationalists and other inerrantists, Ladd confronted those in his own camp whose use of the Bible actually limited their understanding of God. Bultmann was right, in Ladd's view, in that he refused to "let God and his acts become the object of man's control."[42] While God had indeed revealed himself both in history and in the biblical texts, neither of those contexts could contain the totality of that revelation. God's acts can never exhaust his ability to act; God remains free and transcendent. Ladd argued that "there is an ever present danger for orthodox theology to forget this, in practice, if not in theory. God is not *contained* in the past. God is not *contained* in a book. God is not *contained* in our theologies."[43] Finding at least partial common ground with Bultmann, Ladd continued:

> Paradoxically, the past must be present, or it is dead. God is not most present in the most accurate text book on Jesus' life and teachings. A mastery of the contents of the Bible is not synonymous with a knowledge of God. An orthodox theology does not guarantee a Christian life. It is the work of the Holy Spirit to bring the redemptive events out of the past into a living, transforming impact with the present. Orthodoxy is not enough; orthodox doctrine must express itself in vital Christian experience or it is a lifeless thing in the icy grip of a dead past. The final goal of God's revelation in Jesus Christ is not merely enlightened minds, but transformed lives.[44]

For those who measured the quality of faith by one's views on inerrancy or eschatology, Ladd's assertions were a direct challenge. Still, Ladd knew that the task of building credibility for evangelical theology in the broader world required serious reflection and attention to detail. In the context of defending orthodoxy from the attack by Rudolf Bultmann, Ladd argued for a deeper understanding of that orthodoxy from those on his own theological side.

Ladd further pursued this challenge in his next critique of Bultmann, in the *Bulletin of the Evangelical Theological Society (BETS).*[45] Unlike the popular article in *Eternity*, this piece was written for an academic journal produced by the conservative evangelical organization of which Ladd was a founding member. The scholarly audience gave Ladd an opportunity to examine one of the more difficult aspects of Bultmann's thought: the role of the "acts of God." The Evangelical Theological Society had largely ignored Rudolf Bultmann for much of its existence; the Ladd article was not only the first substantive examination of Bultmann to appear in the journal, but it was also virtually the first mention of his name. For the first twenty-five years of its existence, the journal published no reviews of Bultmann's books, and it would be another eleven years after Ladd's article before Bultmann was the subject of another piece in *BETS*.[46]

Ladd must have known that he was treading on controversial ground by writing this article, and he sought to disarm the criticism in the opening line of the piece: "One of the first essentials in any good scholarship is a sympathetic understanding of alternate positions."[47] However, by the second line Ladd is again making the case that evangelicalism was too often marked by substandard—or at least inattentive—scholarship: "One of the besetting sins of orthodox theology is that of condemning unorthodox theologies without adequately understanding them." Ladd's goals in this piece were twofold. First, he is actively engaging in the kind of erudition he believes will earn credibility for evangelicals before a more widespread audience. No one can accuse him of being ignorant of—or resistant to—opposing views when he is writing a fair explication of Rudolf Bultmann for conservative readers. But on a deeper level, Ladd is throwing down the gauntlet before his conservative evangelical colleagues, daring them not only to read about Bultmann but also to learn from that which is instructive in his thought. The first two paragraphs of this article are devoted to making the case for studying Bultmann in the first place.

The central thread of Ladd's critique is a discussion of Bultmann's use of paradox in his theology. For Bultmann, God acts in the present, calling individuals to be transformed by faith to a more authentic existence, completely divorced from questions of historicity. True faith is found only in the existential confrontation between the believer and the risen Christ and is not dependent upon historical proof or scientific evidence:[48] "Since human life is lived out in time and space, man's encounter with God can only be a specific event here and now. This event, our being addressed by God here and now, our being questioned, judged, and blessed by him, is what we mean when we speak of an act of God."[49]

However, Bultmann also claimed that God had acted in the person of Jesus Christ, in the form of the historical Jesus of Nazareth. Criticizing the German liberal tradition for surrendering this point, Bultmann argued that true New Testament faith was rooted in the historical event of Christ's coming and that this faith "had to be revealed; it *came*."[50] Christianity could not exist without the Christ-event, according to Bultmann, despite the mythological nature of that phenomenon. Bultmann clearly struggled with this issue, though in the end he acknowledged both its difficulty and necessity: "It might well appear as though the event of Christ were a relic of mythology which still awaits elimination. This is a serious problem, and if Christian faith is to recover its self-assurance it must be grappled with. For it can recover its certainty only if it is prepared to think through to the bitter end the possibility of its own impossibility or superfluity."[51] This, then, is the paradox upon which Bultmann's theology rests, that while Christian faith may have its origin in a historical event, it continues and exists only in the present reality of each believer. Ladd's article engages Bultmann's thought on precisely this point.

Ladd perceived in Bultmann's paradoxical thinking a useful expression of New Testament faith. After summarizing Bultmann's radical rejection of any information related to the historical Jesus, Ladd acknowledges that Bultmann "does not need such a Jesus nor is he interested in the inner consciousness of Jesus."[52] At this point most conservative evangelicals would have abandoned Bultmann altogether, but Ladd takes the discussion to a deeper level. Allowing Bultmann's belief that past events belong to history but that "faith is reposed directly in God," Ladd was able to observe that Bultmann was not attacking Christian faith but rather attempting to purify it. Still, Bultmann adamantly insisted that God did somehow act in the person and teaching of the historical Jesus, though not in the way evangelicals would have considered. It was not the content of Jesus' message that was important, according to Bultmann, but instead his role as the "bearer of the Word of God which brought men to decision."[53] Bultmann ultimately finds God not contained in any historical person but "only in the *kerygma*—the proclamation of the Gospel."[54]

Ladd recognized that there was a lesson in Bultmann's thought that evangelicals needed to hear. While he defended the greater importance of the historical Jesus, Ladd agreed that no amount of historical information could contain or define the fullness of the saving act of God on the cross as communicated in the kerygma. He left his ETS readers with this challenge from Bultmann: "This proclamation is a word which addresses me personally, and tells me that the prevenient grace of God has already acted on my behalf, though not in such a way that I can look back upon this act of God as a datable event of the past, but in the sense that God's having acted is present as an eschatological Now."[55] Ladd joined this and several other quotations to end the article without critical comment. He was certainly convinced that there was value to the aspect of Bultmann's program that successfully challenged the evangelical understanding of the acts of God in history. Ladd gave Bultmann the last word: "Jesus Christ is the Eschatological Event as the man Jesus of Nazareth, and as the Word which resounds in the mouth of those who preach him."[56] Where evangelicals tended to limit their definition of God to what one could learn through the various means of revelation, Bultmann offered a much larger, indeed infinite God, one who transcended the boundaries of human understanding and met each believer in the moment of faith.

In his next engagement with Bultmann, Ladd turned again to a popular audience and published two short books for the Inter-Varsity Press Series in Contemporary Christian Thought. The first, *Jesus Christ and History*, provides an overview of the development of historical philosophy and its impact on biblical scholarship.[57] The focus in this book is the relationship between history and eschatology, a topic important to both Ladd and his conservative readers. The purpose of the book, according to Ladd, was "to set forth the biblical view of God and history and to expound the role of the second coming of Christ in this biblical perspective."[58] In this context it was crucial to reassert the significance of the evangelical hope of Christ's return, a topic rarely discussed in more critical academic circles. The German liberal tradition had dispensed with the doctrine of the second coming, according to Ladd, by grouping it with other details of ancient apocalyptic thought.[59] Bultmann had revived the positive use of the term, eschatology, but only within his narrowly drawn existential program. How should evangelicals respond to this challenge? How necessary was the doctrine of the second coming to Christian faith? These are the questions Ladd set out to address in this book, and not surprisingly he defends the traditional conclusions. Again, however, this is not so militant defense of doctrine as much as a sober challenge to evangelicals to educate themselves on the critical issues posed by modern historical thought. At the end of this brief book Ladd affirms the evangelical view that "God has invaded human history to defeat the forces of evil that man cannot conquer. In the second coming of Christ God will again invade history to finish the redeeming work He has begun."[60]

Ladd's second book in this series introduced the life and work of Rudolf Bultmann to the same popular audience.[61] Primarily a summary of Bultmann's thought, Ladd's critique contains some important developments that deserve mention. First, Ladd articulates a logical explanation for Bultmann's rejection of the supernatural events of the New Testament and offers a way around the problems his system presents. Bultmann, according to Ladd, applies a careful modern historical methodology in his interpretation of the biblical texts. "History," in the scientific historical framework, "is a closed continuum of interrelated causes and effects and by definition cannot allow for an intrusion from outside" and as such has no place for a deity taking on human flesh, a virgin having a child, or a dead man springing back to life.[62]

This, according to Ladd, is Bultmann's self-imposed limitation. "If a real In-carnation did take place," he argues, "*Bultmann has no way of recognizing it.*"[63] The same is true for the Easter accounts, for "Bultmann's historical presup-positions...make it impossible for him to recognize the reality of the resur-rection as an objective fact in past history." Ladd presents Bultmann as a man not hostile to evangelical faith but rather forced by his own training to reject it.

In his critique of Bultmann at the end of this book, Ladd presents a reasoned evangelical response to his system of thought. He begins this section, typically, by reminding his readers that "this little book has had the aim pri-marily of understanding Bultmann, not of condemning him." He also affirms Bultmann's motivation for writing: He "has asked the right question, whether or not he has provided the right answer." The central motive for Bultmann, in Ladd's estimation, should be the same for those in the evangelical camp: "How are we to interpret the gospel so as to make it relevant to the modern man?"[64] But on a deeper level, Ladd asks whether "Bultmann in his program of de-mythologization [has] cut away the heart of Christian theology." Ladd says that "in spite of his profound and helpful insights which have much to teach us, Bultmann's theology fails at the most crucial point: it makes man the center of theology instead of God."[65]

But Ladd does not end there. For all of his unorthodox conclusions, Bultmann has at least dared to wrestle with a new crucial question, while "evangelical scholarship has been little concerned with this problem."[66] Here again Ladd challenges his own side of the theological fence to avoid the com-placency of believing it had a monopoly on the truth and to begin to engage the difficult questions raised at the intersection of faith and modern life. In the end, Bultmann misses the mark with his answers to these problems, but at least he made the attempt. Ladd summarizes his critique:

> While we must admire him for his intention of trying to translate the gospel into terms compatible with the modern scientific world view, we must conclude that his program of demythologization has cut the historical taproot of redemptive events. The "scandal" of God's re-demptive acts in history has proven to be a real stumbling-block, and Bultmann's solution has failed to solve the problem of the relation-ship between faith and history. Bultmann's understanding of my-thology has led him to deny the objectivity of past redemptive events in history which constitute the heart of the gospel.[67]

Admiring Bultmann's tenacity and pastoral motivation did not equate with acceptance of his conclusions, but in the process Ladd modeled a new style of evangelical engagement with divergent theological views.

Three important observations emerge from Ladd's encounter with the work of Rudolf Bultmann. First, that he engaged Bultmann on his merits at all was a step toward the mainstream of theological scholarship, especially given the silence from the rest of his colleagues in the ETS, and was a clear attempt to earn credibility both for himself as a scholar and for evangelicalism as a system of belief. Ladd rarely missed an opportunity in these works, even when challenging aspects of Bultmann's theology, to point out the fact that evangelicals had long since abandoned this level of critical reflection. Second, Ladd did not simply attack Bultmann but rather engaged him on his own terms. When evangelicals dealt with Bultmann at all, it was often in the form of shrill denunciations that ignored the content of Bultmann's scholarship. Ladd addressed Bultmann's work as an insider (or at least as a close neighbor) and was able to offer a more nuanced critique of his system. Third and most important, Ladd ultimately used Bultmann to expose his conservative audience to the real problems raised by the use of biblical texts as primary historical records. With his critique of Bultmann as a shield, Ladd was able to educate his evangelical readers regarding historical issues without being too closely associated with Bultmann's methods and conclusions.

Ladd's growing involvement in broader historical and theological issues must be seen against the backdrop of the doctrinal and administrative controversies threatening Fuller Seminary.[68] Edward Carnell, who had no administrative experience—or ability, for that matter—was chosen to be the president in 1954 but resigned five years later after several psychological breakdowns and other problems.[69] The presidency of Fuller was an immensely difficult job. It required impeccable academic credentials, the patience to lead a faculty even more shrilly independent than most, the ability to defuse doctrinal attacks from militant enemies, and a knack for raising large sums of money. Carnell had famously complained that as president he "kissed babies, inspected turkey hatcheries, rode around vast ranches, listened to small talk, and sat hours in an unventilated room with children who were in the last stages of Asian flu," all without raising any funds for the seminary.[70] After Carnell's resignation in 1959, with Ockenga again leading the seminary on an interim basis from Boston and with Harold Lindsell consolidating power in Pasadena, the search for a new president served to divide the faculty along conservative and progressive lines.

The presidential search process was a case study in evangelical politics, with opposing factions and behind-the-scenes maneuvering and each side questioning the other's intellectual ability, doctrinal orthodoxy, and spiritual maturity. Ladd, typically preferring to avoid a fight, stayed out of the main fray. He had, however, established a close friendship with Dan Fuller, who was studying in Basel, and kept him abreast of every move. In the midst of the search, there arose a move among the conservatives, led by Lindsell, to require the faculty to sign a statement of faith. Lindsell had asked the faculty to draft a document that would affirm Fuller's defense of conservative doctrine, but they passed the request to Ockenga.[71] The requirement of assent to a rigid doctrinal statement must have revived in Ladd the fear that Fuller would go the way of Western Seminary, where the faculty had been forced to resign. Ockenga's public relations statement apparently did nothing to soothe the anxiety. Ladd wrote the following about the document: "It had two serious defects. First, it was full of loose generalizations and homiletic thinking which was almost tabloid in its naiveté. Secondly its main thrust was to assert that we are really fundamentalists. It made the great issue one's view of the Bible and divided the world up into two camps: fundamentalist-evangelical-conservative on one side and everybody else on the other."[72]

Worse, as a part of the campaign to assure the seminary's constituency of its orthodoxy, each faculty signature was to be reproduced in a promotional mailing. When Ladd hesitated, Lindsell threatened him at a faculty meeting: "Do you sign, or do I turn you over to Dr. Ockenga?"[73] Dan Fuller, after expressing his shock over the incident, replied that "the creed itself damages the future prospects of Fuller" and that he "would like to talk to every person on the Faculty privately, who might be sympathetic to this, and get them behind me." At the bottom of the page he added a handwritten request that Ladd "keep this letter in strictest confidence . . . breathing no thought or word of it to Ockenga or my father or anyone else."[74]

In a response Ladd lamented the pressures of living through both the twin intrigues of the search process and the pressure to conform to a rigid creedal statement.[75] At issue in the process of developing a creed were two sacred cows of the fundamentalist roots of the seminary, premillennialism and the inerrancy of the Bible. Dan Fuller, Paul King Jewett, and the rest of the progressive party were agitating for a less rigid statement, one that would allow the institution to recruit top scholars to the faculty. On the conservative side of the debate, however, were some of the most powerful men in the seminary, including Wilbur Smith and Harold Lindsell, both members of the original faculty, and neither willing to give up the fundamentalist doctrines without a fight. Ladd, while a nondispensational premillennialist himself, aligned himself with the progressives on both issues, presumably as part of his larger strategy of improving the stature of evangelical scholarship.

The division came to the surface when it was learned that David Allan Hubbard was a candidate for the presidency. Hubbard (1928–1996) had been in the second graduating class at Fuller Seminary and had stayed on to complete a ThM in Old Testament with Professor William Sanford LaSor. After

Fuller, Hubbard left for Saint Andrews University in Scotland to pursue doctoral studies in Old Testament with Matthew Black and became the first American student in that department to be retained as a lecturer.[76] When he returned to the United States in 1957, PhD in hand, Hubbard was among the highest regarded of the new generation of evangelical scholars. Ladd wrote on his behalf to Vernon Grounds, president of Conservative Baptist Theological Seminary in Denver, that Hubbard was "not only intelligent, but brilliant . . . the kind of man who comes along once every twenty years. . . . If we [Fuller Seminary] had the money, you couldn't lay your hands on him."[77]

Hubbard joined the faculty of Westmont College, an evangelical liberal arts college in Santa Barbara, California, and immediately became known as a popular teacher and preacher. As early as 1960, when Hubbard just was thirty-two years old, Charles Fuller suggested the possibility of his becoming president of the seminary.[78] At about the same time, Hubbard was contracted by Eerdmans Publishing Company to write an Old Testament survey with Robert Laurin, professor of Old Testament at the fledgling California Baptist Theological Seminary in Covina, and another Fuller graduate with a PhD from Saint Andrews. The draft of this survey, which Hubbard and Laurin were using in their classrooms, became a source of controversy when Hubbard was officially offered the presidency of Fuller in 1963. The text reflected critical challenges to the traditional interpretation of the Pentateuch, as well as other modern conclusions.[79] Hubbard attributed the offending passages to Laurin, and the progressive faction carried the day over the objections of Charles Fuller, Harold Ockenga, and the militant conservatives at the seminary.

Though he was on the side of the progressives, Ladd had doubts about the Hubbard candidacy. He was not concerned about liberal tendencies in Hubbard's thought; he was quite ready to see Laurin's hand in the less orthodox conclusions in the survey. In 1956 Laurin had written Ladd about his struggles with traditional evangelical positions. He told his former professor that he had "been forced to rethink" and was "still rethinking many of the basic problems of our faith." He claimed that his doctoral studies had given him "liberation from a narrow way of thinking."[80] Ironically, Ladd was concerned that Hubbard might be too conservative for Fuller Seminary. In 1960 Ladd wrote to Harold Ockenga, questioning whether Hubbard was "really devoted to the philosophy of the Seminary, for he is both a Conservative Baptist and a dispensationalist."[81] Ladd did not want a president who would align the seminary with John Walvoord and other militant dispensationalist leaders. The seminary's—and, by extension, Ladd's—credibility could only be damaged by a return to the uncritical biblical scholarship of dispensationalism.

Furthermore, Hubbard's identification with the Conservative Baptist movement did not bode well for academic freedom at Fuller. Ladd feared that the Conservative Baptists had become too militant and separatistic. Defending his view to Raymond Buker, a professor at Conservative Baptist Seminary in Denver, Ladd complained that when two Fuller graduates sought ordination from the local Conservative Baptists, they were rejected because they believed "like Calvin." It was acceptable to the Conservative Baptists, according to Ladd, "to believe like Scofield, but if you believe like Calvin ... it is dangerous."[82] Ladd knew that Conservative Baptists were disrupting academic life at Baylor University in Texas, and the purge of faculty members at Western Seminary was never far from his mind.[83] Conservative Baptists continued to use premillennialism as a test of faith and fellowship, and Ladd was concerned that Hubbard might make it a requirement for Fuller faculty. As it turned out, Ladd's fears about Hubbard were unfounded; Hubbard had undergone a transformation during his doctoral studies that mirrored that of Ladd. Hubbard had come back from Scotland with a more sophisticated view of both critical scholarship and academic freedom within the broadening boundaries of conservative evangelicalism.

Hubbard's appointment as president, however, was not met with unanimous approval among the faculty and board of trustees of Fuller Seminary. In an event that has come to be known as "Black Saturday," Hubbard's selection precipitated the resignations of several professors and trustees and solidified the influence of the progressive party in setting the direction of the seminary.[84] In the standard account, at issue was the seminary's formulation of the Scripture clause in its creedal statement. The perception—which proved to be accurate—was that Hubbard would represent the deciding vote on this crucial question, and so his candidacy became the focal point of the debate.

The conservative faction, led by Harold Lindsell, Harold Ockenga, Wilbur Smith, Gleason Archer, and trustee Edward Johnson (a banker and lay leader at the local Lake Avenue Congregational Church) was seeking to reestablish the seminary's defense of a strict formulation of inerrancy. The progressive party, led by William LaSor, Daniel Fuller, and administrator Don Weber (who was also Edward Carnell's brother-in-law), with the support of Ladd and Paul Jewett, wanted to replace "inerrancy" with "infallibility" because they believed it to be a more accurate reflection of critically trained evangelical belief. As with many of the fundamentalist battles, this one had as much to do with political power and personalities as it did with the content of the case at hand. Lindsell, who was seen as desiring the presidency for himself, used his considerable political and debating skill to oppose Hubbard's candidacy. In a strong letter to Ockenga, he stated that the issue of inerrancy was of primary importance for the seminary and that Hubbard's appointment would represent an abdication of "one of the main reasons for its founding."[85] Ockenga responded by putting forth, at the last minute, a new candidate for the presidency, C. Ralston-Smith, hoping to stall Hubbard's election.[86] In the debate over the creed, it is significant that its strongest defender, Johnson, was also its author.[87] Further, the creed in question had been written specifically to prevent the hiring of Bela Vassady in 1949. When this detail was pointed out to the board and faculty by Everett Harrison, Johnson felt his integrity was being questioned and defended the creedal statement with unusual vigor.[88] In the end Johnson, Lindsell, Archer, and Smith resigned over the Black Saturday conflicts, leaving the progressives in firm control of the seminary.

Sensing the more supportive atmosphere coming at Fuller with the hiring of David Hubbard—and the departure of the militant wing on the faculty—Ladd was able to involve himself in a scholarly debate outside the confines of conservative evangelicalism. The issue this time was the historical nature of the resurrection of Jesus, again a topic on the contested border between theology and history. The participants in this engagement were Donald T. Rowlingson of Boston University's School of Theology and John Warwick Montgomery of the Evangelical Theological Society. The articles began appearing in 1962, and the discussion lasted until late 1963. The catalyst for the dialogue actually came from an article by Roy A. Harrisville, "Resurrection and Historical Method," in the spring issue of the newly founded Lutheran journal, *Dialog*.[89] Ladd's response to Harrisville in the next issue drew the challenges from Rowlingson and Montgomery that make up the remaining components of the debate.

Central to the discussion was the technical distinction between *Historie*, or facts of history, and *Geschichte*, the meaning or significance of history. Martin Kähler had drawn this distinction in his attack on the philosophical presuppositions of the life of Jesus movement and its use of the historical-critical method to find the "real Jesus."[90] Still the use of these terms was not without its difficulties. Carl Braaten wrote the following:

> The distinction between historisch and geschichtlich is not evident to the average German-speaking layman. Therefore, a number of theologians argue that it is a meaningless and artificial distinction. It is obviously intended, however, to differentiate two qualitatively different attitudes to historical phenomena.... We have decided to translate historisch as "historical" and geschichtlich as "historic." The historische [sic] Jesus is the man who can be made the object of historical research. The geschichtliche [sic] Jesus is the Christ, my Lord and Savior, my ultimate concern.[91]

In the American context, evangelicals who entered into this discussion tended to champion the historical (*historisch*) nature of the resurrection event and saw any challenge to the biblical accounts as an attack on the foundations of the Christian faith. Those who emphasized a historic (*geschichtlich*) viewpoint, one that taught that the only verifiable aspect of the resurrection was its significance to the faithful, were accused by evangelicals of denying the supernatural origins of the biblical record.

Harrisville's article describes two opposing positions regarding the resurrection in modern thought and proposes a third one of his own. The first is associated with Bultmann, who rejected the historical character of the resurrection in favor of a strictly religious interpretation. Bultmann allowed the event significance, as we have seen, only insofar as the faithful use it to proclaim their faith and hope; the resurrection becomes not the foundation for belief but rather the object of faith itself. Bultmann does not argue against the "objective facticity" of the resurrection, however; instead, he challenges the propriety of calling the event a fact when it cannot be proved by modern methods.[92] Harrisville then summarizes the opposing view, which he attributes to German conservative scholar Ethelbert Stauffer, a professor at the University of Erlangen. In this model the resurrection as historical event can be reconstructed by using the available sources and facts and indeed can be understood only in this way. Contemporary and near-contemporary reports of the event are presented as proof that the resurrection took place and also as the foundation for the faith of the early church. Whereas Bultmann was intentionally indifferent to the first- and second-century sources, Stauffer considered these "witnesses" adequate to verify the historical nature of the resurrection.

Harrisville argued that the positions of both Bultmann and Stauffer led readers into an inescapable "cul de sac," where contemporary theology had been trapped for a generation. He described the problem as follows:

> How is it possible to maintain the meaning of the resurrection, which is Bultmann's great passion and which ultimately prevents his theology from being transmuted into anthropology, but without exalting indifference to the historical aspect to the level of a tenet of faith? And how is it possible, in company with Stauffer, to maintain the nature of the resurrection as a genuine historical occurrence without reducing it to a mere empirical fact?[93]

Both positions strip the resurrection event of an essential part of its character, according to Harrisville, and leave both our understanding and experience of it significantly incomplete.

With Bultmann, Harrisville argues that the resurrection cannot be understood apart from faith and that it is faith that gives the event its eternal significance. But unlike Bultmann, Harrisville allows that historical research has a larger role in our understanding of the resurrection, especially as it demonstrates "the event-character of the revelation" and also as it seeks to show "the church's unwillingness to allow a myth or psychic phenomenon to appear in place of history." With Stauffer, Harrisville agrees that rejecting the historical nature of the resurrection event denies "to faith the conviction that it 'does not begin with itself.' "[94] But Harrisville, using Bultmann, cautions against using the "historical and concrete" to legitimize that which comes at the hand of the "acting redeeming Sovereign who creates the *kairos* for faith."[95]

In the end, Harrisville argues that the question is less about the past than the present—that the New Testament witness of the resurrection is as "an initiation of an activity which has not yet ceased." The authentic kerygma, then, is that the resurrection is neither a fixed historical event nor an individualized existential encounter. For Harrisville, the risen Christ continues to appear in the preaching and sacraments of the church, not only as historical moment but also for "ever-renewed historical activity."[96] Harrisville's article proposes a combination of both *Historie* and *Geschichte*. Historians should continue to search for evidence that a miraculous event took place, but they should recognize that the saving nature of the event can be understood only through the eyes of faith.

The main thrust of Ladd's article, "The Resurrection and History," is to contrast modern historical methodology with the ancient paradigm of the New Testament.[97] Ladd goes to great lengths to admit that "what constituted proofs of Jesus' resurrection to his disciples cannot be considered historical proofs by the modern scholar," thus acknowledging his own willingness to use modern methods to evaluate the biblical record critically.[98] However, this was not an admission that the resurrection could not have taken place. Ladd insists that, despite the modern difficulties with the evidentiary sources, the resurrection must be understood as an event that "happened in history, at a datable time and in a designated place."[99] How does he reconcile these seemingly contradictory positions? While at first adhering to the modern historical principles of causation and analogy, he then builds on his critique of Bultmann and argues that the resurrection should be evaluated by different rules because it is an "unmediated act of God." Though the resurrection stands, according to Ladd, "outside the historian's critical faculties" and is thus by modern standards not a historical event, it is still the best explanation for the behavior and teaching of the disciples in its aftermath.[100]

Again we see Ladd attempt to circumvent the "rules" of scientific history in order to make room for a suprahistorical event. In the end he asks whether the real problem is not the presuppositions of the faithful but rather those of the historical-critical method. Still, he argues that modern historical methods are the best way to interpret historical events, provided they allow for a "dimension within history which transcends historical control." He associates this position with Karl Barth and contends that it is "the only adequate explanation which satisfies the data of redemptive history."[101] At this point Ladd is seeking acceptance for a third way, a method that is at once critically responsible and sensitive to the eyes of faith. Further, by acknowledging a significant point of agreement between his conservative evangelical views and those of Barth, he commits fully to his goal of earning credibility as a critical scholar.

Ladd wrote a longer piece for *Religion in Life* that was published at about the same time.[102] This piece is less open to the difficulties the resurrection poses to modern thinkers and more polemical in its engagement with Bultmann and other theologians in his tradition. Ladd's primary complaint is that a rigid implementation of the historical-critical method rejects, a priori, the possibility of a miracle:

> Such an attitude prejudices the case in advance and makes a decision before the evidence is heard. It assumes that the place where God acts is in the soul and not in history. . . . It rejects the biblical witness as to the nature of redeeming events, which sees God's self-revealing activity not only in the life of men but also in objective events. In other words, the definition of Christianity which is formulated from such presuppositions is bound to be other than the Bible's witness to God's redeeming acts.[103]

Clearly in writing to a more homogeneous evangelical audience Ladd felt little pressure to conform his views to those of the broader academy. He continues his critique by arguing that modern critical theory, with its rigid emphasis on continuity, analogy, and causation, has by its own rules made God's activity in history impossible. And while Bultmann and others tried to circumvent this problem by making human interaction with God an exclusively individualistic and personal event, Ladd rejects that view and maintains instead that no existential encounter can erase the need for an objectively verifiable resurrection. "There is no adequate explanation to account for the rise of the resurrection faith," he states, "except this: that Jesus rose from the dead."[104] Interestingly, this article was actually written before the piece in *Dialog* and, as I have already stated, was intended for a largely evangelical audience. It is also important, however, to note that without the added pressure to be accepted by readers in the broader academy, Ladd presents his argument, which is essentially the same as that in his response to Harrisville, in a much less conciliatory form because he fully expects this audience to agree without question.

The responses to Ladd's articles reflect the problematic relationship the so-called new evangelicals had with the rest of the theological world. In April of 1963, Donald T. Rowlingson of Boston University wrote an article for the *Christian Century* titled "Interpreting the Resurrection."[105] In this article Rowlingson, while stating his belief that the resurrection involved "the mighty working of God in human experience," argues that "our conclusions will to a great extent be influenced by what we presuppose about several things other than the biblical record." Moreover, while he acknowledges that the resurrection event is central to the creation of the church, he clearly admits his sympathy for the view that the disciples were preconditioned to believe that resurrection would take place through "the memory of Jesus' spiritual and moral quality." He asserts that the resurrection must be examined in light of "psychological studies of religious or existential experience" if it is to be "thoroughly dealt with."[106]

Rowlingson uses Ladd's more conservative article in *Religion in Life* as an example of a scholar who is apparently unwilling to risk this kind of thoroughness. He dismisses Ladd's view that the biblical record is a trustworthy source by saying that "it is futile to rest on the assumption that the Bible fully explains itself or is alone a valid body of evidence."[107] Further, he argues that, just as science has expanded human understanding of creation and demon possession (which he attributes solely to mental illness), the resurrection should be subjected to the same scrutiny. In a letter to Ladd before the *Christian Century* piece was published, Rowlingson asked him several questions about his views.[108] Though Rowlingson clearly sees Ladd's work as insufficiently critical, his letter is polite and framed within the boundaries of scholarly dialogue; it represents precisely the sort of engagement Ladd was hoping for. In his response, Ladd restates his confidence in the biblical record and also affirms his approval of modern psychological research by mentioning Fuller's plans for a school of psychology. Ladd defends his views by citing conservative scholars— both American and European—who agree with him and concludes with an acknowledgement of the difficulties involved in understanding the biblical witness.

Ladd closes the letter with the admission that he is "still wrestling with this problem of the relationship between faith and history" and that he "would prefer a faith which was entirely independent of history."[109] Rowlingson responds immediately, not with a rejoinder to Ladd's argument but rather with a newsy, chatty sort of letter in which he acknowledges the quality of the sources Ladd had quoted and mentions a handful of mutual friends. Rowlingson thanks Ladd for inspiring another article, also to be printed in the *Christian Century*, and passes along greetings from one of Ladd's former students, James Mignard, then studying for the PhD under Rowlingson. Importantly, even though these two scholars agreed on little, their discussion was gracious, respectful, and pleasant.

Around the same time as these articles were being written, Karl Barth was visiting the United States, and conservative evangelicals were using the occasion to attack him. John Warwick Montgomery, then affiliated with Waterloo Lutheran University in Canada, wrote an article in *BETS* titled "Karl Barth and Contemporary Theology of History."[110] The bulletin had been a place for serious dialogue on theological issues until the early 1960s, when inerrancy battles began to divide the society. Montgomery, whose PhD was not in theology but rather in library science, would eventually take on the title of guest editor of the bulletin, though his real function was to expose any member not sufficiently strong on the inerrancy of the Bible.[111] In 1966, Gordon Clark invited any who could not sign the society's inerrancy affirmation to leave the organization voluntarily.[112] Montgomery spends the last few pages of the article identifying scholars who he believed were under the influence of Barth and specifically attacks Ladd's conciliatory article in *Dialog*. Ladd had fallen into the trap, according to Montgomery, of "refusing to accept the resurrection as objective *Historie*," a development that "surprised—and pained" Montgomery.[113] Montgomery accuses Ladd of, like Barth, creating "a metahistorical category of interpretation for the resurrection in order to preserve its theological truth from historical criticism," something to which Ladd would have readily admitted, though not for the motives Montgomery attributed to him. Ladd's goal, which he stated in a letter to Vernon Grounds, was "to preserve the real eventfulness and objectivity of the resurrection."[114] Where Ladd had tried to find a place for the supernatural alongside modern historical thought, Montgomery reduced that attempt to the level of heresy.[115]

Montgomery clearly missed the essence of Barth's (and Kähler's for that matter) distinction between *Historie* and *Geschichte* and attributed to him, as many conservative evangelicals did, a hostility to evangelical faith that simply is not there. Barth would not say that the resurrection did not happen, only that its historicity could not be proven by modern methods. Saying that the resurrection, by the rules of modern historical thought, had to be considered *Geschichte*, was taken by Montgomery to be an attack on the historicity of the event. Ladd's agreement, according to Montgomery, was even worse than Barth's original thought because it was seen as an act of accommodation to the enemy. Ladd resented Montgomery's divisive leadership within the ETS and renewed his membership only to avoid the appearance of being unable or unwilling to sign the ETS creed.[116]

Despite the dangers, George Ladd saw an opportunity in Harrisville's article to align his views with a widely known and respected theologian, thereby building credibility both for himself and for evangelical theology. In a contemporary letter to Markus Barth (the son of Karl Barth) at the University of Chicago, Ladd lamented the lack of attention given to conservative scholars in broader academic circles, especially in the area of biblical studies. Ladd pledged that "conservatives like us at Fuller are trying to rethink the question [of the relationship between biblical authority and scholarly engagement] . . . [and] are seeking opportunities for dialogue with any and all who wish to discuss such questions. However, it is not always easy to gain a hearing."[117] Unlike previous generations of fundamentalist scholars and, more to the point, unlike many of his own former colleagues at Fuller Seminary, Ladd wanted a place in the broader world of professional biblical studies. The problem was, at least in Ladd's estimation, that that world did not want to welcome him. He believed that articles submitted to the most respected journals were often routinely rejected because they were written by conservative evangelicals. In the same letter to Markus Barth, Ladd complained that articles of his that *Theology Today* and *Interpretation*, two important journals of biblical theology, had rejected were readily published in the *Journal of Biblical Literature* and *Expository Times*.[118] Thus when Harrisville's article was published, Ladd recognized that a door had been left open for him to contribute an article both faithful to the evangelical doctrine of the resurrection and also sensitive to the terms and conditions of modern historical methodology.

Ladd's entrance into this dialogue was made possible by the fact that he largely agreed with Harrisville's main points, though mere harmony was not his primary goal. He begins by acknowledging the trap in which most conservative scholars found themselves by making the resurrection dependent upon its provability. He then frames the issue in terms that would have been far more familiar to moderate and liberal scholars than to the most conservative wing of American evangelicalism. Echoing Bultmann's pastoral motivation, Ladd writes that "the question of history and the resurrection raises a real problem for any man who wishes to take his stand in the twentieth century and use the categories of thought employed by contemporary scholars."[119] This acknowledgement of the difficulties related to the resurrection also allowed Ladd to identify himself as one who sought to stand in the twentieth century and use modern critical methodologies as well. These were certainly not givens in the conservative evangelical world, and Ladd's willingness to state them at the outset was undoubtedly a plea to be both heard and respected.

During the process of arranging for the publication of this article, Carl Braaten, the editor of *Dialog*, asked Ladd whether the rest of the Fuller faculty shared his views. Ladd stated that while there was some dissent, the "more representative portion of our faculty is trying to interpret orthodox theology in terms of the modern theological dialogue and problems raised by modern historical study."[120] That Edward Carnell of Fuller was in that same year one of six theologians invited to interview Karl Barth at the University of Chicago gives further evidence of the commitment to engagement on the part of Fuller's progressive wing.[121] Nevertheless, this did not mean that the enterprise was without danger. Carnell, and by extension Fuller Seminary, were severely attacked for giving tacit approval to Barth's theology. Ladd acknowledged the difficulties in communicating these critical issues to Fuller's mostly lay constituency and was ready for some to respond by branding him a "liberal" and to accuse him of "denying the factualness of the resurrection of Christ." Still, Ladd was no longer to be deterred by blows from the right. Fuller Seminary in the late 1950s and early 1960s was hit by a series of doctrinal attacks, both from within the faculty and from outside critics.[122] Ladd either did not expect his essay to get much negative attention or more likely decided that this opportunity to represent evangelicalism in a critical discussion of the resurrection was worth the risk.

An important part of that discussion was taking place between Ladd and another member of his own faculty. Dan Fuller, Ladd's former student, was working toward his second doctorate, this time at the University of Basel, and adopting a different position on the historicity of biblical events. Fuller's stance on the relationship between history and faith was actually far more developed than Ladd's, partly because it was central to his doctoral study but also because he was a more systematic thinker than Ladd.[123] Ladd and Fuller disagreed over the manner in which one could know biblical events and understand their meanings. Fuller believed that the resurrection and other phenomena could be known and verified as other facts were, whereas Ladd argued that their uniqueness demanded that they be known in an equally unique way. Fuller— adopting what was essentially a rationalist position—believed that the solution to the post-Enlightenment problem of whether God acted in history was to trust the biblical sources as they would have been read in their own time.[124] Ladd, as we have seen, used the post-Enlightenment boundaries of historical thought to argue that God's actions in history originated outside that history, and were free from its rules and limits. Thus for Fuller the resurrection enters the category of verifiable historical knowledge (with the biblical text as primary source) and necessarily becomes an adequate basis for faith.[125] In the terms of the *Historie* and *Geschichte* discussion, Fuller argued that if the resurrection could be verified, then "the fact of the resurrection leads inescapably to its meaning."[126] Ladd argued, on the other hand, that more of a separation existed between an event and its meaning and that one could accept the historicity of the former while rejecting the significance of the latter.[127]

Fuller did not argue, however, as Montgomery had, that deviation from the objectively provable was tantamount to rejection of the historicity of the event itself. Rather, he and Ladd were able to carry on a friendly dialogue over several years despite their different points of view. Even within progressive evangelicalism, then, there was room for distinct positions on these crucial issues, especially in how they were communicated within the confines of scholarly discourse. The main difference—since they agreed that the resurrection was a "real" event—was that Ladd's strain of historical defense was more acceptable to the mainstream of theological discussion.[128] Thus it makes sense that he would pursue this line of argumentation in his quest for participation in the broader academy.

This greater level of engagement in theological discussion, however, should not be seen as representing a corresponding shift in Ladd's theological position. His understanding of basic—and even peripheral—doctrines actually changed very little throughout his career. What evolved most noticeably during this period were the terms Ladd used to communicate the product of his research and the venues in which he sought to make his views known. It is reminiscent of his Harvard experience, where Ladd claimed not to have changed his belief but rather the way he held it.[129] As he moved into a new level of participation and dialogue within the academic world, Ladd held his conservative evangelical theology in dramatically different containers. He certainly saw the fact that he was largely accepted and fairly treated as affirmation that his strategy for improving the content and image of evangelical thought was working, and he proceeded accordingly.

With David Allan Hubbard installed as the new president of Fuller Seminary in 1963, Ladd was finally able to engage the broader world of theological scholarship in the assurance that it would not cost him his post on the faculty. How the rest of the evangelical world would react to him remained a different story. Still, as the old guard left Fuller for more conservative pastures, Ladd and the progressive faction of Dan Fuller, Paul King Jewett, and David Hubbard began to chart the seminary's new course. For Ladd this meant exploring the intersection of theology and history at a more foundational level than he had before, a development that reshaped the way he communicated his position and provided opportunities to contribute to the general theological discussion. Family life and personal issues remained problematic for the Ladds, but George was becoming adept at separating his private torment from his public roles as scholar and teacher. This would become significantly more difficult in the coming years, but for the moment Ladd was managing. Despite these impediments, Ladd drew confidence from his developing role as a trusted evangelical interpreter of modern theology and set his course for his own ultimate prize, writing his magnum opus, a work of critical scholarship that no one could ignore.

5

The Costs of Engagement
(1963–1966)

In the midst of George Ladd's successful and encouraging interaction with theologians and issues beyond traditional evangelical borders, he learned in 1963 that his magnum opus had been accepted by a major secular publisher. Finally, more than twenty years after he had begun his quest to make an important contribution on behalf of evangelical scholarship, Ladd's time had come. He was not above a little teasing. He wrote to Harold John Ockenga, then in his last few months as president of the seminary: "Now at last I have completed the major work which I had in mind twelve years ago, and have received word from Harper and Row that they will be happy to publish it. I enclose a copy of the report by one of Harper's readers. I trust this vindicates my right to be a member of the Fuller Faculty."[1]

Sarcasm aside, Ladd had done what no other Fuller scholar could manage: publish a critical study on a purely biblical topic with a house outside the evangelical mainstream.[2] In light of his participation in the scholarly debates over the philosophy of history and the nature of the resurrection, Ladd expected a new chapter in his career to begin, one that showed him to be accepted in the broader world of academic discourse. Gone were the petty battles with fundamentalists, along with the attendant wasteful distractions of writing books to debunk their theological positions. Ladd was at the big table now. The process had been long and difficult. The result would be devastating.

Ladd had worked on his magnum opus with near single-minded focus for more than a decade, even as he produced popular works for his conservative audience. The overriding sense for him during this period of preparation was that the other work was merely a distraction from his real reason for being: the creation of a major work of biblical scholarship. To this end Ladd spent several years reading and annotating German and French books related to the Kingdom of God.[3] He wrote to Merrill Tenney, his former classmate at Harvard and later a professor at Wheaton, that his book would be "a rather ambitious project, for it would not only review the entire current literature but would work into the course of the discussion most of the important viewpoints discussed in this literature."[4]

The extent to which Ladd engaged nonevangelical scholarship raised a few eyebrows at Fuller. After sharing some preliminary findings with the faculty in 1955, Ladd said, "The paper incited a lively discussion because I do not use clichés which our tradition and some [other] people expect."[5] He also shared his vision for the scope of the work with Otto Piper (1891–1982), a professor of biblical studies at Princeton Theological Seminary. Piper was a scholar in the *Heilsgeschichte* tradition and had written the influential *God in History* in 1939.[6] Ladd valued his opinion and had corresponded with him about *Crucial Questions*. This time Ladd wrote to let Piper know about the project and to make his case for its necessity before a more established scholar:

> In spite of all that has been written on the subject, I have the conviction that there remains something to be said. I am convinced that the world of scholarship has not yet found a sound position between the extremes of the apocalyptic and neo-prophetic schools, and I am convinced that the biblical position lies in this area. I am trying to assimilate into my thinking all of the important literature in English, German, and French. The book will, of course, be written from a thoroughly conservative point of view, and for this reason I do not know how it will be received; for the modern world of scholarship is not usually generous to any volume which sustains a consistent conservative approach even though the author makes a real effort to obtain a measure of objectivity in his treatment of the problems.[7]

This project dominated Ladd's research time as no other work before or after. He regularly studied until 9:30 each evening, demanding not to be disturbed. At one point he was so frustrated with the competing demands of research and sleep that he threw a book against the wall of his home with such force that it left a gaping hole. Ladd allowed the hole to remain there for years as a monument to his passion for excellence in scholarship.[8]

Ladd's goal was to create a work that would "relate a positive, conservative interpretation of the Kingdom of God to other contemporary optional views among biblical scholars such as Albert Schweitzer, T.W. Manson, William Manson, J.W. Bowman, and others."[9] Ladd knew this was likely to cause problems for him among conservatives. In a preemptive defense of his flank, Ladd wrote to Wayne Christianson, editor of the *Moody Monthly*, and stated that he was "deeply grieved" at the "current situation among evangelicals."[10] Ladd told him about his work in progress and said that the "book is addressed to the broader world of theological thought, and deals almost altogether with what one might call 'liberal' authors. However, I do not condemn them." Ladd knew that the sort of irenic engagement he was attempting with liberal theologians was not happening among conservative evangelicals of even slightly different stripes. He called on Christianson and others to use their "strategic positions" to encourage "Christian dialogue and fellowship." In the end, however, Ladd knew that his true target audience was the theological world of the left, and he proceeded accordingly. In 1960 Ladd wrote to Werner Kümmel (1905–1995), a New Testament scholar who had published a landmark study of the Kingdom of God, and asked for a clarification on several points of detail. In his letter Ladd was clear about his disagreement with Kümmel, who by that time was a professor at the University of Marburg, but he was also civil and appropriately deferential.[11] By his scholarship and attitude, Ladd sought to demonstrate the improved content and image of his own academic work and, by extension, that of evangelicalism.

Ladd's theological position occasionally led him to consider more practical matters. Though he avoided political arguments and rarely expressed his own views during his life, Ladd's Baptist beliefs, coupled with this understanding of the kingdom, led him to take a strong personal position on the issue of race. In 1964 Ladd resigned his membership at the Temple Baptist Church over the decision there to prevent blacks who had been baptized to enter into membership. This was not a new position for Ladd. In 1956, just two years after the landmark *Brown v. Board of Education* decision by the U.S. Supreme Court and in the earliest stages of the civil rights movement, he addressed the race issue at Immanuel Baptist Church, which he then attended. Arguing against any biblically supported divisions between races, Ladd flatly stated that these "distinctions do not exist in Christ" and advised the pastor to proceed appropriately.[12] He was thus appalled in 1964 that someone who had come to faith through the church's ministry still could not then worship with the congregation. Making no pretense of being what he termed a "militant integrationist," Ladd instead argued that, in Christ, "distinctions of race and social status have been transcended."[13] Ladd had resigned from the board of deacons the year before over the issue, but seeing no change he and Winnie left permanently in 1964.

However, the real focus of Ladd's life remained the creation of his major critical work. In the autumn of 1962 the manuscript was complete at a little more than four hundred pages, and Ladd looked for the right company to publish his book. Eerdmans, the publisher of his first three books, "want[ed] it badly," he wrote to a friend, but he was determined to find a nonevangelical house.[14] He initially considered Macmillan since it had worked with Edward Carnell in 1957. Guy Brown, Macmillan's director, had approached Ladd in 1959, after he had mentioned his research, but Ladd was not ready to show them his progress.[15] Though Macmillan showed some interest in the project, Ladd decided to pursue Harper and Row, which was actively seeking contemporary theological texts on a broad range of topics and was in the process of publishing a series of books on Rudolf Bultmann and the relationship between history and theology.[16]

Ladd, whose work was increasingly focused on that same relationship, submitted his manuscript there in late 1962, and Harper sent it to two New Testament scholars for recommendation. One reader was Roger Nicole, Ladd's former colleague at Gordon, but there is no record of the second. Ladd was anxious about the publisher's response and admitted to his friend Glenn Barker that, "if Harper's will not take it, I am going back to the preaching ministry."[17] Ladd also wrote to C. F. D. Moule of Cambridge University, a British evangelical New Testament scholar. Ladd had become acquainted with Moule (1908–2007) at academic conferences and in his letter lamented that "it is not easy to publish a four hundred page technical theological study in America, and I will not be surprised at a negative reaction; but I hope the work will be published in the not too distant future."[18] Perhaps fearing the worst, Ladd complained to John Newport, a professor at Southwestern Baptist Theological Seminary in Fort Worth: "Anyone who writes such long technical works in these days is either a fool or an egotist: take your choice."[19]

As the first to report, Nicole sent a glowing recommendation. He called Ladd's book a "notable contribution" and praised Ladd for his "mastery over the whole material within the field of his study."[20] Of special importance, according to Nicole, was Ladd's ability "to characterize in brief fashion the main trends of the work of scores of other scholars. Those with whom he disagrees are, I feel, fairly dealt with." He also stated that the "work not only embodies a scholarly and stimulating survey of the whole field of interpretations on the question of the Kingdom of God, but it provides a valuable contribution to the exegesis of a number of passages, in the Gospels particularly." Nicole made his final recommendation: "I close with the expression of the hope that you may find it possible to publish this excellent piece of work. If you know me, you will realize that I am not given to superlatives in my opinions and that therefore when I do express myself in that way, it is because there is very significant reason for it."[21]

Nicole later wrote to Ladd to congratulate him for his excellent work and said he had been "honored" to participate in the review process.[22] Melvin Arnold of Harper wrote to Ladd to report that the first reader was "strongly favorable" but that they would "follow [their] usual practice of having two readings."[23] He did, however, communicate that he expected no difficulties. With the first recommendation submitted and favorable, Ladd waited for word on the second.

The second report was not submitted until two months later but was apparently worth the wait. Arnold wrote to Ladd to say that the second recommendation was "as favorable as the first" and that Harper's was "ready to go ahead with a contract."[24] Ladd wrote back immediately and said that he was "gratified and relieved" to learn of Harper's plans. The book, said he mentioned, was "the result of some ten years of work . . . and it would have been a severe blow to my morale if your reviewers had felt it was an unworthy ms."[25] Within a week Harper and Row sent Ladd a contract not only for the publication of *Promise, Fulfillment and Consummation* but also for the standard rights to his next two books.[26] Ladd's sense of relief was palpable. After twenty years of envisioning himself as the writer of a great work of evangelical critical scholarship and more than ten years of actual labor, he had finally earned his opportunity to make an impact on the broader academic world. At long last, Ladd was the scholar he had always wanted to be. In this heady moment, as we have already seen, Ladd gloated a bit to Harold Ockenga.

However, Ladd's achievement was at least partly overshadowed in the Fuller community by the events of Black Saturday.[27] Ladd's book was under review at Harper just as the seminary began to regroup after the conflict, and his joy over the process and result would have fallen on the ears of some very distracted colleagues. Still, his success with Harper and Row was directly related to the transformation that was under way at Fuller Seminary. The resignations and reorganization that occurred in the aftermath of David Hubbard's appointment left the progressive party firmly in control of the institution. The last remnants of militant fundamentalism in Fuller's leadership structure were gone, along with the stifling influence of Harold Ockenga's inconsistent presidency-by-telephone.[28] The seminary was beginning to look like the place

Ladd hoped it would be when he had moved from Gordon College to Pasadena in 1950. He wrote the following to a former student: "Things look real good at the Seminary with Dan Fuller as Dean and Dave Hubbard as President. They are going to make a tremendous team."[29] As he looked forward to the publication of his major book, the emergence of Fuller Seminary as a center for evangelical scholarship, and his growing level of participation in the critical theological discussions of the day, Ladd felt that he had finally arrived.

The marketing plans for *Jesus and the Kingdom* were more extensive than anything Ladd's books had received before. Harper and Row had a much larger audience than Eerdmans and attempted to reach every possible segment of the market for Ladd's book. In August of 1963 Harper sent Ladd a questionnaire that asked him to list any journals, organizations, or individuals who should receive review copies of the book.[30] Eerdmans, with its focus on the evangelical market, never approached this level of sophistication in its advertising plan.[31] In the end, eighty-eight copies of the final work were sent to theological journals, seminary bulletins, Christian magazines, ministry periodicals, and city newspapers.[32] The review list included an impressive array of the most significant academic theological journals in the United States, as well as a lesser number of conservative evangelical publications. Copies were also sent to Otto Piper at Princeton Theological Seminary, as well as to William Barclay and F. F. Bruce in Great Britain.[33] Ladd himself began mentioning the forthcoming book in his public speaking engagements. A local newspaper reported that Ladd would soon publish "his definitive work on the 'Kingdom of God,' a book which has taken 10 years to complete." And in a paraphrase that surely mirrored Ladd's public statements, the article predicts the book "will be the conservative challenge to [liberal] American seminaries, and possibly a history-making volume."[34] Few who mattered would miss the arrival of Ladd's major work.

The marketing effort proposed by Harper and Row provided Ladd an opportunity to offer a rationale for his book to a nonevangelical reader. He wrote a long letter to Marie Cantlon at Harper, in which he described both his motivation and primary audience:

> I represent the conservative, or evangelical (but not fundamentalist) wing of the Protestant church. For a good number of years, a rather distinct gulf has separated what we may call the Evangelicals from the main Church, especially in the area of scholarship. Evangelicals have done relatively little in the area of solid scholarship, but have tended to attack the old line scholars for their liberalism. On the other hand, the old line scholars have tended to look down upon Evangelicals for their uncritical Biblicism.

Evangelicals accept the Bible as the Word of God, and have been themselves sadly divided over different interpretations of the Bible, especially in the area of eschatology. My previous three books have been addressed to these strictly Evangelical discussions.... I do not think I am exaggerating when I say that my books have had considerable influence in Evangelical circles.[35]

However, influence in evangelical circles was not what Ladd now had in mind. With this book he hoped to break out of the narrow boundaries of strict conservative evangelicalism and make an impact on a broader theological audience. This was not an easy task. Evangelical scholarship, according to Ladd, was not often well received, if it was published at all. "I have long since decided that there is a 'bandwagonism' in the publishing of books," Ladd wrote, "and we at Fuller are not on the 'bandwagon.' "[36]

Ladd's contract with Harper represented his emancipation from the boundaries of conservative evangelicalism, and he hoped his success would "make it easier for all of us in the future."[37] He further states that his evangelically oriented books were "only a by-product of my more important studies, which involve interaction and dialogue with the broad stream of Biblical criticism."[38] This represented a significant shift not necessarily in his thinking but certainly in what he was willing to communicate beyond his close friends and colleagues. The engagement with dispensationalism had been a detour at best, but in reality it was more of a negative distraction. Ladd's academic career to that point had been, in his own words, a mere "by-product" of his true calling and interest. Clearly his primary focus was the same as it had been since before he started his graduate education: to write a book in the area of critical biblical scholarship that would be recognized as worthy by those in the nonevangelical world.

With the manuscript for his book in Harper and Row's hands, Ladd began to make plans for his next sabbatical trip to Germany, scheduled for 1964–1965. Hoping to avoid the financial limitations of his first sabbatical, he sought support from both Fuller and beyond for his research. In May of 1963 he wrote to David Hubbard, newly installed as president of the seminary, and made his plea for extra time away from his regular duties. In 1962 Harold Ockenga had rejected his request to take a full sabbatical a year early, so he was ready to make a case.[39] Always looking for extra time to write, Ladd explained to Hubbard—somewhat disingenuously—that the rules had been changed several times and that his own research time had been delayed in the past. Further, according to Ladd, two other members of the faculty had recently been given permission to adjust their sabbatical schedules, thereby providing "ample precedent" for his request. He also worried that his age would be a factor if he waited much longer to complete his second major work, a textbook of New Testament theology. Having turned fifty in 1961, he believed he could not afford to spend ten more years on another book.[40] Ladd probably assumed he held some sway over the new president. He was almost twenty years the president's senior, was a well-known scholar, and had been a professor when Hubbard was a young seminary student. In the end Ladd was granted permission to consolidate his sabbatical time at half salary—$4,800 for the year—and planned to spend fourteen months abroad from July 1964 until September 1965.[41] The critical issue remained, however: how to cover the remainder of the costs.

With the time frame settled, Ladd turned to raising support for his travels and study. He wrote to Charles Taylor, executive secretary of the American Association of Theological Seminaries (AATS; later, the Association of Theological Schools), to solicit funding.[42] Admitting to Taylor that the 1957–1958 sabbatical had been an enormous personal financial burden, he referred dryly to a loan against his home as a "private fellowship," one that had taken more than four years to repay.[43] But Ladd also credited the sabbatical with allowing him the time to complete the necessary research for his new book and stated that his goal for the 1964–1965 study would be "a New Testament Theology which will eventually be a textbook of some 600 pages." The AATS Commission on Faculty Fellowships had agreed to award Ladd a grant of $4,000 toward the expenses related to his overseas research.[44] David Hubbard also solicited Paul C. Doehring, a local physician who had supported faculty studies in the past, on Ladd's behalf. Doehring gave $400 to the seminary's European Research Fund to help pay for Ladd's study abroad.[45]

The added financial assistance allowed Ladd to maintain full support of his son, Larry, who continued to struggle with a variety of developmental problems. Larry's condition had worsened in the early 1960s, and he was just barely able to live independently. Norma and Winnie had been Larry's primary caregivers, but with Norma now married and living elsewhere, the Ladds hoped Larry could finish college and begin to live on his own. Though in his late twenties, Larry still remained financially dependent upon his parents. According to Ladd's arrangements for his sabbatical, Larry was to receive $150 per month, plus all school expenses—an additional $500 for the year.[46]

With the financial arrangements in order, Ladd could concentrate on making plans for his research. What did he hope to accomplish during his time in Europe? His primary goal was to finish the text of a brief book on criticism and to complete the reading for his textbook on New Testament theology. He had been using a syllabus of about 350 pages in his theology classes and now wanted to expand that work into publishable form.[47] He wanted to fill a niche he had identified in the range of available textbooks, a market dominated by Bultmannian existential theologies on one hand and topical studies that, in Ladd's view, overemphasized the unity of the New Testament on the other. Ladd's plan was to write from the *Heilsgeschichte* perspective and to examine the historical development of the diverse types of New Testament writing. In order to accomplish this task, he wanted to spend his time in Germany "study[ing] in depth the tensions between the *Heilsgeschichte* and the contemporary existentialist points of view."[48]

Ladd's choice of a home base for his research revealed his preference in learning environments: "The theological climate at Basel, Erlangen, and Hamburg would be closer to my own position; but since I do my best thinking in dialogue with other positions, I am selecting Heidelberg." This was essentially an accurate self-perception on Ladd's part, within certain limits. He enjoyed dialogue with opposing or divergent views but only if he was allowed to participate as an equal and only if the encounter was free from personal attack. Even with dispensationalists Ladd was willing to debate various issues. What he avoided was any situation in which he would be accused of being an outsider, somehow beyond the boundaries of a prevailing orthodoxy, if he did not agree. As we have already seen, however, Ladd could be inconsistent as to the exact difference between these two types of engagement. Often his sense of inferiority would lead to hypersensitivity when confronted with opposing views and result in severe emotional wounds. But these sorts of wounds were not at issue in 1963 and 1964. Ladd was proud of his acceptance by Harper and Row, comfortable with the new shape of his institution, and ready to make his next major scholarly contribution.

Ladd's time of preparation during the 1963–1964 academic year was interrupted by two important issues related to the publication of his book. First, Frank Elliott at Harper and Row was unhappy with *Promise, Fulfillment and Consummation* as the title of the work, calling it "not sufficiently descriptive of the content to attract the potential audience."[49] Indeed, Ladd later found out, several people had initially thought that the title referred to a marriage manual.[50] They settled on *Jesus and the Kingdom*, and publication of the book proceeded.[51] However, another event posed an even greater challenge to Ladd's achievement. Two books covering virtually the same material were published at about the same time in 1963, just as Ladd's book was going to press. This was an unfortunate turn of events, especially since Ladd had hoped his book would be a thorough interaction with the latest scholarship on the Kingdom of God. Swedish scholar Gösta Lundström (b. 1905) and Norman Perrin (1920–1976), who was British by birth and training but was teaching in the United

States, each published important critical studies of the Kingdom of God in 1963, and both books appeared too late for Ladd to address them in his study. Lündstrom's book, *The Kingdom of God in the Teaching of Jesus: A History of Interpretation from the Last Decades of the Nineteenth Century to the Present Day*, had actually been written in 1947 but was appearing for the first time in English. Perrin's book bore the same main title as Lundström's and approached the topic from a modified Bultmannian perspective, a fact that was particularly galling to Ladd since he was trying specifically to engage existentialist theological scholarship.[52] In the end all Ladd could do was add footnotes in his book, saying that these two books "appeared too late to be of much use in this study."[53]

What was Ladd trying to accomplish in *Jesus and the Kingdom*? The structure of the book followed the pattern of Ladd's original title. Whereas Kümmel and others had focused on promise and fulfillment, Ladd added a futurist sense of apocalyptic consummation to the mix. Even under the new title, his message was that the Kingdom of God existed as promise, fulfillment, and consummation. From the outset he had three goals for the project. First, and in keeping with his strategy for raising the profile of conservative theology, in *Jesus and the Kingdom* Ladd sought to demonstrate the growing level of erudition among the new generation of evangelical scholars, himself especially. He challenges both the process and findings of the "historical Jesus" movement, which endeavored to reduce the understanding of Jesus to only that which scientific historical methods could prove. He demonstrates that he is able to engage this thought on its own terms, something few conservative evangelicals had been able or willing to attempt. His preparation for the writing of this book, as we have seen, was as disciplined and comprehensive as could be expected, and he showed that wide range of reading and reflection throughout the text.

The first main section is a summary of modern scholarship on the Kingdom of God. As Ladd moves from theologian to theologian, he traces the varying views of the doctrine, from fully realized to purely futurist positions. His achievement in this chapter is worthy of note. His critical summary of the existing material on the kingdom is as strong as that in either of the other contemporary monographs by Lundström or Perrin. Further, though he is self-consciously writing from a conservative orientation, he treats a wide range of views respectfully and dispassionately; he is fair and reasoned, even as he writes from his clearly stated presuppositions.[54]

This is Ladd's intentional attempt to distance himself from the reductionistic and reactionary behavior of other conservative critics, who engaged in the "unqualified condemnation" he challenged in his defense of Lundström and tended to brand opposing views as liberal without engaging their perceived error.[55] In his preface Ladd argues for the value of understanding divergent theological views: "Those with whom he [Ladd] most vigorously disagrees are often those from whom he has learned the most."[56] His calm assessment of the state of scholarship on the kingdom stands in contrast to the militant attacks of fundamentalist scholars such as John Warwick Montgomery of the Evangelical Theological Society and represents an important step in the rehabilitation of evangelical scholarship.

The second aim of the book was to make the case, as Ladd had tried to do throughout his career, for understanding the Kingdom of God as the dynamic rule or reign of Christ in history, to be completed in some future event known to all:

> The central thesis of this book is that the Kingdom of God is the re-
> demptive reign of God dynamically active to establish his rule
> among men, and that this Kingdom, which will appear as an apoc-
> alyptic act at the end of the age, has already come into human
> history in the person and mission of Jesus to overcome evil, to
> deliver men from its power, and to bring them into the bless-
> ings of God's reign. The Kingdom of God involves two great mo-
> ments: fulfillment within history, and consummation at the end of
> history.[57]

This was in direct opposition to many in his own conservative world, especially the dispensationalists, who, while affirming the historicity of Jesus' life, death, and resurrection, approached the kingdom in terms of a future earthly realm that was based on an ahistorical and literalistic interpretation of the relevant passages. However, Ladd wanted to challenge the opposite end of the theological spectrum as well. The broader world of critical New Testament scholarship, dominated by the intellectual descendants of Rudolf Bultmann, interpreted the kingdom as a hyperindividualistic encounter with the risen Christ, free from any basis in historical events. Ladd's thought found a niche where the Kingdom of God could be critically examined, yet still defended in conservative terms.

Finally and most importantly, Ladd used his book to champion his mature historical methodology, which allowed for the acts within human history of a God not bound by historical boundaries: "Here is an essential fact in the Gospel: the suprahistorical and the historical are inseparably wedded in *Heilsgeschichte*."[58] Ladd sought to play by the rules of modern scientific history, to a point, even as he described events that could be understood only apart from scientific categories. The crucial issue in relation to most critical scholarship on the New Testament, Ladd wrote in the preface of *Jesus and the Kingdom*, is that it leaves "no room for the acting of God." In Ladd's view, "the biblical records bear witness that God has acted in history," but within the boundaries and rules of modern scientific history, "the secular historian has no critical tools for recognizing it."[59] Here Ladd employs the term "Biblical Realism" to describe a methodology that allows for both the validity of the accounts of the biblical record and the role historical forces played in creating that record. Ascribing a modern scientific worldview to the writers of the New Testament is a trap, he argues, blinding the critic to the thought processes behind the texts being studied. This modern sensibility acts as a filter by creating an understanding that is "alien to the Bible and which therefore distorts the biblical perspective."[60] The solution to this problem, in Ladd's view, is a methodology that separates that which can be evaluated according to scientific methods and that which cannot: "The present study is an effort to understand the Bible's perspective of promise and fulfillment in terms of its own view of God and his relation to history. . . . We employ the term Biblical Realism in the effort to place the emphasis upon these redemptive events, especially the event in Jesus Christ, from within the Bible's own realistic perspective."[61] In *Jesus and the Kingdom* Ladd hoped that his emphasis on the Bible as an accurate witness would be seen as an innovative strategy for the creation of biblical scholarship and not an anachronistic attempt to disguise traditional faith in critical clothing.

The foundation of Ladd's theological and historical method is, then, the idea that God acts in history and that those acts are subsequently interpreted in an authoritative way by the biblical record. "The Kingdom of God," he maintains, "means that God is King and acts in history to bring history to a divinely directed goal."[62] Any theological system that rejects this idea, according to Ladd, "has lost something essential to the biblical faith." But he also understands that this represents a significant problem for modern historians and challenges the very nature of history as understood in the modern sense. He states that in the contemporary world of theology, "the problem of how the absolute and final meaning of life can be embodied in the relativities of history has become acute."[63] Ladd places Bultmann at one end of the spectrum, saying that Bultmann's methodology "requires him to interpret God's acting in existential terms" and that as a result "he is pessimistic about history."

However, this presents too great a problem for faith as Ladd understands it. "This result of demythologizing the biblical teaching of a God who is the Creator and the Lord of history sacrifices an essential element in the gospel and grows out of a philosophical concept of God which is other than the biblical revelation." This is Ladd's dividing line between modernist error and true faith, between that which is provable by the methods of modern scientific history and that which is allowable within an orthodox view of inspiration and revelation. "The fundamental difficulty with Bultmann's theology," Ladd concludes, "is that he has an unbiblical doctrine of God." Here Ladd differentiates his view of history from Bultmann's and states his own mediating position. "If God has acted in history in this Kingdom," Ladd writes, he "will surely establish his Kingdom at the end of history."[64] This, then, is the crux of Ladd's view of both history and the Kingdom of God. Historical method is a valuable tool for demonstrating and interpreting whatever it is able to measure, but God's acts do not fall into that category. Limiting the revelation of the biblical record to only those concepts that can fit within the boundaries of modern historical thought simply costs too much. God must be and must also offer more than simply a personal existential encounter; he must be present and active and *acting*, that is, bringing history to the end he has designed. Quoting British scholar T. W. Manson, Ladd affirms that without a "final victory of good over evil, the kingdom of God becomes an empty dream." Ladd concludes: "The Christian gospel is concerned about mankind as well as about individual men. Its God is the Lord of history who acts in history and who will surely establish his Kingdom at the end of history."[65]

As the 1963–1964 academic year came to an end Ladd learned that his *Jesus and the Kingdom: The Eschatology of Biblical Realism* would be featured on Harper and Row's fall list. He wrote to Henry Cadbury, his Harvard professor, and proudly told him that the book was about to appear. "This is my first piece of scholarship," he wrote, "and it is going to be interesting to see what happens to the book and how it is received."[66] The book was released just as George and Winnie Ladd were settling in at Heidelberg. It was there that Ladd received his first copy, along with several initial reactions to the book. Harold Ockenga, now at Park Street Church full-time, wrote to congratulate Ladd on his accomplishment. Ockenga was an editor at large for *Evangelical Books*, a review publication that inspected books for conservative readers and made regular endorsements to them. In his letter he pledged that he would "strongly recommend that it be used as one of our choices."[67] Ockenga was effusive in his commendation of the book, saying that it "reminded me a great deal of the mode of writing of J. Gresham Machen." This was high praise indeed, especially given Machen's mythic significance at Fuller.[68] Not only was Machen, who was a conservative Presbyterian scholar and helped found Westminster Theological Seminary, the patron saint of Fuller's early faculty and leadership, but Ladd remembered him as the only conservative whose books were read at Harvard.[69] If *Jesus and the Kingdom* was reminding Ockenga of his own hero's work, Ladd was certainly moving in the right direction.

A second letter was even more significant for Ladd. John Bright (1908–1995), an Old Testament scholar who had published several important works, including his own study of the kingdom in the Old Testament, had read a galley copy of Ladd's book.[70] Bright was a professor at Union Seminary in Virginia, a Presbyterian institution, and a theologian in the tradition of *Heilsgeschichte*. He also served as an associate editor of *Interpretation*, an important journal of biblical theology published by his own institution. *Interpretation* offered critical studies of biblical topics for service to the church and was widely read by pastors and scholars alike. Over the years *Interpretation* had rejected Ladd's articles several times, and he was hoping to raise his profile among the editors with his new book. In August of 1964 Bright sent his comments on *Jesus and the Kingdom* to Harper and Row, and the publisher forwarded a copy to Ladd in Germany. Bright was also very complimentary to the volume, saying that he "enjoyed it very much and [thought] it a very worthy book indeed." He continued: "Professor Ladd shows wide acquaintance with the relevant literature and is, as far as I can see, uniformly fair in stating and discussing the opinions of others with whom he disagrees—or agrees for that matter."[71]

This was exactly the sort of response Ladd was hoping for. To be acknowledged as a fair critic of opposing views while maintaining his conservative identity was precisely the evaluation he desired, even craved. Though Bright acknowledged his own disagreement with some aspects of Ladd's conclusions, he wrote that "in [his] opinion this book will have to be considered by all New Testament students as a serious contribution to its subject."[72] Ladd was overjoyed. He wrote to David Hubbard at Fuller, relating the details of Bright's assessment and expressing his delight to see a better-known scholar offer an appraisal that was "*100% favorable.*" "Maybe," he added, "the book will catch on."[73]

Early in his sabbatical Ladd wrote a reflection piece for *the opinion*, Fuller Seminary's student publication.[74] Ladd was reflective about his career to that point, as well as on the new directions it might take. As he rambled through his report on the state of theological study in Germany, he seemed to be somewhat envious of the role theology played in the universities there. "Theology stands first," Ladd wrote, "and heads all other disciplines. . . . Germans cannot understand why our great public universities do not have faculties in theology."[75] Seeing the situation in Germany through the filter of his life's goal of academic respect for evangelical theology, he continued:

> An American type of Evangelicalism is practically non-existent in
> German university faculties of theology, and I fear [they] would view

my theological stance as one of rather naive Biblicism. This is a reproach which Evangelicals must be able to bear. On the other hand, ought it not to be possible to express an Evangelical theology in fresh dynamic terms which will not sound like a reactionary obscurantism but which will meaningfully communicate to theologians standing in other modern traditions?[76]

Now that Ladd felt he had "arrived" as a scholar, he was freer to challenge some of the parochial views he saw as deterrents to excellence among evangelical theologians. "The gravest temptation of orthodoxy," he warned, "is that it become stagnant, defensive, apologetic, traditional." He added that, "While I am convinced that God has communicated eternal, unchanging truth in the inspired Word of God, it remains true that the truth is far greater than our finite minds, that we cannot package it in convenient one-pound chain-store style, that true scholarship must ever be motivated by an open, inquiring mind."[77]

With his own reputation apparently secure, Ladd closed with a challenge to Fuller's students, most of whom were heading into parish ministry or missionary work:

I long to see men of God going from Fuller into the ministry—men not motivated primarily by personal ambition for success, but men completely captivated by Jesus Christ, men unswervingly committed to the Word of God and an evangelical theology, men who can preach the saving, redeeming truth of God with a freshness, creativity, and relevance which will make them prophetic voices of God. Life can offer no greater challenge than this.[78]

This is Ladd at his most confident and unguarded. For these months in Heidelberg Ladd was exactly who he wanted to be. His life's goal was being accomplished. He finally had the stature he had craved for most of his adult life. Assured of his standing, Ladd settled into the life of a visiting scholar, attending lectures, reading books, writing articles, and waiting for the response to his book.

The first major review to appear was from Ladd's old nemesis at Dallas Seminary, John Walvoord, who was highly critical of the book. Ladd and Walvoord had apparently not spoken since Walvoord had preached at Fuller's chapel services—at Ladd's invitation—in 1960, and the negative review of *Jesus and the Kingdom* was anything but unexpected.[79] Still, it must have been at least a little disheartening to have the first major notice of his book turn out to be an attack. Walvoord's assessment proceeds along predictable lines by calling the book a "compromise between historic premillennialism and amillennialism."[80]

In the coded language with which Walvoord protected the boundaries of dispensational orthodoxy, virtually every word in this sentence was meant to damn Ladd's thought. The concept of "compromise" was almost always used pejoratively within militant evangelicalism, in the sense of a weakening of doctrinal limits, and the two millennial views Walvoord associates with Ladd were conspicuously nondispensational.

He continues, again in code, saying that "those who love the intellectual approach will revel in this volume." Walvoord notes Ladd's wide range of reading but is critical of the very limited presence of premillennialist authors in the bibliography. He calls the book "a strange one-sided study that slights the great premillennial scholars of the past, as well as of the present, as being unworthy even of mention."[81] In the end Walvoord argues that Ladd's formulation of the doctrine of the Kingdom of God "is certainly confused" and adds that "readers who want a clear path through the jungle will not find it in this volume." Having played an instrumental role in the removal of premillennialism from Fuller's doctrinal statement, Ladd responded only by stating that Walvoord "does not understand what I am trying to do. This would be funny if it were not so tragic."[82] The approval of dispensationalists was not what Ladd was after. What Ladd was truly hoping for was a review in a mainstream academic journal. He was about to receive it.

Ladd's *Jesus and the Kingdom* was reviewed in *Interpretation* by Norman Perrin, one of the two scholars who had published similar studies just before Ladd's book appeared. The review could hardly have been more scathing. Perrin, at first sympathetic to the unfortunate timing of Ladd's book, found his "initial regret being replaced by an increasing disquietude, for the author's approach and methodology, his understanding of contemporary critical scholarship, and his attitude to its findings all seem to raise rather serious questions."[83] Perrin continued with an attack on Ladd's use of "biblical realism," calling it "an uncritical view of the Gospels as historical sources."[84] He reserved some of his sharpest comments for Ladd's use of Kähler to support both his methods and conclusions. To Ladd's belief that Kähler would have concurred with him in the crucial area of historical methodology, Perrin argued as follows:

> If we are going to invoke the name of Kähler, let us note (a) that
> it takes real eisegesis to make him say that the Jesus who really
> lived in history is the biblical Christ pictured in the gospels,
> and (b) that he certainly would not agree that the Gospels as they
> stand are credible reports of Jesus and his preaching—witness
> his acid comment that the only time we can be sure of the word-

ing of a saying in the tradition is when we have only one witness for it. The point is that Kähler would have set his face as firmly against this kind of "biblical realism" as he did against the older liberalism.[85]

This criticism was particularly difficult for Ladd to bear because he considered himself to be dependent upon Kähler's position as a starting point from which to engage critical scholarship. But Perrin was only getting started.

The review challenged Ladd specifically at the intersection of his handling of biblical and critical texts. Perrin stated that Ladd "gives his presuppositions remarkably free reign [sic] . . . and his approach to biblical exegesis is unusual." Worse, Perrin argued that Ladd

> does not attempt the detailed exegesis of sayings which is a feature of most books on this subject; rather, he treats sayings according to the use he can make of them in the setting of his overall schematic presentation and simply extracts from them what he needs at that point, ignoring everything else. . . . One aspect of Ladd's treatment of sayings and pericopes which the reviewer found annoying is his deliberately one-sided approach to the question of authenticity. Absolved by his approach as stated in the Preface from any necessity to discuss this question, he nonetheless constantly quotes such scholars as he has been able to find who do regard a saying or pericope as authentic, usually without any reference whatever to the points at issue or to dissenting opinions.[86]

Not only was Ladd guilty of this exegesis of convenience, according to Perrin, but he also made inappropriately selective use of critical scholarship as well:

> The book is full of references to contemporary critical scholarship, but they are of such a nature as to arouse grave questions in the mind of the reader. We have already noted Ladd's anxiety to find support for his views on the authenticity of a saying or pericope, and this is but one aspect of what seems to be a ruling passion with him: the search for critical support for his views altogether. . . . Ladd's passion for finding support for his views among critical scholars has as its counterpart an equal passion for dismissing contemptuously aspects of their work which do not support him.[87]

In particular Perrin accused Ladd of misinterpreting, in fundamental ways, the work of both Rudolf Bultmann and Günther Bornkamm. Having launched this broadside against Ladd's methodology and conclusions, Perrin concluded with an assessment of Ladd's place in the world of scholarship: "Ladd thus takes his stand squarely in midstream of the contemporary concern about eschatology—with his face turned resolutely upstream, whence we all came some considerable time ago. It remains to be seen how effective his challenge to the prevailing current of our concern will prove to be."[88] Note the number of subtle references to Ladd as outsider: Perrin contrasted Ladd's work to what happens in "most books on this subject"; he pictured Ladd in some passé stream "whence *we* all came some . . . time ago" and wondered whether Ladd's work would have any impact on the "current of *our* concern."[89] This catalogue of criticisms and the way they are communicated could hardly have cut deeper and were all the worse for being in the first major review to appear.

What do we make of this review? Before addressing the content of Perrin's evaluation, we will find it helpful to understand something about the man himself. In several aspects Norman Perrin's background bears some resemblance to that of George Ladd; by their own divergent paths, Perrin and Ladd had similar origins and personal tensions to overcome on the way to their goals of being highly regarded scholars. Perrin was born in 1920 to a family who worked in the mills of Wellingborough, Northamptonshire, England, and lived in near poverty during his younger years. He showed great promise in his early education, however, and decided to pursue an academic career.[90] According to his biographer, Perrin was "motivated by an intense drive and ambition to succeed . . . due, at least in part, to his earnest desire to repudiate his background by excelling in his profession."[91] Throughout his career Perrin made references to "making it" in the area of critical scholarship and once told a friend that for his eulogy he wanted it said that "While he was here, he made quite a splash."[92]

He obtained his first degree at Manchester University in 1949, where he studied with New Testament scholar T. W. Manson (1893–1958). He obtained his Bachelor of Divinity (1952) and Master of Theology in New Testament (1956) at London University. In 1949 Perrin was ordained as a Baptist minister and served as a pastor during his studies in London. From 1956 to 1959 he studied under Joachim Jeremias (1900–1982) at the University of Göttingen, where he wrote his doctoral dissertation on the Kingdom of God in the teachings of Jesus.

When the time came to begin his academic career, Perrin believed his social standing would keep him from positions in Britain and his Baptist background would prevent him from occupying similar posts in Germany. Further, he was already thirty-nine at the time he received his doctorate—a year older than Ladd when he finished at Harvard—and believed he had to make up for lost time. Motivated as he was by a desire to "develop a scholarly reputation and thereby move upward in the academic world," Perrin moved to the United States after graduation and taught at the Candler School of Theology at Emory University in Atlanta from 1959 until 1964, when he moved to the Divinity School at the University of Chicago.[93] He remained in Chicago until his death from a heart attack in 1976.

Perrin's early years at Candler were spent developing a response to the theology of Rudolf Bultmann; still conservative in his theology and method, Perrin was highly critical of Bultmann in an article published in 1959.[94] He spent the next three years revising his dissertation, which was published in 1963 as *The Kingdom of God in the Teaching of Jesus*. During his Candler years Perrin's own theological position began to change dramatically, and he became convinced that Bultmann's thought represented the future of New Testament studies. Perrin's thought would shift radically several more times in his career, each time placing him at the forefront of a new movement in New Testament scholarship.[95]

In 1964 Perrin moved to the prestigious University of Chicago largely because it allowed him more extended research time and required less classroom teaching—reasons similar to those that prompted Ladd's move from Gordon to Fuller—a situation more conducive to reaching the "big time."[96] Perhaps this is a glimpse into Perrin's own strategy for "making it" in the world of scholarship. It was after his move to Chicago, which occurred just as Ladd left for his sabbatical, that Perrin believed he had "arrived" as a scholar, and there he wrote his review. At the time Perrin penned the review of *Jesus and the Kingdom* he was in the midst of an enormous upheaval in his own belief system, and it is likely that Ladd's book represented the conservatism Perrin had been attempting to escape for much of his early career.

The content of the review, then, should be seen in the light of both the similar and the divergent paths of Ladd and Perrin. Some of the criticisms are fair. Certainly Ladd was prone to relying too much on supportive quotations from scholars or sources better known than he. Nathan Wood had said as much in his evaluation of Ladd's BD thesis at Gordon in 1941, and John Walvoord had observed this trait in his review of *The Blessed Hope*.[97] That Perrin noticed it in Ladd's first major critical work is hardly surprising, though the singling out of Kähler seems strange. Ladd mentions him only twice: once in the preface and once rather late in the book, when his argument had already been made.[98]

On the other hand, Perrin's attack on Ladd's strong presuppositions is more than a little disingenuous. First, Ladd states his biases from the outset of his book. Indeed, the entire reason for writing the book was to present a conservative evangelical exposition of the doctrine of the kingdom in the teachings of Jesus. In this sense Perrin is simply stating the obvious in crueler terms. Further, Perrin himself worked from within strongly held personal biases and a fierce competitiveness that drove his scholarship and criticism. He was "heartbroken, upset and jealous" himself when Gösta Lundström's book on the kingdom was published at the same time as his book and angrily called it a "pile of trash."[99] Perrin was also known to refer to Cullmann's formulation of *Heilsgeschichte* as "Bullgeschichte."[100]

However, some of Perrin's criticisms are a result of own his shift in theological position. Perrin's biographer charts the evolution of his thought as "a continuum on which he moved to positions where history was less and less important for faith."[101] This assessment illustrates the extent to which Ladd and Perrin traveled on a collision course. Ladd was not only working and living within a tradition that was struggling to define its dependence on history as a foundation for faith but was also grappling with these issues in his own faith and scholarship. The matrix of Perrin's evolution from radical historicism to an equally thoroughgoing ahistoricism is mirrored by Ladd's own movement from fundamentalist dispensationalism (with its attendant rejection of the role historical processes may have played in the development of sacred texts) to a moderate version of *Heilsgeschichte*, with a mediating view of how biblical texts came into existence. The results of this collision were catastrophic for Ladd.

Ladd received his copy of Perrin's review in May of 1965, when he had been away from Fuller for almost a year. David Wallace, Ladd's former student and the first Fuller graduate to earn a PhD, was in Basel on his own sabbatical and was visiting Ladd with several friends when the review arrived. The impact of that first reading was evident immediately.[102] According to Wallace, Ladd was "stricken right down to the core" and "on the edge of being manic and out of control." He "had a strange look in his eyes, as though he had been mortally wounded," and paced the room with his guests still there, no longer aware of their presence. Wallace recalls that Ladd repeatedly said that "he was an academic failure" and "a scholarly wipeout." Wallace tried to console him by encouraging him to wait for other reviews, but his words "had absolutely no effect on him." When Wallace left Ladd in his Heidelberg apartment that evening, he remembers thinking that his teacher and mentor looked "destroyed."

That same day Ladd wrote to Dan Fuller, ostensibly about curricular matters for the next academic year but also still in some shock from Perrin's review: "I am being forced to rethink my entire program of scholarship . . . [because] my noble ideal of trying to achieve a sympathetic interaction with other circles of theology is a fool's dream." It "is very obvious," Ladd complained, "that my major life work (which this book embodied) is a complete failure."[103] Within just a day or two after his first reading of Perrin's evaluation,

Ladd was already interpreting it as a death blow to his goal of earning a place for evangelical scholarship in the broader academic world. It is no exaggeration to say that this was the turning point for Ladd's life and career; his already fragile emotional makeup was damaged beyond repair as a direct result of this single review. Almost immediately he began to lash out.

Ladd's initial response to Perrin's review was, ironically, to gather support for his views from a better-known scholar. The day he read Perrin's article Ladd invited Heidelberg professor Günther Bornkamm (1905–1990) to his home "for an evening of theological discussion," which was surely Ladd's barely veiled attempt to enlist the German theologian in his defense against Perrin.[104] Ladd pressed his guest on the allegations that he had misrepresented both Bornkamm and Bultmann in *Jesus and the Kingdom* and came away with some assurance that he had not.[105]

Understanding the context of this discussion, however, casts some doubt on the level of Bornkamm's support for Ladd's case. Certainly Ladd's behavior in the immediate aftermath of reading Perrin's review cannot be seen as stable or rational, a fact that would become more apparent in the months and even years ahead. Further, on a minor question related to Ladd's use—in a footnote—of Bornkamm in *Jesus and the Kingdom*, it appears that Bornkamm was merely acquiescing in the face of Ladd's interrogation.[106] Ladd asked whether Bornkamm had written somewhere that eschatology must retain some element of futurity rather than being limited to the present existential encounter with the Christ of faith. Bornkamm, surely under the withering pressure of Ladd's strong feelings, agreed that he did hold that view, "although he could not remember where he had written it."[107] Without attributing an untruthful statement to Bornkamm in that difficult moment, we must consider it a possibility that he overstated his position in order to calm his host. The theological distinction between the existential present and the futurist eschatological positions—while certainly less central to Bornkamm's thought than it was to Ladd's—remained an important part of the ongoing discussion in New Testament circles, and it seems highly unlikely that Bornkamm would forget where he had stated his own view. Still, his support gave Ladd what he needed (or believed he needed) to defend his case against Perrin's attack.

Armed with Bornkamm's support, Ladd then confronted those whom he held responsible for his humiliation. He wrote a long, rambling letter to Balmer Kelley, the editor of *Interpretation*, demanding to know why he had been singled out for attack. It took several drafts, each progressively calmer in tone, before Ladd actually sent the missive.[108] In the final draft he eased into his complaint, again mentioning the reflection article he had sent to *the opinion*, Fuller's student publication. Ladd quoted himself: "Ought it not to be possible to express an Evangelical theology in fresh dynamic terms which will not sound like a reactionary obscurantism? ... As I see it, this is Fuller's great challenge and one of the most important reasons for which God has raised her up."[109] Ladd made the case that he had been a model of charitable scholarly dialogue between evangelicals and liberals and that his stance had made him "persona non grata" in some conservative circles. "It was in this spirit," he argued, "that I wrote *Jesus and the Kingdom*," only to have the reviewer "damn the book, stooping even to the point of misrepresentation, falsification and vicious insinuation." Ladd concluded, again sounding crushed and defeated, that his "idealistic hope of contributing to an understanding interaction between our conservative stance and a more mediating position is a fool's dream." He ended the letter with bitter sarcasm: "Thank you for your review: it has helped me to become more realistic."

The answer from *Interpretation* was gracious and apologetic in its response to Ladd's complaint. Kelley had passed Ladd's letter to James L. Mays, the associate editor for book reviews at the journal, and Mays responded immediately with remarkable insight into Ladd's pain. He apologized at the start, claiming his overwhelming workload as an excuse.[110] He had read the review in draft form and thought even then "that it neared the limits of acceptability," though he did not see it "as completely damaging and unfortunate" as Ladd did. *Jesus and the Kingdom* was sent to Perrin without malice, according to Mays, simply "because he had published a book in the same field quite recently." Certainly attuned to the level of feeling on Ladd's part regarding the review, Mays expressed sincere concern for the conclusions Ladd appeared to have drawn from it. He encouraged Ladd not to "draw any implications from the review except concerning Perrin himself" and expressed his belief "that the majority of the readers will attribute the critical stance of Perrin to his difference from you in method." "As for *Interpretation*," Mays added, "we did not mean to take up an unsympathetic posture toward your work or position. ... You have done us a service by writing, and we shall try to heed the lessons of this experience." At the close of the letter he stated his hope "that in the future we can carry some of your own work in *Interpretation*."

Ladd seized on this last statement and responded with a letter to Balmer Kelley rather than to Mays. He cited the review editor's apology and conciliatory letter, as well as his invitation to submit an article and let Kelley know that he had been working on a rebuttal for two weeks. "I have tried," he wrote, "to write an essay which has merit in and of itself, using my book and Perrin's review only as occasional illustration. ... I trust you will find room to print it."[111] And then perhaps using his aggrieved state to his advantage, he reminded Kelley: "I sent you an essay several years ago; a year later the essay was

returned unpublished. I thereupon sent it to *Expository Times*, which immediately published it." The new article was accepted for publication and appeared in *Interpretation* in January 1966.[112] Kelley had by this time resigned as
editor, and James Mays was appointed to take his place, so it was Mays who
confirmed the acceptance of the essay, calling it "constructive and interesting."[113] Now Ladd had an article awaiting publication in *Interpretation* and also
a cordial relationship with an editor who understood not only what Ladd was
trying to do but also something of the stakes involved in trying to accomplish it.
Ladd's instinctual response was to offer his services as a book reviewer.[114]

A few days later Ladd wrote to his friend Calvin Schoonhoven, then serving
as both the director of Fuller's library and instructor in biblical interpretation.[115] Schoonhoven was in the progressive group at the seminary and was a
controversial figure based on his resistance to militant formulations of the
doctrine of inerrancy. But he shared Ladd's desire for an academically respectable evangelical presence in the academy, and they were working together to bring prominent lecturers to Fuller's Pasadena campus. This effort
to bring nonevangelical scholars to Fuller held enormous significance for
Ladd. In this work he felt he was demonstrating the openness required of a
respectable institution of higher learning, the same openness he craved from
the rest of the academic world. One of the scholars they were recruiting was
John Bright of Union Seminary. Ladd wrote the following to Schoonhoven:

> I can no longer carry out this duty in good faith. My stomach is sour.
> John Bright is an Associate Editor of *Interpretation*, which pub-
> lished the pathological, falsifying, hateful review of my book. In view
> of the fact that this is my magnum opus which is addressed to spe-
> cifically the audience represented by *Interpretation*, and in view
> of the fact that it represents my major effort to accomplish the end
> expressed in my blurb in *the opinion* about expounding an evangelical
> theology in terms which will be understood and meaningful to
> other traditions, this review and all it represents makes it quite clear
> that I have been living in a fool's world.... I'm going back to
> Eerdmans and fundamentalist consumption, and I can no longer in
> good conscience be the faculty agent trying to promote sympa-
> thetic interaction. The other crowd doesn't want it.[116]

Ladd's wounds even made him suspicious of his friends at this point. Perhaps
feeling that he should have had some warning about the content of Perrin's
article, Ladd wrote in the postscript that "It is curious that neither you nor
anyone else has mentioned the review in *Interpretation*." However, he then
returned to the impact he thought the review would have on his own career:

"I fear this represents to me a major turning point in my objectives as a scholar. If this review is accurate, I should be shipped back to a country parish."[117]

Certainly the depth of Ladd's reaction was exacerbated by the fact that he was away from Fuller and his regular community of friends, colleagues, and students. His alcoholism worsened during his time away, as his marriage almost certainly did as well. Depressed and frustrated, Ladd visited a psychiatrist on a nearby U.S. Army base, only to have him recommend that Ladd abandon his Christian faith.[118] The confidence he felt as a successful scholar studying abroad was thoroughly shattered, and now, trapped in Heidelberg, he had to find a way to survive the last four months of his sabbatical. He spent much of his remaining leave time writing (mostly angry) letters and finishing up the manuscript for his next book.

The Ladds left Germany in early September 1965, just after attending the annual meeting of the Society for New Testament Studies in Heidelberg. At the conference Ladd was stunned to find himself seated at the same table as Norman Perrin and was unable to restrain himself from lashing out. He called Perrin a "fundamentalist," and accused him of being "so prejudiced [that] he couldn't see straight."[119] Perrin replied that he had warned *Interpretation* that his review would be strongly negative but that they had told him to write it anyway.[120] To Ladd's satisfaction, an acquaintance told him later that his attack "shook" Perrin, though there is no indication as to whether Perrin's reaction was to the content of Ladd's complaint or his obvious instability.[121] From Heidelberg the Ladds traveled to Oxford, where George delivered a paper at the Third International Congress on New Testament Studies at Christ Church.[122] George and Winnie Ladd left for home immediately after the conference, surely wondering what lay ahead for George's career.

Ladd returned to Fuller in the fall of 1965 a broken man, drinking heavily, bitter over his treatment by Perrin, humiliated—at least in his eyes—in front of his friends and colleagues, and suddenly unsure of the direction his career should take.[123] In a box of mail Ladd found a copy of the student publication that had printed his letter from Heidelberg. Written before the review by Perrin was published, his letter expressed the hope that evangelical theology might some day be accepted in the broader academy, even if not everyone welcomed its presence. When he wrote the letter he still believed that *Jesus and the Kingdom* could be that "Evangelical theology in fresh dynamic terms," but in the end he realized that his magnum opus had been dismissed as "reactionary obscurantism." The very reproach that Ladd called his fellow scholars and students to weather in his "Sabbatical Reflections" turned out to be more than he himself could bear. Confronted by just one example of hundreds of his own writings about his dream of making an important impact on biblical scholarship, Ladd wrote "No!" on the margin of his copy of the article in a large, unsteady hand. Across the top of the page he added: "This is a fool's dream!"[124]

The dream was not as foolish as Ladd imagined, but neither was it as successful as he had hoped. While he was obsessively focused on Perrin's evaluation, other notices for *Jesus and the Kingdom* were more positive or at least not nearly so negative. The *Pittsburgh Perspective*, the academic journal of Pittsburgh Theological Seminary (Presbyterian), affirmed Ladd's erudition in the varied world of contemporary biblical studies and said that he "[developed] his thesis in exemplary fashion."[125] Further, Ladd was to be complimented for employing an irenic voice for conservative scholarship in the wider academic world, especially since "there has sometimes been more constructive conversation between Protestants and Roman Catholics than between the two Protestant camps." "The academic stature of writers like Ladd," the review concluded, "should help to breach the paper curtain that has kept us from working together in studying the one truth of God." The *Westminster Theological Journal* cheered Ladd's "mastery of the field," even as it pointed out the author's "almost overwhelming interest in the theories of well-known liberal critics."[126] Still, the review concluded that "this is one of the most comprehensive modern treatments by an American evangelical of Jesus and the Kingdom." The *Reformed Theological Review* similarly declared Ladd's book to be "a work of considerable scholarship, and to be valued most highly among books on the Kingdom of God."[127] *Encounter*, the journal of the Christian Theological Seminary (Disciples of Christ), was less sanguine, saying that "in many respects this is a good book. It may provide something of a half-way house for those students who have an a priori [*sic*] commitment to conservative conclusions, but wish to have them expressed in a scholarly idiom."[128] However, for the most part the response was positive from journals across the English-speaking world, at least those that chose to review the book.[129]

The generally favorable response to *Jesus and the Kingdom* continued to have little effect on Ladd's emotional state, however; he spent the 1965–1966 academic year thoroughly discouraged. Ladd was angry at Perrin and bitter toward any publication that either ignored or was critical of his book and grew increasingly frustrated with his publisher. Ladd had written to Melvin Arnold at Harper and Row within days of receiving Perrin's article, warning them that the "psychopathic review" would surely "kill the sales of the book" and asking to be released form his publishing contract, but he never sent the letter.[130]

Later that summer Ladd sent a different letter to Arnold, reiterating his reaction to Perrin's critique and saying that it was "not a review, but an execution."[131] Ladd again questioned his contractual relationship with Harper's by saying "I am not sure that I was wise in publishing with you, thinking that you would help open the door to attain my objective of theological dialogue; I am concluding that such a dialogue is impossible, and I ought to stick with Eerdmans." Ultimately—and catastrophically for Ladd—he was beginning to believe that Fuller Seminary was viewed as an "outside" school and an impossible place from which to earn a fair hearing.[132] For the remainder of the 1965–1966 academic year Ladd continued to complain to anyone who would listen about the article in *Interpretation*, even directly confronting reviewers and editors who had been less than complimentary.[133] But mostly Ladd wrote to scholars all across the theological spectrum, telling of his unfair treatment at the hands of Norman Perrin.[134]

By the end of the academic year, Ladd's reaction to Perrin's review was poisoning even his longest-held friendships. Merrill Tenney, who had been Ladd's teacher at Gordon in the 1930s, fellow student at Harvard, and scholarly colleague in the years since, asked Ladd in 1966 to draw a sharper distinction between his theological position and that of liberal critics.[135] This was the sort of discussion the two men had carried on for more than a quarter century, but in this case Ladd clearly overreacted. He called Tenney's request "perplexing and disturbing" and said that it had sent him "into an emotional tail-spin" that left him "completely frustrated."[136] Tenney, concerned at Ladd's reaction, explained that he had not been making "drastic or destructive comments" but rather asking Ladd to be clear about his position.[137] Tenney's only intent, he wrote to Ladd, was to help his friend avoid any "misunderstanding" from appearing "unnecessarily latitudinarian." Tenney then shifted the conversation to personal matters in an attempt to calm Ladd's emotional state, but Ladd would not be pacified. He wrote to Tenney that he was finished with trying to be so careful with either side's understanding of his work because "the reception of my Harper's book by the "broad stream" has shown me what a fool I have been. I have had to accept failure in my life-long ambition and goal as a scholar."[138]

The emotional fallout from Perrin's review threatened another friendship as well. To his longtime friend Glenn Barker, still on the faculty at Gordon College, Ladd lamented: "Ten years of work has ended in bitter failure. . . . It's obvious I don't have what it takes. . . . I've had it."[139] Barker was concerned, as Tenney had been, by Ladd's tone and told him so. He shared the Gordon students' enthusiastic reactions to Ladd's book and advised him: "In no way must you slow down or give up. Your work and your pen are far too significant for any such thing as that."[140] Barker's assessment of Ladd's impact, though intended to be supportive, represented precisely the opposite of Ladd's own dreams and goals. Barker wrote the following: "I think it is unrealistic to expect the liberal world to accept any writing of ours whatsoever. After all, we would hardly do differently ourselves. What is important is that you have now made available to conservative students, materials which will strengthen their faith and assure them of the basic integrity of our kind of thinking long after both of us have passed from this stage."[141] In his attempt to be encouraging, Barker succeeded only in compounding Ladd's sense of failure. Ladd had spent the better part of two decades hoping that the liberal scholars would accept his writing while doing his best to be accepting of theirs. Further, given that Ladd dismissed his own publishing for the evangelical world as a "by-product" of his real scholarship, hearing that his true achievement was creating advanced devotional works for conservative students was truly galling to him. He wrote back to Barker explaining his feelings, but the damage was done. There is no surviving direct correspondence between them after 1966.[142]

Though few saw Perrin's review as the catastrophic event Ladd believed it to be, Ladd resolved to abandon his dream of engaging the broader academy and write for the evangelical audience alone. In the summer of 1966 he wrote to Vernon Grounds, president of Denver Seminary, a respected leader in the Evangelical Theological Society and a veteran of the Conservative Baptist wars of the 1950s: "I am not a fighter; I am not interested in going into any situation where I have to fight.... The reception of my Harper's book has been a traumatic experience.... I am all through trying to communicate to the 'other crowd.'... I've crawled into my shell and am doing what I have to do."[143] This change in strategy meant that Ladd had to rethink not only his goals as a scholar but his publishing contract as well, yet another humiliation he had to endure. He wrote to Robert Guelich, a favorite student of Ladd's at Fuller, and shared his grief over the current condition of his career: "I only want to get a hearing for what I consider a sound NT theology. I had another reminder this morning of how difficult that is for an 'outsider.' I picked up in the bookstore *A Bibliography of NT Bibliographies* by J.C. Hurd . . . a very convenient tool.... As expected, Ladd was not there.... If you don't belong to the 'club,' you just don't rate."[144] Here the image recurs of Ladd and other evangelicals as "outsiders" who are somehow not welcome at "the club." Ladd concluded that his only hope for seeing his work in print was to return to the evangelical fold and decided that he was "pulling out of Harper's, and crawling back to Eerdmans."[145]

The satisfaction and joy Ladd had felt when he wrote to Harold Ockenga in 1963 was now completely shattered. Ladd would no longer pursue the level of dialogue he had dreamed of—and thought he had accomplished—just three years earlier. His stature as a scholar was now limited, at least in his eyes, to the conservative evangelical world, and the confidence he had felt on the journey to Heidelberg was gone. Ladd's "already but not yet" understanding of the kingdom seemed at once to have become, in reference to his career, "not now and not ever," and he was crushed. Rather than enjoying his place in the broader discussion of biblical scholarship and theology, Ladd found himself shut out of that world, barely tolerated by those to whom he desperately wanted to be considered as an equal. By this time he was also significantly estranged from his family; he had gambled those relationships on his hope of earning his place at the table with the giants of theological scholarship. Extensive work had gone into his quest for acceptance, and now it seemed as if it had been for nothing. At the end of the 1965–1966 academic year Ladd thought his life and career were over. He was fifty-five years old.

6

Surrendering the Quest
(1966–1982)

George Ladd staggered through the remainder of the 1960s and
1970s, convinced that he had been either deluded or victimized or
more likely both. In the winter of 1966 he summed up his condition
in a lament to an old friend:

> I have bet my professional career on the proposition that it
> was now possible for an intelligent conservative theology
> to gain a respectful hearing, IF NOT AGREEMENT, from
> the "other crowd." I have put all my eggs in one basket. . . . It
> is obvious to me that sectarianism and critical orthodoxy
> pervades [sic] American scholarship; I am driven to this
> conclusion against my will. From here on I am writing for
> my "own crowd," and have had to talk myself into the atti-
> tude that I don't give a tinker's damn what anybody thinks or
> says about my writings.[1]

Whether or not Ladd ever actually talked himself into no longer caring
what people thought of his work can remain an open question. His
reaction to the state of his career and the resulting collapse are
much plainer. The last fifteen years of Ladd's life, while giving the
appearance of being productive, saw the man tumble through a process of emotional, physical, and spiritual disintegration. The gambles
he had made during the course of his academic career had failed to
pay off, and he found himself on the one hand a towering figure in
the world of evangelical scholarship, while on the other a failure at

reaching the only real goal he had ever set for himself. He would not set the world of mainstream biblical scholarship on fire. For all of Ladd's intents and purposes his quest was over; he was left with a far smaller and more parochial audience than he had sought at the start of his career. As a result, this final chapter in Ladd's life was marked by an overwhelming sense of surrender—of his quest for acceptance, of his familial relationships, and even of his longest-held friendships—to the darkest impulses of his character.

Some of this darkness centered around Ladd's family life. Ladd was never much of a father to his children. He had long been ashamed of Larry, who had physical and emotional disabilities, and as a result paid little attention to him.[2] Norma, the elder of the two children, resented her father's treatment of her brother and, though married and living away from the family, continued to respond with barely concealed hostility. Both children suffered from Ladd's neglect, first from his obsessive approach to academic work and later from his alcoholism and emotional instability. Winnie was much closer to Norma and Larry and over the years grew highly critical of Ladd's inability to love his children. George in turn blamed the children for their lack of affection for him. Much of this tension played out regularly in the Ladds' home.

The union between George and Winnie had been an increasingly unhappy one, and in these final years it functioned as a marriage in name only. Why did this happen? Ladd often characterized his wife as being cold and joyless and claimed that she was unable or unwilling to participate in activities he enjoyed. Certainly George's stunted sense of self-worth made it difficult for him to form deep connections, and in the aftermath of Perrin's review Ladd perceived even his best qualities as inadequate. Winnie, on the other hand, had been searching for a warm father figure all along, something George could not possibly embody. The couple, one family member recalled, "never seemed to understand each other's needs."[3] By the 1970s the situation had deteriorated to the point that Ladd was making plans to divorce his wife, a serious matter in the world of conservative evangelicalism.[4] And through it all, he was drinking heavily.

Many who knew Ladd during this period have described his alcoholism as "the elephant in the room."[5] While there had been persistent rumors of George's alcohol consumption since the 1950s, the problem became acute in the post-Perrin years.[6] The rules—stated or not—governing the American evangelical subculture at midcentury often made it difficult to distinguish between social drinking and problem drinking. This was, after all, the community that had led the various temperance movements of the nineteenth and early twentieth centuries and continued to ostracize "sipping saints." The consumption of alcohol in any form was a clear boundary issue among evangelicals during Ladd's lifetime, and so any drinking was considered to be a "problem." That Ladd drank at all during his adult life has been characterized as a sign of alcoholism, but by modern standards his addiction became a serious impediment only after 1965. The seriousness of the problem would eventually threaten what was left of Ladd's career.

The overwhelming complex of pressures in Ladd's life led him to look for means of escape, even if only for brief periods. Certainly his abuse of alcohol functioned in this way, but Ladd also found a way to retreat into the simple world of cowboy life he had admired since his childhood. He still read the Zane Grey novels that had captivated him in his youth and continued to idealize the characters in those stories who lived manly, uncomplicated lives in the outdoors.[7] Perhaps in an attempt to experience that life for himself, Ladd slipped away for two weeks each year to a "dude ranch," a place where modern urban men could indulge themselves in a contrived version of Western life, and spent his time riding horses, helping with the cattle, and having meals by campfire.[8] Away from Fuller, away from the Perrins and Walvoords who complicated his life, and away from Winnie, Ladd looked forward to his cowboy days each year and enjoyed them immensely.

It was in these post-Perrin years that Ladd made the conscious decision to abandon his quest to make an impact on the broader world of theological scholarship. The various aspects of that mission—writing critical works for a nonevangelical audience, publishing with houses beyond the narrow conservative world, and participating in dialogues with moderate and liberal scholars—were left behind in favor of a more limited focus on what he called the "enlightened evangelicals."[9] He began talking about staying within "[his] own little circle so far as publication is concerned."[10] To that end he antagonized Harper and Row until the company released him from his contract, even though he owed them two more books. Ladd blamed the poor sales of *Jesus and the Kingdom* on Harper, criticizing its marketing support, its awareness of theological trends, and even its insistence on changing Ladd's original title.[11] Ladd begged to sever the relationship, and in the end Harper was only too happy to comply.[12]

Ladd was formally released from his obligation to Harper and given a check for copies of the book sold in Britain. As if to make sure he received every penny due him from Harper, he calculated the amount of his payment against the current rate of exchange on his copy of the release.[13] After 1967 there was a growing nastiness to Ladd's dealings with Harper and Row. Ladd refused to read a book the company was considering for publication: "It is very obvious to me that any opinion of mine about any of your publications would be quite irrelevant to your constituency."[14] Ladd dashed any hopes of returning to Harper in a bitter letter that he ended as follows: "Eerdmans sent me a contract

without even reading the manuscript. From here out, Eerdmans is my publisher."[15] However, the relationship with Eerdmans had to be reestablished
even as the one with Harper and Row was ended.

Luckily for Ladd, Eerdmans was happy to have him back. In reality, Ladd
had never left his original publisher—he still owed the evangelical company a
book from a previous contract and was negotiating to submit several other titles
even while he was trying to escape from Harper. This was far from "crawling
back to Eerdmans," as Ladd had characterized it to a friend, but it was still
enormously difficult for him because it represented failure in a key aspect of his
quest and a return to a largely conservative audience.[16] Ladd admitted as much
in a letter to Otto Piper: "I have been very ambitious to write theology from an
evangelical stance so well that nobody could ignore my writings. However, this
has proved to be a fool's dream; and from here on I am simply doing what I have
to do."[17] Ladd's mission was over and he knew it, so he settled into his narrower
role as spokesman for—and within—conservative biblical scholarship.

At the same time, Fuller Seminary was coming into its own as a broadly
innovative academic institution. By the mid-1970s Fuller had evolved into a
"megaseminary," with a strong faculty, a large and diverse student body
numbering more than one thousand, and a stable base of financial support; it
was hardly recognizable in comparison to its early years.[18] The original theological faculty was joined in 1965 by two new schools—psychology and world
mission. The missionary enterprise had been a priority for Charles Fuller—
and his students—in the original plan for his seminary. In several of the
earliest classes at Fuller, nearly 40 percent of the graduates had gone into
Christian service outside the United States.[19]

Establishing a well-funded school in support of missions work, complete
with a stellar faculty, was a logical move for Fuller and clearly reflected what
had become the ethos of the seminary. Support for the new School of World
Mission on the part of the existing faculty was assumed, and apart from some
early concerns about its social science orientation, the school was welcomed
into the Fuller community. A school to train Christian psychologists was a
much harder sell, however. Many in the conservative evangelical world perceived psychology to be a secular, naturalistic, and anti-Christian response to
issues that were, in their minds, spiritual in nature.[20] The preliminary plans
for a psychology program were approved at the same meeting that came to be
known as Black Saturday, which should have provided some warning for the
challenges related to folding the new school into Fuller's conservative theological landscape.[21] Still, with key administrators and the most influential
trustees giving their full support, the Graduate School of Psychology opened in
the autumn of 1965.

Ladd played different roles in the creation of the two schools. He was strongly in favor of the School of World Mission, as were most of his faculty colleagues. Ladd's own eschatological beliefs, as we have seen, centered on a literal understanding of Matthew 24:14, which states that Christ's return will come only after the gospel is preached in all nations. The missionary enterprise, therefore, played a crucial role in the culmination of history in the Christian perspective and deserved the support of all who longed for the completion of God's plan. Ladd remained a strong advocate of the missionary enterprise throughout his pastoral and academic career, and he regularly communicated this priority in his classroom teaching. One former student remembered that Ladd "counseled us that we must make our peace with God about missions before we consider an academic teaching ministry."[22] Ladd himself could hardly mention the topic of world evangelization without weeping, often during his classes and seminary chapel sermons.[23] The founding of the School of World Mission at Fuller was a welcome development for Ladd, and he was happy to support it.

Ladd's involvement in the establishment of Fuller's Graduate School of Psychology was more complicated. His initial concerns were practical ones and should be considered in light of his pursuit of academic credibility for both himself and Fuller Seminary. From the beginning, the new school planned to offer the PhD in clinical psychology.[24] The problem was that the theological faculty had not yet begun to offer the same degree. As a result, the administration and some faculty were making hasty moves to design a program for doctoral studies in theology, a development that otherwise might not have occurred for decades. In 1962, during the earliest stages of this planning process, Ladd had expressed to Harold Ockenga a series of objections to offering a theological PhD degree.

First, he believed the doctorate should be offered only by faculties that had received "recognition for first-class scholarship." Fuller's faculty, Ladd argued, had "not yet attained this goal." Ladd himself was still finishing *Jesus and the Kingdom*, and only Edward Carnell and Geoffrey Bromiley had published important works for wider audiences. Second, and in keeping with Ladd's larger remedial goal of seeing evangelical scholars competing for positions in the great universities, he worried that too many of the doctoral candidates would be Fuller's own theological graduates. The seminary should be sending its best and brightest "to Princeton or Harvard or Brandeis or Edinburgh or Basel," where their evangelical theological position could "learn to stand on its own two feet in a hostile environment." Fuller Seminary, Ladd worried, "would do a disservice . . . to the cause of evangelical scholarship by giving the doctoral degree." Third, he was concerned that Fuller might suffer from intellectual "inbreeding." Holding Dallas Theological Seminary up as an example, he thought that the new doctoral offering might cause the seminary to lose the effectiveness of cultural breadth that comes from "interaction in other theological climates."[25] Fourth, he advised the theological faculty to abandon its worry of being overshadowed by the psychology doctorate. The psychology program was highly specialized, Ladd argued, and would probably never eclipse the output of the School of Theology.[26] Finally, Ladd expressed the practical concern that there were not enough members of the theological faculty to meet the demands of a graduate studies program if it were simply added to the present emphasis on divinity training. Ockenga gently dismissed Ladd's concerns, and by December of 1962 the board of trustees had approved the plans.[27]

Ladd also had theological and practical ministry issues. While not a part of the national steering committee that laid out the plans for the school, he was asked by the panel to reflect on both the content of psychological theory and also its compatibility with the seminary's mission and purpose.[28] Ladd's critique can be divided into four main areas. First, he was concerned, typically, with the quality of biblical exegesis employed by the psychological faculty.[29] Second, he questioned the relationship between sanctification (in the theological sense) and psychological healing. In those early days a strain of Christian psychology argued that, if all true healing comes from the hand of God, then Christian therapy can logically be seen as a means of grace. Ladd asked (certainly with his own personal pain in mind), "In what dimension of man does the Holy Spirit effect his sanctifying work? Or to put the matter in different words: Can one be spiritually healthy and still be mentally sick? . . . Are all mental problems spiritual problems?"[30] He was concerned that what he was hearing from the psychology faculty muddied the distinction between emotional health and spiritual salvation, and he called for a more detailed—one presumes a more exegetically sound—understanding of the difference. Third, from a pastoral standpoint, Ladd struggled with the lack of accessibility of psychological treatment to those who could not afford the cost.[31] This issue presented the Christian with a serious dilemma: Can a methodology for restoring emotional and spiritual health—especially one that purports to play some role in the process of sanctification—be denied to willing people if they are not able to pay for it? The psychological profession, conceived as analogous more to medicine than pastoral ministry, by its very structure excluded people from its benefits. In practical terms and in the light of his own lifelong fear of financial difficulty, this was one of Ladd's strongest objections. It was never fully resolved.

Ladd's most revealing objection came even as his own involvement with the school was deepening. In early 1967 Ladd co-taught one of the first integration seminars of the psychology program. His teaching partner was Paul Fairweather (1919–1997), a founding member of the School of Psychology. Fairweather, a former fighter pilot who had earned a PhD in psychology at the University of Southern California, had written extensively on the father's role in a child's development and understanding of God:

> Every child must be related to his father and to the ultimate father with meaning and worth so as to be able to accept his right to act or think or feel non-defensively. To act out of accord with a valid image of authority is impossible without great injury and damage to the psyche. Thus all therapy must involve the therapy of the image of grief and its related value priorities. . . . When the individual cannot imagine grieving meaningfully with others or by himself, he erects a psychic strategy to defend against the experience of grief. Such a strategy is clinically designated as symptomatic and a complex of such symptomatic behaviors is referred to as pathology.[32]

This linking of a human father to a person's emotional health and doctrine of God clearly struck a nerve in Ladd. His own experience with his father had been brief and unsatisfying, and he knew that his wife's relationship with her father had been severely troubled. Further, Ladd must have known at some level that he had been a poor father himself, and to admit that his failings might have damaged the image of God before his own children would have been too bitter a pill to swallow. He instead separated faith struggles from emotional problems and rejected Fairweather's central point. But in the process of making his argument he reveals a high level of awareness of the emotional carnage represented in his own family:

> One of the basic inescapable built-in human needs is security in interpersonal relationships. A child [George] grows up in a home where there is no love. He never knows the security of parental affection. He becomes a lonely introvert who never can relate to people. A girl [Winnie] is reared in a family situation where she can only fear or hate her father. She unconsciously transfers this fear and hatred to all men. If she marries, she is likely to be sexually frigid, for she does not know how to give herself to a man emotionally, and therefore physically. . . . Other emotional problems result from an interaction of physical and interpersonal causes. A baby [Larry] is born with undescended testicles; this impairs his physical development which, in turn, results in a terrible inferiority complex because the individual cannot compete successfully with other children. . . . I myself was a

skinny kid six feet tall, weighing 130 pounds, with a scrawny neck
and receding chin, who bore the nick-name "freak" and "the chinless
wonder." This has caused me severe emotional suffering and given
me a life-long battle to achieve self-acceptance.[33]

This dramatic act of self-disclosure on Ladd's part reveals his inner conflict
over the condition—even those aspects he himself caused—of his wife and
children. Ladd eventually resigned from the seminar after a public disagreement with Fairweather.[34]

That Ladd's involvement did not last can be attributed as much to his
personal struggles as to any objection to the discipline as a whole. Psychological interpretations exposed him to the pain he had experienced—and
inflicted—in his own life. He responded by rigidly defending a narrow view
of biblical exegesis and theology. Still, he remained in his own course of
psychotherapy for years after leaving the integration seminars and later admitted that his therapy had been more beneficial to him in dealing with his
personal struggles than his faith had been.[35] That statement runs parallel to
Ladd's earlier assertions that he had learned more from "liberals" than from
his own evangelical partners and that he thrived best intellectually when in the
company of those with whom he disagreed. Much of Ladd's life had been
spent longing for, reaching for, and trying to experience the benefits of ideas
and groups where he either was not welcome or dared not go. Theological
liberalism and, in this case, the healing impact of psychotherapy, considered
forbidden fruit to most evangelicals, are just two examples of this behavior.

There were redemptive moments during this time, however. One relationship from the pre-Perrin days proved to be especially satisfying in the late
1960s. Robert Guelich (1940–1991) came to Fuller in 1962 and immediately
established himself as one of the seminary's most gifted students. The son of a
Southern Baptist minister in a coal-mining town in West Virginia, Guelich had
gotten an undergraduate degree at Wheaton College in preparation for a career
as a missionary, but a heart condition had made him ineligible for service.
A brilliant linguist, Guelich earned a master's degree in classics at the University of Illinois before coming to Fuller for theological training. He was an
extraordinarily hard worker, carrying twenty credit hours per semester (the
normal rigorous schedule called for twelve to sixteen), all the while earning his
way by teaching elementary Greek and—as Ladd had during his Gordon days—
selling eggs in a local dairy.

Guelich was also exceptionally personable, with an outgoing personality
and an appealing sense of humor. Ladd and Guelich quickly became close
friends and formed a strong bond as mentor and protégé. They played handball

each week and studied the intricacies of biblical and classical Greek, and Guelich regularly joined the Ladds for evening meals. Ladd spoke of being "unusually drawn to the man," perhaps seeing in him some of the "Zane Grey" qualities he so desired for himself, and admitted that he had "never before been so completely taken by the all round abilities and personality and promise of any student here at Fuller."[36] However, even this relationship managed to trigger some of the darker aspects of Ladd's character. He clearly favored his prize student, with his charm and athleticism, over his own son. Many from that era—including Guelich himself—remember with some discomfort the role of surrogate child that Robert came to play.[37] When the time came for Guelich to choose a doctoral program, Ladd was deeply involved in the process. Further, when Guelich was accepted for advanced study under Leonhard Goppelt (1911–1973) at the University of Hamburg, Ladd secretly approached Fuller trustee C. Davis Weyerhauser for financial support. Weyerhauser was convinced by Ladd's recommendation and provided a grant that covered all of Guelich's expenses in Hamburg.[38]

Guelich came to play an important role in Ladd's dream of establishing a presence for conservative scholarship in the larger academic world. Ladd hoped that Guelich "would join the growing circle of evangelical scholars who are dedicating themselves to the attainment of excellence in orthodox theology."[39] Goppelt was a respected German theologian with sympathy for evangelicalism, and Ladd knew that it was a small victory to place a student under his tutelage. Ladd wrote the following:

> As I look upon our task, men like myself are simply making a beginning of something which is rather new in the evangelical church; and the vision which I can impart to men like Guelich will accomplish far more in the coming generation than we can accomplish today. I only wish I had had the opportunity for the kind of training that Guelich can now get. I am confident that he will be able to achieve far more than I have done or will do.[40]

In Guelich Ladd saw a true protégé, one who would carry on his dream of seeing evangelical theology earn a greater measure of acceptance in the academy. Weyerhauser plainly agreed. He quoted Robert McAfee Brown (1920–2001), a religion professor at Stanford University, who had remarked that, when Bultmann and Barth passed from the scene, there would be no one to replace them in influence. Perhaps young Guelich, Weyerhauser dreamed, would "make an impact of worldwide dimensions with a scholarly evangelical emphasis."[41] Note the similarity between Weyerhauser's dream and the letter that inspired Ladd's quest in the first place.[42] This was certainly Ladd's dream as well.

When Ladd returned from Heidelberg, humiliated and thoroughly de-railed in his attempt to make a splash with *Jesus and the Kingdom,* he resumed his relationship with Guelich. It was at this point that Guelich's role as both scholarly protégé and surrogate son took on even greater significance. Ladd lamented to Guelich, as he did with nearly everyone, that his career as he knew it was over. "[T]he most significant work I will ever do," Ladd complained to his younger friend, "is a failure."[43] He may have perceived himself as being de-feated in his mission, but Guelich was just getting started, and for a time the professor poured his energies into encouraging his heir apparent.[44]

The father figure in Ladd emerged at this point. After complaining a bit about the demands placed on him at Hamburg, Guelich thanked Ladd "for the use of [his] shoulder."[45] Ladd responded in an uncharacteristically tender way, saying that his shoulder was "very absorbent."[46] Ladd, while being emotionally generous, was expecting great things from his prized former student, and Guelich, in turn, continued to do well in his doctoral work. He excelled in his program of study with Goppelt and was offered an assistantship in the the-ology department, a rare honor for an American student.[47] Later Guelich was asked to translate one of his doctoral advisor's important theological works into English, a task Guelich performed with distinction.[48] In 1967 Guelich com-pleted his DTheol and returned to the United States to accept a position on the faculty of Bethel College in Minnesota, a Baptist liberal arts institution. Co-incidentally, Guelich's initial hiring—and later his tenure—were delayed be-cause of concerns about his occasional consumption of alcohol while studying in Germany.[49] Ladd never commented on the issue.

Ladd also enjoyed a measure of redemption from an unlikely source, the editors of *Interpretation,* where Perrin's devastating review had appeared. For the journal's twenty-fifth anniversary, a special issue was planned, along with an event to celebrate its quarter century of publication. The commemorative issue was to focus on "the future of Bible and theology" and would comprise articles representing the various areas of the theological enterprise written by important scholars in each field.[50] Ladd was invited to write on New Testament theology, to participate in panel discussions with other theologians, and to present his paper at the 1971 gathering in Virginia.[51]

In the post-Perrin era Ladd had tended to avoid involving himself in general discussions such as this. He had declined an invitation the year before to join a colloquium on the authority of the Bible for the Faith and Order division of the World Council of Churches.[52] In his response to the invitation by prominent New Testament scholar James M. Robinson, Ladd stated his belief "that there can be no real dialogue between liberals and conservatives."

"I have been driven," he complained, "to the place where I have to do my own work in my own way by myself, and let those who are interested listen to what I have to say."[53] Nevertheless, the invitation from *Interpretation* was too significant to let pass. It was an enormous honor, placing Ladd in the same company as luminaries such as James Barr, James M. Robinson, and Dietrich Ristchl. Still, even in this instance, Ladd expressed his fear of being attacked to James Mays, the editor of *Interpretation*. Ladd did not want to spend his time in Virginia defending himself from people who did not "respect [him] as a person."[54] Ladd listed Norman Perrin and John Warwick Montgomery by name as examples in the liberal and conservative camps of those who were "fundamentalistic in mentality," the likes of whom he wished to avoid. In the end, however, Ladd eagerly accepted and devoted two full months to the writing of his essay.[55] To be recognized as representative of an entire category of biblical scholarship was precisely the sort of esteem he craved, and he enjoyed it immensely.

Ladd's essay, titled "The Search for Perspective," is a statement of his mature historical-theological position, which he explicitly classifies as belonging to the *Heilsgeschichte* tradition. Early on Ladd extends an olive branch to those who will not share his view and states again that "theology thrives on debate between competing viewpoints. . . . I have learned most by reading those with whom I disagree."[56] This statement requires some close parsing. Ladd clearly detested debate, as evidenced by his rejection of James Robinson's invitation and his concerns about the *Interpretation* event. However, he is at the same time genuine in his assertion that he has learned much from those outside the evangelical world. From his time under Cadbury until the end of his life, Ladd had been able to take the best of critical scholarship for use in his own theological work.

In this essay Ladd seeks to identify the central question dividing the biblical theological enterprise. Is the Bible a historical record of God's work in history on behalf of his creation, or is it a mythological explanation of the human condition, with a call to find redemption in the cosmic Christ? This had been the essential line of demarcation between the *Heilsgeschichte* and Bultmannian schools for a generation. Ladd firmly comes down on the side of salvation history and reiterates his long-held position that modern historical thought is not equipped to describe the acts of a transcendent God because those acts did not follow the rules of causality and analogy inherited from the Enlightenment. The resurrection and other miraculous signs occurred, Ladd argues, in history, but they are not historical events in the technical sense. They simply do not fit the required categories of scientific history. "[T]he historical-critical method," Ladd states, "places severe limitations upon its methodology before it engages in the quest for Jesus. It has decided in advance the kind of Jesus it must find—or at least the kind of Jesus it may not find."[57]

Ladd proposes instead the "historical-theological" method he had described in *New Testament and Criticism*.[58] Within this methodology the Bible becomes "the record of God's revelatory and saving acts in history, culminating in Jesus of Nazareth; and it is also the prophetic interpretation of these redemptive acts."[59] This is not to negate the existential encounter with God but rather to establish that encounter in the events of history. It is, then, "the Word of God which speaks to me and brings me face to face with the God who was revealed in the person, words, deeds, death, and resurrection of Jesus of Nazareth." This existential language was not new to evangelicalism; conservative piety had long been concerned with "what Jesus means to me" and encountering Jesus "right where I am."[60] But the linkage between the language of personal encounter and a more critical understanding of the biblical text was the essence of Ladd's truly novel mediating position.

Ladd went even further in articulating his theological stance. In "The Search for Perspective" he explicitly joins his academic position to his Christian faith. True to his own evangelical—and evangelistic—orientation, Ladd used this essay to communicate a sort of personal testimony reminiscent of his Baptist upbringing. The experience of Christ, Ladd states,

> is more than authenticity, although it includes all that authenticity means. It means freedom from the past, freedom from the guilt of my sins, freedom from boasting in my own self-righteousness. . . . It means that in the future I shall meet God, for I have already met him in Christ. By faith I have been caught up in Heilsgeschichte. . . . I can only bear witness at this point to what Heilsgeschichte means to me. My sense of God's love and acceptance is grounded not only in the resurrected Christ but also in the Jesus of history. . . . I have only one sure basis for certainty that God is a God of love. I have seen too much of evil in both personal experience and world history to try to rest any assurance of God's love there. But in Jesus of Nazareth I see God identifying himself in love with my humanity, even to the point of sharing my human tragedy.[61]

This is Ladd's best and most effective attempt at integrating the various aspects of his identity. He is unabashedly erudite and faithful, scholarly and evangelistic, but he is also starkly personal. That he was able to appear this way in the pages of *Interpretation* was surely some measure of professional redemption.

He happily reported to a friend that his contribution to the conference was "warmly received."[62]

Much of this good news, however, was eclipsed by persistent issues related to Ladd's abuse of alcohol. The topic of Ladd's alcoholism was rarely discussed, largely because it represented one of the major behavioral taboos in conservative evangelical culture. Also, as Ladd's stature in the evangelical world advanced, it must have been exceedingly difficult to initiate a confrontation on the matter, and, as a result, the drinking continued unabated until it was impossible to ignore. Ladd's alcoholism took over much of his life in the years after the perceived failure of *Jesus and the Kingdom*, a fact that was anything but a well-kept secret. By the early 1970s it was common knowledge that Ladd was regularly slipping away from Fuller's campus at midday to drink at a local bar.[63] Ladd was so inebriated at the funeral of Jaymes Morgan, a Fuller faculty member and close friend, that he had to be helped to his seat.[64]

Ladd's drinking eroded his professional stature. In 1969 he was invited to lecture at Bethel Seminary, the sister school to Bethel College, where Ladd had delivered lectures in 1956. Two former students, Old Testament scholar Ronald Youngblood (1930–) and Robert Guelich, arranged an invitation for their former professor and were looking forward to his presentation. But Ladd's public drinking alarmed the seminary, and the invitation was rescinded. Bethel Seminary at the time enforced a strict abstinence policy, not uncommon for evangelical institutions. Apparently a member of the administration at Bethel had seen Ladd consume several drinks on an airline flight and raised objections to his participation in a seminary program.[65] The task of informing Ladd of the decision fell to Guelich, but he could not bring himself to make the call.[66] Ladd wrote to Youngblood and inquiring about the status of his invitation, and it was Youngblood who explained the seminary's decision. Ladd's reaction to this incident was one of resignation. He wrote that he, too, "used to be in bondage to a rigid legalism" but now had "learned what it means to be a human being." He also stated that "If a glass of scotch renders one unworthy [to be] a member of the gospel, then so be it" but claimed that he harbored "no malice or ill will of any sort."[67] There was no further correspondence between the two.

Ladd's local standing suffered as well. Beginning in 1962 Ladd taught the Chapel Bible Class at Glendale Presbyterian Church near Fuller's campus, a position he had inherited from colleague—and fellow Baptist—Paul King Jewett. The constituency of Fuller Seminary, certainly in Southern California, transcended denominational boundaries and served the conservative believers across a wide range of traditions, so it was not unusual for faculty members to participate in ministries beyond their own affiliations. By all accounts the experience at Glendale Presbyterian Church had been an important and beneficial ministry for Ladd—one member of the class called him "the best Bible teacher I've had."[68] However, in 1970 there were rumors and complaints of Ladd's drinking (some were sent directly to President David Hubbard), and Fuller's administration was compelled to act. Ladd was called before an official review with Hubbard and Daniel Fuller, then the dean of the School of Theology.[69]

Hubbard informed Ladd that Glendale Presbyterian Church had requested that Ladd resign from his post as teacher of the Chapel Bible Class due to his "excessive drinking." Ladd wanted to confront those who had complained, but Hubbard advised him that a quiet resignation was better for the church, the seminary community and constituency, and Ladd himself. At that point the conversation took a bizarre turn, when Ladd abruptly asked whether he could divorce his wife without losing his position on the faculty. Hubbard informed Ladd that a divorce under these circumstances would be grounds for dismissal, and they argued the point for some time. A more compliant Ladd then asked whether Hubbard would help him find a job if he was compelled to leave, and Hubbard promised to do so. In the interim, it was suggested that Ladd be placed on sabbatical immediately and that he focus his work with his psychotherapist on his drinking problem. Later it was decided to make the sabbatical compulsory and to suggest Ladd's participation in group therapy with Adrin Sylling, a member of the School of Psychology faculty.[70]

In June 1970 Ladd resigned from his church position and was placed on administrative leave at Fuller from 1 September 1970 until 31 December 1971. The added quarter was "compensation for the inconvenience caused by the compulsory nature of the sabbatical leave and its arbitrary scheduling."[71] It is a measure of his standing that he was given his full salary for this period, as well as an official invitation to resume a full teaching schedule in January 1972. On the other hand, Ladd was given stringent parameters for his behavior and recovery process, and the penalty for breach would be a review of his status at the seminary. He was expected to get his drinking problem under control and required to participate in a course of psychotherapy with Sylling. In an early draft of the agreement Hubbard wanted to address "other problems," such as Ladd's "attitude toward Winnie" and his "inability to apply his theology to his life," but these were removed from the final version.[72]

How did the Ladds respond? George agreed to the sabbatical but initially refused to attend the required therapy meetings. Worse, his drinking continued without abatement. In late November 1970 he returned to the therapy sessions under protest but was still drinking heavily.[73] Winnie wrote an angry letter to David Hubbard, accusing him of a "lack of Christian love and understanding" and claiming that what had been perceived as the smell of alcohol on George's breath was really caused by "cough drops."[74]

Ladd resumed his teaching responsibilities in 1972, though in a diminished role, even as he continued to drink. Why was he permitted to remain at Fuller? It may be that his stature in the evangelical world was too great and the risk to Fuller's reputation too strong for Hubbard to follow through with his threat of dismissal. The seminary was under some attack in the early 1970s for its progressive views on various theological and social issues, and the controversies threatened to damage Fuller's image before its most important constituents.[75] The public firing of a prominent member of the faculty, especially for a perceived moral failure that involved a major boundary issue in the conservative subculture, might have been catastrophic. So Ladd stayed on. His reputation was unhindered by his personal problems, at least in public discussion, and many of his most prominent students during this period still recall him as their most influential teacher.[76]

During the 1970s the depression and darkness in Ladd's life, however, did not diminish. As he reflected on his own failed quest, Ladd began to resent others he believed should have done more to advance the cause of evangelical scholarship. As his personality became increasingly brittle, he seemed to go out of his way to wound those whom he loved the most. In 1973 Ladd had a chance encounter with David Wallace, a Fuller student from the early days and the first to earn a PhD in Europe. Wallace had served on the faculty at California Baptist Seminary near Pasadena and had achieved moderate success as a teacher and scholar.[77] But Wallace had not been able to find a permanent position as a professor and decided to open a travel agency with his wife. When Ladd and Wallace were catching up, Wallace produced a business card that described his new venture. Ladd read the card, abruptly turned around, and walked away.[78] The two men never spoke again.

More bizarre still was Ladd's treatment of his beloved Robert Guelich. The son of a minister, Guelich had sought to balance his academic work with service to local church ministry; he strongly believed in the role of scholars in the local church and of ministers in the academy. During the early 1970s he had split his time between the position at Bethel and his work as the teaching pastor at Colonial Church in Edina, Minnesota, one of the largest Congregational churches in the United States. However, he also retained his memberships in academic societies and conferences. At one such gathering, at Duke University in 1976, Guelich told Ladd of his decision to divide his time between the academy and the church. As he had with Wallace, Ladd immediately got up to leave, commenting on Guelich's lack of any substantive publication and bluntly telling him, "You are one of my life's greatest disappointments," and walked away.[79] In the light of his own failures, real and perceived, Ladd obsessively expected that others close to him would take up his mission, and when they did not, he lashed out acidly.[80]

Ladd's bitterness damaged other professional relationships as well. The dividing line seemed to be the extent to which he found in others agreement on Perrin's review of *Jesus and the Kingdom*. As we have seen in Ladd's relationship with Glenn Barker, if one did not share Ladd's sense of outrage over Perrin's attack, the friendship was over.[81] Ladd's later interaction with Eldon J. Epp is a case in point. Epp had graduated from Fuller in the early 1950s and had completed his PhD studies at Harvard. Just as Ladd had moved away from dispensationalism under Cadbury, Epp had moved away from Fuller's conservative ethos in the course of his own doctoral studies. By the 1970s Epp was a prominent textual critic and served for many years as a professor at the Case Western Reserve University in Ohio; he was also a friend of Norman Perrin. Epp contributed an essay to the Festschrift for Perrin titled "Norman Perrin on the Kingdom of God: An Appreciation and an Assessment from the Perspective of 1970."[82]

Epp argued that, of the spate of books on the Kingdom of God published in the early 1960s, "it is Perrin's book which stands out not only as the most useful but as the one which carries forward the discussion."[83] Worse, in an extended footnote he states that Perrin's criticism of Ladd "undoubtedly is justified."[84] He goes on to offer a sort of defense of Ladd's position by saying that his former teacher had endured a "soul-searching struggle" with his early fundamentalist stance and that *Jesus and the Kingdom* represented "a position sharply removed from [Ladd's] 'Dispensational' heritage."[85] Epp ends the note with a gracious aside, saying that "while Ladd himself may be facing resolutely upstream, at the same time he has taught a number of his students, including the present writer, those skills which make it possible to navigate the mainstream of modern critical scholarship."[86] Ladd would have loved to see this, as it was an affirmation that he had been successful in a crucially important aspect of his objective, but he probably read little after Epp's positive assessment of Perrin.

Ladd and Epp crossed paths one final time about a year after the Perrin tribute was published. Epp, acting as review editor for the prestigious *Journal of Biblical Literature*, invited Ladd to write a notice of a major work of New Testament scholarship.[87] Ladd's response reveals both the intensity of his continuing rage over Perrin's review and his resulting abandonment of the goal of rehabilitating the evangelical presence in contemporary scholarship. The letter is handwritten—unusual in itself since Ladd preferred to type—in a shaky hand, evidence of both his fierce anger and his deteriorating physical and emotional state. He sarcastically admitted to being "surprised" by Epp's invitation, especially in light of his "agreement with Perrin in his evaluation of my work."[88] He argued that, if Perrin's review "represents sound scholarship," then Ladd is "no scholar but should go back to Podunk as a country preacher."[89]

Clearly Ladd had no ability to be objective regarding any issue related to Perrin. The self-flagellation continued as Ladd said, "I am incompetent, uncritical, and contemptuous. I am surprised that you admitted you had studied under me." However, the fact remained that Epp had admitted to studying under Ladd. Epp had gone out of his way to credit Ladd for helping him develop his academic skills and for preparing him to survive in the larger world of theological scholarship. It is ironic, then, that Ladd subjected Epp to a tirade that announced his surrender of any desire to continue in his quest:

> Ten years ago I would have been honored to [be] ask[ed] to review such a book, but no more. I am all through trying to "build bridges." . . . I am writing for my own circle; I bleed too easily to expose myself any more. I am all through trying to publish in the "standard" journals. I thought that [publishing] had given me some stature, but it is obvious that it has not. My life-long ambition has been to "build bridges," but I have to face it that this ambition has blown up in my face. Frankly, I am not willing to invest the hours in such a review for what negligible status it would give me. I have been categorized, and have got to live with it.[90]

The extent to which Ladd was in reality "categorized," which he uses in the sense of being marginalized, is debatable. What is unquestionable is his perception of being trapped outside the mainstream and of being denied a place in the broader world of theological scholarship.

All of this—the family issues, the excessive drinking, and the failure to achieve the academic success he craved—did little to alter Ladd's theological position. How was this possible? Certainly some level of dissociation was at play in his life. He simply denied that his problems were actually problems and allowed them to fester. Worse, he blamed others for situations he clearly helped to create: His wife was frigid, his children were disappointing, and other theologians were too critical. He would never fully accept responsibility for his own problematic behavior, nor would he allow it to alter or even inform his doctrinal beliefs.[91]

Much of this was to evade the crucial question of just how God intervenes in history. So much of Ladd's theological position rested on an understanding of God as actor in human events, but he experienced little of that intervention in his own life. He had prayed, for example, for Larry to grow into a fully functioning adult, only to see him suffer and withdraw as the years went by.[92] But it was not just Larry. Ladd had prayed for a series of personal issues over the years without seeing any of them resolved. In a chapel sermon titled "God's Answer to the Question, Why?" Ladd recited a litany of unanswered prayers from within his own life. Ladd admitted to asking God why these things had happened, but argued that knowing the answer would not have made him grieve any less. The hope of the believer needed to rest, Ladd preached, on the promise of future resolution, not on present understanding.[93] Still, if he had measured God's involvement in human affairs by his own experience, he would have struggled to sustain his faith. One can deduce, then, that Ladd's separation of his life from his theology was linked to his eschatology, his "already but not yet" understanding of the kingdom of God. If some aspects of the kingdom were present now and the rest reserved for later, then it was relatively easy to believe that some problems that seemed intractable or incomprehensible now would be resolved or redeemed at a future time. Thus Ladd was able to leave those issues that he wanted to ignore in the present, in the belief that they would be resolved when all things were made new.

Ironically, it was during these final years that several of Ladd's most influential books were published, though most were largely written before 1965. In the years between Perrin's review and 1978, Ladd published five new books and more than a dozen important scholarly articles, representing about half of his entire scholarly product, though he perceived himself to be a failure. His audience during this period was limited for the most part to conservative evangelicals, a development that left him frustrated and depressed. Furthermore, there is not much that is new in Ladd's thought in these later years; much of his writing at the time either sums up long-held views or restates them in popular form. Still, given his dream of raising the level of critical discourse among evangelicals and gaining acceptance in the broader academy, these later works—even those that are largely repetitive—represent an important part of his legacy.

In 1967 Ladd published *The New Testament and Criticism*, an introduction for evangelicals to the various critical methods for studying the texts of the New Testament. He had written the bulk of this book on his 1964–1965 sabbatical, but his emotional state had slowed the final revisions and delayed the release of the book. In the introduction to *New Testament and Criticism* Ladd condemned, as he had before, "the dearth of first-rate scholarly production" of evangelicals over the previous half-century and the tendency of some to exhibit "a negative attitude toward interacting with the main stream of culture, philosophy, and theology."[94] In the book Ladd asserts that the tools of biblical criticism can be viewed as neutral—and thus beneficial—if the user avoids the naturalistic a priori assumptions that often accompany them.[95] Critical methods can help reconstruct "the historical side of the process of revelation."[96]

Reviews of the book were generally positive. One credited Ladd with taking on the task of "rehabilitating the use of the word criticism" among evangelicals.[97] David Wallace, Ladd's former student and a biblical scholar himself, challenged Ladd's boundary-less definition of the term "evangelical" but concluded that the book "deserves a wide reading" among evangelicals still suspicious of biblical criticism.[98] The impact was significant, though inadvertent, as it succeeded in making critical methodologies "safe" for generations of evangelicals. However, it was not Ladd's primary intent to drag his evangelical audience into a more critical understanding of the Bible; he would rather have represented the best of evangelical critical scholarship to the mainstream of biblical knowledge. Nevertheless, the book remains in print and continues to enjoy a wide readership among evangelical students of the Bible. It is safe to conclude that Ladd never fully understood what he had accomplished in *The New Testament and Criticism*.

He achieved much less in his next book, *A Commentary on the Revelation of John* (1972), a verse-by-verse study of this crucial source for Christian prophetic thought. It appears inevitable that a scholar of Ladd's stature, who spent so much of his career wrestling with eschatological issues, would publish a study on this important apocalyptic text. However, Ladd was clearly past his day as a critical scholar, and it showed. Across the theological spectrum critics noticed that this book did not reflect his best scholarly work. The introduction, in which one might expect to find a detailed description of the wide range of current critical views on the book, fills barely eight pages, more than half of which are taken up by too-brief summaries of various interpretative methods (preterist, historical, idealist, and futurist). By comparison, the introduction to Ladd's *Jesus and the Kingdom*, which arguably covered more straightforward material than the Apocalypse of John, was thirty-five pages long.

Resting on a fusion of preterist and futurist positions, Ladd's interpretation of John's revelation reflects his "now and not yet" formulation. He writes from his historic premillennialist position and defends a posttribulation rapture as he had in *The Blessed Hope*. Reviews were highly critical, even if gently so. One review challenges Ladd in an area where his earlier work had been recognized for its strength: his fair treatment of critical studies with which he did not agree.[99] Another described Ladd's conservative understanding of apocalyptic literature as "almost totally inadequate" and concluded that the book deserved "harsh judgment."[100] Even John Walvoord, writing for *Bibliotheca Sacra* at

Dallas Seminary, admitted that "this book is not Ladd's best work."[101] However, the commentary had some appeal among conservatives, especially those who were looking for a path away from a strict dispensationalist reading of Revelation, and the book remains in print.

More impressive was Ladd's *Theology of the New Testament* (1974), which was designed as a textbook for seminary students and pastors. This book, a refinement of Ladd's course teaching materials, developed over more than two decades and is his most influential work. In this massive (661 pages) text Ladd reaffirms the historical and theological positions upon which his career had been based, as well as his motivation for writing in the first place. Rehearsing the raison d'être for his career, Ladd states that "American evangelicals have made little contribution to New Testament theological literature.... It is to meet this challenge that the present book was written."[102] He affirms the influence of the *Heilsgeschichte* school of thought, while reiterating his critique of Rudolf Bultmann.[103] He also restates his mature position on the relationship between history and revelation:

> While revelation has occurred in history, revelatory history is not
> bare history. God did not act in history in such a way that historical
> events were eloquent in and of themselves.... The historical events
> are revelatory *only when they are accompanied by the revelatory word*.
> This, however, is not an accurate formulation if it suggests two
> separate modes of revelation. The fact is that God's word is his deed,
> and his deed is his word. We would therefore be more accurate if we
> spoke of the deed-word revelation.[104]

While not particularly innovative, even within his own body of work, Ladd's positions as stated in the introduction to *Theology of the New Testament* establish the boundaries within which we see his fully developed theology.

In *Theology of the New Testament* we see Ladd's understanding of the relationship between history, faith, and the Bible worked out in full. First, Ladd as historian argues that history is not a tool with which to "verify faith by critical findings" but rather the means by which to understand more fully the context of the gospel message.[105] In this sense biblical theology is a descriptive discipline as opposed to the prescriptive role of systematic theology. Second, Ladd restates his argument that the historical events that form the foundation of the Christian faith must also be accompanied by the kerygmatic, revelatory interpretation of the biblical text. The events occurred, but they retain their salvific value only when joined to the authoritative explanation found in the Bible.[106]

"The word of God," according to Ladd, "is both the report about a redemptive event, and is itself a redemptive event, for in the word of the cross, the crucified himself confronts men to communicate to them the benefits of his redeeming death." Similarly on the central doctrine of the atonement, Ladd argues that Paul, while never discussing the details of the crucifixion, nevertheless makes the significance of that event the centerpiece of his theology.[107] Paul "assumes its historicity but is interested primarily in the theological significance of that death." A Theology of the New Testament emerges as a final statement of Ladd's faith as supported and shaped by his critical methodology. The impact of the book was dramatic within the conservative world. Theology of the New Testament has been considered near or equal in significance to John Calvin's Institutes of the Christian Religion among evangelical scholars.[108]

One of Ladd's most important articles in the latter years of his career was his defense of historic premillennialism in a popular collection of essays on eschatology, The Meaning of the Millennium: Four Views, published in 1977.[109] This book gathered together scholars who represented various positions on the millennium and provided each the opportunity to interact with those who held opposing positions. Ladd's presentation was clear and forceful, if not much changed from his earlier writings, and remains one of his best-known published works. Robert Clouse (b. 1931), the editor of the volume, came to the project as a trained and committed dispensationalist but was convinced by Ladd's essay to change his stance. It is a measure of Ladd's influence that more than twenty years later Clouse remained aligned with his position.[110]

Ladd wrote other essays and short books as well. Between 1968 and 1975 he contributed no fewer than four chapters to Festschriften for other scholars.[111] More importantly, he summed up his own position on the relationship between biblical interpretation and historical thought in two essays written before his decline accelerated. The first to appear was "History and Theology in Biblical Exegesis," published in Interpretation largely as a gesture of apology to Ladd for Perrin's review of Jesus and the Kingdom.[112] In the article, which is peppered with footnotes directly challenging Perrin's critique, Ladd restates his long-held position on the relationship between God's acts in history and the revelatory explanation of those acts in biblical texts. "The scandal of the gospel," he argues, "is that the self-revelation of the eternal, transcendent God has occurred in datable historical events."[113]

Two years later, the paper Ladd delivered at Christ Church, Oxford, in 1965, "The Problem of History in Contemporary New Testament Interpretation," was published. Written before the Perrin incident, Ladd writes confidently in favor of an exegetical method that allows for the claims of revelation and faith to be taken seriously. The historical-critical method, which purported to examine biblical texts without the burden of dogma, actually exchanged "one kind of dogma for another," according to Ladd, thereby making it "incompetent to interpret redemptive history."[114] He proposed instead, as he had for most of his career, a critical "response to the apostolic testimony concerning Jesus within the context of the life of the Christian community."[115]

Though Ladd did not publish further in this crucial area of history and the exegesis of biblical texts, he did align his position with that of a younger scholar, British theologian R. T. France. In the inaugural issue of *Themelios*, a journal published by the British Theological Students' Fellowship and International Fellowship of Evangelical Students, France discussed the relationship between constructions of inerrancy and critical New Testament study.[116] The erudite discussion draws on a wide range of sources to recognize what France called the "dual commitment [of the evangelical scholar] as a historian and as a Christian."[117] Ladd agreed wholeheartedly with France's position. Responding to a query regarding his own stance, Ladd recommended France's piece: "I wish I had written this essay. It is a superlative piece of work and represents precisely my view of Scripture."[118]

In 1974 Ladd published *I Believe in the Resurrection of Jesus*, a popular defense of the doctrine in a series edited by British evangelist Michael Green (b. 1930). The book, which relied heavily on Ladd's related articles from the early 1960s, also rehearsed his long-running debate with Daniel Fuller.[119] The central thesis is consistent with his earlier writings: The resurrection of Jesus was an event in history that cannot be explained in the terms of modern historical thought and can be fully understood only through faith.[120] Ladd's final book was appropriately titled *The Last Things: An Eschatology for Laymen*, a last jab at dispensationalism and a call for conservative evangelicals to see the Christian church as the fulfillment of Old Testament prophecy.[121] Despite the impact—uneven as it was—of these new publications, clearly Ladd was just going through the motions and spent much of this final decade depressed at the state of his career.

Tired, broken, and emotionally unstable, Ladd retired in the autumn of 1976 after more than a quarter century at Fuller Seminary. He had seen the seminary grow from a fledgling school, with grand dreams of transforming Western civilization, into a major institution with three separate schools, extension campuses, and a renowned faculty. Its student population had grown almost tenfold during Ladd's tenure, and they were coming from all over the world. Nevertheless, for Ladd it was time to leave the active faculty. At sixty-six years of age Ladd was four years short of the mandatory retirement age at Fuller, but the toll of his alcoholism and emotional problems made him seem significantly older. One colleague recalls that in the span of ten years Ladd had gone from "looking a little like Clark Gable to looking more like Colonel Sanders."[122] A former student who spent time with Ladd during that period saw him as increasingly "out of touch" and "depressed." He was losing track of conversations and showing other "signs of senility."[123] One of his own graduate students remembers Ladd recommending that the young man apply for doctoral studies when he been Ladd's student for three years.[124] A fellow scholar who saw Ladd regularly at various conferences recalls him having "a nervous look in his eyes" and difficulty making eye contact.[125]

Ladd's retirement celebration was hosted by David Hubbard and attended by many in the Fuller community. If the participants in the program shared anything besides their affiliation with Fuller Seminary, it was probably that most of them had been wounded or troubled by Ladd in some way as he declined in his final years. Glenn Barker, Ladd's friend from Harvard and then provost of the seminary, may not have realized the extent to which Ladd had hindered his candidacy at the University of Pennsylvania years before. David Wallace shared his memories (or most of them) of Ladd's mentorship over the previous twenty-five years. Dan Fuller and David Hubbard, both former students of Ladd who were later forced to discipline him, also paid tribute.[126] Ladd left active teaching but retained his office and presence on the Fuller campus.

Ladd's final emotional collapse took place in 1977, after the death of his wife. Winnie Ladd suffered several strokes and eventually died of a pancreatic infection while hospitalized. Still the venerated elder statesman of evangelical biblical scholarship, Ladd maintained his speaking schedule while Winnie was ill, and she passed away while he was at an out-of-town speaking engagement.[127] Only at her death did Ladd seem to realize the depth of the pain he had inflicted on his wife, a fact that served as the catalyst for even more drinking.[128] Overwhelmed by guilt, Ladd slipped farther into the haze of his alcoholism.[129] He lived with his forty-year-old son Larry, who also drank heavily at that time, and they were often seen staggering together around Pasadena. The two of them made an odd and pathetic pair. Both had physical and emotional disabilities, had difficulties with communication, and were occasionally ill tempered. At one seminary gathering George and Larry managed to forget where they had parked their car and spent much of the evening searching for it.[130] They had one very public physical altercation—with each other—at a Christmas party hosted by a faculty member.[131] In a bizarre coda to the events leading up to the end of this strange life, Ladd assembled a gathering on Fuller's campus in 1978, at which he announced his engagement to be married to a "Miss Proctor," but the wedding never took place.[132]

There was one final bright spot, however. In 1978 Ladd was honored with a Festschrift edited by none other than his protégé and surrogate son, Robert Guelich. *Unity and Diversity in New Testament Theology* brought together former students and colleagues spanning the thirty years of Ladd's career as a scholar.[133] In writing the introduction, David Allan Hubbard celebrated Ladd's "probing manner, his driving style, his restless curiosity." "Ladd's passionate fervor for [New Testament studies]," Hubbard wrote, "kept every class alive during the lecture session and awake far into the night trying to pass muster."[134] Some of the most prominent biblical scholars of the day produced essays for the volume, including Fuller colleague Ralph Martin, Leon Morris of Ridley College in Australia, William Barclay of the University of Glasgow, F. F. Bruce of the University of Manchester, Richard Longenecker of the University of Toronto, Bo Reicke of the University of Basel, and I. Howard Marshall of the University of Aberdeen. Several of Ladd's students who had managed to "pass muster" contributed as well, including Robert Meye, W. Ward Gasque, Charles Carlston, Daniel Fuller, and Eldon J. Epp.[135]

It is Epp again who provides a reference point for evaluating Ladd's level of success in his quest. In tribute he wrote the following:

> My debt to George Eldon Ladd is a large one, reaching back twenty-five years when he introduced me not only to the disciplines of New Testament exegesis and biblical theology, but to modern critical scholarship in these fields. Perhaps more than anyone else, he is responsible for my determination to pursue a career in New Testament scholarship, though this is not to suggest that he is responsible either for the course that my scholarship has taken or for its ideological thrust; those decisions rest with me alone. Yet, it was Professor Ladd's infectious enjoyment of both the grand themes and the intricate components of biblical research, his insistence on philological precision, on thoroughness and objectivity, and on fairness in the evaluation of the work of others, and his sincere interest in those who might be inclined to follow a similar scholarly career that were so keenly felt and are so profoundly appreciated.[136]

Here again we see a former student willing to forgive—if not forget—the often painful excesses of Ladd's behavior and express gratitude for his mentorship and inspiration. We also see, ironically, Ladd acknowledged to have accomplished a key component of his quest: to encourage and enable young academics to produce quality scholarship. Though Epp did not stay within the conservative fold—he was certainly the farthest from traditional evangelicalism among the contributors—his work remains highly regarded, and he has never disavowed the fact that his life as a scholar began at the feet of George Ladd.

Ladd's final chapel sermon at Fuller served as a reminder of the reason he was held in such high regard, even as it showed the seminary community the extent of his decline. The gathered community, seeing a clearly weakened Ladd take the pulpit, rose with thunderous applause, reducing Ladd to tears. He could barely complete the first line of his message: "I am simple enough to believe the Word of God: This gospel must be preached in all the world and to all nations and then shall the Lord come."[137] He then quipped, "Is that apocalyptic?"—and gestured to New Testament scholar Ralph Martin while saying, "Well, you were the one who said it."[138] The room was his, and he continued in a voice halting and tremulous but still reminiscent of his earlier power. He forgot several details at the start but made light of the problems, putting his audience at ease.

The sermon was vintage Ladd. Preaching on his favorite text, Matthew 24:14, he challenged his listeners never to forget the call to preach the message of the kingdom wherever they went. This was the true call of the Christian leader, and to abdicate that responsibility was to ignore a direct command from the Almighty. Ladd rambled and found his way into several tangential points, but he also communicated a clear and passionate message of exhortation. Straying into the topic of dispensationalism and its use of the Bible, Ladd asked his listeners: "How wrong can a man be in his head and yet be right in his heart?" The question reveals Ladd's sense of regret over too much time wasted in petty squabbles, while the real task of preaching the gospel "in all the world and to all nations" went unfinished. However, it also showed Ladd's conflicted understanding of the exact nature of what evangelicals call "saving faith." To illustrate, Ladd told of his experience at Harvard under Henry Cadbury. At the mere mention of his professor's name, Ladd began to sob and barely managed to get the words out: "He died in his agnosticism but I pray to God that I'll meet him in heaven. He was a devout man, in spite of the fact that he had a wrongheaded theology."

Ladd asked the congregation a question that had both driven and vexed him throughout much of his career: "What is the meaning of history?" Ladd restated the passage from Matthew, then told his listeners that they embodied the answer to the question. "What this group of men and women do with the Gospel," he thundered, "is more important in the long run, than what happens in Washington, or Geneva, or Paris, or Moscow. God has put the times in our hands. We have a mission, and that mission is first of all, evangelization." To preach the gospel to every nation on earth, in Ladd's view, would somehow automatically trigger the return of Christ and the end of history. For someone who had suffered so much and so consistently throughout the years of his life, this was both a call and a message of hope. The wounds that had not found healing or resolution during Ladd's life, he hoped, would be reconciled at the close of the age. And so he charged his students to hasten that end, not least so that he could finally find some peace. When the service was over Ladd staggered back to his campus office alone, exhausted. A former student recalled that he looked confused and broken and that his trousers were partially undone.[139] Ladd gradually retreated from the scene as the 1970s came to a close.

In August of 1980 Ladd suffered a major stroke. Within a few weeks he was able to move one arm and began to recover some of his speech, but he still required hospitalization.[140] In September of that year he was moved to a care facility near Pasadena, and the prognosis was hopeful that he might be able to go home within three to six months.[141] Ladd gradually lost his ability to speak, and the effects of the stroke also prevented him from reading. Robert Meye, former student of Ladd's at Fuller and now dean of the School of Theology, spent hours with Ladd, reading the Bible to him. On one such occasion Meye was reading from the eighth chapter of Paul's letter to the Romans. When he reached the twenty-third verse, which reads, "we wait eagerly for our adoption as sons, the redemption of our bodies," Ladd lifted his head and said clearly, "I long for that day."[142] Later Meye's son John visited Ladd and played traditional hymns on the piano in the facility. Ladd, who could no longer speak, was able to sing the hymns of his childhood, weeping in his bed. He lingered in this semiconscious state for two years. On 5 October 1982 Ladd died from complications of pneumonia.

Conclusion

How do we assess George Ladd's life and achievements? George Marsden has said that the various aspects of Ladd's personality "were not always well integrated."[1] Certainly this is a valuable insight, but it is also incomplete. Virtually every wound from Ladd's early life bore some bitter fruit in the end, a terrible sort of continuity. At the last, Ladd's theological position became a defense against the overwhelming evidence of the unfairness of human experience. So much had gone astray in his life: His family, his faith, his ministry, and his career—all had missed the mark he had envisioned when he went off to Gordon College in 1929. His decision—and then his compulsion—to dull the pain with alcohol and work thus makes some perverse sense. All around him Ladd saw scholars and young seminary students, happy in their lives and confident in their transcendent faith—they were Zane Grey characters in the evangelical tradition.

Yet while he could not relate to their apparent comfort and happiness, he bravely resisted the temptation to envy. In the final years, however, it became increasingly difficult for Ladd to reconcile the path his life had taken with the God he sought to serve. Still, he chose not to interpret the Bible according to his own experience because that would have left him with a capricious God, deaf to his passionate concerns and prayers. He chose instead to press on in his eschatological belief in the already-but-not-yet kingdom, where whatever was left incomplete in this life would be made new in the next. Ladd's collapse in his last years must be seen through the filter of the bedridden evangelical Baptist minister, singing the hymns of his youth and still believing that healing and reconciliation lay just ahead.

George Ladd remains a pivotal figure in the postwar evangelical resurgence in America, and its most important biblical scholar. In his own time he was overshadowed, at least in part, by philosopher-theologians such as Edward John Carnell, but in the closing decades of the twentieth century Ladd emerged as having had the greatest influence on this era of American evangelicalism. Even dispensationalist leaders continue to move closer to Ladd's positions on various key doctrines of theology and eschatology.[2] Most significantly, there are growing numbers of evangelical scholars who have embraced the life of the mind as an expression of their Christian faith, many directly and still more indirectly through the example Ladd set.[3] How did he accomplish this? It is a central thesis of this book that Ladd's influence derives more from the simple fact that he published the work that he did than it does from the content or originality of that work.

The pattern of Ladd's career follows a strategy—partly of conscious design and partly reactive to contemporary situations—in order to achieve his ultimate goal of a rehabilitated evangelicalism, in both content and image. This strategy began with the time of preparation at Gordon College and Harvard, during which Ladd tested and refined his intellectual abilities under the mentorship of Henry Cadbury and others. In this sense Ladd fits well into Joel Carpenter's view of a thriving evangelicalism by developing new means for engaging the broader culture.[4] Jon Stone has argued that Ladd and the other new evangelical scholars attended elite universities because they were looking for professional "advantage."[5] However, this estimate overlooks Ladd's sincere desire to act as a catalyst for the rehabilitation of evangelical scholarship from within. If anything, degrees from secular institutions were more likely to be seen as handicaps in the suspicious and conflicted world of fundamentalism, and the young men who sought that training cannot be defined so cynically.

Along the way Ladd was inspired—and then driven—to create a work of scholarship that would earn for evangelicalism a place in the larger discussion of theology. After laying the foundation but before the engagement with the mainstream, Ladd began his quest by fighting a rear-guard action. In his critique of dispensationalism at the start of his career Ladd sought to correct the understanding and use of the Bible in the creation of theological writing, arguing instead for a more historically sensitive approach to texts he defended as divinely inspired. He also engaged dispensational ecclesiology for its tendency toward militancy and separation, in part because he did not find any biblical basis for such behavior but mostly because he believed it prevented the mainstream from accepting evangelical scholarship—and evangelicalism as a movement. At first Ladd was careful to tread lightly in his interaction with the powerful John Walvoord and other dispensationalist leaders, but as he grew in stature and influence he was able to confront more aggressively those whom he believed were a threat to the evangelical scholarly enterprise. This challenge to the most powerful faction within American evangelicalism was a dangerous gamble professionally, but it served to establish Ladd as the preeminent biblical scholar within conservative Christianity.

From this position of strength within evangelicalism Ladd moved to the next element of his strategy: engagement with the mainstream of theological scholarship. Within the broader discussion of the relationship between Christian theology and historical understanding, he made the case for a conservative defense of the resurrection of Jesus by using the critical methods of contemporary biblical study. Again Jon Stone misreads the motivation of Ladd and conservative Protestantism. It is a major conclusion of Stone's study that postwar evangelicalism was "captivated by the issue of defining its boundaries . . . with both liberalism and fundamentalism."[6] But certainly Ladd does not fit into this narrow mold; he was far more concerned with connection and participation than with simple boundary making. If anything, Ladd showed along the way that he was willing to abandon (as he did with the premillennialism clause in Fuller Seminary's doctrinal statement) deeply held beliefs to further the rehabilitation of his movement. He aligned himself with those who were "willing to recognize truth wherever it is found" and criticized those who were overly concerned with "defending their own position."[7]

Ladd thus engaged—as an unabashed evangelical—the most important theologian of his day, Rudolf Bultmann, and articulated both the strengths and dangers of his existential theology. At the same time, Ladd made his way to the margins of the broader theological discussion and achieved in part that for which he had set the course of his career. Nonetheless, he had grander designs, and with the publication of his magnum opus in 1964 he hoped to be welcomed as an equal among theologians beyond the evangelical world. That he perceived himself as a failure in this effort certainly had as much—if not more—to do with his emotional makeup and personal demons as it did with Norman Perrin's evaluation of his work. Ladd's quest, while not succeeding in the way he had envisioned, still opened doors for later evangelical scholars to accomplish what he could not, and therein lies his lasting significance.

How did Ladd's mind develop over the course of his life and career? The answer to this question lies in the evolution of Ladd's thought as it relates to three main areas: his understanding of history and historical thought, his view of the Bible as revelation and his eschatology. In each of these Ladd sought, as a part of his strategy to rehabilitate evangelical scholarship, to embrace critical viewpoints and methods while defending traditional Christian orthodoxy. He was not always successful in finding a workable balance within each of these areas, but he made the attempt; as a result, doors were opened for others who followed to take up the standard.

Ladd's developing historical understanding is the foundation for assessing the rest of his thought. During his years at Harvard and early in his career Ladd moved away from the simple view of history as an accumulation of objective facts in favor of a more sophisticated understanding of history as science. Influenced by Martin Kähler, Ladd began to use a more refined distinction between *Historie* and *Geschichte* in his theological writings. At the core of this effort was his desire to make use of critical principles and methods while maintaining the essence of his conservative theological position. In order to accomplish this Ladd rejected the Enlightenment idea of history as an unbroken chain of demonstrable causes and effects.[8] He thus defended the historicity of the resurrection of Jesus not simply as an objective event but rather one that had meaning only when interpreted by the revelatory word of the Bible.

Later influenced by Oscar Cullmann, Ladd embraced the *Heilsgeschichte* movement and began to speak of "redemptive history" and the continuity of the biblical message throughout human time. Rudolph Bultmann's formulation of the relationship between history and faith forced Ladd to sharpen his own view. And while Ladd agreed with Bultmann that history cannot be the foundation for faith, he rejected his radical pronouncement that history was irrelevant for theological understanding. Robert Yarbrough is thus correct in his conclusion that "Ladd's view of history may be seen as a measure designed to offset criticism's historiographical excesses and thereby to hear the biblical message in fuller dimension."[9] Ladd rejected the limitations of modern historical methods, which denied the miracles and other crucial events in the biblical writings, even as he used those tools in his own scholarship.

Ladd's view of the Bible also changed dramatically over the course of his years as a scholar. He embraced the dispensationalism of "Miss Cash" from the start and presumably an understanding of inspiration that leaned strongly toward the supernatural, with little influence from historical forces. However, by the time he graduated from Gordon College and was searching for employment in the preaching roster of the New England Fellowship, he had already abandoned his dispensational views and held an understanding of the Bible that allowed for "the personality and training of men" in the shaping of its message.[10] At Harvard Ladd was exposed to—and adopted—critical methods that approached biblical texts as the product of historical processes in order to determine their meaning and significance for contemporary readers. This was the most important step in the development of Ladd's thought, and it set the course for his scholarly work to come. Ladd's defense of the Revised Standard Version of the Bible thus shifted focus from the translators' doctrinal positions to the accuracy of the translation itself. In Ladd's later mature view of the Bible he saw it in light of his historical understanding as the revealed interpretative guide to the acts of God in history. This "deed-word complex" came to define how he understood the way God's intervention into human history became saving faith for succeeding generations.

Ladd's opinions on historical thought and the Bible influenced his eschatology. As a young dispensationalist he adopted its complex scheme for understanding both the Bible and God's plan for human history. But under the influence of Merrill Tenney, who would become his lifelong friend and colleague, Ladd jettisoned dispensationalism's interpretation of prophecy and replaced it with an eschatological position that changed only slightly throughout the rest of his career. Joel Carpenter has emphasized Ladd's desire to create an eschatological position more in line with classic Christian orthodoxy.[11] However, this attributes to Ladd too much of a retrograde position. Ladd was more forward looking than that and hoped for a time when a reasoned evangelical eschatology might be accepted among opposing views in the theological academy.

As a direct result of his critical exegetical method, Ladd rejected the dispensationalist interpretation of biblical texts and adopted what he would later term "historic premillennialism," in which Christ's return would take place at some future date, after which he would establish a literal thousand-year reign on earth. Ladd did not abandon the eschatology of dispensationalism in full, however—he retained his belief in a rapture of believers after a time of tribulation—but he was strongly critical of the dispensationalist tendency to read signs of the times to determine the timing of Christ's appearing.

Central to Ladd's eschatology is his understanding of the Kingdom of God. This doctrine was emerging as an important object of critical study just as Ladd's career as a scholar was beginning, and he made it the focus of his attempt to engage the broader academic world as a critically astute evangelical. Ladd introduced to his popular evangelical audience the critical understanding of the Kingdom of God as an infinite reign rather than a finite realm, thereby providing an alternative eschatology to that of dispensationalism. Bradley Harper has demonstrated that Ladd's view of the Kingdom of God, with its already-but-not-yet formulation, remains the dominant view of the kingdom across the spectrum of evangelical thought.[12] It is important to add to this assessment, however, that it was a part of Ladd's strategy to develop a critically reasoned eschatology as a means of rehabilitating evangelical scholarship.

Little of what Ladd wrote after 1965 was especially original, though it was groundbreaking in a way. Ladd's reaction to the critique of his major work was to surrender his quest to force his way into the broader academic world and retreat to the safer zones of his evangelical audience. Still, in several important ways Ladd's failed quest—or more accurately, his incomplete achievement—did open doors for the next generation to succeed in places where he had never been fully welcome. The best of Ladd's former students (and their students after them) enjoyed access to academic circles that had been largely closed—or at least resistant—to him. Thus his influence on a generation of scholars remains his most enduring legacy. We have seen this in the careers of diverse scholars such as Daniel Fuller, Robert Guelich, and Eldon Epp, but there are dozens more whom Ladd's tutelage inspired directly, and hundreds more whose horizons were broadened through his published work. This is the essence of his legacy and lasting appeal. Tragically—and typically—he would never fully know it.

And so it is Ladd's emotional breakdown that stands out as an oddly tragic event in a career that accomplished so much. Perrin's review of *Jesus and the Kingdom* acted as a gust of wind against Ladd's psychological house of cards, which arguably was destined to fall in any case. Certainly the disintegration of his relationships acted as a cause—rather than a result—of his overreaction to the response to his book. It is thus an overstatement to say that Perrin broke Ladd, as if one review of a single book could be the sole cause of Ladd's collapse. It is more accurate to say that Perrin's review permanently laid open a wound that had existed in Ladd's psyche from his earliest days, one that had grown virtually unabated during his adult life. Ladd's sense of himself as an outsider, which had as its root causes the relationship with his father and his childhood self-perception as a "freak," made him especially vulnerable to criticism in any form, let alone a negative review of his most cherished work. His response—estrangement from his family, bitterness toward friends, and the serious alcoholism that haunted his later life—must be seen in light of the wounds that made his quest appealing in the first place. Ladd desperately wanted to be heard and loved and welcomed into the groups and communities he valued most. That he found little of what he wanted either in his career or personal life is one of the tragic side-stories in the history of modern evangelicalism. In the end, however, Ladd's life—with all its conflict and messiness—fitted manageably into his understanding of a broken world, having caught a glimpse of the kingdom in part, waiting for the fullness to come at a later date. Only his eschatology, which formed the bedrock of his academic career, gave Ladd the hope he needed to survive the pain of his private and professional lives.

Later evangelicals have had a somewhat easier time. Most relevant to the present study is the dynamic presence of evangelical scholars in the more general American academy. No longer relegated to specifically conservative religious institutions, evangelicals work alongside secular colleagues in many public or otherwise nonreligious universities and even create scholarship together through academic associations and societies. The American academy, to be sure, remains largely secular in tone and content, but the willingness to accept as equals (or nearly so) evangelical scholars on their own merits is a dramatic shift from the situation just a few decades earlier. On the other hand, this new level of participation has posed problems for progressive evangelical institutions such as Fuller Seminary, which struggle to compete for faculty with elite institutions that offer higher salaries and greater research privileges (ironically, the same enticements that brought Ladd and others to Fuller).[13] This development—despite the difficulties it creates for Fuller Seminary and others— is a positive result of the influence of George Ladd and other evangelical scholars who sought acceptance in the academy at large. Further, it would be welcome news for Ladd, as it represents precisely the sort of fair treatment he craved during his own career.

The published work of George Ladd also continues to have an impact to the present day. In conservative traditions that have maintained the anti-intellectualism against which Ladd and the other new evangelicals rebelled, many find their way out by way of Ladd's books and articles. His *New Testament and Criticism* demystified critical methods for generations of evangelical students of the Bible and made possible for many a deeper understanding of the biblical message. Regarding dispensationalism, Daniel Fuller has commented that, in the year 2000, Dallas Seminary had finally caught up to where George Ladd was in 1955.[14]

If this is true for an institution, one may surmise that individuals around the nation and world might similarly experience liberation from the interpretative limitations and ecclesiological militancy of dispensationalism. Recall the informal town hall meetings over which Ladd presided after the publication of his first two books. A simple search of the Internet will reveal that his work continues to spark discussion, initiate change, and inspire a new generation to explore the ancient texts of the Christian faith using the critical tools of the modern age.[15] One can argue that, in separatistic or otherwise closed traditions, many conservative evangelicals who desire a greater level of participation and engagement with the broader culture find that Ladd's published work represents a key point of entry. It may be that a "Ladd door" remains through which conservative Christians may pass on their way to a more critical understanding and expression of the old, old story.

For evangelicals in the mainstream academy, the path to acceptance—and the rehabilitation of their intellectual content and image—came and continues to advance not through the demonstration of the truth of their message or doctrinal position but rather by their technical excellence in disciplines that can be evaluated with some measure of objectivity. In this sense Ladd was truly a trailblazer. It is this emphasis on method and technical virtuosity—which Ladd inspired and demanded of others—that accounts for his enduring influence in contemporary evangelicalism, even as his more philosophically oriented colleagues have drifted into obscurity.[16]

Ladd's scholarly work was not groundbreaking in the broader academic world—the audience to whom his major work was directed—but it functioned as such for the subculture from which he wrote, and this is another of his lasting achievements. Nearly four decades before a new generation of evangelicals would lament the scandal of the evangelical mind and propose the outrageous idea that scholarship could be distinctively Christian, Ladd bet his reputation and professional life on both of these ideas.[17] That he was largely unsuccessful in his own time is beside the point. He set a standard that later evangelical scholars would have to reach or exceed if their work was to find acceptance in the broader academy. Generations of highly regarded evangelical scholars owe an unpaid debt to George Ladd for opening doors to them at the highest levels of academic discourse, and making possible their place at the table.

Notes

NOTES TO INTRODUCTION

1. George Eldon Ladd (hereafter GEL) to Merrill Tenney, 23 August 1971, George Eldon Ladd Papers. Unless otherwise noted, all references to correspondence, manuscripts, and other materials are to Ladd's own papers.

2. Survey methodology and results are found in Mark A. Noll, *Between Faith and Criticism: Evangelicals, Scholarship, and the Bible in America* (San Francisco: Harper & Row, 1986), 209–14.

3. William G. McLoughlin, "Introduction," in McLoughlin, ed., *The American Evangelicals, 1800–1900* (New York: Harper Torchbooks, 1968), 1, 26. For a definition of "evangelicalism" see the excursus below, 18–25.

4. On the various issues related to social and religious change at the turn of the twentieth century see Timothy L. Smith, "Religion and Ethnicity in America," *The American Historical Review* 83 (December 1978), 1155–85; Ferenc Morton Szasz, *The Divided Mind of Protestant America, 1880–1930* (University: University of Alabama Press, 1982); Paul A. Carter, *The Spiritual Crisis of the Gilded Age* (DeKalb: Northern Illinois University Press, 1971). On the impact of these issues within evangelicalism see Douglas Frank, *Less Than Conquerors: How Evangelicals Entered the Twentieth Century* (Grand Rapids, Mich.: Eerdmans, 1986).

5. There is a vast amount of literature on all three of these factors and their impact on evangelicalism. On the influence of modern science see David Lindberg and Ronald Numbers, *God and Nature: Historical Essays on the Encounter Between Christianity and Science* (Berkeley: University of California Press, 1986); V. Elving Anderson, "Evangelicals and Science: Fifty Years After the Scopes Trial, 1925–1975," in David Wells and John

Woodbridge, eds., *The Evangelicals: What They Believe, Who They Are, Where They Are Changing* [rev. ed.] (Grand Rapids, Mich.: Baker Books, 1977), 269–88; Mark Noll, "Science, Theology, and Society: From Cotton Mather to William Jennings Bryan," and David N. Livingstone, "Situating Evangelical Responses to Evolution," in Livingstone, D. G. Hart, and Noll, eds., *Evangelicals and Science in Historical Perspective* (New York: Oxford University Press, 1999), 99–119 and 193–219, respectively.

On the secularization of the American academy see George M. Marsden, *The Soul of the American University: From Protestant Establishment to Established Nonbelief* (New York: Oxford University Press, 1994), and Marsden and Bradley Longfield, eds., *The Secularization of the Academy* (New York: Oxford University Press, 1992).

On the rise and impact of biblical criticism see Grant Wacker, "The Decline of Biblical Civilization," in Nathan Hatch and Mark Noll, eds., *The Bible in America: Essays in Cultural History* (New York: Oxford University Press, 1982), 121–38, and *Augustus H. Strong and the Dilemma of Historical Consciousness* (Macon, GA: Mercer University Press, 1985); Roy Harrisville and Walter Sundberg, *The Bible in Modern Culture: Theology and Historical-Critical Method from Spinoza to Käsemann* (Grand Rapids, Mich.: Eerdmans, 1995); Mark S. Massa, *Charles Augustus Briggs and the Crisis of Historical Criticism* (Minneapolis: Fortress Press, 1990).

6. On the rise and influence of the prophecy conferences see Ernest R. Sandeen, *The Roots of Fundamentalism: British and American Millenarianism, 1800–1930* (Chicago: University of Chicago Press, 1970), 132–61; George Marsden, *Fundamentalism and American Culture: The Shaping of Twentieth-Century Evangelicalism, 1870–1925* (New York: Oxford University Press, 1980), 46, 51, 66–71; Timothy Weber, *Living in the Shadow of the Second Coming: American Premllennialism, 1875–1982*, 2nd ed. (Chicago: University of Chicago Press, 1987 [1979]), 28, 105, 125–29; and W. V. Trollinger, "Niagara Conferences," in Daniel G. Reid, et al., eds., *Dictionary of Christianity in America* (Downers Grove: InterVarsity Press, 1990), 824–25.

7. Marsden, *Fundamentalism and American Culture*, 117.

8. See *The Fundamentals: A Testimony to the Truth*, 12 vols. (Chicago: 1910–1915). The term "fundamentalist" was coined by Baptist pastor Curtis Lee Laws in a 1920 article he wrote titled "Convention Side Lights." Laws stated that the term was reserved for those "who still cling to the great fundamentals and who mean to do battle royal for the faith."

Several helpful studies of the fundamentalist movement are Marsden, *Fundamentalism and American Culture*; Sandeen, *The Roots of Fundamentalism: British and American Millenarianism, 1800–1930*; Louis Gasper, *The Fundamentalist Movement* (The Hague: Mouton, 1963); C. Allyn Russell, *Voices of American Fundamentalism: Seven Biographical Studies* (Philadelphia: Westminster Press, 1976); Stewart G. Cole, *The History of Fundamentalism* (New York: Richard Smith, 1931); and Marsden, *Understanding Fundamentalism and Evangelicalism* (Grand Rapids, Mich.: Eerdmans, 1991); a partisan conservative viewpoint can be found in George Dollar, *A History of Fundamentalism in America* (Greenville: 1973).

9. On the history and cultural impact of this incident, see Edward J. Larson, *Summer for the Gods: The Scopes Trial and America's Continuing Debate over Science and Religion* (New York: Basic Books, 1997).

10. See Mark Noll, *The Scandal of the Evangelical Mind* (Grand Rapids, Mich.: Eerdmans, 1994), esp. 109–45.

11. On the rise of Bible colleges as a response to secularization in higher education, see Virginia Lieson Brereton, *Training God's Army: The American Bible School, 1880–1940* (Bloomington: Indiana University Press, 1990).

12. Marsden, *Soul of the American University*, 317–31 passim.

13. Quoted in ibid., 325.

14. Ibid., 365.

15. See Mark Silk, "The Rise of the 'New Evangelicalism': Shock and Adjustment," in William R. Hutchison, ed., *Between the Times: The Travail of the Protestant Establishment in America, 1900–1960* (New York: Cambridge University Press, 1989), 278–99.

16. On the rise of the NAE see Joel Carpenter, *Revive Us Again: The Reawakening of American Fundamentalism* (New York: Oxford University Press, 1997), 141–60.

17. For a detailed description of these and other missionary organizations see ibid., 177–86.

18. Rudolph Nelson, "Fundamentalism at Harvard: The Case of Edward John Carnell," *Quarterly Review* 2 (Summer 1982), 79–98.

19. See George Marsden, *Reforming Fundamentalism: Fuller Seminary and the New Evangelicalism* (Grand Rapids, Mich.: Eerdmans, 1987).

20. Carpenter, *Revive Us Again*. This is the central thesis of the book.

21. Noll, *Between Faith and Criticism*, esp. 142–61.

22. Gary Dorrien, *The Remaking of Evangelical Theology* (Louisville: Westminster John Knox Press, 1998), 1, 148–51.

23. David Lee Russell, "Coming to Grips with the Age of Reason: An Analysis of the New Evangelical Intellectual Agenda, 1942–1970 (PhD diss., Michigan State University, 1993), 7.

24. Jon R. Stone, *On the Boundaries of American Evangelicalism: The Postwar Evangelical Coalition* (New York: St. Martin's Press, 1997), 10.

25. George Marsden, *Reforming Fundamentalism*. James Bradley, professor of church history at Fuller Seminary, makes this criticism in his review of Marsden's book in *Pneuma* 10 (Spring 1988), 67–72.

26. Carl F. H. Henry, Paul King Jewett, Edward John Carnell, and George Ladd served on the Gordon faculty before coming to Fuller Seminary.

27. Rudolph Nelson, *The Making and Unmaking of an Evangelical Mind: The Case of Edward Carnell* (New York: Cambridge University Press, 1987).

28. Ibid., 12–13.

29. See, for example, the biographical sketches by Markus McDowell, in Kenneth T. Jackson, ed., *The Scribner Encyclopedia of American Lives*, vol. 1 (New York: Charles Scribner's Sons, 1998), 481–83; Lee M. McDonald, in Donald McKim, ed., *Historical Handbook of Major Bible Interpreters* (Downers Grove: InterVarsity Press,

1998), 588–94; Donald Hagner in Walter Elwell and J. D. Weaver, eds., *Biblical Interpreters of the Twentieth Century* (Grand Rapids, Mich.: Baker Books, 1993), 228–45; Molly Marshall-Green in Timothy George and David Dockery, eds., *Baptist Theologians* (Nashville: Broadman Press, 1990), 480–95; John A. D'Elia, in Timothy Larsen, ed., *Biographical Dictionary of Evangelicals* (Downers Grove: InterVarsity Press, 2003), 354–56.

30. The colleague was David Allan Hubbard, then president of Fuller Seminary. Hubbard interviewed Ladd for the biographical sketch Hubbard was to contribute to Ladd's *Festschrift*, but Ladd recalled some details of his life incorrectly, and these have been repeated in other treatments since 1978. See Hubbard, "Biographical Sketch and Appreciation," in Robert Guelich, ed., *Unity and Diversity in New Testament Theology: Essays in Honor of George E. Ladd* (Grand Rapids, Mich.: Eerdmans, 1978), xi–xv.

31. James Bibza, "A Critical Analysis of the Publications of D. P. Fuller, G. E. Ladd, I. H. Marshall and M. C. Tenney on the Resurrection of Jesus Christ with Special Attention to the Problem of the Locale of the Post-Resurrection Appearances" (PhD diss., Princeton Theological Seminary, 1985), 75–86.

32. Robert Yarbrough, "The *Heilsgeschichtliche* Perspective in Modern New Testament Theology" (PhD diss., University of Aberdeen, 1985).

33. Ibid., 409.

34. Bradley J. Harper, "The Kingdom of God in the Theology of George Eldon Ladd: A Reflection of 20th-Century American Evangelicalism" (PhD diss., Saint Louis University, 1994).

35. Rebecca Jane Duncan, "The Spiritual Formation of George Eldon Ladd, 1911–1982," unpublished paper, Fuller Theological Seminary, Fall 1989.

36. See, for example, Marsden, "Can Jonathan Edwards (and His Heirs) Be Integrated Into the American History Narrative?" *Historically Speaking: The Bulletin of the Historical Society* 5 (July–August 2004), 13–15.

37. Ibid., 13.

38. Virtually every monograph on the history of American evangelicalism begins with some statement of definitions. Some examples: James D. Hunter, *American Evangelicalism: Conservative Religion and the Quandary of Modernity* (New Brunswick: Rutgers University Press, 1983), 3–9; Marsden, *Reforming Fundamentalism*, 10–11, and "The Evangelical Denomination," in Marsden ed., *Evangelicalism in Modern America* (Grand Rapids, Mich.: Eerdmans, 1984), vii–xix; Noll, *Between Faith and Criticism*, 1–5, and Noll, David Bebbington and George A Rawlyk, eds., *Evangelicalism: Comparative Studies of Popular Protestantism in North America, the British Isles, and Beyond, 1700–1990* (New York: Oxford University Press, 1994), 6; Stone, *On the Boundaries of American Evangelicalism*, 1–21.

39. David Bebbington, *Evangelicalism in Modern Britain: A History from the 1730s to the 1980s* (London: Unwin Hyman, 1989), 2–19.

40. This is the central thesis of Farley Butler's dissertation, "Billy Graham and the End of Evangelical Unity" (PhD diss., University of Florida, 1976).

41. The best short summary of dispensational theology is the first chapter of Daniel P. Fuller, *Gospel and Law, Contrast or Continuum? The Hermeneutics of*

Dispensationalism and Covenant Theology (Pasadena: Fuller Seminary, 1990) 1–17. See also Fuller's "The Hermeneutics of Dispensationalism" (ThD diss., Northern Baptist Theological Seminary, 1957). A more recent assessment can be found in Timothy Weber, *On the Road to Armageddon: How Evangelicals Became Israel's Best Friend* (Grand Rapids, Mich.: Baker Academic, 2004), 19–43. This summary of dispensationalism, unless otherwise noted, leans heavily upon Fuller's chapter.

For representative participant descriptions of the traditional dispensationalist system see C. I. Scofield, *Rightly Dividing the Word of Truth* (Findlay: Fundamental Truth Publishers, 1940); Charles Ryrie, *The Basis of the Premillennial Faith* (Neptune: Loizeaux Bros., 1953) and *Dispensationalism Today* (Chicago: Moody Press, 1965); John Walvoord, *The Millennial Kingdom* (Findlay: Dunham, 1959); Arnold Ehlert, *A Bibliographic History of Dispensationalism* (Grand Rapids, Mich.: Baker, 1965). For a summary of a newer, slightly more moderate form of dispensationalism see Craig Blaising and Darrell L. Bock, *Progressive Dispensationalism* (Wheaton: BridgePoint, 1993).

For critiques of dispensationalism see Curtis I. Crenshaw and Grover E. Gunn, III, *Dispensationalism Today, Yesterday, and Tomorrow* (Memphis: Footstool, 1985); Keith A. Mathison, *Dispensationalism: Rightly Dividing the People of God?* (Phillipsburg: Presbyterian and Reformed Publishing, 1995); George Eldon Ladd, *The Blessed Hope* (Grand Rapids, Mich.: Eerdmans, 1956); Paul B. Fischer, *Ultra-Dispensationalism is Modernism: Exposing a Heresy Among Fundamentalists* (Chicago: Weir Bros., 1936) Fischer was an attorney in Chicago and a charter member of the Full Gospel Business Men's Fellowship. For mediating positions from outside the dispensationalist tradition see Kraus, *Dispensationalism in America* [Mennonite]; and Vern S. Poythress, *Understanding Dispensationalists*, 2nd ed. [Reformed] (Phillipsburg: Presbyterian and Reformed, 1994).

For comparisons of the various millennial positions see Millard J. Erickson, *Contemporary Options in Eschatology: A Study of the Millennium* (Grand Rapids, Mich.: Baker, 1977); Timothy Weber, *Living in the Shadow of the Second Coming*; and Robert G. Clouse, *The Meaning of the Millennium: Four Views* (Downers Grove: InterVarsity Press, 1977). Clouse's collection consists of essays and responses by George Eldon Ladd (historic premillennialism), Herman Hoyt (dispensational premillennialism), Loraine Boettner (postmillennialism), and Anthony Hoekema (amillennialism).

42. Ehlert, *Bibliographic History*, 83.

43. Fuller, *Gospel and Law*, 12.

44. Ibid., 3–4

45. Roger Robins, "*American Millennarian and Prophetic Review*," in Mark Fackler and Charles Lippy, eds., *Popular Religious Magazines of the United States* (New York: Greenwood Press, 1995), 48.

46. Sandeen, *Roots of Fundamentalism*, 38.

47. This summary is dependent on Paul Boyer, *When Time Shall Be No More: Prophecy Belief in Modern American Culture* (Cambridge: Belknap Press of Harvard University Press, 1992), 87–88.

48. James Barr, *Fundamentalism*, 2nd ed. (London: SCM Press, 1981), 191; Sandeen, *Roots of Fundamentalism*, 222; Boyer, *When Time Shall Be No More*, 97–98.

49. Boyer, *When Time Shall Be No More*, 97–98. Boyer claims that this is a conservative estimate, and that the true figure was between 5 and 10 million.

50. Ibid., 92.

51. Barr, *Fundamentalism*, 191.

52. Quoted in Boyer, *When Time Shall Be No More*, 98. The melody is from the hymn, "On Christ the Solid Rock I Stand."

53. Sandeen, *Roots of Fundamentalism*, 224.

54. Matt. 24:14 (KJV).

NOTES TO CHAPTER I

1. This account of Ladd's early life, unless otherwise noted, is distilled from a series of interviews conducted by Rebecca Jane Duncan for a class at Fuller Seminary. She has graciously shared her original interview notes with me. The conversations with Muriel Ladd, the wife of George Ladd's brother, James, and Judy Ladd Rylander, daughter of James and Muriel Ladd, are especially helpful and revealing. Both interviews were conducted in December 1989.

2. Dartmouth College General Catalogue, 1769–1940 (Hanover: Dartmouth College Publications), 878. Rauner Special Collections Library, Dartmouth College, Hanover, New Hampshire.

3. The link between Ladd and the fiction of Zane Grey was mentioned in interviews with Muriel Ladd, George's sister-in-law, 15 December 1989, and John Wipf, a former student of Ladd's at Fuller Seminary, n.d. (c. December 1989). Rebecca Jane Duncan Papers.

4. From the biographical sketch for Zane Grey at www.classicreader.com. [accessed 21 February 2004.] For a more recent full-length biography of Grey see Thomas H. Pauly, *Zane Grey: His Life, His Adventures, His Women* (Champaign, Ill.: University of Illinois Press, 2005).

5. Kent L. Steckmesser, "Lawmen and Outlaws," published online by the Texas Christian University, at http://www2.tcu.edu/depts/prs/amwest/html/wl0119.html (accessed 21 February 2004).

6. All of these qualities are listed in the interview with Muriel Ladd, 15 December 1989. Duncan Papers.

7. Interview with John Wipf, n.d. (c. December 1989). Duncan Papers.

8. George Eldon Ladd, autobiographical sketch, in an application to join the New England Fellowship, c.1936.

9. Ibid.

10. Ibid.

11. Interview with Bruce Dreon, 25 September 2003. Dreon is a former student of Ladd's at Fuller Theological Seminary. Ladd shared this recollection with his classes.

12. Interview with Muriel Ladd, 15 December 1989, and Judy Ladd Rylander, n.d. (c. December 1989). Duncan Papers

13. Interview with Muriel Ladd, 15 December 1989, who recalls that, as a child, George was whipped with a leather belt. Duncan Papers.

14. Ibid.

15. *The Hypernikon*, the yearbook of Gordon College of Theology and Missions, 1926, p.53. When Ladd was interviewed for the biographical sketch in his *Festschrift* in 1977, he said that Cash had been a student at Moody Bible Institute, and this has been repeated in every subsequent biographical treatment of Ladd—usually as a way of identifying him as a strict fundamentalist in his earlier years. But an earlier recollection (in his 1935 application to work with the New England Fellowship) casts doubt on this detail, and the discovery of Cash's name in the *Hypernikon* confirms that she was indeed a graduate of Gordon College and not Moody Bible Institute.

16. Margaret Lamberts Bendroth, *Fundamentalism and Gender: 1875 to the Present* (New Haven: Yale University Press, 1993), 75. See also Julie Ingersoll, *Evangelical Christian Women: War Stories in the Gender Battles* (New York: New York University Press, 2003).

17. Ladd, autobiographical sketch, in his application to join the New England Fellowship, ca.1936.

18. George M. Marsden, *Fundamentalism and American Culture: The Shaping of Twentieth-Century Evangelicalism, 1870–1925* (New York: Oxford University Press, 1980), 71.

19. On the growth and dominance of "upstart" Methodist and Baptist churches in New England see Roger Finke and Rodney Stark, *The Churching of America, 1776–1990: Winners and Losers in Our Religious Economy* (New Brunswick, N.J.: Rutgers University Press, 1992), 66–71.

20. Ladd, autobiographical sketch, in an application to preach with the New England Fellowship, c.1936.

21. Ibid.

22. Interview with Muriel Ladd, 15 December 1989. Duncan Papers.

23. GEL to Rudolph Nelson, 22 June 1978. Nelson has generously provided me with a copy.

24. Recollection of Carl Dolloff, a member of the Gilford church when Ladd was the pastor there. Quoted in a letter to me from Raymond Wixson, pastor of Gilford Community Church, 4 June 1991.

25. On the treatment of women in New England's textile industry, see William Moran, *The Belles of New England: The Women of the Textile Mills and the Families Whose Wealth They Wove* (New York: Thomas Dunne's/St. Martin's Press, 2002), especially 225–43.

26. Ladd autobiographical sketch, in an application to preach with the New England Fellowship, c.1936.

27. See Virginia Lieson Brereton's comprehensive study, *Training God's Army: The American Bible School, 1880–1940* (Bloomington: Indiana University Press, 1990).

28. Wood is quoted in ibid., 105.

29. I am indebted to Thomas Askew of Gordon College for this insight.

30. Brereton, *Training God's Army*, 83.

31. Several minor controversies occurred at the school over the years, however. In 1919, in order to ensure its Baptist identity, Gordon's board of trustees amended

the institutional by-laws to require that a minimum of twenty-four of the thirty-
six members of the board, as well as the president and chairman, be committed
members of Baptist churches (Board of Trustee Minutes [9 April 1919], Gordon
College of Theology and Missions, Gordon College Archives, 5[G2], Book 3 [1914–
1924]). This regulation, though challenged occasionally, remained in effect until it
was rescinded in 1945 (Board of Trustee Minutes [21 May 1945], Gordon College of
Theology and Missions, Gordon College Archives, 5[G2], Book 4 [1924–1952]). More
important in the context of the doctrinal controversies during that time, Gordon
struggled with its identification with the Newton Theological Institution, a Baptist
seminary founded in 1825. Newton had sponsored Gordon's nascent program of
theological education from 1907 to 1914, when Gordon's own faculty was ready
to take over full responsibility for training (Askew, "Educational Legacy of A. J.
Gordon," 34). In 1931 Newton merged with Andover Seminary, precipitating
a minor controversy at Gordon. Andover had been founded in 1808 as a Trini-
tarian alternative to Harvard's Unitarian theological position but over the years had
drifted into theological liberalism. By the early twentieth century Andover had become a symbol for conservative evangelicals of what would happen to an institution if it did not enforce a strict doctrinal statement. Newton's partnership with
Andover thus threatened to taint Gordon's own standing within conservative evangelicalism. At the 1931 board meeting, however, the board averted a division by
prohibiting any Gordon trustee from serving on the governing body of "any other
New England Theological Institution" (Board of Trustee Minutes [19 November
1931], Gordon College of Theology and Missions, Gordon College Archives,
5[G2], Book 4 [1924–1952]). Despite these near crises Gordon College managed to
avoid the militant divisions that damaged or destroyed other schools in the movement, no mean feat in the fractious landscape of 1920s' and 1930s' American
evangelicalism.

32. Gordon College of Theology and Missions Catalog for 1915, 29. Gordon
College Archives.

33. Board of Trustee Minutes (14 April 1915), Gordon College of Theology and
Missions. Gordon College Archives, 5(G2), Book 3 (1914–1924).

34. Ibid. (12 April 1916).

35. Gordon College of Theology and Missions Catalog for 1933, 35.

36. Brereton, *Training God's Army*, 104–105. The influence of Gordon College
was relatively broad. In Ladd's senior year (1933) 288 regular students were enrolled at
the school, with others taking occasional courses. Of the 288 attending, 94 (32.6
percent) were women. See the Gordon College for Theology and Missions Bulletin for
1933.

37. *Hypernikon*, 1933, 86. Gordon College Archives.

38. Ladd, autobiographical sketch, in an application to preach with the New
England Fellowship, ca. 1936.

39. *Gordon News-Letter*, June 1932, 5. Gordon College Archives.

40. David Allan Hubbard, handwritten notes for a biographical sketch of Ladd,
ca. 1976, David Allan Hubbard Papers, Fuller Seminary Archives.

41. Recollection of Carl Dolloff, a member of the Gilford church when Ladd was the pastor there. Quoted in a letter to me from Raymond Wixson, pastor of Gilford Community Church, 4 June 1991.

42. Board of Trustee Minutes (March 1933), Gordon College of Theology and Missions, Gordon College Archives, 5(G2), Book 4 (1924–1952).

43. From Ladd's self-reported transcript, ca. 1941.

44. George Eldon Ladd, "Life of Saul," unpublished undergraduate paper, ca. 1930.

45. "George Eldon Ladd," entry in *Contemporary Authors Online*, Gale Group, 2001 (accessed on my behalf by a librarian at Dartmouth College on 26 April 2004).

46. Ladd's personal diary, 11 July 1933 (the Ladds' wedding day).

47. Interview with Muriel Ladd, 15 December 1989. Duncan Papers.

48. Ladd's personal diary, n.d. (ca. May 1930).

49. Recollection of Carl Dolloff.

50. Salary information is reported in the Registry of Ministers and Missionaries Benefit Board of the Northern Baptist Convention. Personal information form for George Eldon Ladd, dated 6 June 1936, American Baptist Historical Society, Archives Center, Valley Forge, Pennsylvania.

51. Unless otherwise noted, I am indebted to Roland Nelson ("Fundamentalism and the Northern Baptist Convention," PhD diss., University of Chicago, 1964, 119–25, 386) for the following discussion.

52. GEL to Richard Clearwaters, 15 October 1953. Clearwaters was a leader in the Conservative Baptist (CB) movement.

53. GEL to R. T. Ketcham, 4 November 1936. This letter does not survive but is referenced in Ketcham's reply.

54. William H. Brackney, "Robert Thomas Ketcham," in *The Baptists* (New York: Greenwood Press, 1988), 209–10.

55. Ketcham to GEL, 9 November 1936.

56. Ibid.

57. See Elizabeth Evans' study of the NEF, *The Wright Vision: The Story of the New England Fellowship* (Lanham: University Press of America, 1991). See also Joel A. Carpenter, *Revive Us Again: The Reawakening of American Fundamentalism* (New York: Oxford University Press, 1997), 154–55.

58. On the founding of the NAE see Joel A. Carpenter, "The Fundamentalist Leaven and the Rise of an Evangelical United Front," in Leonard I. Sweet, ed., *The Evangelical Tradition in America* (Macon: Mercer University Press, 1984), 257–88.

59. Evans, *Wright Vision*, 11.

60. Quoted in ibid., 10.

61. Evans, *Wright Vision*, 26, 28. The manuscripts of several radio sermons survive in the GEL papers.

62. *The Gordon* 4(2) (October 1948): 5. Gordon College Archives.

63. Ladd, "Statement of Doctrinal Belief," in an application to join the New England Fellowship, ca. 1936.

64. Ibid., 11.

65. Ibid., 6.

66. The salary was recalled by Ladd in David Allan Hubbard's notes for a biographical sketch of Ladd, ca. 1976, Hubbard Papers.

67. Letter from Juelia Desilets Cerutti to me, 21 May 1991. Cerutti and her husband were members of the Montpelier church and neighbors of the Ladds.

68. Ibid.

69. Letter from Sherwood and Helen Murray to me, 21 May 1991. Both were members of Ladd's youth group at the Montpelier church, and both were baptized by him. Ladd performed their wedding service in 1940, and in 1991 they were still active members of the Montpelier church.

70. Ibid.

71. Registry of Ministers and Missionaries Benefit Board of the Northern Baptist Convention. Personal information form for George Eldon Ladd, dated 1 October 1948, American Baptist Historical Society, Archives Center, Valley Forge, Pennsylvania. The document lists Ladd's salary at Gordon as $3,600 per year, a significant difference even in light of the better economic conditions in the postwar years.

72. Interview with Muriel Ladd, 15 December 1989. Duncan Papers.

73. On Wheaton's significance in the evangelical world see Michael S. Hamilton, "The Fundamentalist Harvard: Wheaton College, 1919–1965" (PhD diss., University of Notre Dame, 1994).

74. These biographical details are from Joel Carpenter, "[J]ames Oliver Buswell, Jr.," in Daniel G. Reid et al., eds., *Dictionary of Christianity in America* (Downers Grove, Ill.: InterVarsity Press, 1990), 203–204.

75. James Oliver Buswell to GEL, 21 November 1938. Ladd's letter does not survive, but its level of detail is mentioned in Buswell's response.

76. GEL to John R. Sampey, 7 February 1939. This letter does not survive, but its date and contents are referenced in Sampey's response.

77. John R. Sampey to GEL, 15 February 1939.

78. W. Hersey Davis to GEL, 21 March 1939.

79. GEL to Davis, 20 October 1939. This letter does not survive, but its date is mentioned in Davis's response.

80. Davis to GEL, 31 October 1939.

81. Davis to GEL, 21 November 1939. Ladd's letter of 2 November does not survive, but its details are mentioned in Davis's response.

During this courtship with Southern Baptist Seminary, Ladd was also making overtures to Dallas Theological Seminary, which was the intellectual home of dispensationalism, the dominant theological system among American fundamentalists, and would still have been a reasonably comfortable fit for Ladd at that point. A degree from Dallas (though it would not be the university degree he hoped for) would solidify his credentials as a conservative scholar and move him slightly nearer to his goal. But it was not to be. John Walvoord (1910–2002), registrar of the seminary and heir apparent to the presidency, wrote to Ladd with the news that his Gordon degree would not meet the requirements for admission to the seminary. Further, even Dallas required a divinity degree for acceptance to doctoral work, and unless Ladd either had the BD in hand or could state that it was near completion, he could not be admitted to the program. Walvoord was encouraging; Bible college credentials were certainly not rare among American fundamentalist applicants, and Dallas offered several remedial courses for students who lacked sufficient academic preparation. According to Walvoord, Dallas generally recognized "any theological degree provided its standards are reasonable and includes both Scriptural languages" (John Walvoord to GEL, 14 February 1939).

82. "Tentative Study for the MA Degree," ca. 1939.

83. Edgar Brightman to GEL, 22 December 1939. Ladd had rendered *Timaeus* as *Timeas* in his proposal.

84. Luther Weigle to GEL, 19 October 1940.

85. Self-reported transcripts in GEL Papers.

86. Letter from Juelia Desilets Cerutti to me, 21 May 1991.

87. J. Homer Slutz to GEL, 1 February 1941.

88. H. Earl Myers to GEL, 10 February 1941.

89. Carl H. Morgan to GEL, 4 April 1941.

90. Ibid. Emphasis in Morgan's letter.

91. Paul C. Kitchen to GEL, 31 March 1941.

92. Kitchen to GEL, 21 April 1941.

93. GEL to Kitchen, 24 April 1941. This letter does not survive but is mentioned in Kitchen's response, dated 9 May 1941.

94. Registry of Ministers and Missionaries Benefit Board of the Northern Baptist Convention, personal information form for George Eldon Ladd, dated 17 September 1938. American Baptist Historical Society, Archives Center, Valley Forge, Pennsylvania.

95. Ibid.

96. Interviews with Muriel Ladd, 15 December 1989, and Judy Ladd Rylander, George's niece, n.d. (ca. December 1989). Duncan Papers.

97. Service information is taken from the U.S. Army personnel record for James Mathon Ladd (1942–1950). Courtesy of the U.S. Army Chaplain Museum, Fort Jackson, South Carolina.

98. "Serious and Humorous Incidents Told by N.H. [New Hampshire] Chaplain," *Gordon Alumni Chronicle* 10(4) (October 1944), 1. Gordon College Archives.

99. James Ladd's dissertation was titled "Dwight L. Moody's Use of the Aristotelian Modes of Persuasion" (PhD diss., Oklahoma State University, 1960).

100. Interview with Judy Ladd Rylander, n.d. (ca. December 1989). Duncan Papers.

101. Ibid.

102. Interview with Muriel Ladd, 15 December 1989. Duncan Papers.

103. Bernard Loomer to GEL, 16 January 1942.

104. Allen Wikgren to GEL, 24 January 1942. Wikgren was the chair of the scholarship committee at the divinity school.

105. Ladd, "Did Paul Change His Mind about the Time of the Second Coming of Christ?" (BD thesis, Gorden Divinity School, 1941).

106. Ibid., 6.

107. Ladd makes this argument in ibid., 80. Matt. 24:36 reads as follows: "But of that day and hour knoweth no man, no, not the angels of heaven, but my father only" (KJV).

108. Nathan Wood, typescript comments, n.d. (ca. 1941).

109. Ibid.

110. Ladd, "Did Paul Change His Mind about the Time of the Second Coming of Christ?" 1.

111. Registry of Ministers and Missionaries Benefit Board of the Northern Baptist Convention. Personal information form for George Eldon Ladd, dated 29 October 1944. American Baptist Historical Society, Archives Center, Valley Forge, Pennsylvania. The parsonage where the Ladds lived still survives, but Blaney Memorial Baptist Church was closed and its property sold to a local bank in the 1980s. A parking lot now occupies the site.

112. On the influence of fundamentalism within Boston churches see Margaret Lamberts Bendroth, *Fundamentalists in the City: Conflicts and Division in Boston's Churches, 1885–1950* (New York: Oxford University Press, 2005).

113. Carroll Bingham to GEL, 16 April 1942. Bingham was the clerk of the congregation and in this role extended the invitation to Ladd.

114. Merrill Tenney to GEL, 23 January 1942.

115. Minutes of the Boston South Baptist Association, 1943, 10, and 1944, 10. American Baptist–Samuel Colgate Library, Rochester, New York.

116. Ladd's copy of the minutes of the Program Committee of the Massachusetts Baptist Convention, 13 June 1945.

117. Ibid.

118. GEL to George F. Beecher, 14 June 1945. Beecher was the secretary of the Conference of Baptist Ministers in Massachusetts.

119. Gordon H. Clark to GEL, 12 September 1942.

120. William A. Mueller to GEL, 14 September 1942.

121. H. Emerson Rosenberger to GEL, 23 September 1942.

122. T. Leonard Lewis to GEL, 9 October 1942. Lewis would later become president of Gordon School of Theology and a colleague of Ladd's.

123. Gordon College and Divinity School Catalog 1948–1949, 16–17. Gordon College Archives.

124. See, for example, Robert H. Pfeiffer, *Excavations at Nuzi Conducted by the Semitic Museum and the Fogg Art Museum of Harvard University* (Cambridge: Harvard University Press, 1929); *State Letters of Assyria: A Transliteration and Translation of 355 Official Assyrian Letters Dating from the Sargonid Period, 722–625 B.C.* (New Haven: American Oriental Society, 1935); and *Introduction to the Old Testament* (New York and London: Harper & Brothers, 1941).

125. File titled "Inter-Testamental Period," the seminar taught by Pfeiffer at Boston University School of Theology, n.d. (ca. 1943).

126. Unless otherwise noted, I am indebted to Rudolph Nelson for this discussion. See Nelson, *Making and Unmaking of an Evangelical Mind: The Case of Edward Carnell* (New York: Cambridge University Press, 1987), 54–72.

127. Ibid., 55.

128. See David Callahan, *Kindred Spirits: Harvard Business School's Extraordinary Class of 1949 and How They Transformed American Business* (Hoboken, N.J.: John Wiley and Sons, 2007). This fascinating book traces the background and training of these businessmen and the impact of their leadership on the U.S. economy and beyond.

129. See Nelson, *Making and Unmaking of an Evangelical Mind*, 56–58.

130. In his annual report to the president of the university, Willard L. Sperry, dean of the divinity school, defended Harvard's intentional historical approach:

> In particular our emphasis upon the historical approach to religion, as against the psychological, social and aesthetic approaches to the subject, should be defended.... Meanwhile our more than three hundred years of history and our constant concern over all these years for our religious heritage in America suggest not merely the propriety, but the inevitability of our construing religion historically.... The emphasis in this School upon the historical approach to the Christian religion is not, therefore, to be construed as a mere matter of academic antiquarianism, an engaging ivory tower which offers attractive escape from the challenge of modernity. It aims steadily at an interpretation of the present. (Sperry, "Report of the Dean of the Divinity School," 1948–1949 Academic Year, 415–16. Harvard University Archives)

131. Ladd, in notes from an interview with Rudolph Nelson in December 1977. Nelson shared a copy of his notes with me.

132. Ladd, in Nelson, *Making and Unmaking of an Evangelical Mind*, 69. See also 235n22.

133. Noted in Ladd's Fulbright Fellowship application, 5 November 1949.

134. GEL to the officers and congregation of Blaney Memorial Baptist Church, 1 July 1945.

135. Nelson, *Making and Unmaking of an Evangelical Mind*, 59.

136. GEL to Cadbury, 8 April 1964.

137. For a detailed and sympathetic biography of Cadbury see Margaret Hope Beacon, *Let This Life Speak: The Legacy of Henry Joel Cadbury* (Philadelphia: University of Pennsylvania Press, 1987).

138. Henry J. Cadbury, *The Making of Luke-Acts* (New York: Macmillan, 1927), 3.

139. Richard I. Pervo, "On Perilous Things," in Mikeal Parsons and Joseph Tyson, eds., *Cadbury, Knox, and Talbert: American Contributions to the Study of Acts* (Atlanta: Scholars Press, 1992), 38.

140. Nelson, *Making and Unmaking of an Evangelical Mind*, 58.

141. Marsden, *Fundamentalism*, 51–55.

142. Ladd's class notes from Cadbury's New Testament seminar, n.d. (ca. 1945).

143. Ibid. The quote is written across the top of the page and is specifically attributed to Cadbury.

144. Levering Reynolds Jr., "The Later Years," in Williams, ed., *The Harvard Divinity School* (Boston: Beacon Press, 1954), 226.

145. Ralph Lazzaro, "Theological Scholarship at Harvard from 1880 to 1953," in ibid., 259.

146. From the dedication to Henry Joel Cadbury in ibid., v.

147. GEL to Cadbury, 8 April 1964.

148. George Eldon Ladd, "The Eschatology of the *Didache*" (PhD diss., Harvard University, 1949). Ladd's degree in biblical and patristic Greek was granted by the graduate school of the university rather than the divinity school.

149. Ibid., 42.

150. Ibid., 14.

151. Ibid., 176.

152. Ibid.

153. Raymond Elliott, interview by Chris Matthews, 28 April 1980. Tape T1, Collection 115. Archives of the Billy Graham Center, Wheaton, Ill.

154. Registry of Ministers and Missionaries Benefit Board of the Northern Baptist Convention. Personal information form for George Eldon Ladd, dated 1 October 1948. American Baptist Historical Society, Archives Center, Valley Forge, Pennsylvania.

155. Notes from GEL interview by Rudolph Nelson, ca. 1978. Details are repeated in a letter from GEL to Glenn Barker, 17 October 1955.

156. GEL to H. H. Rowley, 20 July 1965. See also Ladd's 1949 application for a Fulbright Grant (#6-49-355-197).

157. Ibid., 4. Ladd is quoting Harnack in the *Encyclopaedia Britannica*, 9th ed., vol. 16, 330.

158. Ibid., 5, 6.

159. This story is ably told in George M. Marsden, *Reforming Fundamentalism: Fuller Seminary and the New Evangelicalism* (Grand Rapids, Mich.: Eerdmans, 1987), 13–30 and passim.

160. Harold Ockenga to Charles Fuller, 9 April 1947. Quoted in ibid., 56.

161. Ladd recounted this reason for coming to Fuller repeatedly during his career. Daniel Fuller to George Marsden, 10 June 1986. Marsden-Fuller Correspondence.

162. Registry of Ministers and Missionaries Benefit Board of the Northern Baptist Convention. Personal information form for George Eldon Ladd, dated 16 October 1950. American Baptist Historical Society, Archives Center, Valley Forge, Pennsylvania.

NOTES TO CHAPTER 2

1. On these early years see George M. Marsden, *Reforming Fundamentalism: Fuller Seminary and the New Evangelicalism* (Grand Rapids, Mich.: Eerdmans, 1987), 94–118.

2. For this discussion, unless otherwise noted, I am indebted to Robert S. Elwood, *1950: Crossroads of American Religious Life* (Grand Rapids, Mich.: Eerdmans, 1987), 94–118.

3. Ibid., 99.

4. Statistics are from Paul A. Crow Jr., "National Council of Churches of Christ in the U.S.A.," in Daniel G. Reid et al., eds., *Dictionary of Christianity in America* (Downers Grove, Ill.: InterVarsity Press, 1990), 798–99.

5. Elwood, *1950*, 117, 131.

6. On these organizations see Joel Carpenter, *Revive Us Again: The Reawakening of American Fundamentalism* (New York: Oxford University Press, 1997), 124–40 (*Old Fashioned Revival Hour*), 141–60 (National Association of Evangelicals), 161–76 (Youth for Christ), and 211–32 (early Billy Graham).

7. Ellwood, *1950*, 56.

8. See Carl F. H. Henry, *The Uneasy Conscience of Modern Fundamentalism* (Grand Rapids, Mich.: Eerdmans, 1947).

9. See, for example, Harold Lindsell's *Battle for the Bible* (Grand Rapids, Mich.: Zondervan, 1976).

10. Marsden, *Reforming Fundamentalism*, 26.

11. Ibid., 69.

12. The Vassady story can be found in ibid., 97–111.

13. On the significance of Ladd and Woodbridge see ibid., 120–22.

14. Ibid., 17–20, 24–25, 53–63.

15. Ibid., 18.

16. Ibid., 24.

17. Rudolph Nelson, *The Making and Unmaking of an Evangelical Mind: The Case of Edward Cornell* (New York: Cambridge University Press, 1987), 70–71, 75–78.

18. GEL to Kenneth L. Pike, 21 February 1951. Pike (1912–2000) was a classmate of Ladd's at Gordon and had become an expert linguist with a specialty in phonetics. He was the first president of the Summer Linguistic Institute (1942–1979), an organization affiliated with Wycliffe Bible Translators and in 1951 published a translation of the New Testament in the Miztec language of San Miguel, Mexico. Pike was professor of linguistics at the University of Michigan from 1948 until 1979. See his biographical sketch at the website of the Summer Linguistic Institute, http://www .sil.org/klp/klp-chronology.htm (accessed 6 November 2007).

19. Interview with Judy Ladd Rylander (ca. December 1989). Rebecca Jane Duncan Papers.

20. On this condition see the article at http://www.llu.edu/lluch/pedsurg/cryptorchidism.htm (accessed 6 November 2007).

21. B. Myron Cedarholm to GEL, 2 April 1953. Cedarholm was a CB leader who tried to recruit Ladd to the movement.

22. Earl S. Kalland to GEL, 7 November 1950.

23. Daniel Fuller to George Marsden, 10 June 1986. Marsden-Fuller Correspondence.

24. On the rise of the CBA see Roland T. Nelson, "Fundamentalism and the Northern Baptist Convention" (PhD diss., University of Chicago, 1964), 421–71.

25. Catalog for the 1952–1953 academic year, Western Conservative Baptist Theological Seminary, 10.

26. Ibid., 11.

27. On the ministry of Paul Rader see Larry Eskridge, "Only Believe: Paul Rader and the Chicago Gospel Tabernacle" (MA thesis, University of Maryland, 1985).

28. See GEL to Howard Ferrin, 23 November 1951, and Ferrin to GEL, 29 November 1951.

29. GEL to Ferrin, 23 November 1951.

30. Ibid.

31. Ibid.

32. Ibid.

33. Carpenter, *Revive Us Again*, 202–203.

34. J. C. Macaulay to GEL, 8 November 1952.

35. GEL to J. C. Macaulay, 10 November 1952.

36. Ladd was not alone in this effort. While liberal theologians remained largely indifferent to dispensationalism, conservative Reformed scholars had leveled detailed attacks on various aspects of the system for years. William Rutgers, a professor at the Dutch Reformed Calvin College, dismissed dispensationalism as a "novel system of theology [that] . . . gives the semblance of profundity which is in reality little more than analytic skill coupled with a fruitful imagination" (William P. Rutgers, *Premillennialism in America* [Goes, Holland: Oosterbaan & LeCointre, 1930], 237–38). Oswald Allis focused his critical attention on dispensationalist ecclesiology, challenging its notion of the church as a parenthesis. Dispensationalism is flawed by its "arbitrary and sweeping assertions," in Allis's view, a charge he lays at the feet of the Scofield Bible. This primary text of dispensationalism is exegetically flawed, Allis believed, and "tends to give the reader an utterly false impression of the biblical record" (Oswald T. Allis, *Prophecy and the Church* [Philadelphia: Presbyterian and Reformed Publishing Co., 1945], 52–54, 267–77, 53). However, the most devastating critique came from Louis Berkhof, former president of Calvin College and a highly regarded conservative theologian. In his view, premillennialism itself was unsupportable, and dispensationalism was its weakest variant. The representation of the gospel found in dispensationalism, according to Berkhof, "is not warranted by Scripture and grates upon our Christian sensibility" (Louis Berkhof, *The Kingdom of God* [Grand Rapids, Mich.: Eerdmans, 1951], 176). These challenges, though they came from scholars who believed in the supernatural origins of both the Christian faith and the Bible, could be dismissed by the most conservative wing of American evangelicalism because of the writers' millennial views. As conservative Reformed thinkers, Rutgers, Allis, and Berkhof were committed amillennialists who rejected the literal thousand-year reign of Christ on earth. Ladd's critique, coming from inside the conservative premillennialist camp, would be far more difficult to ignore and represents a significant development in the intellectual history of American evangelicalism.

37. Earl S. Kalland, "Preface," in George Eldon Ladd, *Crucial Questions about the Kingdom of God* (Grand Rapids, Mich.: Eerdmans, 1957), 7.

38. Ibid.

39. GEL to William B. Eerdmans, 8 October 1951.

40. Ibid.

41. Peter de Visser to GEL, 2 January 1952. Peter de Visser was the general manager of Wm. B. Eerdmans Publishing Company.

42. Report of the Committee for Faculty Club Research, January 1951.

43. Ockenga to GEL, 2 February 1951.

44. Ibid.

45. GEL to Ockenga, 16 April 1951.

46. Ockenga to GEL, 22 April 1952.

47. GEL to Ockenga, 28 June 1952.

48. GEL to Ockenga (unsent), 28 June 1952.

49. GEL to Ockenga, 28 June 1952.

50. Ladd, *Crucial Questions*, table of contents.

51. Ibid., 21–22.

52. Wilbur M. Smith in preface to *Crucial Questions*, 12.

53. Ibid.

54. Smith to GEL, 5 November 1952.

55. Ibid.

56. Ladd, *Crucial Questions*, 48–52. The Sperry work is *Systematic Theology*, 8 vols. (Dallas: Dallas Seminary Press, 1948).

57. Ladd, *Crucial Questions*, 64.

58. Ibid., 78.

59. Ibid., 80.

60. Ibid., 84. The emphasis is Ladd's.

61. Rev. 20:1–6 reads as follows:

And I saw an angel come down from heaven, having the key of the bottomless pit and a great chain in hand. And he laid hold on the dragon, that old serpent, which is the Devil and Satan, and bound him a thousand years, and cast him into the bottomless pit, and shut him up, and set a seal upon him, that he should deceive the nations no more, till the thousand years should be fulfilled: and after that he must be loosed a little season. And I saw thrones, and they sat upon them, and judgment was given unto them: and I saw the souls of them that were beheaded for the witness of Jesus, and for the word of God, and which had not worshipped the beast, neither his image, neither had they received his mark upon their foreheads, or in their hands; and they lived and reigned with Christ a thousand years. But the rest of the dead lived not again until the thousand years were finished. This is the first resurrection. Blessed and holy is he that hath part of the first resurrection: on such the second death hath no power, but they shall be priests of God and of Christ, and shall reign with him a thousand years. (KJV)

62. Ladd, *Crucial Questions*, 135.

63. Ibid., 149.

64. See ibid., 78n3 and 88n22. An examination of books by early Fuller faculty shows that most of Ladd's contemporaries (including Smith, Woodbridge, Ockenga,

and Lindsell) did not cite German critical sources in their work. Everett Harrison, on the other hand, used Kittel and Kümmel extensively in his graduate studies. See Harrison, "The Use of *Doxa* in Greek Literature with Special Reference to the New Testament" (PhD diss., University of Pennsylvania, 1950). Ladd's future colleague, British scholar Geoffrey Bromiley, would translate Kittel's *Wörterbuch* for use by English-speaking students.

65. Delbert Rose, review of *Crucial Questions, The Journal of Bible and Religion* 21 (July 1953) 208. A slightly different version of this review also appeared in the *Asbury Seminarian* 8 (Fall–Winter 1954): 63–65.

66. Bruce, review of *Crucial Questions,* 114.

67. F. F. Bruce, *In Retrospect: Remembrance of Things Past,* 2d ed. (Grand Rapids, Mich.: Baker Book House, 1993), 12–19, 52–55, 154–61, 313–17, and passim.

68. Bruce, review of *Crucial Questions,* 115.

69. Ibid.

70. James F. Scott, ed., *An Analytical Index to* Bibliotheca Sacra (Dallas: Axminster Press, 1971).

71. Walvoord wrote full-length review articles on just three books in *Bibliotheca Sacra:* Lewis Sperry Chafer's *Systematic Theology* (1948), Ladd's *Crucial Questions* (1953), and *The Blessed Hope* (1956).

72. GEL to Walvoord, 23 August 1951.

73. Walvoord to GEL, 24 November 1952.

74. Walvoord to GEL, 2 December 1952.

75. GEL to Walvoord, 26 November 1952.

76. The four articles in *Bibliotheca Sacra* were "Kingdom of God in the Jewish Apocryphal Literature: Introduction," 109 (Winter 1952), 55–62; "Kingdom of God in the Jewish Apocryphal Literature: Jubilees," 109 (Spring 1952), 164–74; "Kingdom of God in the Jewish Apocryphal Literature: Enoch," 110 (Fall 1952), 318–31; and "Kingdom of God in I Enoch," 110 (Winter 1953), 32–49. The final article appeared in the same issue as Walvoord's review of *Crucial Questions.*

77. John F. Walvoord, review of *Crucial Questions,* in *Bibliotheca Sacra* 110 (Winter 1953), 1.

78. Ibid., 4, 8.

79. Ibid., 6, 10.

80. Walvoord to GEL, 19 December 1952.

81. Ibid.

82. GEL to Walvoord, 20 December 1952. Ladd's carbon copy of this letter is printed on the back of an early draft page of *Crucial Questions.*

83. The sentence in question read as follows: "Dr. Ladd evidently embraces covenant theology which views the whole purpose of God as essentially soteriological and concerned with the unfolding of the plan of salvation." The revised sentence reads this way: "Although not a covenant theologian, Dr. Ladd's view is similar to covenant theology which regards the whole purpose of God as essentially soteriological and concerned with the unfolding of the plan of salvation."

84. GEL to Walvoord, 6 December 1952.

85. Raymond Buker to GEL, 18 November 1952.

86. GEL to Buker, 20 November 1952.

87. Vincent Brushwyler to GEL, 19 November 1952.

88. GEL to Brushwyler, 25 November 1952.

89. Bernard Ramm to GEL, postmarked 3 January 1953.

90. Vernon Grounds to GEL, 17 February 1953.

91. Sherman Roddy to GEL, 20 February 1953.

92. See Sherman Roddy, "Fundamentalists and Ecumenicity," *Christian Century* (1 October 1958), 1109–10.

93. Tenney to GEL, 24 November 1952.

94. Ibid.

95. Smith to GEL, 5 November 1952.

96. See Bruce M. Metzger, "The Revised Standard Version," *The Duke Divinity School Review* 44 (Spring 1979), 70–87.

97. William A. Irwin, *An Introduction to the Revised Standard Version of the Old Testament* (New York: Thomas Nelson and Sons, 1952), 13.

98. Ibid., 14.

99. Metzger, "Revised Standard Version," 75.

100. David Ewert, "Bible, English Translations and Versions in North America," in Daniel G. Reid et al., eds., *Dictionary of Christianity in America* (Downers Grove, Ill.: InterVarsity Press, 1990), 139.

101. When I took an introductory course on the Bible at a state university in 1981, the RSV was the required textbook.

102. Robert G. Lee, "The Revised Standard Version," newspaper clipping, n.d.

103. Quoted in an unattributed newspaper clipping, n.d.

104. T. S. Jackson, *This New Bible, the Genius of Modernism* (Little Rock: American Baptist Publishing, n.d.), 4. Quoted in Gerald A. Larue, "Another Chapter in the History of Bible Translation," *Journal of Bible and Religion* 31 (October 1963), 301.

105. Quoted in F. F. Bruce, *The English Bible: A History of Translations from the Earliest English Versions*, 196. The author of the article is not named.

106. Reported in Metzger, "Revised Standard Version," 76.

107. Bruce, *English Bible*, 196. Ladd was aware of this incident—and horrified by it. See GEL to Edward Hart, 26 December 1956, and Hart's response to GEL, 29 December 1956. Hart was Ladd's pastor at the time.

108. C. F. Lincoln, ed., et al., "Critique of the Revised Standard Version," *Bibliotheca Sacra* 110 (Winter 1953), 50–66. This is the same issue of *Bibliotheca Sacra* that contained John Walvoord's review of Ladd's *Crucial Questions*.

109. Ibid., 50.

110. Ibid., 54.

111. Ibid., 62.

112. Ibid., 65.

113. Ibid., 66. This page contains a notice that extra copies of this issue of *Bibliotheca Sacra* would be printed for wider distribution and available from the publisher for 75 cents each.

114. This represents a correction to the record as published by Marsden in *Reforming Fundamentalism*, 137. He quotes LaSor's recollection of the project in a 1976 publication, in which he lists Charles Woodbridge and not Ladd as the fourth member of the team. Woodbridge was a strict inerrantist who later left Fuller over changes to its doctrinal statement and would not have shared LaSor's generally positive view of the RSV. All of the extant papers related to the project show Ladd and not Woodbridge as the fourth member.

115. Lincoln, et al. "Critique of the Revised Standard Version."

116. "Suggested Outline of Critique of Revised Standard Version." GEL Papers.

117. This letter does not survive. Eerdmans's response gives the details contained in the previous letter, as well as its date. Eerdmans to GEL, 26 December 1952.

118. GEL to Eerdmans, 5 January 1953.

119. Several notes in Ladd's RSV file describe the routing path.

120. Hitt to GEL, 12 May 1954.

121. GEL to Hitt, 3 June 1954.

122. On the democratic nature of evangelical enterprises and the authority of public opinion in shaping their decisions, see Nathan O. Hatch, "Evangelicalism as a Democratic Movement," in George Marsden, ed., *Evangelicalism and Modern America* (Grand Rapids, Mich.: Eerdmans, 1984), 78–80.

123. Summarized in Marsden, *Reforming Fundamentalism*, 137–38.

124. Quoted in ibid., 138.

125. Ibid. Several important chapters of the book existed in draft form when the project was cancelled. See William Sanford La Sor, "Preliminary Considerations," unpublished draft, n.d.; Ladd, "Chapter 2: Accuracy of Translation (New Testament)," unpublished draft, n.d.; Ladd, "The RSV as a Tool for Bible Study," unpublished draft, n.d.; and Ladd, untitled draft of chapter 8, n.d. These drafts are in the GEL Papers.

126. Ladd, "Accuracy of Translation (New Testament)." These first two points represent the argument of the chapter.

127. This is a nearly unanimous recollection from alumni throughout Ladd's career. Ladd was clearly more like Arthur Darby Nock than Henry Cadbury in teaching style.

128. GEL to Nicole, 13 November 1952.

129. Nicole to GEL, 20 November 1952.

130. Marsden, *Reforming Fundamentalism*, 138–40. The case can be made that Ockenga liked the idea of an intellectually progressive evangelical seminary more than the practice of such.

131. Ibid., 141–43.

132. Carnell to Ockenga, 14 October 1955. Quoted in Marsden, *Reforming Fundamentalism*, 150.

133. Interview with Muriel Ladd, George's sister-in-law, 15 December 1989. Rebecca Jane Duncan Papers.

134. The headaches at Harvard and their recurrence at Fuller are mentioned in a letter from GEL to Daniel Fuller, 20 May 1954.

135. GEL to Kenneth Monroe, 26 January 1953. Monroe was then dean of Westmont College in Santa Barbara, California. Ladd wrote to recommend the treatment for Monroe's headaches. The psychologist, referred to only as "Dr. Sandblom," is never mentioned again in Ladd's papers. For a full discussion of this method of treatment see http://www.lightparty.com/Health/Radionics.html (accessed 8 November 2007).

136. See the account of the trial in 1951 of Ruth Drown, inventor of instruments used in radionics, at http://www.chirobase.org/12Hx/drown.html (accessed 8 November 2007).

137. GEL to Alex Crossan Jr., 8 October 1954.

NOTES TO CHAPTER 3

1. GEL to Richard Clearwaters, 24 November 1953.

2. Ibid.

3. B. Myron Cedarholm to GEL, 2 April 1953.

4. *Yearbook of the American Baptist Convention: 1956*, 472. The yearbooks list members active from the previous year, so Ladd may have left in 1955. American Baptist Historical Society, American Baptist Archives Center, Valley Forge, Penn.

5. George M. Marsden, *Reforming Fundamentalism* (Grand Rapids, Mich.: Eerdmans, 1987), 147–50. See Carnell's inaugural address, "The Glory of a Theological Seminary," published by Fuller Seminary in 1967. The text of the address had been impounded by Charles Fuller immediately after it was delivered, and George Ladd was instrumental in having it made public. See Rudolph Nelson, *Making and Unmaking of an Evangelical Mind* (New York: Cambridge University Press, 1987), 237n40.

6. See Robert S. Ellwood, *The Fifties Spiritual Marketplace: American Religion in a Decade of Conflict* (New Brunswick: Rutgers University Press, 1997), 123–24. *Brown v. Board of Education* struck down segregated public education in the United States. See Kermit Hall, ed., *Oxford Companion to the Supreme Court of the United States* (New York: Oxford University Press, 1992), 93–96.

7. Marsden, *Reforming Fundamentalism*, 141–52.

8. Harold Lindsell and Charles J. Woodbridge, *A Handbook of Christian Truth* (Westwood: Fleming Revell, 1953).

9. Marsden, *Reforming Fundamentalism*, 150–52, 198–200.

10. Ibid., 150.

11. Carnell's story is ably told in Nelson, *Making and Unmaking of an Evangelical Mind*.

12. Interviews with Daniel Fuller and other members of the class of 1951 at the fiftieth anniversary reunion, Fuller Theological Seminary, 7–9 June 2001.

13. GEL to Daniel Fuller, 8 February 1954. As late as 1989 Fuller was still teaching a course (titled "The Unity of the Bible") at the seminary based on this research. I took the course. He published the work as *The Unity of the Bible: Unfolding God's Plan for Humanity* (Grand Rapids, Mich.: Zondervan, 1992).

14. Fuller to GEL, 17 March 1954.

15. Fuller to GEL, 7 May 1954.

16. Daniel Payton Fuller, "The Hermeneutics of Dispensationalism" (ThD diss., Northern Baptist Theological Seminary, 1957). This dissertation was later published in expanded form as *Gospel and Law, Contrast or Continuum? The Hermeneutics of Dispensationalism and Covenant Theology* (Pasadena: Fuller Seminary Press, 1990).

17. Fuller to GEL, 12 June 1954.

18. Students who questioned dispensationalism could, within limits, pursue studies at Fuller as well. From 1954 to 1956 Ladd supervised the graduate work of Wesley Gerig, who stayed at Fuller after his Bachelor of Divinity studies to complete a Master of Theology (ThM) with an emphasis in New Testament exegesis. Fuller's ThM degree program was a rigorous one that included seminars and research work. Pedagogically it fit well into Ladd's and the other critically trained professors' plans to gain credibility for the seminary by preparing Fuller graduates for doctoral studies at other universities. Gerig's thesis challenges the dispensationalist doctrine of the secret pretribulational rapture of the church and argues instead for a posttribulational, premillennial position, the stance shared by Ladd (see Gerig, "Church and the Tribulation," ThM thesis, Fuller Theological Seminary, 1956). It methodically summarizes the various positions on the issue and makes his case based on his own study of the relevant biblical texts. Showing the influence of Ladd's objective ideal, Gerig acknowledges in his last chapter that a textual difficulty exists in Matthew 24:15 that clouds the relationship between the church and Israel, making it impossible to argue unequivocally for one position over the other. Still, he writes, "it must be admitted by this author ... that the advantages of a posttribulational interpretation of the teaching regarding the Church and the Great Tribulation far outweigh this one difficulty." Gerig's thesis is evidence not only of the direction of Ladd's research in the mid-1950s but also of the relative freedom at Fuller to stray outside traditional fundamentalist boundaries. After completing his degree, Gerig enrolled in the PhD program in religion at the State University of Iowa, where he earned his degree in 1965.

19. GEL to Walter Wessel, 27 September 1955.

20. The details related to the founding of Western Seminary, unless otherwise noted, are summarized from Albert W. Wardin, *Baptists in Oregon* (Portland: Judson Baptist College, 1969), 423–34.

21. The community of Portland was, for the most part, less conservative than Western Seminary. The local newspaper carried extensive advertising for dance halls and liquor sales and published editorials against Sen. Joseph McCarthy. Still, in 1955 a car dealer was tried for selling a car on Sunday (he was eventually acquitted). See the *Oregonian*, 9 July 1955, 1.

22. Wardin, *Baptists in Oregon*, 431. See the account of the pivotal 1946 Northern Baptist Convention in Roland T. Nelson, "Fundamentalism and the Northern Baptist Convention" (PhD diss., University of Chicago, 1964), 249–53, 455–71, 481–86.

23. Wardin, *Baptists in Oregon*, 431. See the account of the pivotal 1946 Northern Baptist Convention in Roland T. Nelson, "Fundamentalism and the Northern Baptist Convention," 249–53, 455–71, 481–86.

24. In his speech Kalland stated:

> We are not obscurantists nor isolationists. . . . We attempt to be aware of every theological wind that blows. . . . We are endeavoring to make known to our students every angle of every proposition. . . . We do not predigest what we give to our students. We insist that they must learn for themselves from the totality of knowledge or at least the great amount of it which we can bring to them. (Address to the convention, minutes of the Oregon Baptist State Convention, 1948; quoted in Wardin, *Baptists in Oregon*, 434.)

25. Bruce Shelley, *Conservative Baptists: A Story of Twentieth-Century Dissent* (Denver: Conservative Baptist Theological Seminary, 1960), 90–91.

26. Executive Committee of the Board of Trustees, Western Conservative Baptist Theological Seminary, *The Seminary Situation: A Factual Record of Our Stewardship to Our Local and National Conservative Baptist Constituency* (Portland: Western Conservative Baptist Theological Seminary, 1955), 1.

27. Ibid., 5.

28. Bruce Shelley, *A History of Conservative Baptists* (Wheaton: Conservative Baptist Press, 1971), 114. See also the article "Western Seminary," in *Conservative Baptist Association News of Oregon VII* (October 1955), 5, which lists those who resigned. In addition to Kalland, Arthur Collins, Neil Winegarden, Paul Finlay, Walter Wessel, and Stuart Hackett left Western as a direct result of the controversy.

29. *Seminary Situation*, 2.

30. Ibid.

31. GEL to Wesley Gerig, 7 March 1956.

32. The letters do not survive, but doctrinal statements from the following are in Ladd's files: Calvary Baptist Church of New York, Beth Eden Baptist Church of Denver, and *Baptist Outlook Quarterly* of Denver.

33. GEL to de Visser, 27 December 1955.

34. See GEL to Rev. Vance Webster, 27 September 1955. Webster was the pastor of the First Baptist Church in Eugene, Ore., and signatory to the trustees' report (*Seminary Situation*) on the Western controversy.

35. GEL to Charles Erdman, 17 October 1955.

36. Erdman to GEL, 27 October 1955, 7 December 1955.

37. Erdman to GEL, 27 October 1955.

38. See Ladd, *The Blessed Hope: A Biblical Study of the Second Advent and the Rapture* (Grand Rapids, Mich.: Eerdmans, 1956), 159.

39. John McNicol to GEL, 30 September 1955.

40. GEL to G. Allen Fleece, 27 September 1955.

41. Fleece to GEL, 3 October 1955.

42. Philip Newell to GEL, 4 October 1955.

43. GEL to Howard Ferrin, 27 September 1955. The Providence and Barrington Bible Colleges had merged since Ladd's 1951 communication with Ferrin (see chapter 2.).

44. Ferrin to GEL, 5 October 1955.

45. Ibid.

46. Ibid.

47. Ladd discussed this danger with a former colleague at Gordon College, Glenn Barker (d. 1984). See GEL to Barker, 19 March 1956, and Barker to GEL, 31 March 1956.

48. GEL to Merrill Tenney, 21 May 1956.

49. GEL to E. Schuyler English, 24 January 1953.

50. GEL to English, 8 May 1956.

51. English to GEL, 15 May 1956.

52. See Ladd's "Blessed Hope," speech manuscript, n.d. Unless otherwise noted, all quotes in this section are from this manuscript.

53. Ibid., 18.

54. These quotations are from Ladd's handwritten notes made at the convention.

55. GEL to Harold Ockenga, 15 June 1956. This letter also refers to the favorable response to Ladd's presentation.

56. GEL to English, 30 August 1956.

57. See, for example, GEL to Bernard Ramm, 29 April 1957. Ramm (1916–1992) was a lifelong friend and confidant of Ladd's and another important progressive evangelical scholar. Ladd refers to "the wrong-headedness of dispensationalism" and its occasional "exegetical double-talk": "I have been careful in my own writing to avoid the emotional element. In fact, as you have doubtless noted, I have gone out of my way to pay compliments to the other crowd although, frankly, I have said far more than I actually think."

58. The quote is from GEL to English, 30 August 1956. The sentiment regarding dispensationalism is in GEL to Bernard Ramm, 29 April 1957. Ladd's private disdain for dispensationalist views is clear throughout his correspondence with Bernard Ramm from 1954 to 1957.

59. GEL to English, 30 August 1956.

60. *Yearbook of the American Baptist Convention: 1960*, 500. American Baptist Historical Society, American Baptist Archives Center, Valley Forge, Penn.

61. Ladd, *Blessed Hope*, 8.

62. Ibid., 9.

63. Ibid.

64. Ibid., 10.

65. Ibid., 11.

66. Ibid.

67. Ibid., 12, 14. The final quote is a reference to Ephesians 4:3.

68. Ibid., 19.

69. Ibid., 59.
70. Ibid., 60.
71. Ibid., 130.
72. Ibid.
73. Ibid., 136.
74. Ibid., 140–41.
75. Ibid., 167. The quote is from Titus 2:13.
76. GEL to Wilbur Smith, 5 December 1955.
77. Smith to GEL, 12 December 1955.
78. Smith to GEL, 15 December 1955.
79. Marsden, *Reforming Fundamentalism*, 190–92.
80. Harold Lindsell to GEL, 22 December 1955.
81. Homer Stanley Morgan to Charles Fuller, 27 November 1955.
82. The claim to have participated in Ladd's conversion is not corroborated by Ladd's own recollection. Ladd does, however, mention a revival meeting in which he made a commitment to enter Christian service. See Ladd, autobiographical sketch, in his application to join the New England Fellowship, ca. 1936.
83. Ibid.
84. See Marsden, *Reforming Fundamentalism*, 177–80, 215, for a description of the seminary's financial difficulties. This assessment is confirmed in a letter from Daniel Fuller to George Marsden, 14 July 1986, Marsden-Fuller Correspondence. Marsden's account of Fuller's history was informed by Dan Fuller's recollections of critical details.
85. E. B. Hart to GEL, 2 December 1955.
86. GEL to Hart, 4 December 1955.
87. J. E. Fison, review of *Blessed Hope*, in *Encounter* 18 (Winter 1957), 121. On Bruce's review of *Crucial Questions*, see chapter 2.
88. Fison, review of *Blessed Hope*.
89. Ibid.
90. John F. Walvoord, review of *Blessed Hope*, in *Bibliotheca Sacra* 113 (Fall 1956), 289–307. See statement on 307.
91. Ibid., 289.
92. Ibid., 290.
93. Ladd's copy of Walvoord's review.
94. Walvoord, review of *Blessed Hope*, 290.
95. Ibid., 291–92.
96. Ibid., 293.
97. Ibid., 294.
98. Ibid., 306.
99. Ibid., 304.
100. GEL to Walvoord, 7 May 1956.
101. Walvoord to GEL, 21 May 1956.
102. Ibid.
103. GEL to Walvoord, 26 June 1956.

104. Walvoord to GEL, 11 July 1956.

105. See Joel Carpenter's excellent account of the rise of Billy Graham in *Revive Us Again: The Reawakening of American Fundamentalism* (New York: Oxford University Press, 1997), 211–32.

106. Farley Butler, "Billy Graham and the End of Evangelical Unity" (PhD diss., University of Florida, 1976), 79, 147, and passim.

107. Carl McIntire, *Servants of Apostasy* (Collingswood, N.J.: Christian Beacon Press, 1955).

108. Ibid., 336.

109. Butler, "Billy Graham and the End of Evangelical Unity," 66–89.

110. Ibid., 81.

111. Ibid., 158–59.

112. Donald Grey Barnhouse, "Billy in Manhattan," *Eternity* 8 (May 1957), 7.

113. See Butler, "Billy Graham and the End of Evangelical Unity." This is a main thesis of his dissertation. See also Marsden, *Reforming Fundamentalism*, 162–65.

114. 2 Corinthians 6:17 (KJV). An example of how separatism is taught can be found in Gary G. Cohen, *Biblical Separation Defended: A Biblical Critique of Ten New Evangelical Arguments* (Philadelphia: Presbyterian and Reformed Publishing Co., 1966).

115. Interview with Catherine Kroeger, 14 June 2001. Kroeger was the wife of a Fuller student and later a biblical scholar herself.

116. GEL to Merrill Tenney, 20 June 1952.

117. GEL to Jaymes P. Morgan, 31 January 1964. The reference is to Ladd's hearing loss in the late 1950s.

118. The family vacations are mentioned in GEL to Norman Lavers, 19 September 1952. Lavers was a professor of English at Gordon College.

119. Interview with Muriel Ladd, 15 December 1989. Rebecca Jane Duncan Papers.

120. Ibid.

121. Interview with James Mignard, 17 May 2001. Mignard, a former student of Ladd's, long felt responsible for introducing his mentor to alcohol, though this was certainly not the case. Muriel Ladd also places the genesis of Ladd's serious drinking to his 1957 trip to Heidelberg.

122. Interview with Catherine Kroeger, 14 June 2001. The evidence of a drinking problem in the late 1950s was corroborated by David Wallace, former student and colleague of Ladd's, in an interview on 2 May 2002.

123. Interview with Catherine Kroeger, 14 June 2001.

124. Ibid.

125. Interview with Paul King Jewett, n.d. (ca. December 1989). Duncan Papers.

126. GEL to Glenn Barker, 17 October 1955.

127. Barker to GEL, 19 January 1956.

128. See Charles Carlston, "*Metanoia* and Church Discipline in the New Testament" (PhD diss., Harvard University, 1958).

129. Interview with Charles Carlston, 25 March 2004.

130. GEL to Eldon J. Epp, 23 March 1956.

131. Epp to GEL, 24 April 1956.

132. See David H. Wallace, "Semitic Origin of the Assumption of Moses" (PhD diss., New College, University of Edinburgh, 1955).

133. Much of this influence and engagement is examined in the following chapter.

134. GEL to Jaymes P. Morgan, 31 January 1964. Ladd recalled his study of Kähler and Cullmann in this letter to a former student who was pursuing doctoral studies at the University of Basel.

135. GEL to Edward Carnell, 23 September 1957.

136. See the brief description of the Tyndale Fellowship in F. F. Bruce, *In Retrospect: Remembrance of Things Past* (Grand Rapids, Mich.: Baker Book House, 1993), 122–27.

137. This account is taken from GEL to Carnell, 23 September 1957.

138. Ibid. The Fuller alumni who had pursued doctoral studies under Black to that point were David Wallace, who earned his PhD at New College, and David Allan Hubbard and Robert Laurin, who earned their degrees at Saint Andrews. Robert Emery, a 1954 graduate of Fuller, who is also mentioned in the letter, studied at the Free University of Amsterdam. Ladd later thanked Black for his support in furthering Ladd's nomination (GEL to Black, 10 January 1964).

139. See Edward Carnell to GEL, 11 December 1957, and GEL to Carnell, 18 December 1957. Ladd says, "My heart is singing to have the word from you and several others that the Seminary is now fully accredited."

140. Major articles published in 1957 include "Biblical Theology, History, and Revelation," in *Review and Expositor* 54 (April 1957), 195–204; "Eschatology and the Unity of New Testament Theology," in *Expository Times* 68 (June 1957), 268–71; "The Modern Problem of Biblical Scholarship," *Bethel Seminary Quarterly* 5 (February 1957), 10–20; "The Revelation and Jewish Apocalyptic," in *Evangelical Quarterly* 29 (April–June 1957), 94–100; "Revelation, History, and the Bible," in *The Journal of the American Scientific Affiliation* 9 (September 1957), 15–18; and "Why Not Prophetic-Apocalyptic?," *Journal of Biblical Literature* 76 (Part III 1957), 192–200.

141. George Eldon Ladd, "Biblical Theology, History, and Revelation," *Review and Expositor* 54 (Apr. 1957), 195.

142. Ibid., 197.

143. Ibid., 199.

144. George Eldon Ladd, "RSV Appraisal: New Testament," *Christianity Today* 1 (8 July 1957), 7–11.

145. George Eldon Ladd, "Why Not Prophetic-Apocalyptic?," *Journal of Biblical Literature* 76 (Part III 1957), 193.

146. Ibid., 200.

147. The immersion in the contemporary scene did not allow Ladd to completely escape his place as the resident expert in eschatology at Fuller Seminary. Grace Fuller (ca. 1888–1966), wife of the founder of the seminary, had engaged Ladd in a debate over his writings in the spring of 1957 and come away with a promise from him to summarize the various eschatological positions and recommend the most

biblically sound. This was more dangerous territory for Ladd. The Fullers were committed dispensationalists, though of a nonmilitant variety, and worried that the seminary that bore their name was drifting from its theological moorings. Further, the vast majority of their radio constituency—and by extension that of the seminary— shared those views as well, and they were aware of the financial repercussions of any perceived deviation from dispensational truth. Nonetheless, Ladd traced the various positions in eschatology and concluded—perhaps too hastily—that "dispensationalism is on the wane." Ladd endorsed what he called "premillennialism in its historical form," the position for which he would become known, which emphasized God's "single redemptive purpose in the future" over the dual redemptive purposes (Israel and the Church) found in dispensational thought. He fulfilled his obligation to Grace Fuller with a detailed but accessible outline of the issues but was hoping soon to shake off his role as the authority on dispensationalism and focus on the broader world of theological scholarship—and the creation of his magnum opus. (See GEL to Grace Payton Fuller, 29 July 1957, and Ladd, "Evangelical Types of Eschatology," unpublished paper sent to Grace Fuller on 29 July 1957.)

148. George Eldon Ladd, *The Gospel of the Kingdom: Scriptural Studies in the Kingdom of God* (Grand Rapids, Mich.: Eerdmans, 1959).

149. Ibid., 123–40. Matt. 24:14 reads as follows: "And this gospel of the kingdom shall be preached in all the world for a witness to all nations; and then shall the end come" (KJV).

150. Ibid., 107.

151. Ibid., 32.

152. Ibid., 60.

153. Ibid., 141.

154. See, for example, the index to Ladd's *Crucial Questions About the Kingdom of God* (Grand Rapids, Mich: Eerdmans, 1952), 189–190.

155. Frederick Danker, review of *Gospel of the Kingdom*, in *Concordia Theological Monthly* 31 (June 1960), 393.

156. Curtis Vaughan, review of *Gospel of the Kingdom*, in *Southwestern Journal of Theology* 3 (October 1960), 85.

157. Harold N. Englund, review of *Gospel of the Kingdom*, in *Reformed Review* 13 (May 1960), 46–47.

158. Ibid., 47.

159. J. Ramsey Michaels, review of *Gospel of the Kingdom*, in *Westminster Theological Journal* 23 (January 1960), 47–50. Michaels would later be ousted from his position at Gordon-Conwell for his "soft" views on inerrancy. See Nelson, *Making and Unmaking of an Evangelical Mind*, 203–204.

160. John Walvoord, review of *Gospel of the Kingdom*, in *Christianity Today* 4 (28 March 1960), 36–37.

161. Ibid., 37.

162. Ladd had written a long letter of critique after Walvoord's *Millennial Kingdom* was published in 1959, but he did not send the letter. Ladd mentions this in his

response to the advance draft of Walvoord's review of *Gospel of the Kingdom*; GEL to Walvoord, 20 January 1960.

163. There was at least one more meeting, however. Ladd had invited Walvoord to speak for Fuller's chapel service on 19 February 1960. The letter from Walvoord accepting the invitation and making the changes to the review that Ladd had requested was the last written exchange between them (Walvoord to GEL 2 February 1960).

NOTES TO CHAPTER 4

1. George Eldon Ladd, "Renaissance in Evangelicalism," speech manuscript, first delivered at the North American Baptist Theological Seminary, Spring 1959.

2. Ibid., 5.

3. Ibid., 8.

4. Ibid., 13, 16.

5. Ibid., 18.

6. Ibid., 20.

7. Ibid., 22.

8. Ladd describes this idea to Daniel Fuller in a letter dated 1 August 1961.

9. Robinson's father was William Childs Robinson (b. 1897), long-time professor of biblical studies at Columbia Theological Seminary (then Southern Presbyterian) in Georgia, who was affiliated with the conservative Presbyterian Church in the United States.

10. That Ladd found Robinson "refreshing" was a response to seeing these views in the work of an American theologian. Ladd was probably aware of the origin of these ideas in the work of Wilhelm Herrmann and, before him, Albrecht Ritschl. For a summary of the Marburg School see Bruce L. McCormack, *Karl Barth's Critically Realistic Dialectical Theology: Its Genesis and Development, 1909–1936* (New York: Oxford University Press, 1995), 31–77.

11. Ladd, review of James M. Robinson, *A New Quest of the Historical Jesus* (London: SCM, 1959), in *Christianity Today* 4 (18 January 1960), 36. Italics and quotation marks are Ladd's.

12. Interview with Muriel Ladd, 15 December 1989. Rebecca Jane Duncan Papers.

13. Ibid.

14. Ibid., and interview with Robert Guelich, n.d. (ca. December 1989), Duncan Papers.

15. GEL to Günter Dulon, 20 February 1961.

16. Two separate sources confirm that Ladd engaged in some inappropriate behavior on this trip but asked not to be cited by name.

17. Roger A. Johnson, *Rudolf Bultmann: Interpreting Faith for the Modern Era* (San Francisco: Collins, 1987), 9. This biographical section is indebted to Johnson's introduction.

18. I am indebted to McCormack, *Karl Barth's Critically Realistic Dialectical Theology*, 31–125, for this discussion of the Marburg School.

19. This section on Bultmann's theology, unless otherwise noted, is summarized from Johnson, *Rudolf Bultmann*, 9–43.

20. Raymond F. Collins, *Introduction to the New Testament* (New York: Image, 1987), 47–55.

21. Albert Schweitzer, *Quest of the Historical Jesus*, 2d ed. (New York: Macmillan, 1950), 401.

22. Johnson, *Rudolf Bultmann*, 12.

23. Rudolph Bultmann, "New Testament and Mythology," in Hans W. Bartsch, ed., R. H. Fuller, trans., *Kerygma and Myth: A Theological Debate* (London: SPCK, 1957), 3.

24. Ibid., 19.

25. Ibid.

26. Ibid., 38.

27. Ibid., 39.

28. In the United States, Bultmann's theology, while controversial, did not initially provoke an intense response, for several reasons. First, most of his work was not immediately available in English; thus, until the 1950s it was limited to scholars with knowledge of theological German. The first English-language volume of Bultmann's *Theology of the New Testament* was published in 1951, and the second volume was released in 1955 (New York: Charles Scribner's Sons). Other major works followed, some within the same year: *Primitive Christianity in Its Contemporary Setting* (New York: Meridian, 1956); *History and Eschatology* and *Jesus and the Word* (New York: Scribner's, 1958); *Jesus Christ and Mythology* and *History of the Synoptic Tradition* (Oxford: Blackwell, 1963).

Second, early American evaluations were uneven, as is apparent from a journal article that classifies Bultmann as a "Barthian" in 1935 (see Gilbert Theodore Rowe, "Bultmann as a Barthian" in *Religion in Life* 4 [Summer 1935], 447–54). According to their correspondence, Barth and Bultmann were well aware of their theological disagreement as early as 1922, certainly by the early 1930s, and it seems difficult to miss the fundamental differences with a careful reading of their works. Third, it was Barth and the neo-orthodox school that dominated discussion in the United States in the years immediately before and after World War II. Conservative magazines offered very little in the way of a challenge to Bultmann's theology until *Christianity Today* in 1961.

Finally, while most conservatives in the United States were focusing their attacks on Barth and neo-orthodoxy, the writers who did discuss Bultmann were generally either supportive or primarily explanatory of his position. Conservatives did not see Bultmann as a significant threat until it became apparent that his influence had come to rival that of Barth in Germany. There is no mention of Bultmann in conservative magazines such as the *Moody Monthly*, which was content to avoid the mention of specific theologians, and instead condemned a monolithic "modernism" (indices of *Moody Monthly*, 1925–1970). Other journal articles merely translate Bultmann's philosophical and methodological views into accessible English. Many of the earliest prominent American and British writers who mentioned Bultmann functioned as apologists for his work. For examples, see Dennis E. H. Whiteley, "Religion of the New Testament Writers," *Modern Churchman* 40 (September 1950), 227–38; Erich Dinkler, "Existentialist Interpretation of the New Testament," *Journal of Religion* 32 (April 1952), 87–96; Sherman E. Johnson, "Two Great New Testament Interpreters," *Religion in Life* 21 (Spring 1952), 288–97; and Ronald G. Smith, "What Is Demythologizing?" *Theology Today* 10 (April 1953), 34–44. For a Catholic critique of Bultmann's theology see D. M. Stanley, "Rudolf Bultmann: A Contemporary Challenge to the Catholic Theologian," *Catholic Biblical Quarterly* 19 (July 1955), 347–55.

29. 1 Cor. 15:19.

30. The "Dare We Follow Bultmann?" articles were written by Geoffrey Bromiley, 5 (27 March 1961), 6–8; Herman Ridderbos, 5 (22 May 1961), 5–8; Johannes Schneider, 5 (5 June 1961), 6–9; and Walter Künneth, 5 (13 October 1961), 25–28.

31. *Christianity Today* 5 (27 March 1961), 542–44.

32. *Christianity Today* 5 (22 May 1961), 717–20.

33. Ibid., 719.

34. GEL to DPF, 20 May 1954. This letter refers to Ladd's reading of Bultmann in English in 1954. See also Hans Werner Bartsch, *Kerygma und Mythos: Ein theologisches Gespräch*, a series in five volumes published between 1948 and 1962. A selection of these essays in English was published as *Kerygma and Myth: A Theological Debate*.

35. Ladd, "What Is Rudolf Bultmann Trying to Do?" *Eternity* (May 1962), 26–28, 38.

36. Ibid., 26.

37. Ibid.

38. Ibid., 27.

39. Ibid., 28.

40. Ibid.

41. Ibid.

42. Ibid.

43. Ibid. The italics are Ladd's.

44. Ibid., 28, 38. Interestingly, adjacent to the last paragraph of this article is an advertisement for leather-bound Scofield Bibles.

45. Ladd, "What Does Rudolf Bultmann Understand by the Acts of God?" *Bulletin of the Evangelical Society* 5 (Summer 1962), 91–97.

46. Alfred A. Glenn, "Rudolf Bultmann: Removing the False Offense," *Bulletin of the Evangelical Theological Society* 16 (Spring 1973), 73–81.

47. Ladd, "What Does Rudolf Bultmann Understand by the Acts of God?" 91.

48. According to Bultmann, "Nothing preceding the faith which acknowledges the risen Christ can give insight into the reality of *Christ's resurrection.* The resurrection cannot—in spite of 1 Cor. 15:3–8—be demonstrated or made plausible as an objectively ascertainable fact on the basis of which one could believe. But insofar as the risen Christ is present in the proclaiming word, it can be believed—and only so can it be believed." *Theology of the New Testament*, vol. 1 (New York: Charles Scribner's Sons, 1951), 305.

49. Bultmann, in Bartsch, ed., *Kerygma and Myth*, 196–97. Quoted in Ladd, "What Does Bultmann Mean by the Acts of God?" 91.

50. Bultmann, in Bartsch, ed., *Kerygma and Myth*, 22. The italics are Bultmann's. Quoted in Ladd, "What Does Bultmann Mean by the Acts of God?" 92.

51. Bultmann, in Bartsch, ed., *Kerygma and Myth*, 23.

52. Ladd, "What Does Bultmann Understand by the Acts of God?" 95.

53. Ibid.

54. Ibid., 96.

55. Bultmann, in *Kerygma and Myth*, 209. Quoted in ibid.

56. Bultmann, *Essays Philosophical and Theological* (London: SCM, 1955), 286. Quoted in Ladd, "What Does Bultmann Mean by the Acts of God?" 97.

57. Ladd, *Jesus Christ and History* (Chicago: InterVarsity Press, 1963).

58. Ibid., 7.

59. Ibid., 7–12.

60. Ibid., 59.

61. Ladd, *Rudolf Bultmann* (Chicago: InterVarsity Press, 1964).

62. Ibid., 19.

63. Ibid. The italics are Ladd's.

64. Ibid., 37.

65. Ibid., 38.

66. Ibid., 45.

67. Ibid., 49–50.

68. This discussion, unless otherwise noted, is dependent upon Marsden, *Reforming Fundamentalism*, 53–65, 138–40, and passim.

69. Rudolph Nelson, *The Making and Unmaking of an Evangelical Mind: The Case of Edward Carnell* (New York: Cambridge University Press, 1987), 86–106. See also Marsden, *Reforming Fundamentalism*, 141–50, 172–94.

70. Marsden, *Reforming Fundamentalism*, 180.

71. GEL to Daniel Fuller, 25 November 1960.

72. GEL to Daniel Fuller, 7 December 1960.

73. Ibid.

74. Daniel Fuller to GEL, 14 December 1960. Fuller continues his complaint: "I'm getting bald, I can't work so hard as I used to, I can't sleep so well, Kennedy is elected, the Catholics are growing in power, the faculty at Fuller is divided, and we haven't a President."

75. GEL to Daniel Fuller, 19 December 1960.

76. GEL to Vernon Grounds, 5 February 1957.

77. Ibid.

78. Marsden, *Reforming Fundamentalism*, 198.

79. Ibid., 208.

80. Robert Laurin to GEL, 20 September 1956.

81. GEL to Harold John Ockenga, 6 April 1960.

82. GEL to Raymond Buker, 5 June 1959.

83. GEL to Vernon Grounds, 20 April 1959; Bernard Ramm to GEL, 21 April 1959 (Baylor); Earl S. Kalland to GEL, 29 September 1954 (Western).

84. This summary of the Black Saturday events, unless otherwise noted, is taken from Marsden, *Reforming Fundamentalism*, 208–15.

85. Lindsell to Ockenga, 13 December 1962. Harold Lindsell Papers, Folder 34, Box 4, Collection 192. Archives of the Billy Graham Center, Wheaton, Ill.

86. GEL to Paul Jewett, 14 January 1963. Ralston-Smith was a Presbyterian minister from Oklahoma and virtually unknown to the Fuller faculty, according to Ladd's account.

87. GEL to Paul Jewett, 27 December 1962. This is not in Marsden's retelling of the story but is in Ladd's firsthand account. On Johnson see Marsden, *Reforming Fundamentalism*, 215.

88. GEL to Paul Jewett, 27 December 1962.

89. Roy A. Harrisville, "Resurrection and Historical Method," *Dialog* 1 (Spring 1962), 30–37.

90. Martin Kähler, trans. Carl Braaten, *The So-called Historical Jesus and the Historic Biblical Christ* (Philadelphia: Fortress Press, 1964). See especially the helpful introduction by Braaten, 1–38.

91. Braaten, "Martin Kähler on the Historic Biblical Christ," 80n3.

92. Harrisville, "Resurrection and Historical Method," 33.

93. Ibid., 36.

94. Ibid. Harrisville quotes Günther Bornkamm, *Jesus of Nazareth*, trans. Irene and Fraser McLuskey (New York: Harper, 1960), 23.

95. Harrisville, "Resurrection and Historical Method," 36–37.

96. Ibid., 37.

97. Ladd, "Resurrection and History," *Dialog* 1 (Fall 1962).

98. Ibid., 55.

99. Ibid., 56.

100. Ibid., 55.

101. Ibid., 56.

102. Ladd, "Resurrection and History," *Religion in Life* 32 (Spring 1963).

103. Ibid., 248.

104. Ibid., 251.

105. Donald T. Rowlingson, "Interpreting the Resurrection," *Christian Century* 80 (10 April 1963), 459–61.

106. Ibid., 459.

107. Ibid., 460.

108. Rowlingson to GEL, 16 March 1963.

109. GEL to Rowlingson, 20 March 1963.

110. John Warwick Montgomery, "Karl Barth and Contemporary Theology of History," *Bulletin of the Evangelical Society* 6 (Spring 1963), 39–49.

111. See John Warwick Montgomery, "The Libraries of France at the Ascendancy of Mazarin: Louis Jacob's '*Traicté des plus belles bibliotheques*' " (PhD diss., University of

Chicago, 1962). Montgomery remains a vocal and opportunistic critic of evangelicals who stray from his strict rationalist approach to historical-theological issues.

112. Daniel L. Swinson, "The Bulletin/Journal of the Evangelical Theological Society," in Lippy, ed., *Religious Periodicals of the United States: Academic and Scholarly Journals* (New York: Greenwood Press, 1986), 305–9.

113. Montgomery, "Karl Barth and Contemporary Theology of History," 47.

114. GEL to Vernon Grounds, 12 July 1966.

115. The ETS continues to struggle with the relationship between faith and historical criticism, as is evidenced by a recent series of articles in what is now called the *Journal of the Evangelical Theological Society*: Grant Osborne, "Historical Criticism and the Evangelical," 42 (June 1999), 193–210; Robert Thomas, "Historical Criticism and the Evangelical: Another View," 43 (March 2000), 97–111; and Osborne, "Historical Criticism: A Brief Response to Robert Thomas," 43 (March 2000), 113–17.

116. GEL to Vernon Grounds, 12 July 1966.

117. GEL to Markus Barth, 16 October 1962.

118. The articles in question are "Kingdom of God—Reign or Realm?," *Journal of Biblical Literature* 81 (September 1962), 230–38; and "Eschatology and the Unity of New Testament Theology," *Expository Times* 68 (June 1957), 268–71.

119. Ladd, "Resurrection and History," 55.

120. GEL to Carl Braaten, 1 August 1962. Braaten's question to Ladd is unambiguously referred to in Ladd's letter.

121. Marsden, *Reforming Fundamentalism*, 194–96. See also Nelson, *Making and Unmaking of an Evangelical Mind*, 186–89.

122. See Marsden, *Reforming Fundamentalism*.

123. Fuller's dissertation was later published as *Easter Faith and History* (Grand Rapids, Mich.: Eerdmans, 1965).

124. Fuller, *Easter Faith and History*, 253–56.

125. Ibid., 154–55, 257–61, and passim. Fuller also makes this argument in letters to Ladd dated 30 January 1961 and 20 May 1961 and in another with no date but probably sent in the summer of 1961.

126. Dan Fuller to GEL, 30 January 1961.

127. GEL to Fuller, 1 August 1961.

128. Ladd later proposed that "real" replace "*geschichtliche*" as a clearer way to discuss questions of historicity in relation to biblical events. Ladd, "History and Theology in Biblical Exegesis," *Interpretation* 20 (January 1966), 60n19.

129. Quoted in Nelson, *Making and Unmaking of An Evangelical Mind*, 69, 235–36n22.

NOTES TO CHAPTER 5

1. GEL to Harold John Ockenga, 6 March 1963.

2. Edward John Carnell had published a book with the Macmillan Company, but his was a work of apologetics. See Carnell's *Christian Commitment* (New York:

Macmillan, 1957). Further, the book sold poorly and was remaindered soon after publication. See Rudolph Nelson's biography of Carnell, *The Making and Unmaking of an Evangelical Mind: The Case of Edward Carnell* (New York: Cambridge University Press, 1987), 103. Harold Lindsell was also slated to have his devotional book, *When You Pray*, published by Harper's in the spring of 1964, but it was eventually released by Tyndale Press in 1969.

3. GEL to Ockenga, 28 June 1952.

4. GEL to Merrill Tenney, 28 November 1952.

5. GEL to Bernard Ramm, 21 November 1955. Ramm was then a member of the Baylor University faculty.

6. Otto Piper, *God in History* (New York: Macmillan, 1939).

7. GEL to Piper, 14 March 1956.

8. Interview with Dr. James Mignard, 17 May 2001. Mignard was a former student of Ladd's at Fuller and later earned a PhD at Boston University.

9. GEL to John Bradbury, 2 November 1956. Bradbury was editor of the *Watchman-Examiner*, a conservative Baptist publication.

10. GEL to Wayne Christianson, 10 August 1960.

11. GEL to Werner Kümmel, 11 July 1960.

12. GEL to Edward Hart, 16 April 1956.

13. GEL to the Board of Deacons, Temple Baptist Church, 31 January 1964.

14. GEL to Robert Meye, 21 September 1962.

15. Guy Brown to GEL, 21 October 1959, and GEL to Brown, 27 October 1959.

16. On the interest Harper and Row showed in publishing theological works see Mark Noll, *Between Faith and Criticism: Evangelicals, Scholarship, and the Bible in America* (San Francisco: Harper and Row, 1986), 104. For examples of titles see Daniel Day Williams, *What Present-day Theologians Are Thinking* (1952), Walter M. Horton, *Christian Theology: An Ecumenical Approach* (1958), Heinz Zahrnt, *The Historical Jesus* (1960), and John Macquarie, *The Scope of Demythologizing: Bultmann and His Critics* (1960). Most significant was the series (then in progress) titled *New Frontiers in Theology: Discussions among Continental and American Theologians*, which included James M. Robinson, ed., *The Later Heidegger and Theology* (1963); Robinson and John B. Cobb Jr., eds., *The New Hermeneutic* (1964); and Robinson and Cobb, eds., *Theology as History* (1967).

17. GEL to Glenn Barker, 8 November 1962.

18. GEL to C. F. D. Moule, 28 November 1962.

19. GEL to John Newport, 14 December 1962.

20. Roger Nicole to Melvin Arnold of Harper and Row, n.d. (probably in early December 1962).

21. Ibid.

22. Nicole to GEL, 21 March 1963.

23. Arnold to GEL, 17 December 1962.

24. Arnold to GEL, 1 March 1963.

25. GEL to Arnold, 4 March 1963.

26. Arnold to GEL, 11 March 1963. The contract also bears the same date.

27. See the discussion above, chapter 4.

28. George M. Marsden, *Reforming Fundamentalism: Fuller Seminary and the New Evangelicalism* (Grand Rapids, Mich.: Eerdmans, 1987), 208–19. The characterization of Ockenga's presidency is wholly my own.

29. GEL to Bill Beuhler, 13 August 1963. Buehler was studying in Basel at the time.

30. Marie Cantlon of Harper and Row to GEL, 28 August 1963.

31. The Eerdmans file in the GEL Papers contains more than three hundred documents, but there is no surviving list of potential review publications such as the one that Harper sent to Ladd.

32. Harper and Row Publicity/Review Copy List.

33. Ibid.

34. Ladd, speaking at the First Southern Baptist Church of Gardena, Calif., quoted in the *Gardena Alondra Park Tribune*, 6 June 1963.

35. GEL to Cantlon, 4 September 1963.

36. Ibid.

37. GEL to Adrian Heaton, president of California Baptist Theological Seminary, 6 September 1963.

38. GEL to Cantlon, 4 September 1963.

39. Ockenga to GEL, 8 June 1962, David Allan Hubbard Papers.

40. GEL to David Allan Hubbard, 9 May 1963.

41. Ladd's annual salary was $9,600 at the time. Reported by Ladd in a grant application to the American Council of Learned Societies, 9 March 1964.

42. GEL to Charles Taylor, 3 June 1963.

43. Ibid. Ladd mentions a payment of $100 per month and says, "I do not know how I did it."

44. Charles Taylor to GEL, 10 February 1964.

45. Richard Curley to Paul C. Doehring, 19 August 1964, David Allan Hubbard Papers. Curley was the seminary's business manager at the time. Doehring was a prominent physician and president of the board of directors for the nearby Glendale Memorial Hospital in California from 1964 to 1968.

Ladd also applied to the American Council of Learned Societies (ACLS) for a grant to support his sabbatical, as he had done for his brief study trip in 1961 (GEL to Gordon Turner of ACLS, 9 March 1964). The ACLS was a consortium of academic guilds established in 1919 to represent the United States within the Union Académique Internationale (International Union of Academies). See the ACLS website, http://www.acls.org/mor-hist.htm (accessed 12 November 2007). In a strong letter in support of Ladd's proposal for a $1,000 grant, David Hubbard called him "well suited to make a significant contribution to Biblical scholarship during this year of study" (Hubbard to ACLS, n.d. Ladd's request for a letter of reference is dated 15 July 1964). This application, however, appears to have been unsuccessful.

46. Ila Mae Harris to GEL, 27 July and 15 September 1964. Harris, the faculty secretary at Fuller, assisted with personal matters while professors were on extended leave.

47. This description of Ladd's research plan is taken from his "Proposed Program for Sabbatical, 1964–65," submitted to the seminary's sabbatical committee, n.d. (ca. June 1964).

48. Ibid.

49. Frank Elliott of Harper and Row to GEL, 11 February 1964.

50. Melvin Arnold of Harper and Row to GEL, 10 December 1965.

51. GEL to Elliott, 12 February 1964. GEL to Elliott, 24 February 1964.

52. Gösta Lundström, *The Kingdom of God in the Teaching of Jesus: A History of Interpretation from the Last Decades of the Nineteenth Century to the Present*, trans. Joan Bulman (Richmond: John Knox Press, 1963); Norman Perrin, *The Kingdom of God in the Teaching of Jesus* (Philadelphia Westminster Press, 1963).

53. Ladd, *Jesus and the Kingdom: The Eschatology of Biblical Realism* (New York: Harper and Row, 1964), 3n2. If Ladd saw these events as bad omens, he certainly gave no indication of it. When *Christianity Today* published a negative review of Lundström's book in early 1964, Ladd wrote in its defense. The review, by Herman Waetjen of San Francisco Theological Seminary (Presbyterian), was thoroughly brutal. Waetjen attacked the book as "ineptly written" and "badly translated" and said that, after close examination, one "can only conclude that [it] is not worth buying or reading" (Herman Waetjen, review of Lundström, *The Kingdom of God in the Teaching of Jesus*, in *Christianity Today* 8 [27 March 1964], 32). While some of the criticisms had validity, the tone of the review struck Ladd as inappropriate. "The fact that there are several notable flaws in the book," he argued, "does not merit its unqualified condemnation. . . . We need such books [so] that every scholar may carry on his own studies in light of the history of interpretation" (GEL to *Christianity Today*, 30 March 1964). Perhaps attempting to pave the way for his own forthcoming book, Ladd championed Lundström's conclusions about the kingdom and affirmed that he "stands with a growing number of scholars who see the Kingdom as both present and future." (The most notable of these "scholars" was indeed Ladd himself.) Foreshadowing some of the criticisms that would strike at his own work, Ladd defended Lundström against the accusation that he was "merely selecting bits and pieces from the scholars he has reviewed in an entirely uncreative synthesis." As a postscript Ladd notes that "It is interesting that another study has appeared with precisely the same title which attempts the same history of interpretation . . . by Norman Perrin as a doctoral dissertation under Professor [Joachim] Jeremias at Göttingen. Apparently we have needed such a book for some time." Certainly Ladd had needed his own book for a long time.

54. Ladd, *Jesus and the Kingdom*, 3–38.

55. See note 53 of this chapter.

56. Ladd, *Jesus and the Kingdom*, xv.

57. Ibid., 214.

58. Ibid., 151.

59. Ibid., xii.

60. Ibid., xiii.

61. Ibid., xiv.

62. Ibid., 327.

63. Ibid., 328.

64. Ibid., 328–29.

65. Ibid., 329. The Manson quote is from *The Teaching of Jesus*, 2d ed. (Cambridge UK: Cambridge University Press, 1935), 284.

66. GEL to Henry J. Cadbury, 8 April 1964.

67. Ockenga to GEL, 22 October 1964.

68. On the relationship between J. Gresham Machen and the early faculty at Fuller, see Marsden, *Reforming Fundamentalism*, 31–36.

69. GEL to Merrill Tenney, 1 August 1966. Ladd wrote that he wanted to produce scholarship that "would be read by theological students in non-evangelical seminaries, as I read Machen when I was studying at Harvard under Cadbury." On Machen see D. G. Hart, *Defending the Faith: J. Gresham Machen and the Crisis of Conservative Protestantism in Modern America* (Baltimore: Johns Hopkins Press, 1994).

70. John Bright, *The Kingdom of God* (Nashville: Abingdon-Cokesbury Press, 1953) and *A History of Israel* (Philadelphia: Westminster Press, 1959).

71. Bright to Janice Prussack of Harper and Row, 5 August 1964.

72. Ibid.

73. GEL to Hubbard, n.d. (early October 1964). In Ladd's letter the phrase is underlined multiple times. Copy in David Allan Hubbard Papers.

74. Ladd, "Sabbatical Reflections," in *the opinion* 4 (January 1965). This piece may have been written as early as November of 1964. GEL Papers.

75. Ibid., 5.

76. Ibid., 5–6.

77. Ibid., 6.

78. Ibid.

79. See the discussion above, 168–170.

80. John Walvoord, review of *Jesus and the Kingdom*, in *Bibliotheca Sacra* 122 (Jan–Mar 1965), 74–76.

81. Ibid. Indeed, Walvoord is not mentioned in either the text or bibliography of *Jesus and the Kingdom*.

82. Ladd to Melvin Arnold at Harper and Row, 23 August 1965.

83. Norman Perrin, "Against the Current," review of *Jesus and the Kingdom*, in *Interpretation* 19 (April 1965), 228–29.

84. Ibid., 229.

85. Ibid.

86. Ibid., 229–30.

87. Ibid., 230.

88. Ibid., 231.

89. The italics are mine.

90. This biographical sketch, unless otherwise noted, is taken from Calvin R. Mercer, *Norman Perrin's Interpretation of the New Testament: From "Exegetical Method" to "Hermeneutical Process"* (Macon, Ga: Mercer University Press, 1986), 1–12. Mercer also allowed me access to the correspondence related to his study of Perrin.

91. Ibid., 3.

92. Ibid., 3n5.

93. Ibid., 5.

94. See Norman Perrin and William Farmer, "The Kerygmatic Theology and the Question of the Historical Jesus," *Religion in Life* 29 (Winter 1959–60), 86–97.

95. This is the thesis of Mercer's study.

96. Mercer, *Norman Perrin's Interpretation of the New Testament*, 6.

97. See above, chapters 1 and 3.

98. Ladd, *Jesus and the Kingdom*, xiii, 332.

99. David Abernathy to Calvin Mercer, n.d. ("June 1984" is handwritten at the top). Abernathy was a colleague of Perrin's at Emory University. Mercer Papers.

100. Abernathy to Mercer, 28 April 1985. Mercer Papers.

101. Mercer, *Norman Perrin's Interpretation of the New Testament*, 34.

102. This account of Ladd's first reading of Perrin's review is reconstructed from interviews with David Wallace, 2 May 2002 and 15 May 2003. Wallace's recollections are confirmed by another Fuller alumnus who was present that evening, Rae Heimbeck, in a letter to the author dated 24 January 2004. The event itself took place on 19 May 1965.

103. GEL to Dan Fuller, 19 May 1965.

104. GEL to Balmer Kelley of *Interpretation*, 20 May 1965. This source is actually the first unsent draft of a letter. See note 107, this chapter.

105. Ibid.

106. See Ladd, *Jesus and the Kingdom*, 329n7.

107. Bornkamm, quoted in GEL to Balmer Kelley, 20 May 1965. This is a second unsent draft of Ladd's letter (cf. note 104, this chapter). The meeting probably took place on the evening of 19 May (it is not mentioned in a letter written earlier that day).

108. The versions Ladd kept are at least as revealing as the one he finally mailed. In what appears to be the first attempt, Ladd complained that Perrin's review unfairly called *Jesus and the Kingdom* "uncritical, incompetent, and contemptuous," then proceeded systematically to list Perrin's perceived misunderstandings in short paragraphs that alternately began with either "The review:" or "The facts:" (GEL to Kelley, 20 May 1965; first unsent draft). Ladd expressed his apprehension that the review "will effectively kill my book for the readers of *Interpretation*."

Perhaps uncomfortable with the pedantic look and angry feel of his first attempt, he wrote another draft of the letter on the same day. This second draft was fully twice as long and only slightly calmer in tone. Ladd began abruptly with a reference to his defense of Lundström in the face of the negative review in *Christianity Today* and lamented his similar treatment in *Interpretation* (GEL to Kelley, 20 May 1965; second unsent draft). He listed ten charges against Perrin's evaluation of *Jesus and the*

Kingdom and answered each with quotes from his book. He then said that he "had expected this kind of review from *Bibliotheca Sacra,* but hardly from *Interpretation*" and expressed his disappointment that he was not treated with as much respect by liberals as he had tried to show to them. Employing Edward Carnell's critique of fundamentalism, Ladd accused those who would concur with the views expressed in *Interpretation* of being guilty of achieving "status by negation" (ibid.; see Carnell's article, "Post-fundamentalist Faith," in *Christian Century* 76 [26 August 1959], 971). The full quote regarding fundamentalist attitudes reads as follows: "Status by negation, not a humble reliance on the grace of God, served as the base for Christian security." Ladd closed the letter sounding defeated and reiterated that the review had convinced him that his life's goal had been "a fool's dream." These drafts were set aside, however, after Ladd had allowed himself some time to regain his composure.

109. GEL to Balmer Kelley, 24 May 1965.

110. James Mays to GEL, 3 June 1965.

111. GEL to Balmer Kelley, 21 June 1965.

112. Ladd, "History and Theology in Biblical Exegesis," *Interpretation* 20 (January 1966), 54–64.

113. Mays to GEL 30 June 1965.

114. GEL to Mays, 8 July 1965. Ladd eventually wrote a single review for *Interpretation* in 27 (July 1974): 361–62.

115. See Marsden, *Reforming Fundamentalism,* 225–26. Proof that Schoonhoven remains a controversial figure among militant fundamentalists can be found on the Internet, where a simple search of his name turns up several sites attributing the alleged erosion of orthodoxy at Fuller Seminary, at least in part, to him.

116. GEL to Schoonhoven, 24 May 1965.

117. Ibid.

118. George Eldon Ladd, "Man as Spirit," unpublished paper, School of Psychology Integration Seminar, 25 January 1967.

119. GEL to Robert Guelich, 7 January 1966.

120. GEL to Melvin Arnold of Harper and Row, 18 November 1965.

121. Ibid. There is no record of who the "acquaintance" was. To his credit, Perrin later regretted writing the review as intensely as he had. Interview with Martin Marty, a colleague of Perrin's at the University of Chicago, October 1991.

122. The paper was later published as "The Problem of History in Contemporary New Testament Interpretation," in F. L. Cross, ed., *Studia Evangelica* V (Berlin: Akademic-Verlag, 1968), 88–100.

123. The reports of Ladd's drinking during this period are too numerous to list individually.

124. Ladd, "Sabbatical Reflections," 6. These handwritten comments were likely written sometime in the fall of 1965.

125. James A. Walther, review of *Jesus and the Kingdom,* in *Pittsburgh Perspective* 6 (June 1965), 37.

126. George W. Knight, III, review of *Jesus and the Kingdom,* in *Westminster Theological Journal* 28 (November 1965), 64–73; quotes from 65, 67.

127. Francis Foulkes, review of *Jesus and the Kingdom*, in *Reformed Theological Review* 25 (May–August 1966), 72–73.

128. M. Eugene Boring, review of *Jesus and the Kingdom*, in *Encounter* 29 (Spring 1968), 230–32.

129. See, for example, Walter Dunnett, *Moody Monthly* 65 (March 1965), 7; Robert Bryant *United Church Herald* 8 (1 February 1965), 3; Lloyd Dean, *Eternity* 16 (March 1965), 44–46; Herman Waetjen, *Christianity Today* 9 (4 June 1965), 31–32; R. Lunt, *Expository Times* 27 (Spring 1966), 365–66; F. H. Borsch, *Journal of Theological Studies* 18 [new series] (April 1967), 195–97; Robert Maddox, *Australian Biblical Review* 15 (December 1967), 46–47; G. C. Golding, *Indian Journal of Theology* 15 (April–June 1966), 81–83; Stanley B. Marrow, *Biblica* 47 (Fall 1966), 604–6; George Macrae, *New Blackfriars* 48 (November 1966), 106–7; W. Gordon Robinson, *Ecumenical Review* 19 (July 1967), 335.

130. GEL to Arnold, 24 May 1965. Across the top of the page Ladd wrote "not sent."

131. GEL to Arnold, 23 August 1965.

132. GEL to Marie Cantlon of Harper and Row, 17 December 1965.

133. See the correspondence between Ladd and George McKnight, who reviewed *Jesus and the Kingdom* for the *Westminster Theological Review* (19 November 1965). Ladd had written a similar statement of defense to James Daane, editor of *Christianity Today*, regarding a small detail in Herman Waetjen's review.

134. There are more than a hundred examples of these letters in the GEL Papers.

135. Tenney to GEL, 1 June 1966.

136. GEL to Tenney, 6 June 1966.

137. Tenney to GEL, 26 July 1966.

138. GEL to Tenney, 1 August 1966.

139. GEL to Barker, 4 April 1966.

140. Barker to GEL 26 April 1966.

141. Ibid.

142. GEL to Barker, 2 May 1966. In a strange but revealing coda to this episode, Ladd was asked in 1968 to provide a reference for Barker in support of his application to join the faculty of the Conwell School of Theology in Philadelphia. Ladd wrote that, while he had been well acquainted with Barker during their time at Harvard in the 1940s, since then he had "had almost no contact with him, either by correspondence or through scholarship" (GEL to Stuart Babbage of the Conwell School of Theology, 8 May 1968). This was patently false. There are more than forty extant letters between Barker and Ladd between 1955 and 1966, covering a wide range of topics from personal to theological and including accounts of several visits to each other's homes. Still, in his recommendation Ladd expressed his disappointment that Barker had not been very productive as a scholar but suggested weakly he might make a good administrator. Ladd sent a copy of the letter to Barker, who ironically would become the dean and provost of Fuller Seminary—and Ladd's immediate superior—in 1972. For a discussion of Barker's impact on Fuller see Marsden, *Reforming Fundamentalism*, 271–72.

143. GEL to Vernon Grounds, 1 August 1966.

144. GEL to Guelich, 24 June 1966. The book to which Ladd refers is John C. Hurd, *A Bibliography of New Testament Bibliographies* (New York: Seabury Press, 1966). The relationship between Ladd and Guelich is examined in the following chapter.

145. GEL to Guelich, 24 June 1966.

NOTES TO CHAPTER 6

1. GEL to Robert Kraft, 15 February 1966. The emphasis and internal quotation marks are Ladd's.

2. The following details of Ladd's family life are found in an interview with Mrs. James Mathon Ladd, George's sister-in-law, 15 December 1989. Rebecca Jane Duncan Papers.

3. Ibid.

4. Notes from a conversation between Ladd, Daniel Fuller, and David Allan Hubbard, 4 May 1970. David Allan Hubbard Papers.

5. Interview with Timothy Weber, 3 April 2003. This precise phrase was frequently used during the course of my research (cf. interview with David Wallace, 2 May 2002).

6. Interview with David Wallace, 2 May 2002. Numerous others confirm the rumors in the 1950s.

7. Interview with John Wipf, 14 September 2004. Wipf was a student of Ladd's in the early 1970s.

8. Interview with C. Mel Robeck, 26 September 2004 (date of email response). Robeck was a former student of Ladd's and is now a professor and an administrator at Fuller Theological Seminary.

9. GEL to Glenn Barker, 2 May 1966.

10. GEL to Harvey McArthur, 3 March 1966. McArthur was a professor of New Testament at the Hartford Seminary Foundation in Connecticut.

11. See GEL to Erik Langkjaer (marketing), 24 February 1967. GEL to Tadashi Akaishi (theological trends), 6 February 1967, and GEL to Melvin Arnold (title), 18 November 1965. All held various positions at Harper and Row.

12. GEL to Langkjaer, 3 April 1967.

13. Langkjaer to GEL, 12 April 1967. According to Ladd's calculations Harper's payment was about $56.00 short. He did not pursue the matter.

14. GEL to Laura Paull, 28 October 1968.

15. GEL to Akaishi, 15 November 1968.

16. GEL to Robert Guelich, 24 June 1966.

17. GEL to Otto Piper, 15 October 1970.

18. See George M. Marsden, *Reforming Fundamentalism: Fuller Seminary and the New Evangelicalism* (Grand Rapids, Mich.: Eerdmans, 1987), 263–76.

19. Report of the reunion classes of 1950–1953. Fuller Theological Seminary Office of Church and Alumni Relations.

20. Details of the founding of the Graduate School of Psychology are found in H. Newton Malony, *Psychology and the Cross: The Early History of Fuller Seminary's School of Psychology* (Pasadena: Fuller Theological Seminary, 1995), 1–11.

21. Ibid., 14–15.

22. Unidentified alumnus, quoted in Marsden, *Reforming Fundamentalism*, 248.

23. See chapel sermons "Keep Awake" and "The Gospel Must Be Preached," tapes 0109a and 0222b, respectively. Fuller Seminary Academic Technology Center. Ladd's weeping in class is reported by virtually every student after 1965.

24. Marsden, *Reforming Fundamentalism*, 234.

25. GEL to Harold John Ockenga, 22 June 1962.

26. Ibid. Ladd was clearly wrong on this point: Nineteen doctoral-level students were enrolled in the inaugural class of the School of Psychology, and twenty-four were in the second. Fuller Seminary conferred at least sixty-nine PhD degrees in clinical psychology before the first student completed the PhD program in theology (during that same period eight ThD degrees were earned). That first graduate, Howard Loewen (PhD, 1976), became dean of the School of Theology at Fuller in 2002.

27. Ockenga to GEL, 27 June 1962. The approval process is chronicled in Malony, *Psychology and the Cross*, 14–15.

28. Information on the steering committee can be found in Malony, *Psychology and the Cross*, 24–28.

29. George Eldon Ladd, "Problems in the Integration of Theology and Psychology," unpublished internal assessment, Fuller Theological Seminary, n.d. (ca. 1965), 11–14.

30. Ibid., 22.

31. Ibid., 20–22.

32. Paul Fairweather and Carroll J. Wright, *Image Therapy* (self-published, 1967), 32–33.

33. George Eldon Ladd, "Man as Spirit," unpublished paper for a School of Psychology integration seminar, 25 January 1967. I have added the identity of the persons to whom Ladd refers.

34. Malony, *Psychology and the Cross*, 88–89. Ladd made several attempts to reconcile with Fairweather, whom he liked, but after 1967 there was little contact. See GEL to Fairweather, 12 January and 29 September 1967.

35. GEL to David Hubbard, 1 October 1969. Hubbard Papers. Marianne Meye Thompson, the daughter of Robert Meye and a former student of Ladd's, confirmed that Ladd often expressed this view (interviewed on 17 February 2004).

36. GEL to C. Davis Weyerhauser, 21 May 1963.

37. Interviews with Robert Guelich, n.d. (ca. December 1989) and Mrs. James Mathon Ladd, 15 December 1989. Duncan Papers.

38. Ladd's request is found in GEL to C. Davis Weyerhauser, 21 May 1963. The grant was confirmed in a letter from Weyerhauser's treasurer, C. A. Black, to Robert Guelich, 16 July 1963. Guelich was teaching a class at the Fuller-affiliated Winona Lake Bible Institute when he received the letter.

39. GEL to Weyerhauser, 21 May 1963.

40. GEL to Weyerhauser, 28 July 1963.

41. Weyerhauser to GEL, 22 August 1963.

42. See the discussion of this letter above (note 122 of chapter 1), 60–62.

43. GEL to Guelich, 29 March 1966.

44. See, for example, GEL to Guelich, 7 January 1966, 29 March 1966, 24 June 1966, and 14 December 1966.

45. Guelich to GEL, 11 December 1966.

46. GEL to Guelich, 14 December 1966. One wonders whether Ladd ever made a similar gesture to his own son.

47. Guelich to GEL, n.d. (ca. April 1966).

48. See Leonhard Goppelt, *Apostolic and Post-apostolic Times*, trans. Robert A. Guelich (London: A&C Black, 1970).

49. Guelich to GEL, 25 November 1967. Guelich went on to have a distinguished career as a scholar and pastor, serving at Bethel College and Seminary, the University of Aberdeen, Colonial Church in Minnesota, and Fuller Seminary, where he was a professor of New Testament Studies. He died of heart failure in 1991.

50. See *Interpretation* 25n1 (January 1971).

51. James L. Mays, editor of *Interpretation*, to GEL, 20 February 1970. An example of Ladd's lifelong obsession with financial matters is found on his copy of the invitation letter. Dividing the number of words required for the article by the honorarium he was offered, Ladd determined precisely what he would earn for each word submitted.

52. James M. Robinson to GEL, 27 January 1969.

53. GEL to Robinson, 5 February 1969.

54. GEL to James Mays, 20 March 1970.

55. GEL to Floyd Roseberry, 6 July 1971. Roseberry was a Fuller alumnus who was serving as a missionary in the Philippines in the early 1970s.

56. Ladd, "The Search for Perspective," *Interpretation* 25 (January 1971), 47.

57. Ibid., 51.

58. Ibid., 55. See also Ladd, *The New Testament and Criticism* (Grand Rapids, Mich.: Eerdmans 1967), 14, 40.

59. Ladd, "Search for Perspective," 55.

60. I am indebted to Marianne Meye Thompson for her help with this insight.

61. Ladd, "Search for Perspective," 56–57.

62. GEL to Floyd Roseberry, 6 July 1971.

63. Interview with Timothy P. Weber, 3 April 2003.

64. Ibid. Weber did not remember at whose funeral this took place, but it is mentioned in a letter from Winnie Ladd to David Allan Hubbard, 8 June 1970. Hubbard Papers.

65. Interview with Ronald Youngblood, 23 February 2004. Unless otherwise noted, this account is taken from my interview with Youngblood.

66. Ronald Youngblood to GEL, 9 May 1969.

67. GEL to Youngblood, 12 May 1969.

68. John L. Novak to David Allan Hubbard, 17 May 1970. Hubbard Papers.

69. The following account is from "A Summary of Conversation with George Ladd," confidential meeting notes, dated 4 May 1970. Hubbard Papers.

70. The meeting was scheduled for 13 May 1970, though the notes do not survive.

71. Memorandum from David Allan Hubbard to GEL, 16 November 1970. Hubbard Papers. The following details are from this document.

72. Ibid. The remarks are in Hubbard's hand but are crossed out in the earlier draft.

73. Notes from a phone conversation between David Allan Hubbard and Adrin Sylling, 2 December 1970. David Allan Hubbard Papers. Sylling reported that Ladd had consumed "a pint of something yesterday," knowing that he was about to be interviewed on the progress of his recovery.

74. Winnie Ladd to David Allan Hubbard, 8 June 1970. Hubbard Papers.

75. See Marsden, *Reforming Fundamentalism*, 277–90.

76. This is as anecdotal as it is revealing. Timothy Weber (seminary president), Darrell Johnson (pastor and professor), Marianne Meye Thompson (professor), John Thompson (professor), and John Ortberg (pastor and author), have all shared with me essentially this same point.

77. See his assessment of Oscar Cullmann in Philip Edgecombe Hughes, ed., *Creative Minds in Contemporary Theology*, 2nd ed. (Grand Rapids, Mich.: Eerdmans, 1969), 163–202. Ladd was actually offered the Cullmann chapter before Wallace but refused, presumably to focus on the completion of *Jesus and the Kingdom*. See Philip Hughes to GEL, 30 June 1962. Though no letter survives, it is likely that Ladd recommended Wallace for the task.

78. Interview with David Wallace, 2 May 2002.

79. Interview with Robert Guelich, n.d. (ca. December 1989). Rebecca Jane Duncan Papers. This incident took place at the 1976 meeting of the Studiorum Novi Testamenti Societas at Duke University. Guelich had actually not published much before that year: only his dissertation, which was published as an institutional requirement by the University of Hamburg, and two journal articles. Two major scholarly books and at least a dozen articles appeared after their meeting in 1976.

80. It is a mark of Ladd's impact that both Wallace and Guelich loved him until the end. Wallace could not tell his story without weeping—for Ladd. Guelich was the catalyst and inspiration for the present project, insisting that Ladd deserved an honored place in the history of evangelical scholarship.

81. GEL to Barker, 2 May 1966. See discussion in previous chapter, 257–58.

82. See Epp, "Norman Perrin on the Kingdom of God.

83. Ibid., 114.

84. Ibid., 119n6.

85. Ibid., 120n6.

86. Ibid.

87. The letter from Epp to Ladd does not survive, and the title of the book to be reviewed is not named in Ladd's response.

88. GEL to Eldon J. Epp, 17 January 1972.

89. Ibid.

90. Ibid.

91. In the immediate aftermath of receiving Perrin's review in 1965, Ladd wrote the following to David Hubbard: "I recognize that my own emotional problems are

tied up with this for my drive in scholarship has been in substantial part neurotically motivated. I have been a failure as a husband and father (I woke up to this fact four years ago), and now it is obvious that the product of my life's work and my high aspirations as an evangelical scholar are a failure" (GEL to Hubbard, 21 May 1965). This letter, however, was not sent, and this blunt acknowledgment of his failures in familial relationships does not appear in other letters.

92. GEL to C. W. Fishburne, 15 May 1968.

93. George Eldon Ladd, "God's Answer to the Question, Why?," chapel sermon at Fuller Theological Seminary, 20 April 1976. Fuller Seminary Academic Technology Center, tape 0073a.

94. Ladd, *New Testament and Criticism*, 9, 11.

95. Ibid., 183.

96. Ibid., 215.

97. Edgar Krentz, review of *The New Testament and Criticism*, in *Concordia Theological Monthly* 38 (November 1967), 668.

98. David H. Wallace, review of *The New Testament and Criticism*, in *Christianity Today* 12 (13 October 1967), 32–33.

99. Elisabeth Schüssler Fiorenza, review of *A Commentary on the Revelation of John*, in *Theological Studies* 33 (December 1972), 760.

100. R.C. Briggs, review of *A Commentary on the Revelation of John*, in *The Journal of Religious Thought* 30 (Spring–Summer 1973), 86.

101. John F. Walvoord, review of *A Commentary on the Revelation of John*, in *Bibliotheca Sacra* 130 (April–June 1973), 177.

102. George Eldon Ladd, *A Theology of the New Testament* (Grand Rapids, Mich.: Eerdmans, 1974), 25. Again one expects to hear "but the attempt must be made..."

103. Ibid., 21–23.

104. Ibid., 30–31. The italics are Ladd's.

105. Ibid., 179.

106. Ibid., 390–91.

107. Ibid., 424.

108. See Mark Noll, *Between Faith and Criticism: Evangelicals, Scholarship and the Bible in America* (San Francisco: Harper and Row, 1986), 212.

109. Robert G. Clouse, ed., *The Meaning of the Millennium: Four Views* (Downers Grove, Ill.: InterVarsity Press, 1977). This book remains in print and continues to generate discussion among students of eschatological issues. See the reader review section of Amazon.com; http://www.amazon.com/gp/product/customer-reviews/ 0877847940/ref=cm_rev_all_1/104-6493948-7337533?%5Fencoding=UTF8&me= ATVPDKIKX0DER (accessed 15 November 2007).

110. Interview with Robert Clouse at the Conference on Faith and History, 19 October 2000. Clouse received his theological training at the dispensationalist Grace Theological Seminary in Indiana.

111. See "Paul and the Law," in J. M. Richards, ed., *Soli Deo Gloria: Festschrift for William Childs Robinson* (Richmond: John Knox Press, 1968), 50–67; "Revelation and Tradition in Paul," in W. W. Gasque and Ralph P. Martin, eds., *Apostolic*

History and the Gospel: Festschrift for F. F. Bruce (Grand Rapids, Mich.: Eerdmans, 1970), 223–30; "Apocalyptic and New Testament Theology," in Robert Banks, ed., *Reconciliation and Hope: Festschrift for Leon Morris* (Grand Rapids, Mich.: Eerdmans, 1974), 285–96; and "The Holy Spirit in Galatians," in G. F. Hawthorne, ed., *Current Issues in Biblical and Patristic Interpretation: Festschrift for Merrill Tenney* (Grand Rapids, Mich.: Eerdmans, 1975), 211–16.

112. That this piece functioned as an apology is clear in the correspondence between Ladd and the editors of *Interpretation* in the aftermath of Perrin's review. See, for example, James Mays to GEL, 3 June 1965; GEL to Balmer Kelley, 21 June 1964; Mays to GEL, 30 June 1965; GEL to Mays, 8 July 1965; Miriam Blake to GEL, 2 November 1965.

113. George Eldon Ladd, "History and Theology in Biblical Exegesis," *Interpretation* 70 (January 1966), 54–64. The Perrin-related footnotes are 54n4, 59n15, 61n22, and 63n24.

114. George Eldon Ladd, "The Problem of History in Contemporary New Testament Interpretation," in F. L. Gross, ed., *Studia Evangelica V* (Berlin: Akademie-Verlag, 1968), 89, 99.

115. Ibid., 100.

116. R. T. France, "Inerrancy and New Testament Exegesis," *Themelios* 1 (Autumn 1975), 12–18.

117. Ibid., 16.

118. GEL to Mark Jeremias, 27 April 1976.

119. George Eldon Ladd, *I Believe in the Resurrection of Jesus* (Grand Rapids, Mich.: Eerdmans, 1974).

120. Ibid., 22–27.

121. George Eldon Ladd, *The Last Things: An Eschatology for Laymen* (Grand Rapids, Mich.: Eerdmans, 1978). On the church as the new Israel see 23–28.

122. Interview with Colin Brown, 4 December 2003.

123. Handwritten notes from a conversation between W. Ward Gasque and David Hubbard, n.d. (ca. 1976). Gasque earned a PhD in New Testament at the University of Manchester, England, and was later a cofounder of Regent College in Vancouver, British Columbia. Hubbard Papers.

124. Interview with C. Mel Robeck, 26 September 2004 (date of email response).

125. Interview with Jack Dean Kingsbury, 13 September 2003. Kingsbury is a prominent New Testament scholar, now retired from Union Seminary in Virginia.

126. The event took place on 12 October 1976. See copy of program and note from David Hubbard to Glenn Barker, 16 September 1976. Hubbard Papers.

127. Interview with Robert Guelich, n.d. (ca. December 1989). Duncan Papers.

128. Interview with Mrs. James Ladd, 15 December 1989. Duncan Papers.

129. Interview with Robert Guelich, n.d. (ca. December 1989). Duncan Papers.

130. Interview with Colin Brown, 4 December 2003. The event was at the home of British scholar Ralph P. Martin, then professor of New Testament at Fuller.

131. Ibid.

132. Ibid. The engagement was confirmed in an interview with Mrs. James Ladd, 15 December 1989. Duncan Papers. No source reveals the woman's full name or anything further about this episode.

133. See Robert A. Guelich, ed., *Unity and Diversity in New Testament Theology: Essays in Honor of George E. Ladd* (Grand Rapids, Mich.: Eerdmans, 1978).

134. David Allan Hubbard, "Biographical Sketch and Appreciation," in Guelich, ed., *Unity and Diversity in New Testament Theology,* xi.

135. At the time the Festschrift was published, Meye was dean of the School of Theology at Fuller. Gasque was cofounder and professor of New Testament at Regent College in Canada. Charles Carlston, the first Fuller graduate to earn a PhD at Harvard, was then professor of New Testament at Andover Newton Theological School in Massachusetts. Daniel Fuller was professor of hermeneutics at Fuller Seminary. Epp was professor of biblical literature and dean of humanities and social sciences at Case Western Reserve University in Ohio.

136. Eldon J. Epp, "Paul's Diverse Imageries of the Human Situation and His Unifying Theme of Freedom," introductory note, in Guelich, ed., *Unity and Diversity in New Testament Theology,* 100.

137. George Eldon Ladd, "The Gospel Must Be Preached," chapel sermon at Fuller Theological Seminary, 20 April 1979. Fuller Seminary Academic Technology Center, tape 0222b.

138. Ibid. Ladd and Martin had carried on a peaceful debate over the relationship between prophetic and apocalyptic literature.

139. Interview with John McKenna, then assistant to David Allan Hubbard, November 1991.

140. Robert Meye, memo to the Fuller community, 27 August 1980. Hubbard Papers.

141. Robert Meye, memo to the Fuller community, 10 September 1980. Hubbard Papers.

142. Interview with Robert Meye, n.d. (ca. December 1989). Duncan Papers.

NOTES TO CONCLUSION

1. George Marsden, *Reforming Fundamentalism: Fuller Seminary and the New Evangelicalism* (Grand Rapids, Mich.: Eerdmans, 1987), 248.

2. On dispensationalists moving closer to Ladd's position see Bradley Harper, "The Kingdom of God in the Theology of George Eldon Ladd: A Reflection of 20th Century American Evangelicalism" (PhD diss., Saint Louis University, 1994), 276–78.

3. Among those former students who went on to distinguish themselves in scholarly careers are Clarence Bass, James Bradley, William Buehler, Fred Bush, Eldon Epp, Daniel Fuller, Ward Gasque, Wesley Gerig, Robert Guelich, Donald Hagner, Rae Heimbeck, James Mignard, Robert Mounce, Donald Tinder, David Wallace, Timothy Weber, and Ronald Youngblood.

4. Joel Carpenter, *Revive Us Again: The Reawakening of American Fundamentalism* (New York: Oxford University Press, 1997), 31 and passim.

5. Jon R. Stone, *On the Boundaries of American Evangelicalism: The Postwar Evangelical Coalition* (New York: St. Martin's Press, 1997), 146.

6. Ibid., 179.

7. George Eldon Ladd, *The New Testament and Criticism* (Grand Rapids, Mich.: Eerdmans, 1967), 11.

8. Ladd, "History and Theology in Biblical Exegesis," *Interpretation* 20 (January 1966), 57.

9. Robert Yarbrough, "The *Heilsgeschichtliche* Perspective in Modern New Testament Theology" (PhD diss., University of Aberdeen, 1985), 415.

10. George Eldon Ladd, "Statement of Doctrinal Belief," in an application to join the New England Fellowship, ca. 1936. GEL Papers.

11. Carpenter, *Revive Us Again*, 195.

12. Harper, "Kingdom of God in the Theology of George Eldon Ladd," 274–76.

13. An example of this struggle is that of theologian Miroslav Volf, who left Fuller Seminary for Yale University in 1998. Other top faculty members at Fuller report receiving regular offers from secular universities or mainstream divinity schools.

14. Interview with Daniel Fuller, 8 June 2001.

15. See, for example, www.peninsulabible.org/perspectives/reading/3/Ladd _TheGospelof.pdf; www.geocities.com/hebrews928/ladd.html; and www.hakesher .org/hakesher2/Frankovic9.htm.

16. The marketplace highlights this point. None of Edward John Carnell's books remains in print, while in 2004 no fewer than six of Ladd's books were still being published.

17. See Mark Noll, *The Scandal of the Evangelical Mind* (Grand Rapids, Mich.: Eerdmans, 1994), and George Marsden, *The Outrageous Idea of Christian Scholarship* (New York: Oxford University Press, 1997).

Bibliography

PRIMARY SOURCES

THE GEORGE ELDON LADD PAPERS: A BIBLIOGRAPHIC ESSAY

The George Eldon Ladd Papers (GELP) are a rich and diverse collection that documents one scholar's role in the resurgence of evangelical scholarship in the years after the Second World War. Robert P. Meye, then dean of the School of Theology at Fuller Theological Seminary, preserved the collection after Ladd's death, and it is largely intact as Ladd left it. The papers were stored in their original filing cabinets from 1980 until 1999, at which time they were transferred into my possession. The permanent owner of the collection is Fuller Seminary in Pasadena, California, and interested readers should contact the seminary librarian regarding access.

The earliest documents in the GELP are course notes and essays from Ladd's undergraduate years at Gordon College (1929–1933). These files are not comprehensive but rather reflect those items that Ladd chose to keep. In particular, there are essays related to his study of the New Testament, often with markings from his professors at the time. Ladd also briefly kept a handwritten journal of his courtship with Winifred Webber, who was to become his wife in 1933. In addition to the details of this important relationship, the journal helps to identify Ladd's early handwriting, thereby allowing early undated writings to be distinguished from those of later years.

Relatively few documents in the GELP relate to Ladd's years of active pastoral service and work within the Northern Baptist Convention (1933–1945). Several letters describe the terms of call for pastoral positions, and Ladd's letter of resignation from his final full-time pastorate (Blaney Memorial Baptist Church in Dorchester, Massachusetts) survives. Also from this era are two farm boxes (approx. 60cm × 40cm × 20cm) that contain more than two hundred sermons. Ladd preached from spare outlines, handwritten on halved letter-sized sheets (approximately 14cm × 21.5cm), with Bible passages at the top and key points identified with only a sentence or even a single word. These sermons are difficult to assess with any accuracy since they rarely if ever reflect what Ladd actually preached. It was during this period that Ladd joined the New England Fellowship (NEF), a cooperative evangelistic organization, and preached several times on regional radio. Because these sermons were scripted, they give a better indication of Ladd's early preaching style. More significantly, Ladd was required to write a statement of his beliefs as a part of the application to join the NEF. This document provides a glimpse into Ladd's spiritual history and doctrinal positions circa 1936.

Ladd's years at Harvard are represented by several seminar papers and some course and study notes. The course notes help to chronicle some of Ladd's development as a scholar but are not complete enough to provide a full picture. More difficult still are Ladd's peculiar—and voluminous—notes on Greek texts, which demonstrate his diligence as a student. These notes are written on quartered letter-sized sheets (approximately 10.5cm × 14cm) and fastened together according to the passage under study. Ladd would maintain this practice throughout his career, leaving thousands of pages of notes on various Greek texts. The collection also includes a copy of Ladd's doctoral thesis.

The most important components of the GELP are Ladd's correspondence files. Ladd exchanged letters with friends, colleagues, and scholars in the United States and Europe and kept carbon copies of his own side of the various discussions. The GELP correspondence is arranged in simple alphabetical order by last name, though on occasion a letter is filed according to the institution represented. The incoming letters are autograph originals, except when one came to Ladd after having been addressed to the seminary president or other official, in which case a photocopy was made. No original outgoing letters of Ladd's were consulted, primarily because his own collection is so extensive. The carbon copies occasionally identify errata, which presumably represent corrections made to the outgoing letters. There is at least one unsent letter whose carbon copy contains errata that are corrected on the final version.

In his letters to Fuller Seminary faculty members who were away on sabbatical, Ladd discussed issues related to the political conflicts at the institution, and this favor was returned during Ladd's extended visits to Europe during his career. These letters provide firsthand accounts, often written within hours or a few days of the actual events, of some of the most dramatic developments in the seminary's history. Ladd also debated various themes related to theology and biblical study. The correspondence with John Walvoord of Dallas Theological Seminary is especially descriptive of the issues that conservative evangelicals faced in the postwar era. But beyond the conservative camp, Ladd maintained relationships with some of his contemporaries who were far better known than he. From these people he sought advice, and with them he argued points of theology and attempted to assert his own voice in the theological discussions of the day. These letters—perhaps more than a journal could accomplish—chart Ladd's growth as a scholar, his involvement in contemporary theological issues, and his progress in his quest for acceptance in the broader academic world. This collection has provided the most important source material for the present study.

MANUSCRIPT COLLECTIONS

American Baptist Historical Society Archives, Valley Forge, Pennsylvania
American Baptist–Samuel Colgate Library, Rochester, New York
Billy Graham Center Archives, Wheaton, Illinois
Calvin Mercer Papers, Personal Holdings
David Allan Hubbard Papers, Fuller Seminary, Pasadena, California
Fuller Seminary Academic Technology Services Records, Pasadena, California
Fuller Seminary Archives, Pasadena, California
George Marsden-Daniel P. Fuller Correspondence, Personal Holdings
Gordon College Archives, Wenham, Massachusetts
Harvard University Archives, Cambridge, Massachusetts
Rauner Special Collections Library, Dartmouth College, Hanover, New Hampshire
Rebecca Jane Duncan Papers, Personal Holdings
Rudolph Nelson–George Eldon Ladd Interview Notes, Personal Holdings
U.S. Army Chaplain Museum Archives, Fort Jackson, South Carolina
Western (Conservative Baptist) Seminary Library and Archives, Portland, Oregon

WORKS BY GEORGE ELDON LADD

UNPUBLISHED DISSERTATIONS

"Did Paul Change His Mind about the Time of the Second Coming of Christ?" BD thesis, Gordon Divinity School, 1941.
"The Eschatology of the *Didache*." PhD diss., Harvard University, 1949.

BOOKS

The Blessed Hope: A Biblical Study of the Second Advent and the Rapture. Grand Rapids, Mich.: Eerdmans, 1956.
Commentary on the Revelation of John. Grand Rapids, Mich.: Eerdmans, 1972.
Crucial Questions about the Kingdom of God. Grand Rapids, Mich.: Eerdmans, 1952.
The Gospel of the Kingdom: Scriptural Studies in the Kingdom of God. Grand Rapids, Mich.: Eerdmans, 1959.
I Believe in the Resurrection of Jesus. Grand Rapids, Mich.: Eerdmans, 1975.
Jesus and the Kingdom: The Eschatology of Biblical Realism. New York: Harper and Row, 1964.
Jesus Christ and History. Chicago: InterVarsity Press, 1963.
The Last Things: An Eschatology for Laymen. Grand Rapids, Mich.: Eerdmans, 1977.
The New Testament and Criticism. Grand Rapids, Mich.: Eerdmans, 1967.

The Pattern of New Testament Truth. Grand Rapids, Mich.: Eerdmans, 1968.

The Presence of the Future (2d ed. of *Jesus and the Kingdom*). Grand Rapids, Mich.: Eerdmans, 1974.

Rudolf Bultmann. Chicago: InterVarsity Press, 1964.

A Theology of the New Testament. Grand Rapids, Mich.: Eerdmans, 1974.

The Young Church: Acts of the Apostles. London: Lutterworth, 1964.

ARTICLES AND CHAPTERS

"The Acts of the Apostles." Pfeiffer and Harrison, eds., *Wycliffe Bible Commentary*, 1123–78.

"Age." Harrison, ed., *Baker's Dictionary of Theology*, 31–33.

"Apocalyptic." Douglas, ed., *New Bible Dictionary*, 43–44.

"Apocalyptic/Apocalypse." Harrison, ed., *Baker's Dictionary of Theology*, 50–54.

"Apocalyptic Literature." Tenney, ed., *Zondervan Pictorial Bible Dictionary*, 49–50.

"Biblical Theology, History, and Revelation." *Review and Expositor* 54 (April 1957): 195–204.

"The Christian and the State." *His* (December 1967): 2–5.

"The Christology of Acts." *Foundations* 11 (January–March 1968): 27–41.

"Consistent or Realized Eschatology in Matthew." *Southwestern Journal of Theology* 5 (October 1962): 55–63.

"Eschatology." Douglas, ed., *New Bible Dictionary*, 386–94.

"Eschatology and Ethics." Henry, ed., *Baker's Dictionary of Christian Ethics*, 214–17.

"Eschatology and the Unity of New Testament Theology." *Expository Times* 68 (June 1957): 268–71.

"The Evangelical's Dilemma: Doctrinal Purity or Visible Unity." *Eternity* (June 1962): 7–9, 33.

"Faith and History." *Bulletin of the Evangelical Theological Society* 6 (Summer 1963): 86–91.

"He Shall Come Again." Roddy, ed., *Things Most Surely Believed*, 63–75.

"The Hermeneutics of Prophecy." *Asbury Seminarian* 22 (April 1968): 14–18.

"Historic Premillennialism." Clouse, ed., *Meaning of the Millennium*, 17–40.

"History and Faith." *Foundations* 7 (January 1964): 5–14.

"History and Theology in Biblical Exegesis." *Interpretation* 20 (January 1966): 54–64.

"The Holy Spirit in Galatians." G. F. Hawthorne, ed., *Current Issues in Biblical and Patristic Interpretation: Festschrift for Merrill Tenney.* Grand Rapids, Mich.: Eerdmans, 1975, 211–16.

"Interim Ethics." *Interpretation* 25 (January 1971): 332.

"Is There a Future for Israel?" *Eternity* (May 1964): 25–28, 36.

"Israel and the Church." *Evangelical Quarterly* 36 (October–December 1964): 206–14.

"Justification." *Eternity* (July 1958): 10.

"Kingdom of God." Harrison, ed., *Baker's Dictionary of Theology*, 307–14.

"Kingdom of God." *Journal of Biblical Literature* 81 (September 1962): 466–67.

"Kingdom of God." *Interpretation* 25 (January 1971): 369–70.

"The Kingdom of God." Carl E. Amerding and W. Ward Gasque, eds., *Dreams, Visions, and Oracles: The Layman's Guide to Biblical Prophecy.* Grand Rapids, Mich.: Eerdmans, 1977, 131–42.

"The Kingdom of God in I Enoch." *Bibliotheca Sacra* 110 (Winter 1953): 32–49.

"The Kingdom of God in the Jewish Apocryphal Literature: Enoch." *Bibliotheca Sacra* 110 (Fall 1952): 318–31.

"The Kingdom of God in the Jewish Apocryphal Literature: Introduction." *Bibliotheca Sacra* 109 (Winter 1952): 55–62.

"The Kingdom of God in the Jewish Apocryphal Literature: Jubilees." *Bibliotheca Sacra* 109 (Spring 1952): 164–74.

"The Kingdom of God—Reign or Realm?" *Journal of Biblical Literature* 81 (September 1962): 230–38.

"The Knowledge of God: The Saving Acts of God." Henry, ed., *Basic Christian Doctrines,* 7–13.

"The Life-setting of the Parables of the Kingdom." *Journal of Bible and Religion* 31 (July 1963): 193–99.

"The Lion Is the Lamb." *Eternity* (April 1965): 20.

"The Lord's Return." *His* (April 1961): 9–11.

"Matthew." Henry, ed., *Biblical Expositor,* 23–72.

"The Modern Problem of Biblical Scholarship." *Bethel Seminary Quarterly* 5 (February 1957): 10–20.

"More Light on the Synoptics." *Christianity Today* 3 (2 March 1959): 12–16.

"The Need of Eschatology." *Watchman-Examiner* 40 (16 October 1952): 960–61.

"The Origin of Apocalyptic in Biblical Religion." *Evangelical Quarterly* 30 (July–September 1958): 140–46.

"The Parable of the Sheep and the Goats in Recent Interpretation." R. N. Longe-necker, ed., *New Dimensions in New Testament Study.* Grand Rapids, Mich.: Zondervan, 1974, 191–99.

"Paul and the Law." J. M. Richards, ed., *Soli Deo Gloria: Festschrift for William Childs Robinson.* Richmond, Va.: John Knox Press, 1968, 50–67.

"The Place of Apocalyptic in Biblical Religion." *Evangelical Quarterly* 30 (April–June 1958): 75–85.

"Pondering the Parousia." *Christian Century* 78 (13 September 1961): 1072–73.

"The Problem of History and Faith in Contemporary New Testament Studies." F. L. Cross, ed., *Studia Evangelica V.* Berlin: Akademie Verlag, 1968, 88–100.

"The Rapture Question." *Eternity* (May 1957): 8–10.

"A Redactional Study of Mark." *Expository Times* 92 (October 1981): 10–13.

"The Resurrection and History." *Dialog* 1 (Fall 1962): 55–56.

"The Resurrection and History." *Religion in Life* 32 (Spring 1963): 247–56.

"The Resurrection of Christ." Henry, ed. *Christian Faith and Modern Theology,* 261–84.

"The Revelation and Jewish Apocalyptic." *Evangelical Quarterly* 29 (April–June 1957): 94–100.

"Revelation and Tradition in Paul." W. Ward Gasque and Ralph P. Martin, eds., *Apostolic History and the Gospel.* London: Paternoster Press, 1969, 223–30.

"Revelation, History, and the Bible." *Christianity Today* 1 (30 September 1957): 5–8.

"Revelation, History, and the Bible." *Journal of the American Scientific Affiliation* 9 (September 1957): 15–18.

"The Revelation of Christ's Glory." *Christianity Today* 2 (1 September 1958): 13–14.

"Revelation 20 and the Millennium." *Review and Expositor* 57 (April 1960): 167–75.

"The Revival of Apocalyptic in the Churches." *Review and Expositor* 72 (Summer 1975): 263–70.

"Righteousness in Romans." *Southwestern Journal of Theology* 19 (Fall 1976): 6–17.

"The Role of Apocalyptic in New Testament Theology." Robert Banks, ed., *Reconciliation and Hope: Festschrift for Leon Morris*. London: Paternoster Press, 1974, 285–96.

"The Role of Jesus in Bultmann's Theology." *Scottish Journal of Theology* 18 (March 1965): 57–68.

"RSV Appraisal: New Testament." *Christianity Today* 1 (8 July 1957): 7–11.

"Sabbatical Reflections." *the opinion* 4 (January 1965): 1, 3–6.

"The Search for Perspective." *Interpretation* 25 (January 1971): 41–62.

"Searching for the Historical Jesus." *Eternity* (October 1966): 17–19, 28–30.

"The *Sitz im Leben* of the Parables of Matthew 13: The Soils." F. L. Cross, ed., *Studia Evangelica II*. Berlin: Akademie Verlag, 1964, 203–10.

"The Theology of the Apocalypse." *Gordon Review* 7 (1963–1964): 73–86.

"Trends in New Testament Theology." *Theology, News, and Notes* (June 1977): 6–7.

"Unity and Variety in New Testament Faith." *Christianity Today* 10 (19 November 1965): 21–24.

"What Does Rudolf Bultmann Understand by the Acts of God?" *Bulletin of the Evangelical Theological Society* 5 (Summer 1962): 91–97.

"What Does 'The Forward Movement' Mean?" *Watchman-Examiner* 24 (26 November 1936): 1317.

"What I Want to Communicate." Interview with George Eldon Ladd. *Christian Life* 22 (June 19, 1960): 36–39.

"What Is Rudolf Bultmann Trying to Do?" *Eternity* (May 1962): 26–28, 38.

"When?" *Decision* (February 1968): 3.

"Why?" *Decision* (October 1967): 6.

"Why Did God Inspire the Bible?" W. Ward Gasque and William Sanford LaSor, eds., *Scripture, Tradition, and Interpretation*. Grand Rapids, Mich.: Eerdmans, 1978, 49–59.

"Why Not Prophetic-apocalyptic?" *Journal of Biblical Literature* 76 (Part 3, 1957): 192–200.

SELECTED BOOK REVIEWS BY GEORGE ELDON LADD

Review of A. Guillaumont et al., eds., *The Gospel according to Thomas*. New York: Harper and Row, 1959. *Christianity Today* 4 (29 February 1960): 470–71.

Review of Alva McClain, *The Greatness of the Kingdom*. Grand Rapids, Mich.: Zondervan, 1959. "Dispensational Theology," *Christianity Today* 4 (12 October 1959): 38–40.

Review of Béda Rigaux, *Dieu l'a ressucité: Exégèse et théologie biblique*. *Interpretation* 28 (July 1974): 361–62.

Review of Edward Blair, *Jesus in the Gospel of Matthew*. Nashville: Abingdon, 1960. *Christianity Today* 5 (24 October 1960): 35–36.

Review of G. C. Berkouwer, *The Return of Christ*. Grand Rapids, Mich.: Eerdmans, 1972. *Eternity* (September 1972): 54.

Review of Herman Ridderbos, *Paul: An Outline of His Theology*. Grand Rapids, Mich.: Eerdmans, 1975. *Christian Scholar's Review* 6 (January 1976): 91–92.

Review of J. Barton Payne, *The Imminent Appearing of Christ*. Grand Rapids, Mich.: Eerdmans, 1962. *Christianity Today* 7 (22 June 1962): 34–35.

Review of James M. Robinson, *A New Quest of the Historical Jesus*. London: SCM Press, 1959. *Christianity Today* 4 (18 January 1960): 36.

Review of John Walvoord, *Thy Kingdom Come*. Chicago: Moody Press, 1975. *Westminster Theological Journal* 28 (Winter 1976): 251–53.

Review of Joseph Clower, *The Church in the Thought of Jesus*. Richmond, Va.: John Knox Press, 1961. *Eternity* (September 1961): 50.

Review of Paul Minear, *Commands of Christ: Authority and Implications*. Nashville: Abingdon, 1972. *Foundations* 16 (July–September 1973): 285.

Review of Ralph P. Martin, *New Testament Foundations: A Guide for Christian Students*. Grand Rapids, Mich.: Eerdmans, 1975. *Virginia Seminary Journal* 27 (Fall 1976): 21–22.

Review of Raymond Zorn, *Church and Kingdom*. Philadelphia: Presbyterian and Reformed, 1962. *Christianity Today* 8 (28 September 1962): 49.

Review of Rudolf Schnackenburg, *The Church in the New Testament*. New York: Herder and Herder, 1965. *Journal of Biblical Literature* 85 (September 1966): 249–50.

Review of T. W. Manson, *Ethics and the Gospel*. New York: Charles Scribner's Sons, 1960. *Christianity Today* 7 (13 October 1961): 59–60.

Review of Werner Georg Kümmel, *The Theology of the New Testament according to Its Major Witnesses, Jesus, Paul, and John*. Nashville: Abingdon, 1973. *Theological Students Fellowship* (Autumn 1974): 21–22.

SELECTED REVIEWS OF BOOKS BY GEORGE ELDON LADD

Aune, David. Review of *A Theology of the New Testament*. *Interpretation* 29 (October 1975): 424–27.

Barrosse, Thomas. Review of *A Commentary on the Revelation of John*. *Catholic Biblical Quarterly* 35 (January 1973), 100–101.

Boring, M. Eugene. Review of *Jesus and the Kingdom*. *Encounter* 20 (Spring 1968): 230–32.

Borsch, F. H. Review of *Jesus and the Kingdom*. *Journal of Theological Studies*, n.s., 18 (April 1967): 46–47.

Briggs, R. C. Review of *A Commentary on the Revelation of John*. *Journal of Religious Thought* 30 (Spring–Summer 1973): 86.

Bruce, F. F. Review of *Crucial Questions about the Kingdom of God*. *Evangelical Quarterly* 25 (April 1953): 114–15.

Bryant, Robert. Review of *Jesus and the Kingdom*. *United Church Herald* 8 (1 February 1965): 3.

Danker, Frederick. Review of *The Gospel of the Kingdom*. *Concordia Theological Monthly* 31 (June 1960): 393.

Dean, Lloyd. Review of *Jesus and the Kingdom*. *Eternity* 16 (March 1965): 44–46.

Dunnett, Walter. Review of *Jesus and the Kingdom*. *Moody Monthly* 65 (March 1965): 7.

Efird, James M. Review of *A Theology of the New Testament*. *Duke Divinity Review* 41 (Spring 1977): 38–39.

Englund, Harold. Review of *The Gospel of the Kingdom*. *Reformed Review* 13 (May 1960): 46–47.

Fiorenza, Elizabeth Schüssler. Review of *A Commentary on the Revelation of John*. *Theological Studies* 33 (December 1972): 760.

Fison, J. E. Review of *Blessed Hope*. *Encounter* 18 (Winter 1957): 121.

Foulkes, Francis. Review of *Jesus and the Kingdom*. *Reformed Theological Review* 25 (May–August 1966): 72–73.

Fuller, Reginald H. Review of *A Theology of the New Testament*. *Anglican Theological Review* 58 (July 1976): 381–84.

Golding, G. C. Review of *Jesus and the Kingdom*. *Indian Journal of Theology* 15 (April–June 1966): 81–83.

Guelich, Robert A. Review of *A Commentary on the Revelation of John*. *Christianity Today* 16 (9 June 1972), 33–36.

———. Review of *A Theology of the New Testament*. *Christianity Today* 20 (23 April 1976): 39–40.

Heinecken, Martin J. Review of *Crucial Questions about the Kingdom of God*. *Lutheran Quarterly* 6 (November 1954): 371.

Holst, Robert. Review of *A Theology of the New Testament*. *Current Theology Monthly* 2 (April 1975): 118.

Knight, George W. Review of *Jesus and the Kingdom*. *Westminster Theological Journal* 28 (November 1965): 64–73.

Krentz, Edgar. Review of *The New Testament and Criticism*. *Concordia Theological Monthly* 38 (November 1967): 668.

Lunt, R. Review of *Jesus and the Kingdom*. *Expository Times* 27 (Spring 1966): 365–66.

Macrae, George. Review of *Jesus and the Kingdom*. *New Blackfriars* 48 (November 1966): 106–107.

Maddox, Robert. Review of *Jesus and the Kingdom*. *Australian Biblical Review* 15 (December 1967): 46–47.

Marrow, Stanley. Review of *Jesus and the Kingdom*. *Biblica* 47 (Fall 1966): 604–606.

Marshall, I. Howard. Review of *I Believe in the Resurrection of Jesus*. *Scottish Journal of Theology* 29 (May–June 1976): 279–80.

Mason, Clarence E. Review of *Crucial Questions about the Kingdom of God*. *Our Hope* 61 (September 1954): 189–90.

McKnight, George. Review of *Jesus and the Kingdom*. *Westminster Theological Journal* 28 (Fall 1965): 64–73.

Michaels, J. Ramsey. Review of *The Gospel of the Kingdom*. *Westminster Theological Journal* 23 (January 1960): 47–50.

Perrin, Norman. Review of *Jesus and the Kingdom*. "Against the Current," *Interpretation* 19 (April 1965): 228–29.

Robinson, W. Gordon. Review of *Jesus and the Kingdom*. *Ecumenical Review* 19 (July 1967): 335.

Rose, Delbert. Review of *Crucial Questions about the Kingdom of God*. *Journal of Bible and Religion* 21 (July 1953): 208–209.

Ryan, Thomas J. Review of *A Theology of the New Testament*. *Catholic Biblical Quarterly* 38 (January 1976): 114–16.

Seitz, Oscar. Review of *Jesus and the Kingdom*. *Anglican Theological Review* 47 (April 1965): 245–46.

Vaughan, Curtis. Review of *The Gospel of the Kingdom*. *Southwestern Journal of Theology* 3 (October 1960): 85.

Waetjen, Herman. Review of *Jesus and the Kingdom*. *Christianity Today* 9 (4 June 1965): 31–32.

Wallace, David H. Review of *The New Testament and Criticism*. *Christianity Today* 12 (13 October 1967): 32–33.

Walther, James A. Review of *Jesus and the Kingdom*. *Pittsburgh Perspective* 6 (June 1965): 37–38.

Walvoord, John. Review of *Blessed Hope*. *Bibliotheca Sacra* 114 (Fall 1956): 289–307.

———. Review of *A Commentary on the Revelation of John*. *Bibliotheca Sacra* 130 (April–June 1973): 177.

———. Review of *Crucial Questions about the Kingdom of God*. *Bibliotheca Sacra* 110 (Winter 1953): 1–10.

———. Review of *The Gospel of the Kingdom*. *Christianity Today* 4 (28 March 1960): 36–37.

———. Review of *Jesus and the Kingdom*. *Bibliotheca Sacra* 122 (January–March 1965): 74–76.

———. Review of *The Last Things*. *Bibliotheca Sacra* 136 (April–June 1979): 182–83.

OTHER PRIMARY WORKS

Alderman, R. J. "Evolution Leads to Sodom." *Moody Monthly* 23 (September 1922): 12.

Allis, Oswald T. *Prophecy and the Church: An Examination of the Claim of Dispensationalists that the Christian Church Is a Mystery Parenthesis Which*

Interrupts the Fulfillment to Israel of the Kingdom Prophecies of the Old Testament.
   Philadelphia: Presbyterian and Reformed, 1945.

Association Minutes for the South Boston Association of the Northern Baptist
   Convention. American Baptist–Samuel Colgate Library, Rochester, New York.

Barnhouse, Donald Grey. "Billy in Manhattan." *Eternity* 8 (May 1957): 7.

Bartsch, Hans W., ed. *Kerygma and Myth: A Theological Debate*, trans. Reginald H.
   Fuller. London: SPCK, 1957.

Bender, Harold, Millard C. Lind, and Chester Lehman. *The Revised Standard Version:
   An Examination and Evaluation.* Scottdale, Penn.: Herald Press, 1953.

Berkof, Louis. *The Kingdom of God: The Development of the Idea of the Kingdom,
   Especially since the Eighteenth Century.* Grand Rapids, Mich.: Eerdmans, 1951.

Betz, Hans Dieter, ed. *Christology and a Modern Pilgrimage: A Discussion with Norman
   Perrin.* Claremont, Calif.: New Testament Colloquium, 1971.

Blackwood, Andrew, ed. *Evangelical Sermons of Our Day: Thirty-seven Examples of Bible
   Preaching.* New York: Harper and Brothers, 1959.

Bradbury, John. "The Northern Baptist Convention Fundamentalists." *Watchman-
   Examiner* (12 August 1937): 916–18.

Bromiley, Geoffrey. "Dare We Follow Bultmann?" *Christianity Today* 5 (27 March
   1961): 6–8.

Bultmann, Rudolf. *Essays Theological and Philosophical.* London: SCM Press, 1955.

———. *History and Eschatology.* New York: Charles Scribner's Sons, 1958.

———. *The History of the Synoptic Tradition.* New York: Harper and Row, 1963.

———. *Jesus and the Word.* New York: Charles Scribner's Sons, 1958.

———. *Jesus Christ and Mythology.* New York: Charles Scribner's Sons, 1958.

———. "New Testament and Mythology." Bartsch, ed., *Kerygma and Myth*, 1–44.

———. *Primitive Christianity in Its Contemporary Setting.* New York: Meridian, 1956.

———. *Theology of the New Testament.* 2 vols. New York: Charles Scribner's Sons,
   1951, 1955.

Cadbury, Henry J. *The Book of Acts in History.* London: A&C Black, 1955.

———. *The Making of Luke-Acts.* New York: Macmillan, 1927.

Carlston, Charles. "*Metanoia* and Church Discipline in the New Testament." PhD
   diss., Harvard University, 1958.

Carnell, Edward John. *Christian Commitment.* New York: Macmillan, 1957.

———. "The Glory of a Theological Seminary." Inaugural address delivered on 17
   May 1955. Published by Fuller Seminary, n.d. (ca. 1970).

———. "Post-fundamentalist Faith." *Christian Century* 76 (26 August 1959): 971.

Chafer, Lewis Sperry. *Systematic Theology.* 8 vols. Dallas: Dallas Seminary Press, 1948.

Clouse, Robert, ed. *The Meaning of the Millennium: Four Views.* Downers Grove, Ill.:
   InterVarsity Press, 1977.

Cohen, Gary G. *Biblical Separation Defended: A Biblical Critique of Ten New Evangelical
   Arguments.* Philadelphia: Presbyterian and Reformed, 1966.

Cullmann, Oscar. *Christ and Time: The Primitive Christian Conception of Time and
   History*, trans. Floyd V. Filson. Philadelphia: Westminster, 1950.

———. *The Early Church.* London: SCM Press, 1956.

———. *Salvation in History*, trans. Sidney G. Sowers et al. London: SCM Press, 1967.

Douglas, J. D., ed. *The New Bible Dictionary*. Grand Rapids, Mich.: Eerdmans, 1962.

Draper, James T. *Authority: The Critical Issue for Southern Baptists*. Old Tappan, N.J.: Fleming Revell, 1984.

Ehlert, Arnold. *A Bibliographic History of Dispensationalism*. Grand Rapids, Mich.: Baker, 1965.

Epp, Eldon J. "Norman Perrin on the Kingdom of God: An Appreciation and an Assessment from the Perspective of 1970." Betz, ed., *Christology and a Modern Pilgrimage*, 113–22.

———. "Paul's Diverse Imageries of the Human Situation and His Unifying Theme of Freedom." Guelich, ed., *Unity and Diversity in New Testament Theology*, 100–116.A

Fairweather, Paul D., and Carroll J. Wright. *Image Therapy*. Self-published, 1967.

Feinberg, Charles Lee. *The Revised Standard Version: What Kind of Translation?* Los Angeles: Talbot Theological Seminary, n.d. (ca. 1952).

Ferm, Robert O. *Cooperative Evangelism: Is Billy Graham Right or Wrong?* Grand Rapids, Mich.: Zondervan, 1958.

France, R. T. "Inerrancy and New Testament Exegesis." *Themelios* 1 (Autumn 1975): 12–18.

Fuller, Daniel P. *Easter Faith and History*. Grand Rapids, Mich.: Eerdmans, 1965.

———. *Give the Winds a Mighty Voice*. Waco, Tex.: Word Publishing, 1972.

———, and George M. Marsden. Comments on an early draft of *Reforming Fundamentalism*, 30 May 1986.

Fuller, David Otis. *Whose Unclean Fingers Have Been Tampering with the Holy Bible, God's Pure, Infallible, Verbally Inspired Word?* Grand Rapids, Mich.: Wealthy Street Baptist Church, n.d. (ca. 1952).

Fuller, Grace Payton, ed. *Heavenly Sunshine: Letters to the "Old-fashioned Revival Hour."* Westwood, N.J.: Fleming Revell, 1956.

The Fundamentals: A Testimony to the Truth. 12 vols. Chicago: 1910–1915. Since they were privately published, there is no publisher listed in the pamphlets. Marsden and other authors have referenced them as I have done.

Gerig, Wesley Lee. "The Church and the Tribulation." ThM thesis, Fuller Theological Seminary, Pasadena, Calif., 1956.

Gordon, Adoniram Judson, and Maria Hale Gordon. John Beauregard, ed., *Journal of Our Journey (1888)*. Wenham, Mass.: Gordon College Archives, 1989.

Gordon College of Theology and Missions Catalogs, 1929–1950.

Gray, Clayton Howard. *The Revised Standard Version: A Friend or Traitor to the Faith?* Butler, Penn: First Baptist Church, n.d. (ca. 1952).

Griffis, Paul. *Let's Be Fair about the Versions: An Appraisal of the Criticisms of the Revised Standard Version*. Conklin, New York: Little White Church, n.d. (ca. 1952).

Guelich, Robert, ed. *Unity and Diversity in New Testament Theology: Essays in Honor of George Eldon Ladd*. Grand Rapids, Mich.: Eerdmans, 1978.

Harrison, Everett F., ed. *Baker's Dictionary of Theology*. Grand Rapids, Mich.: Baker, 1960.

Harrisville, Roy. "Resurrection and Historical Method." *Dialog* 1 (Spring 1962): 30–37.

Henry, Carl F. H., ed. *Baker's Dictionary of Christian Ethics.* Grand Rapids, Mich.: Baker, 1973.

————, ed. *Basic Christian Doctrines.* New York: Holt, Rinehart, and Winston, 1962.

————, ed. *The Biblical Expositor.* Philadelphia: Holman, 1960.

————, ed. *Christian Faith and Modern Theology.* Great Neck, N.Y.: Channel Press, 1964.

————, ed. *Contemporary Evangelical Thought.* Great Neck, N.Y.: Channel Press, 1957.

————. *The Uneasy Conscience of American Fundamentalism.* Grand Rapids, Mich.: Eerdmans, 1947.

Irwin, William A. *An Introduction to the Revised Standard Version of the Old Testament.* New York: Thomas Nelson and Sons, 1952.

Jackson, T. S. *This New Bible, the Genius of Modernism.* Little Rock, Ark.: American Baptist Publishing, n.d. (ca. 1952).

Jewett, Paul King. *The Ordination of Women: An Essay on the Office of Christian Ministry.* Grand Rapids, Mich.: Eerdmans, 1980.

Kähler, Martin. *The So-called Historical Jesus and the Historic Biblical Christ*, trans. Carl Braaten. Philadelphia: Fortress, 1964.

Kantzer, Kenneth S., ed. *Evangelical Affirmations.* Grand Rapids, Mich.: Academie Books, 1990.

————, ed. *Evangelical Roots: A Tribute to Wilbur Smith.* Nashville: Thomas Nelson Publishers, 1978.

Kinney, Kenneth. *Satan's Master Plan to Destroy the Work of God.* Johnson City, New York: First Baptist Church, n.d. (ca. 1952).

Künneth, Walter. "Dare We Follow Bultmann?" *Christianity Today* 6 (13 October 1961): 25–28.

Laws, Curtis Lee. "Convention Side Lights." *Watchman-Examiner* 8 (1 July 1920).

————. "Fundamentalism from the Baptist Viewpoint." *Moody Bible Institute Monthly* 23 (September 1922): 14–17.

Lee, Robert G. "The Revised Standard Version." Unidentified newspaper clipping, n.d. (ca. 1952).

Lightner, Robert P. *Neo-evangelicalism.* Findlay, Ohio: Dunham, n.d. (ca. 1959).

————. *Neoevangelicalism Today.* Schaumburg, Ill.: Regular Baptist Press, 1965.

Lincoln, C. F. "A Critique of the Revised Standard Version." *Bibliotheca Sacra* 110 (Winter 1953): 50–66.

Lindsell, Harold. *Abundantly Above*, 2d ed. Grand Rapids, Mich.: Eerdmans, 1944.

————. *The Battle for the Bible.* Grand Rapids, Mich.: Zondervan Press, 1976.

————, and John Woodbridge. *A Handbook of Christian Truth.* Westwood, N.J.: Fleming Revel, 1953.

Lindsey, Hal. *The Late Great Planet Earth.* Grand Rapids, Mich.: Zondervan, 1970.

————. *The Liberation of Planet Earth.* Grand Rapids, Mich.: Zondervan, 1974.

————, with C. C. Carlson. *Satan Is Alive and Well on Planet Earth.* Grand Rapids, Mich.: Zondervan, 1972.

Lundström, Gosta. *The Kingdom of God in the Teaching of Jesus: A History of Inter-pretation from the Last Decades of the Nineteenth Century to the Present Day*, trans. Joan Bulman. Richmond, Va.: John Knox Press, 1963.

Machen, J. Gresham. *Christianity and Liberalism*. New York: Macmillan, 1923.

———. *The Origin of Paul's Religion*. New York: Macmillan, 1921.

———. *The Virgin Birth of Christ*. New York: Harper and Row, 1930.

McIntire, Carl. "The New Bible: Why Christians Should Not Accept It." Collingswood, N.J.: Christian Beacon, n.d. (ca. 1952).

———. *Servants of Apostasy*. Collingswood, N.J.: Christian Beacon Press, 1955.

Montgomery, John Warwick. *History and Christianity: A Vigorous, Convincing Presentation of the Evidence for a Historical Jesus*. Minneapolis: Bethany House, 1964.

———. "Karl Barth and Contemporary Theology of History." *Bulletin of the Evangelical Theological Society* 6 (Spring 1963): 39–49.

National Association of Evangelicals Executive Committee, eds. *Evangelical Action: A Report of the Organization of the National Association of Evangelicals for United Action*. Boston: United Action Press, 1942.

Ness, Henry. *An Analysis of Criticisms of the New Revised Standard Version of the Bible*. Seattle: Henry Ness, n.d. (ca. 1952).

"New Testament Theology: A Tribute to George Eldon Ladd." Special issue, *Theology, News, and Notes* (June 1983). This is the title of the full issue.

An Open Letter concerning the Revised Standard Version of the Bible. New York: Division of Christian Education, National Council of Churches, n.d. (ca. 1952).

Perrin, Norman. *The Kingdom of God in the Teaching of Jesus*. Philadelphia: Westminster, 1963.

———. *The Promise of Bultmann*. Philadelphia: Fortress, 1969.

———. *The Resurrection according to Matthew, Mark, and Luke*. Philadelphia: Fortress, 1977.

———, and William Farmer. "The Kerygmatic Theology and the Question of the Historical Jesus." *Religion in Life* 29 (Winter 1959–60): 86–97.

Pfeiffer, C. F., and Everett Harrison, eds. *The Wycliffe Bible Commentary*. Chicago: Moody Press, 1962.

Pickering, Ernest D. *The Tragedy of Compromise: The Origin and Impact of the New Evangelicalism*. Greenville, S.C.: Bob Jones University Press, 1994.

Ramm, Bernard. *The Christian View of Science and Scripture*. Grand Rapids, Mich.: Eerdmans, 1955.

———. *The Pattern of Religious Authority*. Grand Rapids, Mich.: Eerdmans, 1957.

Registry, Ministers and Missionaries Benefit Board. American Baptist Historical Society Archives Center, Valley Forge, Penn.

Ridderbos, Herman. "Dare We Follow Bultmann?" *Christianity Today* 5 (22 May 1961): 5–8.

Robinson, James M., ed. *The Later Heidegger and Theology*. New York: Harper and Row, 1963.

———. *A New Quest of the Historical Jesus*. London: SCM Press, 1959.

―――. *The Problem of History in Mark*. Naperville, Ill.: Alec R. Allenson, 1957.

―――, and John B. Cobb Jr., eds. *The New Hermeneutic*. New York: Harper and Row, 1964.

―――, eds. *Theology as History*. New York: Harper and Row, 1967.

Roddy, Clarence, ed. *Things Most Surely Believed*. New York: Fleming Revel, 1963.

Roddy, Sherman. "Fundamentalists and Ecumenicity." *Christian Century* 75 (1 October 1958): 1109–10.

Rowe, Gilbert Theodore. "Bultmann as a Barthian." *Religion in Life* 4 (Summer 1935): 447–54.

Rowlingson, Donald T. "Interpreting the Resurrection." *Christian Century* 80 (10 April 1963): 459–61.

Ryrie, Charles. *The Basis of the Premillennial Faith*. Neptune, N.J.: Loizeaux Bros., 1953.

―――. *Dispensationalism Today*. Chicago: Moody Press, 1965.

Schneider, Johannes. "Dare We Follow Bultmann?" *Christianity Today* 5 (5 June 1961): 6–9.

Schweitzer, Albert. *The Quest of the Historical Jesus*, 2d ed. New York: Macmillan, 1950.

Scofield, Cyrus I. *Rightly Dividing the Word of Truth: Being Ten Outline Studies of the More Important Divisions of Scripture*. Findlay, Ohio: Fundamental Truth Publishers, 1940.

The Seminary Situation: A Factual Record of Our Stewardship to Our Local and National Conservative Baptist Constituency. Portland, Ore.: Executive Committee of the Board of Trustees, Western Conservative Baptist Theological Seminary, 1955.

Sider, Ronald, ed. *The Chicago Declaration*. Carol Stream, Ill.: Creation House, 1974.

Smith, Wilbur. "The Need for a Vigorous Apologetic in the Present Battle for the Christian Faith." Part 1: *Bibliotheca Sacra* 399 (July–September 1943): 407–21; Part 2: 400 (October–December 1943): 532–45.

Tenney, Merrill C., ed. *Zondervan Pictorial Bible Dictionary*. Grand Rapids, Mich.: Zondervan, 1963.

"Theologian Speaks." *Gardena Alondra Park Tribune*, 6 June 1963.

Tulga, Chester. *The Foreign Missions Controversy in the Northern Baptist Convention: 30 Years of Struggle for a Pure Missionary Testimony*. Chicago: Conservative Baptist Fellowship, 1950.

Wallace, David H. "The Semitic Origin of the Assumption of Moses." PhD diss., New College, University of Edinburgh, 1955.

Walvoord, John. *The Blessed Hope and the Tribulation: A Historical and Biblical Study of Posttribulationism*. Grand Rapids, Mich.: Zondervan, 1976.

―――. *Inspiration and Interpretation*. Grand Rapids, Mich.: Eerdmans, 1957.

―――. *The Millennial Kingdom*. Findlay, Ohio: Dunham Press, 1959.

Western Conservative Baptist Theological Seminary Catalogs, 1949–1956.

"Western Seminary." *Conservative Baptist Association News of Oregon* 7 (October 1955): 1.

Youngblood, Ronald, ed. *Evangelicals and Inerrancy: Selections from the Journal of the Evangelical Theological Society*. Nashville: Thomas Nelson, 1984.

SECONDARY SOURCES

Ahlstrom, Sydney. *A Religious History of the American People.* New Haven, Conn.: Yale
University Press, 1972.
————. "The Scottish Philosophy and American Theology." *Church History* 24
(September 1955): 257–72.
Ammerman, Nancy Tatom. *Bible Believers: Fundamentalists in the Modern World.* New
Brunswick, N.J.: Rutgers University Press, 1987.
Anderson, V. Elving. "Evangelicals and Science: Fifty Years after the Scopes Trial,
1925–1975. Wells and Woodbridge, eds., *Evangelicals,* 269–88.
Archer, Gleason, Jr., Paul Feinberg, Douglas Moo, and Richard Reiter. *The Rapture:
Pre-, Mid-, or Post-tribulational.* Grand Rapids, Mich.: Zondervan, 1984.
Askew, Thomas. "The Educational Legacy of A. J. Gordon." Ferguson, ed., *Shaping
a Heritage,* 23–35.
Balmer, Randall Herbert. *Blessed Assurance: A History of Evangelicalism in America.*
Boston: Beacon Press, 1999.
————. *Encyclopedia of Evangelicalism.* Louisville, Ky.: Westminster John Knox Press,
2002.
————. *Mine Eyes Have Seen the Glory: A Journey into the Evangelical Subculture in
America.* New York: Oxford University Press, 1989.
Barr, James. *Beyond Fundamentalism: Biblical Foundations for Evangelical Christianity.*
Philadelphia: Westminster, 1984.
————. *Fundamentalism,* 2d ed. London: SCM Press, 1981.
————. *Holy Scripture: Canon, Authority, Criticism.* Philadelphia: Westminster, 1983.
Bass, Clarence. *Backgrounds to Dispensationalism: Its Historical Genesis and Ecclesiastical
Implications.* Grand Rapids, Mich.: Eerdmans, 1960.
Beacon, Margaret Hope. *Let This Life Speak: The Legacy of Henry Joel Cadbury.*
Philadelphia: University of Pennsylvania Press, 1987.
Bebbington, D. W. "Evangelicalism in Its Settings: The British and American Move-
ments since 1940." Noll, Bebbington, and Rawlyk, eds., *Evangelicalism,* 365–88.
————. *Evangelicalism in Modern Britain: A History from the 1730s to the 1980s.* London
and Winchester, Mass.: Unwin Hyman, 1989.
Bell, William E., Jr. "A Critical Evaluation of the Pretribulation Rapture Doctrine in
Christian Eschatology." PhD diss., New York University, 1967.
Bendroth, Margaret Lamberts. *Fundamentalism and Gender: 1875 to the Present.* New
Haven, Conn.: Yale University Press, 1993.
————. *Fundamentalists in the City: Conflict and Division in Boston's Churches, 1885–
1950.* New York: Oxford University Press, 2005.
Bibza, James. "A Critical Analysis of the Publications of D. P. Fuller, G. E. Ladd, I. H.
Marshall, and M. C. Tenney on the Resurrection of Jesus Christ with Special
Attention to the Problem of the Locale of the Post-resurrection Appearances."
PhD diss., Princeton Theological Seminary, Princeton, N.J., 1985.
Biel, Steven. *Independent Intellectuals in the United States, 1910–1945.* American Social
Experience Series 25. New York: New York University Press, 1992.

Blaising, Craig, and Darrell L. Bock. *Progressive Dispensationalism*. Wheaton, Ill.: BridgePoint, 1993.

Bloesch, Donald G. *The Evangelical Renaissance*. Grand Rapids, Mich.: Eerdmans, 1973.

Blumhofer, Edith L., ed. *Religion, Education, and the American Experience: Reflections on Religion and American Public Life*. Tuscaloosa: University of Alabama Press, 2002.

———— and Joel A. Carpenter, eds. *Twentieth-century Evangelicalism: A Guide to the Sources*. New York: Garland, 1990.

Bornkamm, Günther. *Jesus of Nazareth*, trans. Irene McLuskey and Fraser McLuskey. New York: Harper and Brothers, 1960.

————. "Myth and Gospel: A Discussion of the Problem of Demythologizing the New Testament Message." Braaten and Harrisville, eds., *Kerygma and History*, 172–96.

Bowden, Henry Warner. *Church History in an Age of Uncertainty: Historiographical Patterns in the United States, 1906–1990*. Carbondale: Southern Illinois University Press, 1991.

Bowman, John Wick. "The Bible and Modern Religions: Dispensationalism." *Interpretation* 10 (April 1956): 170–87.

Boyer, Paul S. *When Time Shall Be No More: Prophecy Belief in Modern American Culture*. Cambridge, Mass.: Belknap Press of Harvard University Press, 1992.

Braaten, Carl. "Martin Kähler on the Historic Biblical Christ." Braaten and Harrisville, eds., *Historical Jesus and the Kerygmatic Christ*, 79–105.

————, and Roy Harrisville, eds. *The Historical Jesus and the Kerygmatic Christ*. New York: Abingdon, 1964.

————, eds. *Kerygma and History: A Symposium on the Theology of Rudolf Bultmann*. New York: Abingdon, 1962.

Brackney, William. *The Baptists*. New York: Greenwood, 1988.

Brereton, Virginia Lieson. *Training God's Army: The American Bible School, 1880–1940*. Bloomington: Indiana University Press, 1990.

Bruce, F. F. *The English Bible: A History of Translations from the Earliest English Versions to the New English Bible*. New York: Oxford University Press, 1970.

————. *In Retrospect: Remembrance of Things Past*, 2d ed. Grand Rapids, Mich.: Eerdmans, 1993.

Bryant, M. Darrol, and Donald W. Dayton, eds. *The Coming Kingdom: Essays in American Millennialism and Eschatology*. Barrytown, N.Y.: International Religious Books, 1983.

Butler, Farley. "Billy Graham and the End of Evangelical Unity." PhD diss., University of Florida, 1976.

Callahan, David. *Kindred Spirits: Harvard Business School's Extraordinary Class of 1949 and How They Transformed American Business*. Hoboken, N.J.: John Wiley and Sons, 2002.

Carpenter, Joel A. "Contending for the Faith Once Delivered: Primitivist Impulses in American Fundamentalism." Hughes, ed., *American Quest for the Primitive Church*, 99–119.

————. "Fundamentalist Institutions and the Rise of Evangelical Protestantism, 1929–1942." *Church History* 49 (March 1980): 62–75.

———. "The Fundamentalist Leaven and the Rise of an Evangelical United Front." Sweet, ed., *Evangelical Tradition in America*, 257–88.

———. *Revive Us Again: The Reawakening of American Fundamentalism*. New York: Oxford University Press, 1997.

———, and Wilbert R. Shenk, eds. *Earthen Vessels: American Evangelicals and Foreign Missions, 1880–1980*. Grand Rapids, Mich.: Eerdmans, 1990.

Carter, Paul A. *The Spiritual Crisis of the Gilded Age*. DeKalb: Northern Illinois University Press, 1971.

Case, Shirley Jackson. *The Christian Philosophy of History*. Chicago: University of Chicago Press, 1943.

———. *The Millennial Hope: A Phase of War-time Thinking*. Chicago: University of Chicago Press, 1918.

Cauthen, Kenneth. *The Impact of American Religious Liberalism*. New York: Harper and Row, 1962.

Coben, Stanley, and Lorman Ratner. *The Development of an American Culture*, 2d ed. New York: St. Martin's Press, 1983.

Cohen, Norman, ed. *The Fundamentalist Phenomenon: A View from Within; a Response from Without*. Grand Rapids, Mich.: Eerdmans, 1990.

Cole, Stewart G. *The History of Fundamentalism*. New York: Harper and Row, 1931.

Collins, Raymond. *Introduction to the New Testament*. New York: Image, 1987.

Commager, Henry Steele. *The American Mind: An Interpretation of American Thought and Character since the 1880s*. New Haven, Conn.: Yale University Press, 1950.

———. *Documents of American History*, 9th ed. New York: Appleton-Century-Crofts, 1973.

Cox, William E. *Amillennialism Today*. Phillipsburg, N.J.: Presbyterian and Reformed, 1966.

Crenshaw, Curtis I., and Grover E. Gunn III. *Dispensationalism Today, Yesterday, and Tomorrow*. Memphis: Footstool Press, 1985.

Dayton, Donald W. *Discovering an Evangelical Heritage*. New York: Harper and Row, 1976.

———, and Robert K. Johnston, eds. *The Variety of American Evangelicalism*. Knoxville: University of Tennessee Press, 1991.

Dean, William D. *History Making History: The New Historicism in American Religious Thought*. SUNY Series in Philosophy. Albany: State University of New York Press, 1988.

D'Elia, John A. "George Eldon Ladd." Timothy Larsen, ed., *Biographical Dictionary of Evangelicals*. Downers Grove, Ill.: InterVarsity Press, 2003, 354–56.

Dinkler, Erich. "Existentialist Interpretation of the New Testament." *Journal of Religion* 32 (April 1952): 87–96.

Dittberner, Job L. *The End of Ideology and American Social Thought, 1930–1960*. Ann Arbor: UMI Research Press, 1979.

Dollar, George. *A History of Fundamentalism in America*. Greenville, S.C.: Bob Jones University Press, 1973.

Dorrien, Gary. *The Making of American Liberal Theology: Idealism, Realism, and Modernity, 1900–1950*. Louisville, Ky.: Westminster John Knox Press, 2003.

———. *The Remaking of Evangelical Theology*. Louisville, Ky.: Westminster John Knox Press, 1998.

"The Incredible Drown Case." http://www.chirobase.org/12Hx/drown.html (accessed 3 November 2007).

Duncan, Rebecca Jane. "The Spiritual Formation of George Eldon Ladd, 1911–1982." Unpublished paper, Fuller Theological Seminary, Pasadena, Calif., 1989.

Ellwood, Robert S. *1950: Crossroads of American Religious Life*. Louisville, Ky.: Westminster John Knox Press, 2000.

———. *The Fifties Spiritual Marketplace: American Religion in a Decade of Conflict*. New Brunswick, N.J.: Rutgers University Press, 1997.

———. *The Sixties Spiritual Awakening: American Religion Moving from Modern to Postmodern*. New Brunswick, N.J.: Rutgers University Press, 1994.

Epp, Eldon J. "Mediating Approaches to the Kingdom: Werner Georg Kümmel and George Eldon Ladd." Willis, ed., *Kingdom of God in 20th-century Interpretation*, 35–52.

Erickson, Millard J. *Contemporary Options in Eschatology: A Study of the Millennium*. Grand Rapids, Mich.: Baker, 1977.

———. *The New Evangelical Theology*. London: Marshal, Morgan, and Scott, 1968.

Eskridge, Larry. "Only Believe: Paul Rader and the Chicago Gospel Tabernacle." MA thesis, University of Maryland, 1985.

Evans, Elizabeth. *The Wright Vision: The Story of the New England Fellowship*. Lanham, Md.: University Press of America, 1991.

Evans, Rod, and Irwin M. Berent. *Fundamentalism: Hazards and Heartbreaks*. La Salle, Ill.: Open Court, 1988.

Fackler, P. Mark, and Charles Lippy. *Popular Religious Magazines of the United States*. New York: Greenwood, 1995.

Ferguson, Ann D., ed. *Shaping a Heritage: Celebrating the Centennial*. Wenham, Mass.: Gordon College, 1989.

Fink, Leon. *Progressive Intellectuals and the Dilemmas of Democratic Commitment*. Cambridge, Mass: Harvard University Press, 1997.

Finke, Roger, and Rodney Stark. *The Churching of America, 1776–1990: Winners and Losers in Our Religious Economy*. New Brunswick, N.J.: Rutgers University Press, 1992.

Fischer, Paul B. *Ultra-dispensationalism Is Modernism: Exposing a Heresy among Fundamentalists*. Chicago: Weir, 1936.

Flake, Carol. *Redemptorama: Culture, Politics, and the New Evangelicalism*. Garden City, N.Y.: Anchor, 1984.

Fraker, Anne T., ed. *Religion and American Life: Resources*. Urbana: University of Illinois Press, 1989.

Frank, Douglas. *Less than Conquerors: How Evangelicals Entered the Twentieth Century*. Grand Rapids, Mich.: Eerdmans, 1986.

Fuller, Daniel P. *Gospel and Law, Contrast or Continuum? The Hermeneutics of Dispensationalism and Covenant Theology*. Pasadena, Calif.: Fuller Seminary, 1990.

———. *The Unity of the Bible: Unfolding God's Plan for Humanity.* Grand Rapids, Mich.: Zondervan, 1992.

Gasper, Louis. *The Fundamentalist Movement.* The Hague: Mouton, 1963.

Gerstner, John. *A Primer on Dispensationalism.* Phillipsburg, NJ: Presbyterian and Reformed Publishing, 1982.

Gilbert, James Burkhart. *Redeeming Culture: American Religion in an Age of Science.* Chicago: University of Chicago Press, 1997.

Glenn, Alfred. "Rudolf Bultmann: Removing the False Offense." *Journal of the Evangelical Theological Society* 16 (Spring 1973): 73–81.

Gogarten, Friedrich. *Demythologizing and History,* trans. Neville H. Smith. London: SCM Press, 1955.

Goodwin, Everett, ed. *Baptists in the Balance: The Tension between Freedom and Responsibility.* Valley Forge, Penn.: Judson Press, 1997.

Goppelt, Leonhard. *Apostolic and Post-apostolic Times,* trans. Robert Guelich. London: A&C Black, 1970.

Green, Jay D. "A Creed for Modernism: Shirley Jackson Case and the Irony of Modern Approaches to 'Faith and History.'" *Fides et Historia* 29 (Fall 1997): 38–49.

"Grey, Zane." Biographical sketch. http://www.classicreader.com (accessed 21 February 2004).

Hagner, Donald. "George Eldon Ladd." Walter Elwell and J. D. Weaver, eds., *Biblical Interpreters of the Twentieth Century.* Grand Rapids, Mich.: Baker, 1993, 228–45.

Hall, Kermit L., ed. *The Oxford Companion to the Supreme Court of the United States.* New York: Oxford University Press, 1992.

Hamilton, Michael S. "The Fundamentalist Harvard: Wheaton College, 1919–1965." PhD diss., University of Notre Dame, 1994.

———, and Margaret Lamberts Bendroth. "Keeping the 'Fun' in Fundamentalism: The Winona Lake Bible Conferences, 1895–1968." Jacobsen and Trollinger, eds., *Re-forming the Center,* 300–17.

Hammond, Phillip. "In Search of a Protestant Twentieth Century: American Religion and Power since 1900." *Review of Religious Research* 24 (June 1983): 281–94.

Handy, Robert T. "Biblical Primitivism in the American Baptist Tradition." Hughes, ed., *American Quest for the Primitive Church,* 143–52.

Hankins, Barry. "History Is Written by the Losers: A Case Study in Historiography and Religious Conflict." *Fides et Historia* 29 (Fall 1997): 50–65.

Harper, Bradley J. "The Kingdom of God in the Theology of George Eldon Ladd: A Reflection of 20th-century American Evangelicalism." PhD diss., Saint Louis University, 1994.

Harris, Harriet A. *Fundamentalism and Evangelicals.* New York: Oxford University Press, 1998.

Harrison, Paul M. *Authority and Power in the Free Church Tradition: A Social Case Study of the American Baptist Convention.* Princeton, N.J.: Princeton University Press, 1959.

Harrisville, Roy, and Walter Sundberg. *The Bible in Modern Culture: Theology and Historical-critical Method from Spinoza to Käsemann*. Grand Rapids, Mich.: Eerdmans, 1995.

Hart, D. G. *Defending the Faith: J. Gresham Machen and the Crisis of Conservative Protestantism in Modern America*. Baltimore: Johns Hopkins University Press, 1994.

————. *The Lost Soul of American Protestantism*. Lanham, Md.: Rowman and Littlefield, 2002.

————, ed. *Reckoning with the Past: Historical Essays on American Evangelicalism from the Institute for the Study of American Evangelicals*. Grand Rapids, Mich.: Baker, 1995.

Hartshorne, Hugh, and Milton C. Froyd. *Theological Education in the Northern Baptist Convention*. Philadelphia: Board of Education of the Northern Baptist Convention, 1945.

Harvey, Van A. "On the Intellectual Marginality of American Theology." Lacey, ed., *Religion and Twentieth-century American Intellectual Life*, 172–92.

Hatch, Nathan O. "Evangelicalism as a Democratic Movement." George Marsden, ed., *Evangelicalism and Modern America*, 71–82.

————, and Mark A. Noll, eds. *The Bible in America: Essays in Cultural History*. New York: Oxford University Press, 1982.

Hedlund, Roger E. "Conservative Baptists in Mid-passage: The Study of a Movement, Its Growth and Self-understanding, Its Present Crisis of Uncertainty." DMiss diss., Fuller Theological Seminary, Pasadena, Calif., 1974.

Henry, Carl Ferdinand Howard. *Confessions of a Theologian: An Autobiography*. Waco, Tex.: Word Books, 1986.

Hofstadter, Richard. *Anti-intellectualism in American Life*. New York: Knopf, 1963.

————. *The Paranoid Style in American Politics and Other Essays*. New York: Knopf, 1965.

————, De Witt Hardy, and the Commission on Financing Higher Education. *The Development and Scope of Higher Education in the United States*. New York: Columbia University Press, 1952.

————, and Walter P. Metzger. *The Development of Academic Freedom in the United States*. New York: Columbia University Press, 1955.

————, and Wilson Smith, eds. *American Higher Education: A Documentary History*. Chicago: University of Chicago Press, 1961.

Hollinger, David A. *In the American Province: Studies in the History and Historiography of Ideas*. Bloomington: Indiana University Press, 1985.

————. "Justification by Verification: The Scientific Challenge to the Moral Authority of Christianity in Modern America." Lacey, ed., *Religion and Twentieth-century American Intellectual Life*, 116–35.

————. *Science, Jews, and Secular Culture Studies in Mid-twentieth-century American Intellectual History*. Princeton, N.J.: Princeton University Press, 1996.

————, and Charles Capper. *The American Intellectual Tradition: A Sourcebook*. New York: Oxford University Press, 1989.

Holman, Charles. *Till Jesus Comes: Origins of Christian Apocalyptic Expectation.* Peabody, Mass.: Hendrickson, 1996.

Hubbard, David A. "Biographical Sketch and Appreciation." Guelich, ed. *Unity and Diversity in New Testament Theology,* xi–xv.

——. *What We Evangelicals Believe: Expositions of Christian Doctrine Based on "The Statement of Faith" of Fuller Theological Seminary.* Pasadena, Calif.: Fuller Theological Seminary, 1979.

Hudson, Winthrop S. "The Divergent Careers of Southern and Northern Baptists." *Foundations* 16 (April–June 1973): 171–83.

Hughes, Philip Edgecombe, ed. *Creative Minds in Contemporary Theology,* 2d ed. Grand Rapids, Mich.: Eerdmans, 1969.

Hughes, Richard T., ed. *The American Quest for the Primitive Church.* Urbana: University of Illinois Press, 1988.

Hunter, James Davison. *American Evangelicalism: Conservative Religion and the Quandary of Modernity.* New Brunswick, N.J.: Rutgers University Press, 1983.

——. *Evangelicalism: The Coming Generation.* Chicago: University of Chicago Press, 1987.

Hurd, John C. *A Bibliography of New Testament Bibliographies.* New York: Seabury Press, 1966.

Hutchison, William R., ed. *Between the Times: The Travail of the Protestant Establishment in America, 1900–1960.* New York: Cambridge University Press, 1989.

——. *The Modernist Impulse in American Protestantism.* Cambridge, Mass.: Harvard University Press, 1976.

Iggers, Georg G. *The German Conception of History: The National Tradition of Historical Thought from Herder to the Present.* Middletown, Conn.: Wesleyan University Press, 1968.

——. *Historiography in the Twentieth Century: From Scientific Objectivity to the Postmodern Challenge.* Hanover, N.H.: Wesleyan University Press, 1997.

Ingersoll, Julie. *Evangelical Christian Women: War Stories in the Gender Battles.* New York: New York University Press, 2003.

Jacobsen, Douglas, and William Vance Trollinger Jr., eds. *Re-forming the Center: American Protestantism, 1900 to the Present.* Grand Rapids, Mich.: Eerdmans, 1998.

Johnson, Roger A. *Rudolf Bultmann: Interpreting Faith for the Modern Era.* San Francisco: Collins, 1987.

Johnson, Sherman E. "Two Great New Testament Interpreters." *Religion in Life* 21 (Spring 1952): 288–97.

Johnston, Robert K. *Evangelicals at an Impasse: Biblical Authority in Practice.* Atlanta: John Knox Press, 1979.

——, ed. *The Use of the Bible in Theology: Evangelical Options.* Atlanta: John Knox Press, 1985.

Jorstad, Erling. *Popular Religion in America: The Evangelical Voice.* Westport, Conn.: Greenwood, 1993.

Kramer, Hilton. *The Twilight of the Intellectuals: Culture and Politics in the Era of the Cold War.* Chicago: Ivan R. Dee, 1999.

Krapohl, Robert, and Charles Lippy, eds. *The Evangelicals: A Historical, Thematic, and Biographical Guide.* Westport, Conn.: Greenwood, 1999.

Kraus, Norman C. *Dispensationalism in America: Its Rise and Development.* Richmond, Va.: John Knox Press, 1958.

Kuhn, Thomas S. *The Structure of Scientific Revolutions,* 3d ed. Chicago: University of Chicago Press, 1996.

Kuklick, Bruce. *Churchmen and Philosophers from Jonathan Edwards to John Dewey.* New Haven, Conn.: Yale University Press, 1985.

————. "John Dewey, American Theology, and Scientific Politics." Lacey, ed., *Religion and Twentieth-century American Intellectual Life,* 78–93.

————. *The Rise of American Philosophy, Cambridge, Massachusetts, 1860–1930.* New Haven, Conn.: Yale University Press, 1977.

————, and D. G. Hart, eds. *Religious Advocacy and American History.* Grand Rapids, Mich.: Eerdmans, 1997.

Lacey, Michael J., ed. *Religion and Twentieth-century American Intellectual Life.* New York: Cambridge University Press, 1989.

Ladd, James Mathon. "Dwight L. Moody's Use of the Aristotelian Modes of Persuasion." PhD diss., Oklahoma State University, 1960.

Larson, Edward J. *Summer for the Gods: The Scopes Trial and America's Continuing Debate over Science and Religion.* New York: Basic Books, 1997.

Larue, Gerald A. "Another Chapter in the History of Bible Translation." *Journal of Bible and Religion* 31 (October 1963): 301–10.

Lasch, Christopher. *The New Radicalism in America, 1889–1963: The Intellectual as a Social Type.* New York: Knopf, 1965.

Lawrence, Bruce. *Defenders of God: The Fundamentalist Revolt Against the Modern Age.* Columbia: University of South Carolina Press, 1989.

Lears, Jackson. *No Place of Grace: Antimodernism and the Transformation of American Culture, 1880–1920.* New York: Pantheon, 1981.

Lindberg, David, and Ronald Numbers, eds. *God and Nature: Historical Essays on the Encounter between Christianity and Science.* Berkeley: University of California Press, 1986.

Lindsell, Harold. *Park Street Prophet: The Story of Harold Ockenga.* Wheaton, Ill.: Van Kampen, 1951.

Lippy, Charles, ed. *Religious Periodicals of the United States: Academic and Scholarly Journals.* New York: Greenwood, 1986.

Livingstone, David N. "Situating Evangelical Responses to Evolution." Livingstone, Hart, and Noll, eds., *Evangelicals and Science in Historical Perspective,* 193–219.

————, D. G. Hart, and Mark A. Noll., eds. *Evangelicals and Science in Historical Perspective.* New York: Oxford University Press, 1999.

Lotz, David W., ed. *Altered Landscapes: Christianity in America, 1935–1985; Essays in Honor of Robert T. Handy.* Grand Rapids, Mich.: Eerdmans, 1989.

Malony, H. Newton. *Psychology and the Cross: The Early History of Fuller Seminary's School of Psychology.* Pasadena, Calif.: Fuller Seminary, 1995.

Marsden, George M. "Can Jonathan Edwards (and His Heirs) Be Integrated into the American History Narrative?" *Historically Speaking: The Bulletin of the Historical Society* 5 (July–August 2004): 13–15.

———, ed. *Evangelicalism and Modern America*. Grand Rapids, Mich.: Eerdmans, 1984.

———. *Fundamentalism and American Culture: The Shaping of Twentieth-century Evangelicalism, 1870–1925*. New York: Oxford University Press, 1980.

———. *The Outrageous Idea of Christian Scholarship*. New York: Oxford University Press, 1997.

———. *Reforming Fundamentalism: Fuller Seminary and the New Evangelicalism*. Grand Rapids, Mich.: Eerdmans, 1987.

———. *Religion and American Culture*. San Diego: Harcourt Brace Jovanovich, 1990.

———. *The Soul of the American University: From Protestant Establishment to Established Nonbelief*. New York: Oxford University Press, 1994.

———. *Understanding Fundamentalism and Evangelicalism*. Grand Rapids, Mich.: Eerdmans, 1991.

———, and Bradley J. Longfield, eds. *The Secularization of the Academy*. New York: Oxford University Press, 1992.

——— and Frank Roberts, eds. *A Christian View of History?* Grand Rapids, Mich.: Eerdmans, 1975.

Marshall-Green, Molly. "George Eldon Ladd." Timothy George and David Dockery, eds., *Baptist Theologians*. Nashville: Broadman, 1990, 480–95.

Marty, Martin E. *Modern American Religion*. Vol. 1: *The Irony of It All, 1893–1919*. Chicago: University of Chicago Press, 1986.

———. *Modern American Religion*. Vol. 2: *The Noise of Conflict, 1910–1941*. Chicago, University of Chicago Press, 1991.

———. *Modern American Religion*. Vol. 3: *Under God, Indivisible, 1941–1960*. Chicago: University of Chicago Press, 1996.

———. "Religion in America since Mid-century." *Daedalus* 111 (Winter 1982): 149–63.

Massa, Mark S. *Charles Augustus Briggs and the Crisis of Historical Criticism*. Minneapolis: Fortress, 1990.

Mathison, Keith A. *Dispensationalism: Rightly Dividing the People of God?* Phillipsburg, N.J.: Presbyterian and Reformed, 1995.

May, Henry F. *The Divided Heart: Essays on Protestantism and the Enlightenment in America*. New York: Oxford University Press, 1991.

———. *The Enlightenment in America*. New York: Oxford University Press, 1976.

———. *Ideas, Faiths, and Feelings: Essays on American Intellectual and Religious History, 1952–1982*. New York: Oxford University Press, 1983.

McBeth, H. Leon. *The Baptist Heritage: Four Centuries of Baptist Witness*. Nashville: Broadman, 1987.

McCormack, Bruce L. *Karl Barth's Critically Realistic Dialectical Theology: Its Genesis and Development, 1909–1936*. New York: Oxford University Press, 1995.

McDonald, Lee M. "George Eldon Ladd." Donald McKim, ed., *Historical Handbook of Major Bible Interpreters*. Downers Grove, Ill.: InterVarsity Press, 1998, 588–94.

McDowell, Markus. "George Eldon Ladd." Kenneth T. Jackson, ed., *The Scribner Encyclopedia of American Lives*, vol. 1. New York: Charles Scribner's Sons, 1998, 481–83.

McLoughlin, William G. "The Illusions and Dangers of the New Christian Right." *Foundations* 25 (April–June 1982): 128–43.

————. "Introduction." McLoughlin, ed., *The American Evangelicals, 1800–1900: An Anthology*. New York: Harper Torchbooks, 1968, 1–26.

————. *Modern Revivalism: Charles Grandison Finney to Billy Graham*. New York: Ronald Press, 1959.

Mercer, Calvin. *Norman Perrin's Interpretation of the New Testament: From "Exegetical Method" to "Hermeneutical Process."* Macon, Ga.: Mercer University Press, 1986.

Metzger, Bruce M. "The Revised Standard Version." *Duke Divinity School Review* 44 (Spring 1979): 70–87.

Moberg, David. *The Great Reversal: Evangelism and Social Concern*, rev. ed. Philadelphia: Holman, 1977.

Moore, R. Laurence. *Religious Outsiders and the Making of Americans*. New York: Oxford University Press, 1986.

Moorhead, James H. *World without End: Mainstream American Protestant Visions of the Last Things, 1880–1925*. Bloomington: Indiana University Press, 1999.

Moran, William. *The Belles of New England: The Women of the Textile Mills and the Families Whose Wealth They Wove*. New York: Thomas Dunne's/St. Martin's Press, 2002.

Mouw, Richard J. *The Smell of Sawdust: What Evangelicals Can Learn from Their Fundamentalist Heritage*. Grand Rapids, Mich.: Zondervan, 2000.

Nash, Ronald H. *Evangelicals in America: Who They Are, What They Believe*. Nashville: Abingdon, 1987.

————. *Faith and Reason: Searching for a Rational Faith*. Grand Rapids, Mich.: Academie Books, 1988.

————. *The New Evangelicalism*. Grand Rapids, Mich.: Zondervan, 1963.

Nelson, Roland T. "Fundamentalism and the Northern Baptist Convention." PhD diss., University of Chicago, 1964.

Nelson, Rudolph. "Fundamentalism at Harvard: The Case of Edward John Carnell." *Quarterly Review* 2 (Summer 1982): 79–98.

————. *The Making and Unmaking of an Evangelical Mind: The Case of Edward Carnell*. New York: Cambridge University Press, 1987.

Niebuhr, H. Richard. *The Kingdom of God in America*. New York: Harper, 1959.

————. *Radical Monotheism and Western Culture*. New York: Harper, 1960.

————. *The Social Sources of Denominationalism*. New York: Henry Holt, 1929.

Niebuhr, Reinhold. *Faith and History: A Comparison of Christian and Modern Views of History*. London: Nisbet, 1949.

————. *The Irony of American History*. New York: Scribner's Sons, 1954.

————. *The Nature and Destiny of Man: A Christian Interpretation.* Gifford Lectures, 1939. New York: Scribner's Sons, 1946.

Niebuhr, Richard R. *Resurrection and Historical Reason: A Study of Theological Method.* New York: Charles Scribner's Sons, 1957.

Noll, Mark A. *Between Faith and Criticism: Evangelicals, Scholarship, and the Bible in America.* San Francisco: Harper and Row, 1986.

————. *A History of Christianity in the United States and Canada.* Grand Rapids, Mich.: Eerdmans, 1992

————. "Primitivism in Fundamentalism and American Biblical Scholarship: A Response." Hughes, ed., *American Quest for the Primitive Church*, 120–28.

————. *The Scandal of the Evangelical Mind.* Grand Rapids, Mich.: Eerdmans, 1994.

————. "Science, Theology, and Society: From Cotton Mather to William Jennings Bryan." Livingstone, Hart, and Noll, eds., *Evangelicals and Science in Historical Perspective*, 99–119.

————, D. W. Bebbington, and George A. Rawlyk, eds. *Evangelicalism: Comparative Studies of Popular Protestantism in North America, the British Isles, and Beyond, 1700–1900.* New York: Oxford University Press, 1994.

————, Nathan O. Hatch, and George M. Marsden. *The Search for Christian America.* Colorado Springs: Helmers and Howard, 1989.

Nordbeck, Elizabeth. *Thunder on the Right: Understanding Conservative Christianity in America.* New York: United Church Press, 1990.

Novick, Peter. *That Noble Dream: The "Objectivity Question" and the American Historical Profession.* New York: Cambridge University Press, 1988.

Numbers, Ronald. *God and Nature: Historical Essays on the Encounter between Christianity and Science.* Berkeley: University of California Press, 1986.

Ohlmann, Eric H. "Baptists and Evangelicals." Dayton and Johnston, eds., *Variety of American Evangelicalism*, 148–60.

Parris, David P. "The Resurrection and the Philosophy of History." ThM thesis, Fuller Theological Seminary, Pasadena, Calif., 1994.

Parsons, Mikeal, and Joseph Tyson, eds. *Cadbury, Knox, and Talbert: American Contributions to the Study of Acts.* Atlanta: Scholars Press, 1992.

Pauly, Thomas H. *Zane Grey: His Life, His Adventures, His Women.* Champaign: University of Illinois Press, 2005.

Pfeiffer, Robert H. *Excavations at Nuzi Conducted by the Semitic Museum and the Fogg Art Museum of Harvard University.* Cambridge, Mass.: Harvard University Press, 1929.

————. *Introduction to the Old Testament.* New York: Harper and Brothers, 1941.

————. *State Letters of Assyria: A Transliteration and Translation of 355 Official Assyrian Letters Dating from the Sargonid Period, 722–625 B.C.* New Haven, Conn.: American Oriental Society, 1935.

Pierard, Richard V. "The Quest for the Historical Evangelicalism: A Bibliographical Excursus." *Fides et Historia* 11 (Spring 1979): 60–72.

Piper, Otto. *God in History.* New York: Macmillan, 1939.

Poythress, Vern S. *Understanding Dispensationalists*, 2d ed. Phillipsburg, N.J.: Presbyterian and Reformed Press, 1994.

Pyles, Volie. "Bruised, Bloodied, and Broken: Fundamentalism's Internecine Controversy in the 1960s." *Fides et Historia* 18 (Summer 1986): 45–55.

Quebedeaux, Richard. *By What Authority: The Rise of Personality Cults in American Christianity*. New York: Harper and Row, 1982.

————. *The Worldly Evangelicals*. San Francisco: Harper and Row, 1978.

————. *The Young Evangelicals: Revolution in Orthodoxy*. New York: Harper and Row, 1974.

Ramm, Bernard L. *After Fundamentalism: The Future of Evangelical Theology*. San Francisco: Harper and Row, 1983.

————. *The Evangelical Heritage*. Waco, Tex.: Word Books, 1973.

Rawlyk, George A., and Mark A. Noll, eds. *Amazing Grace: Evangelicalism in Australia, Britain, Canada, and the United States*. Grand Rapids, Mich.: Baker, 1993.

Reid, Daniel G., Robert Linder, Bruce L. Shelley, and Harry S. Stout, eds. *Dictionary of Christianity in America*. Downers Grove, Ill.: InterVarsity Press, 1990.

Reuben, Julie A. *The Making of the Modern University: Intellectual Transformation and the Marginalization of Morality*. Chicago: University of Chicago Press, 1996.

Rogers, Jack, ed. *Biblical Authority*. Waco, Tex.: Word Publishers, 1977.

————, and Donald McKim. *The Authority and Interpretation of the Bible: An Historical Approach*. New York: Harper and Row, 1979.

Rosell, Garth. *The Evangelical Landscape: Essays on the American Evangelical Tradition*. Grand Rapids, Mich.: Baker, 1996.

Rosenberg, Stuart E. *More Loves Than One: The Bible Confronts Psychiatry*. New York: Thomas Nelson and Sons, 1963.

Rowley, H. H. *The Relevance of Apocalyptic: A Study of Jewish and Christian Apocalypses from Daniel to the Revelation*, rev. ed. New York: Harper and Brothers, 1946.

Roy, Ralph Lord. *Apostles of Discord: A Study of Organized Bigotry and Disruption on the Fringes of Protestantism*. Boston: Beacon, 1953.

Russell, C. Allyn. *Voices of American Fundamentalism: Seven Biographical Studies*. Philadelphia: Westminster, 1976.

Russell, David L. "Coming to Grips with the Age of Reason: An Analysis of the New Evangelical Intellectual Agenda, 1942–1970." PhD diss., Michigan State University, 1993.

Rutgers, William H. *Premillennialism in America*. Goes, the Netherlands: Oosterbaan and Le Cointre, 1930.

Sandeen, Ernest R., ed. *The Bible and Social Reform*. Philadelphia: Fortress, 1982.

————. *The Roots of Fundamentalism: British and American Millenarianism, 1800–1930*. Chicago: University of Chicago Press, 1970.

Saucy, Mark. *The Kingdom of God in the Teaching of Jesus: In 20th-century Theology*. Dallas: Word Publishing, 1997.

Schlosser, Ronald E. "Chronology of the American Baptist Churches, USA." *American Baptist Quarterly* 14 (June 1995): 108–75.

Schuster, Robert D., James Stambaugh, and Ferne Weimer, eds. *Researching Modern Evangelicalism: A Guide to the Holdings of the Billy Graham Center, with Information on Other Collections*. New York: Greenwood, 1990.

Scott, James F., ed. *An Analytical Index to* Bibliotheca Sacra, *a Theological Journal Published by Dallas Theological Seminary: From 1934 through 1970*. Dallas: Axminster, 1971.

Shelley, Bruce L. *Conservative Baptists: A Story of Twentieth-century Dissent*. Denver: Conservative Baptist Theological Seminary, 1960.

———. *Evangelicalism in America*. Grand Rapids, Mich.: Eerdmans, 1967.

———. *A History of Conservative Baptists*. Wheaton, Ill.: Conservative Baptist Press, 1971.

———. *Transformed by Love: The Vernon Grounds Story*. Grand Rapids, Mich.: Discovery House, 2002.

Silk, Mark. "The Rise of the 'New Evangelicalism': Shock and Adjustment." Hutchison, ed. *Between the Times*, 278–99.

Sittser, Gerald. *A Cautious Patriotism: The American Churches and the Second World War*. Chapel Hill: University of North Carolina Press, 1997.

Sloan, Douglas. *The Scottish Enlightenment and the American College Ideal*. New York: Teachers College Press, 1971.

Smith, Christian. *American Evangelicalism: Embattled and Thriving*. Chicago: University of Chicago Press, 1998.

———. *Christian America? What Evangelicals Really Want*. Berkeley: University of California Press, 2000.

Smith, Richard Norton. *The Harvard Century: The Making of a University to a Nation*. New York: Simon and Schuster, 1986.

Smith, Ronald G. "What Is Demythologizing?" *Theology Today* 10 (April 1953): 34–44.

Smith, Timothy L. "Religion and Ethnicity in America." *American Historical Review* 83 (December 1978): 1155–85.

Stanley, D. M., S.J. "Rudolf Bultmann: A Contemporary Challenge to the Catholic Theologian." *Catholic Biblical Quarterly* 19 (July 1955): 347–55.

Steckmesser, Kent. "Lawmen and Outlaws." Texas Christian University, http://www2.tcu.edu/depts/prs/amwest/html/wl0119.html (accessed 21 February 2004).

Stone, Jon R. *A Guide to the End of the World: Popular Eschatology in America*. New York: Garland, 1993.

———. *On the Boundaries of American Evangelicalism: The Postwar Evangelical Coalition*. New York: St. Martin's Press, 1997.

Susman, Warren. *Culture as History: The Transformation of American Society in the Twentieth Century*. New York: Pantheon, 1984.

Sweeney, Douglas. "The Essential Evangelicalism Dialectic: The Historiography of the Early Neo-evangelical Movement and the Observer-participant Dilemma." *Church History* 60 (March 1991): 70–84.

———. "Fundamentalism and the Neo-evangelicals." *Fides et Historia* 24 (Winter–Spring 1992): 81–96.

———. "Historiographical Dialectics: On Marsden, Dayton, and the Inner Logic of Evangelical History." *Christian Scholar's Review* 23 (September 1993): 48–61.

Sweet, Leonard I., ed. *The Evangelical Tradition in America*. Macon, Ga.: Mercer University Press, 1984.

———. "Wise as Serpents, Innocent as Doves: The New Evangelical Historiography." *Journal of the American Academy of Religion* 56 (Fall 1988): 397–416.

Szasz, Ferenc Morton. *The Divided Mind of Protestant America, 1880–1930*. Tuscaloosa: University of Alabama Press, 1982.

Tallack, Douglas. *Twentieth-century America: The Intellectual and Cultural Context*. New York: Longman, 1991.

Throckmorton, Burton H., Jr. *The New Testament and Mythology*. Philadelphia: Westminster, 1959.

Tinder, Donald. "Fundamentalist Baptists in the Northern and Western United States, 1920–1950." PhD diss., Yale University, 1969.

Tweedie, Donald F. *Logotherapy and the Christian Faith: An Evaluation of Frankl's Existential Approach to Psychotherapy*. Grand Rapids, Mich.: Baker, 1961.

——— and Paul Clement, eds. *Psychologist Pro Tem: Essays in Honor of the 80th Birthday of Lee Edward Travis*. Los Angeles: University of Southern California Press, 1976.

Wacker, Grant. *Augustus H. Strong and the Dilemma of Historical Consciousness*. Macon, Ga.: Mercer University Press, 1985.

———. "The Decline of Biblical Civilization." Hatch and Noll, eds., *Bible in America*, 121–38.

Wallace, David H. "Oscar Cullmann." Hughes, ed. *Creative Minds in Contemporary Theology*, 163–202.

Walters, Ronald G. *Scientific Authority and Twentieth-century America*. Baltimore: Johns Hopkins University Press, 1997.

Wardin, Albert, Jr. *Baptists in Oregon*. Portland, Ore.: Judson Baptist College, 1969.

Watt, David Harrington. *A Transforming Faith: Explorations of Twentieth-century American Evangelicalism*. New Brunswick, N.J.: Rutgers University Press, 1991.

Webber, Robert, and Donald G. Bloesch, eds. *The Orthodox Evangelicals: Who They Are and What They Are Saying*. Nashville: Nelson, 1978.

Weber, Timothy P. *Living in the Shadow of the Second Coming: American Premillennialism, 1875–1982*, 2d ed. Chicago: University of Chicago Press, 1987.

———. *On the Road to Armageddon: How Evangelicals Became Israel's Best Friend*. Grand Rapids, Mich.: Baker Academic, 2004.

———. "Premillennialism and the Branches of Evangelicalism." Dayton and Johnston, eds., *Variety of American Evangelicalism*, 5–21.

Wells, David F. "On Being Evangelical: Some Theological Differences and Similarities." Noll, Bebbington, and Rawlyk, eds., *Evangelicalism*, 389–410.

———, and John D. Woodbridge, eds. *The Evangelicals: What They Believe, Who They Are, Where They Are Changing*. Nashville: Abingdon, 1975.

Wells, Ronald, ed. *History and the Christian Historian*. Grand Rapids, Mich.: Eerdmans, 1998.

Wenger, Robert. "Social Thought in American Fundamentalism, 1918–1933." PhD diss., University of Nebraska, 1973.

Whiteley, Denys E. H. "Religion of the New Testament Writers." *Modern Churchman* 40 (September 1950): 227–38.

Williams, George Hunston, ed. *The Harvard Divinity School: Its Place in Harvard University and in American Culture.* Boston: Beacon, 1954.

Willis, Wendell, ed. *The Kingdom of God in 20th-century Interpretation.* Peabody, Mass.: Hendrickson, 1987.

Wirt, Sherwood Eliot. *The Social Conscience of the Evangelical.* New York: Harper and Row, 1968.

Wood, Nathan R. *A School of Christ.* Wenham, Mass.: Gordon College of Theology and Missions, 1953.

Woodbridge, John D., Mark A. Noll, and Nathan O. Hatch. *The Gospel in America: Themes in the Story of America's Evangelicals.* Grand Rapids, Mich.: Zondervan, 1979.

Wright, J. Elwin. *The Old-Fashioned Revival Hour and the Broadcasters.* Boston: Fellowship Press, 1940.

Wuthnow, Robert. *The Struggle for America's Soul: Evangelicals, Liberals, and Secularism.* Grand Rapids, Mich.: Eerdmans, 1989.

Yarbrough, Robert. "The *Heilsgeschichtliche* Perspective in Modern New Testament Theology." PhD diss., University of Aberdeen, 1985.

Index